A Guide to Recreation and Leisure

Donald C. Weiskopf

Coordinator of Recreation Leadership
American River College, Sacramento

ALLYN and BACON, Inc.

BOSTON   LONDON   SYDNEY

Copyright © 1975 by Allyn and Bacon, Inc.,
470 Atlantic Avenue, Boston, Massachusetts 02210

Library of Congress Cataloging in Publication Data

Weiskopf, Don.
  A guide to recreation and leisure.

  Bibliography: p.
  Includes index.
  1. Recreation. 2. Leisure. 3. Recreation
leadership. I. Title.
GV171.W44   790   74-23720

ISBN   0-205-04589-8

Second printing . . . November, 1975

TO THE LATE
DR. CHARLES K. BRIGHTBILL,
WHOSE PIONEER EFFORTS AS A LEADER,
TEACHER, AND PHILOSOPHER HAVE LEFT A
LASTING MARK ON THE FIELD OF
RECREATION AND LEISURE, UNDER WHOM
I HAD THE PRIVILEGE TO LEARN AND
STUDY, WHOSE ATTITUDE TOWARD LIFE
HAS SO MUCH INFLUENCED MY OWN.

Contents

Preface

A *Guide to Recreation and Leisure* provides an introduction to the field of organized recreation and leisure services. In describing the rapid expansion of community recreation, the author has tried to analyze the total field of recreation and leisure, with particular emphasis on what has occurred during the past two decades.

As we stand on the threshold of a leisure-oriented society, the potential of recreation and leisure time services for satisfying and creative living is almost unlimited. The determining factor, of course, will be *how people use their leisure time*. Leisure hours must be spent in a constructive rather than a destructive manner, in activities that are satisfying and enjoyable.

To meet the challenge of such a society, this book has attempted to provide a basis for understanding organized recreation service and its further development. In describing the growing significance of recreation services, the author has placed considerable stress on the vital importance of education for leisure.

If this text can contribute to more effective recreation services on all levels and settings, better understanding of the recreation movement, and a stronger quality of recreation leadership, the author will feel that the intent and purpose of the book will have been served.

This comprehensive, attractively illustrated, and up-to-date book has been designed to serve as a text in college and university courses and as a basic guide for professional recreators on all levels of organized recreation service. The author hopes that this book will prove beneficial not only to professors and students in college courses but to citizens in all settings of life. The book should also serve as an excellent reference and source guide for community and civic leaders, agencies, and organizations of all types, including members of boards and commissions, volunteer leaders, club leaders, and planning committees.

Parts I, II, and III provide an understanding of recreation and leisure as an important part of American life. A comprehensive study of today's organized recreation services is presented, which involves sponsorship of a diverse array of governmental, voluntary, private, and commercial agencies and organizations. The economic, social, and psychological aspects of recreation and play are covered in depth and in an appealing fashion. The history and background of the recreation movement receive thorough study, with particular emphasis on the rapid development of recreation and leisure as a growing profession.

The functions and services of governmental agencies on all levels, from the local unit up, receive a careful and up-to-date treatment. The author's approach to international recreation is perhaps the most comprehensive and appealing ever documented, a chapter that can be useful in exchanging program practices among the countries of the world.

Part IV, The Recreation Program, offers a practical and challenging study of organizational practices and program methods, those that have proven their worth in communities and areas throughout America. The major program areas and activities are presented in considerable detail, followed by planning and organizational data that can produce exciting and stimulating programs.

Parts V and VI, in describing recreation as "a challenging profession," discuss the role of the professional and the preparation and training necessary to meet new and stronger professional standards. An absorbing and challenging approach to the problems and major issues confronting the field is offered in Chapter 17, including an updated report on the energy shortage. Through his exhaustive research and investigation, the author, with the assistance of many authorities, has attempted to provide solutions to the difficult problems and issues facing our society. While many texts in the past have failed to mention the problems of minorities and the needs of the disadvantaged, the author has taken an objective and direct approach to the social, cultural, and recreational inequities that have befallen these groups (especially black people) in the past.

In looking to the future, he strives to describe the type of "leisure-oriented society" toward which the nation is moving. An exciting and challenging list of trends is presented in Chapter 18—trends that should have a profound effect on the leisure and recreation movement.

D. C. W.

Acknowledgments

Sincere thanks must go to the outstanding professional recreators and educators who shared their experiences, provided materials, and appeared in photographs. Many distinguished authors and writers gave their permission to use quotations and material from their works. The author is particularly grateful to Richard Kraus, regarded by many as America's most prolific writer on recreation and leisure.

The author would like to acknowledge and express his appreciation to a number of agencies, organizations, and individuals who provided information, data, and photographs relative to their programs and activities. Heading the list is Miss Susan Lee, daughter of the late Joseph Lee, regarded by many as the "father of the playground movement." Special recognition should go to the United States Forest Service in the Department of Agriculture; The National Park Service in the Department of Interior; National Recreation and Park Association; State of California Department of Parks and Recreation; Alameda, California Park and Recreation Department; Elizabethtown, Pennsylvania State Hospital for Crippled Children; Metro-Dade County Park and Recreation Department in Miami, Florida; Naperville Park District, Illinois; Wheeling Park Commission, Wheeling, West Virginia; Oregon State Highway Division; City of Ottawa, Canada Department of Recreation and Parks; Auckland Regional Authority, New Zealand; New Zealand Forest Service; Canadian Parks and Recreation Association; The Sports Council, London, England; Norges Idrettsforbund, Oslo, Norway; German Sports Federation; Recreation Center for the Handicapped, City of San Francisco; and the President's Council on Fitness and Sports.

The author received information from many administrators and staff members of park and recreation departments on all levels of government and in every area in the United States and from many nations of the world.

Chapter Nine, on international recreation, could not have been such a comprehensive and well illustrated chapter if it had not been for those organizations and officials who responded so thoughtfully and generously. Special recognition should go to Woodrow Hutchison of Sacramento,

California, who visited many European countries on behalf of the President's Council on Physical Fitness and Sports. Woody's survey on sports and fitness programs was most helpful in gaining up-to-date information on sports and recreation programs in Europe. This valuable data was most useful in the implementation of the President's Sports Award in this country by the President's Council under Carson "Casey" Conrad, Executive Director.

During the past 25 years, the author has had the opportunity and the privilege to serve and associate with many outstanding professional recreators and educators to whom much of the philosophy and knowledge presented in this text can be attributed. While attending the University of Illinois, the author was privileged to study under such outstanding educators as professors Charles K. Brightbill, Allen Sapora, Alfred Hubbard, C. O. Jackson, and S. C. Staley. Later, as a member of the teaching faculty of the University of Idaho, the author served under Dr. Leon Green, head of the Physical Education and Recreation Division, who had studied at New York University under Jay B. Nash, regarded universally as one of the greatest recreators and philosophers the recreation field has produced.

Perhaps the author's most rewarding experiences in the recreation and park field took place in Spokane, Washington, as program director under Stanley Witter, for many years the city's highly popular superintendent of recreation. He will always remember the countless hours when Mr. Witter, one of the Northwest's pioneers, shared his wealth of knowledge, philosophy, and outlook on life. As a consultant with the Los Angeles City Schools Youth Services Section, the author was involved in the planning and organization of school recreation under such outstanding administrators and educators as Ted Gordon, John Merkley, and Larry Houston. An expression of appreciation should go to Professor Jerome

"Shocky" Needy, California State University at Sacramento, who was most helpful in the author's move to Sacramento.

In the sports field, the author has had the opportunity to make many contributions in the form of textbooks and articles. In collaborating on books with coach George Allen and manager Walter Alston, the author had the rare privilege of associating closely with two of the great leaders in sports history, whose exceptional qualities of leadership and personality made a great impression. As an athlete in Libertyville, Illinois, the writer had the opportunity to play for Arthur Bergstrom, an outstanding coach whose organizational and planning abilities were put to good use later as one of the top administrators of the National Collegiate Athletic Association in Kansas City.

Grateful appreciation must go to the author's wife, Annegrete, who devoted many hours of her time typing and handling many of the details necessary in the development of this manuscript. The strong encouragement and support of his parents, Mr. and Mrs. H. Alan Weiskopf of Pasadena, California, and his wife, have done much to further his education-journalism career. He is grateful to his wife and two daughters, Christine and Lisa, whose leisure participation, like his, had to be restricted while this manuscript was being prepared.

James Negley, recreation instructor at American River College, should be cited for his assistance in collecting resource material on behalf of this book, particularly information on the growing Community School movement.

Finally, editor Russell P. Mead and the staff of Allyn and Bacon should be specially acknowledged for their editorial and production assistance and constructive ideas.

Donald C. Weiskopf
El Dorado Hills, California

I

The Nature and Significance of Recreation and Leisure

1

The Growth of Leisure Time

Today, Americans have more leisure than any other people have ever had in the history of the world. People are working less and experiencing more leisure. Furthermore, the amount of leisure available to most individuals is increasing as a result of our automated existence and the common feeling that one should enjoy the fruits of one's labors. Never before have the people of any country had at their disposal so much leisure and such varied outlets for its use.

LEISURE—WHAT IS IT?

The most common definition and interpretation of leisure is that it represents the free time that people have after they take care of their necessities and after their work has been performed. Leisure time has been defined as ". . . that period of time at the complete disposal of an individual, after he has completed his work and fulfilled his other obligations. Leisure hours are a period of freedom, when man is able to enhance his value as a human being and as a productive member of his society."[1]

According to Sebastian de Grazia, "Free time cannot be identified directly with leisure, since leisure implies such things as a state of being, a mental attitude involving contemplation and serenity."[2] As de Grazia points out, anyone can have free time but not every person can have leisure.

According to the late Charles K. Brightbill, there are two types of leisure—true leisure and enforced leisure. "True leisure is the kind of leisure which is not imposed upon the individual. Enforced leisure, however, is not the leisure which people seek or want. It is the time one has on his hands when he is unemployed, ill, or made to retire from his work when he wants to continue."[3]

Fig. 1-1 THE LEISURE TO ESCAPE. Americans are escaping at a rapidly accelerating rate and heading for the outdoors as if the year were one long weekend. Here, a young family enjoys the camping facilities at Smokehole Recreation Area in West Virginia. (Courtesy of the U.S. Forest Service.)

[1] Editorial Advisory Board, "Charter for Leisure," *Leisure Today*, 1972, p. 15.

[2] Sebastian de Grazia, *Of Time, Work and Leisure* (New York: Doubleday-Anchor, 1962), p. 5.

[3] Harold Meyer, Charles Brightbill, and H. Douglas Sessoms, *Community Recreation—A Guide to Its Organization* (Englewood Cliffs, N.J.: Prentice-Hall, Inc., 1969), p. 30.

A leading French sociologist, Joffre Dumazedier, defines leisure as nonwork activity that people engage in during their free time. "Leisure is activity—apart from the obligations of work, family, and society—to which the individual turns at will, for either relaxation, diversion, or broadening his knowledge and his spontaneous social participation, the free exercise of his creative capacity."[4]

A LEISURE-ORIENTED SOCIETY

Indeed, we live in an age of urbanization, mechanization, automation, computers, nuclear energy, spaceships, and jet-propelled transportation. Although these changes have been nothing short of fantastic, the end is not in sight. We stand at the threshold of a leisure-oriented society, a nuclear age with unlimited possibilities for the enrichment of human life. The potential of recreation and leisure time services for satisfying, creative, and enriched living is limitless.

In 1850, the average work week in industry and farming was approximately seventy hours. In 1950, it had dwindled to forty hours. Today, an estimated seven million persons work thirty-seven hours, thirty-five hours, or even less, with predictions of a thirty-two-hour work week by the end of the decade.

On the basis of a forty-hour work week, the average industrial worker spends over 2,000 hours a year on the job and has approximately 3,000 hours off the job. However, it should be noted that this free time is reduced by "moonlighting," commuting to and from work, working at "do-it-yourself" jobs, doing household chores, and shopping.

Americans, then, are involved in an economic and social revolution. The past half century has brought technological changes at such an accelerated pace that our lives have been revolutionized. New industrial machinery, incredible mobility, television, and miracle drugs are just a few of the new and exciting influences that have changed the lives of Americans.

The implications of such a revolution are so vast that every aspect of our lives will be affected. Many Americans will be experiencing shorter working hours and a greater amount of free time. Predictions for the future indicate a work year of 1,100 hours with four-day weeks and at least thirteen weeks of vacation.

Leisure has increased particularly among older people. A longer life span—and early retirement with social security and pensions—have combined to give them considerably more leisure time.

While a continued world fuel shortage could result in a major setback to the leisure industry, there have been positive indications that the current crisis will ease in the years ahead. Certainly, the leisure society that this text will describe in the chapters ahead will depend on an abundance of energy and natural resources.

EDUCATION FOR LEISURE TIME

Unfortunately, for many citizens, the gift of free time will come more as a detriment than as a blessing. Too many of us are unprepared for it. This is because leisure carries no guarantee of Utopian happiness. True, it may bring opportunities for the enjoyment of art, music, and science; for development of health, strength, and satisfaction. Conversely, a great amount of leisure may bring boredom, idleness, escape through drugs, overindulgence, deterioration, or corruption.

> THE WISE USE OF LEISURE TIME IS THE CHALLENGE OF OUR TIME.

In order to have a strong society, leisure hours must be spent in a constructive rather than a destructive manner. Individuals must be given help in developing those areas where deficiencies exist in their personal development. For example, the person who spends long hours every day at a desk doing mental work should be given the opportunity to spend some time engaging in physical activity.

In a democratic society the use of leisure will always remain the prerogative of the individual. However, with the great increase in leisure time, society should be entrusted with some obligations

---

[4] Joffre Dumazedier, *Toward a Society of Leisure* (New York: Free Press, 1967), pp. 16–17.

Fig. 1-2 A FAMILY TRIES ITS LUCK at Hungry Horse Reservoir in Montana. (Courtesy of the U.S. Forest Service.)

and responsibilities for making adequate provisions for its use.

The role of community leaders—recreators, teachers, social workers, and others—in helping people to develop the various qualities and competencies of good living will be a vital one. Society can do much to provide the skills, understanding, appreciations, attitudes, and values that will motivate its people to spend their leisure hours in a profitable manner.

THE THREAT OF LEISURE

A major problem for society will be the task of creating a civilization that does not degenerate under leisure. We have already learned that leisure can be either an asset or a liability. What we do with it will determine our fate. Leisure that cannot be used constructively can be just as dangerous as no leisure at all.

Fig. 1-3 AMERICANS WORK SO HARD AT FUN! Here a father uses some of his free time to play in the sand with his children. Sun, surf, and sand attract millions of Americans.

Fig. 1-4 MORE LEISURE FOR MOM, TOO. Thanks to many labor-saving devices in the home, the housewife has less work, which has lessened the drudgery of household chores.

Do we know how to choose? Indeed, the danger of choice can be a problem if we cannot distinguish between what is helpful and what is hurtful. To be able to choose, an individual must have a trained intellect and possess a wide range of skills. Intelligent and constructive choices cannot be made unless the individual has the broad knowledge and emotional make-up to want to use his leisure constructively. The ability to make wise choices, perhaps, is the key to man's existence.

LEISURE AND THE SCHOOLS

It is becoming increasingly clear to a growing number of people that the school can be a vital instrument in converting leisure into an asset of major significance. Although the education field has always advocated the optimum use of leisure time as one of its cardinal principles, schools have failed to devote sufficient emphasis on its execution and application. "In a nation where leisure constitutes more than half of the waking hours of its citizens," wrote Howard Danford, "there can be no possible justification for the failure of

the schools to prepare young people for the creative use of their leisure time."[5]

Now, it appears that there is a growing trend by all areas and departments of education to prepare students for a better education for leisure than they have ever been provided before. Schools, in greater numbers, are assuming responsibility for helping students acquire life-long interests, appreciations, and skills in art, music, reading, outdoor education, sports and games, and many other worthwhile activities. These leisure pursuits may continue throughout their lifetimes.

Few people actually know how to play. They lack skills, interests, and other motivating factors. In short, they do not feel that recreation and play has an important place in their lives. Generally, most people prefer to participate in those activities which are satisfying and enjoyable. The interest and enjoyment of the students largely will be determined by the manner in which teachers present their subjects.

Leisure is a time when choices must be made.

[5] Howard G. Danford and Max Shirley, *Creative Leadership in Recreation*, 2nd ed. (Boston: Allyn and Bacon, Inc., 1970), p. 23.

But to be able to choose, we must have the intelligence, along with a sense of values, appreciations, interests, and skills. Furthermore, people must be disciplined in making choices not only for their own good but for the good of society as a whole. In short, an individual must have the ability to determine that which is good.

THE CHALLENGE OF LEISURE

For many Americans, work fails to provide opportunities for optimum growth and development. Therefore, leisure must assume a more important role than mere freedom from work. To be enjoyable to the individual, as well as constructive to society, leisure must provide some satisfaction to people's basic needs. It must serve a rehabilitative or therapeutic function.

People should have opportunities to express themselves through cultural activities, such as painting a picture or enjoying a good book. To experience satisfaction and enjoyment, though, they should have developed the necessary skills, interests, and appreciations.

Quite often, an individual is unfit for leisure simply because the schools have neglected this important aspect of his education. Furthermore, his work has not provided opportunities for practice in the art of creative self-expression.

CHARTER FOR LEISURE

A charter for leisure was developed by a symposium held in Geneva, Switzerland in 1967. Convened by the International Recreation Association, the symposium was attended by some sixteen organizations operating internationally in the field of leisure, recreation, and play. A resolution was adopted calling for the development of a charter for leisure that could be used by all agencies, governmental and voluntary, concerned with leisure and its use.

The Recreation Division of the American Association for Health, Physical Education, and Recreation believes this document can be an im-

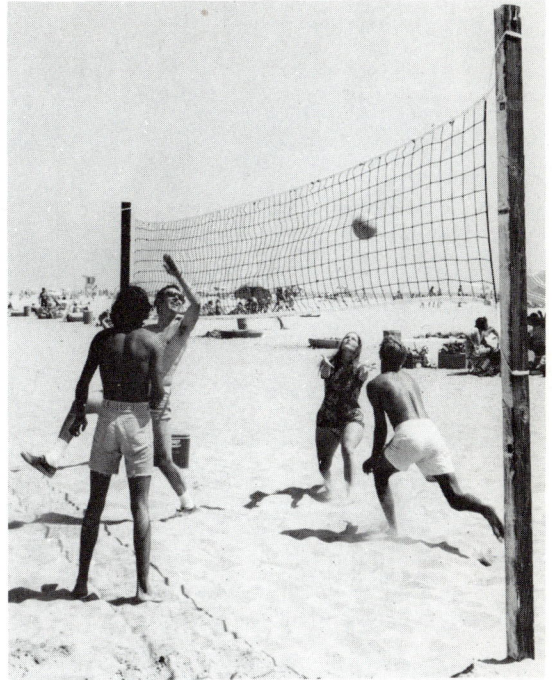

Fig. 1-5 GOOD USE OF LEISURE TIME. A vigorous, stimulating game of volleyball can be an ideal activity for the person who spends long hours at his desk doing mental work.

portant tool for planning the recreation and leisure time services for all age groups.

Article 1: Every man has a right to leisure time.

Article 2: The right to enjoy leisure time with complete freedom is absolute.

Article 3: Every man has a right to recreational facilities open to the public, and to nature reserves by lakes, seas, wooded areas, in the mountains, and to open spaces.

Article 4: Every man has a right to participate in and be introduced to all types of recreation during leisure time.

Article 5: Leisure time should be unorganized in the sense that official authorities, urban planners, architects and private groups of individuals do not decide how others are to use their leisure time.

Article 6: Every man has a right to the opportunity for learning how to enjoy his leisure time.

Fig. 1-6 THE QUALITY OF LEADERSHIP will determine to a great degree whether leisure in America becomes an asset or a liability.

Article 7: The responsibility for education is still divided among a large number of disciplines and institutions.[6]

Although curricula in the schools will likely remain work-centered for many years to come, there is some evidence that "education for leisure" is not a visionary dream but a commitment to be achieved.

RECREATION—WHAT IS IT?

Recreation takes on a great variety of forms. Some activities involve active participation; others involve quiet relaxation, listening, or watching. Indeed, the appeal of recreation varies as the interests and needs, age, physical and intellectual capacity of the participants change.

> RECREATION IS ANY ENJOYABLE LEISURE EXPERIENCE IN WHICH THE PARTICIPANT VOLUNTARILY ENGAGES AND FROM WHICH HE RECEIVES IMMEDIATE SATISFACTION.
> *Reynold Carlson, Theodore Deppe,*
> *and Janet MacLean*

[6] "Charter for Leisure," a resolution adopted at an International Recreation Association symposium in Geneva, Switzerland, 1967.

What is considered recreation for one person may be boring and lacking in interest for another. The attitude of the individual toward the activity is of prime importance. According to S. R. Slavson, the quality of the experience, and the feeling the participant has about it, are most essential to satisfying recreation activity. In summing up this point, Slavson wrote: "Recreation does not consist of what one does; it is rather the motive, attitude, and value of the doing to the individual that gives an activity a recreational significance."[7] For example, building a sailboat can be an ideal form of recreation to one individual; to another, it would be work.

> RECREATION MAY BE THOUGHT OF AS ACTIVITY VOLUNTARILY ENGAGED IN DURING LEISURE AND PRIMARILY MOTIVATED BY THE SATISFACTION OR PLEASURE AND PRIMARILY MOTIVATED BY THE SATISFACTION OR PLEASURE DERIVED THEREFROM.
> *Charles K. Brightbill and*
> *Harold Meyer*

Although many educators have written many different definitions of recreation, several components are common to each of them. Recreation must not only be chosen voluntarily and be

[7] S. R. Slavson, *Recreation and the Total Personality* (New York: Association Press, 1946), p. 2.

8

enjoyable but it must be socially acceptable and morally sound. It must help meet certain basic human needs and interests, otherwise it will not be satisfying. The activity should have the potential to make a significant contribution to the well-being of the individual and society as a whole.

> RECREATION IS THE NATURAL EXPRESSION OF HUMAN INTERESTS AND NEEDS SEEKING SATISFACTION DURING LEISURE.
> *Gerald B. Fitzgerald*

DEFINITIONS OF RECREATION

The term "recreation" comes from the Latin word *recreatio,* meaning that which refreshes or restores. Max Kaplan wrote: "In its traditional sense, recreation has been as a period of light and restful activity, voluntarily chosen, which restores one for heavy, obligatory activity, or work."[8]

A modern point of view was expressed by Sebastian de Grazia: "Recreation is activity that rests men from work, often by giving them a change, and restores them for work. When adults play—as they do, of course, with persons, things and symbols—they play for recreation. Like the Romans, our own conception of leisure is mainly recreative."[9]

However, Richard Kraus feels this concept of recreation lacks acceptability today.

First, as most work in modern society becomes less demanding, many people become more fully engaged, both physically and mentally, in their recreation, than in their work. Second, the idea that recreation is primarily intended to restore one for work has no meaning for such groups as aging persons who have no work but who certainly need recreation to make their life meaningful.[10]

[8] Max Kaplan, *Leisure in America: A Social Inquiry* (New York: John Wiley, 1960), p. 19.

[9] de Grazia, op. cit., p. 233.

[10] Richard Kraus, *Recreation and Leisure in Modern Society* (New York: Appleton-Century-Crofts, 1971), pp. 260–61. © 1971 by Meredith Corporation. Reprinted by permission of Prentice-Hall, Inc., Englewood Cliffs, N.J.

Fig. 1-7 EDUCATION FOR LEISURE. The schools have a vital responsibility to prepare young people for the creative use of leisure time. Lifetime sports such as archery should receive major emphasis.

Motivation is often the decisive factor that determines the recreation nature of the activity or experience. Howard Danford writes: "If the individual engages in an activity for the sheer fun of doing so, it is recreation. If he does so because of an outer compulsion, such as the need for money, the activity is work."[11]

Today, recreation provides employment for large numbers of people in the "recreation and parks industry," or the rapidly expanding "leisure economy." Thus, recreation becomes more than a concept or a form of activity. Instead, it refers to all the governmental agencies and social institutions that have been formed to meet the leisure and recreation needs of our society.

[11] Danford and Shirley, op. cit., p. 25.

Fig. 1-8 A LEISURELY BICYCLE RIDE. Guy and Ralna Hovis, popular singing stars on the Lawrence Welk television show, take a break from their busy schedule to go bicycling, their favorite recreation activity.

In recent years, the public has accepted recreation, along with leisure, as the terms most applicable to the broad field of leisure services and experiences, including such institutional forms as community agencies, professional organizations, and occupational involvement.

Community recreation is commonly thought of as those recreation activities that society provides through various social institutions such as the municipal recreation department, the school, the home, and the church.

CHARACTERISTICS OF RECREATION

The term *recreation* implies certain basic characteristics:

• The choice of activity is voluntary.
• Recreation occurs during leisure time.
• Recreation provides enjoyment.
• Recreation is activity as opposed to idleness.
• Recreation is broad in concept.
• Recreation provides a refreshing change-of-pace.

• Recreation should be wholesome and constructive.
• Recreation should be socially acceptable.
• Recreation contributes to the physical, mental, and moral welfare of the participant.

THE MEANING OF PLAY

The term *play* is generally regarded as an activity carried on within leisure for purposes of pleasure, satisfaction, and self-expression. It is often carried on in a spirit of competition, exploration, fun, or make-believe.

Although the words *recreation* and *play* have often been used interchangeably or synonymously, most textbooks have distinguished between these two terms in various ways. Both describe play as spontaneous, physical activity, while recreation is re-creative, organized, and relaxing activity. Generally, most textbook authors accept recreation as the broad term that includes play. Play is generally carried on by children, while recreation is an adult's concern. However, adults may engage in both play and recreation, as may children.

De Grazia wrote that "Play is what children do, frolic and sport. Adults play too, though their games are less muscular and more intricate. Men may play games in recreation; indeed except for men who work, play is a form of recreation. When adults play, as they do, of course, they play for recreation."[12]

According to Richard Kraus, "Both play and recreation may be examined in their relationship to work. While, by definition, recreation cannot exist within work, play (both in terms of the spirit of participation and the manner in which one approaches a task) certainly is part of work for many individuals."[13]

THEORIES OF PLAY AND RECREATION

Why do people play? This question has been asked for centuries, and down through the years, educators and scholars have attempted to answer it

---

[12] de Grazia, op. cit., p. 233.
[13] Kraus, op. cit., p. 265.

Fig. 1-9 A THRILLING RIDE DOWN THE SALMON RIVER. People who experience boredom and monotony on the job need leisure activities that provide thrills and excitement, like running the rapids with a rubber raft down the Salmon River in Idaho. (Courtesy of the U.S. Forest Service.)

with a variety of theories. In re-examining play and its theories, M. J. Ellis said: "Theories are important because they are simplifying explanations of previous experiences and data that seem to have the capacity to predict what will come about. A theory has no worth beyond its value to promote insights into and predictions of outcomes. A theory, then, is an ordered way of moving from previous experience into the future."[14]

There have been many theories that attempted to explain the development of the modern concept of recreation and play. Their inadequacy can be attributed in part to the fact that many of these theories were partial and incomplete. Many were based upon the play of children, rather than the recreation of people of all ages. Although these theories present a number of differences, there are also points of agreement. None of the theories limit the forms that play and recreation take.

Classical Theories

The classical theories are the best known play theories and are regularly discussed in introductory texts. Surplus energy, instinct, recapitulation, preparation, and relaxation are theories that originated before the beginning of the twentieth century. In general, classical theories have been concerned

with those elements in the nature of man that led him to play and with the purposes that play served.

Surplus Energy Theory. According to this theory, play is the expression of "animal spirits"; the individual is so charged with muscular energy that he cannot keep still. Play is caused by the existence of energy that is surplus to the needs of survival. Although energy can be stored, storage is limited. Therefore, excess energy must be expended.

The fallacy of this theory is revealed by the fact that children play when fatigued or near the point of fatigue. Thus, a surplus is not necessary for play. Many people engage in recreational activity even though their physical or mental energy has largely been depleted. We cannot, then, explain their motivations by the surplus energy theory.

Instinct Theory. Play is caused by the inheritance of unlearned capacities to emit playful acts. The determinants of our behavior are inherited in the same way we inherit the genetic code that determines our structure.

This theory can be criticized because it ignores the obvious capacity of people to learn new responses that we classify as play.

Recapitulation Theory. Play is caused by the player recapitulating the history of the development of the species during its development. However, the theory has been criticized because there

[14] M. J. Ellis, "Play and Its Theories Re-Examined," *Parks and Recreation,* August 1971, p. 51.

11

Fig. 1-10 THE VARIETY OF RECREATION. Paddling a canoe offers an outlet for physical power. The young lady, meanwhile, finds sketching a very creative and relaxing way to spend her leisure moments.

is no linear progression in our play development that seems to mirror the development of a species.

Relaxation Theory. According to this theory, play relieves the stresses and strains of the individual. Play is viewed as being pleasurable and sought for its own sake; it is a release from work, compulsion, and the struggle to live.

Applying more to the play and recreation of adults, the relaxation theory is similar to the surplus energy view that play is an outlet for pent-up emotions.

Recent Theories of Play

Many additional explanations of play were introduced after the turn of the century, theories such as generalization, compensation, catharsis, psychoanalytic development, and learning. These theories had a different character than the classic theories, being more concerned with the content of the play behavior and the play of an individual.

According to M. J. Ellis, "The explanations of generalization and compensation are in the process of being tested and they have some appeal since work still features as a powerful influence in the lives of schoolchildren and adults."[15]

Compensation Theory. Play is caused by players using their play to satisfy psychic needs not satisfied in or generated by their work. In play or leisure the player will avoid behaviors that are unsatisfying in the work setting. The player selects leisure experiences that meet his psychic needs.

The theory has been criticized because it seems to exclude the play of pre-school children. Furthermore, it assumes that work is damaging.

_____
[15] Ibid., p. 53.

Generalization Theory.   According to this theory, play is caused by the player using experiences that have been rewarding at work. The player transfers to his play or leisure those types of behavior that are rewarded in another setting. This theory can be criticized because it seems to exclude the play of pre-school children and because it assumes that at least some aspects of work are rewarding.

Catharsis Theory.   This theory suggests that play is caused in part by the need to express disorganizing emotions in a harmless way by transferring them to a socially sanctioned activity. Play is viewed as a safety valve for pent-up emotions such as anger.

Although it has some validity, the theory fails to explain the nature of recreation for relaxation that characterizes many forms of play.

Psychoanalytic Theories.   Play is caused in part by the players repeating in a playful form some strongly unpleasant experiences, thereby reducing their seriousness and allowing their assimilation.

As yet, however, there is no very clear-cut contribution to the play behavior of people not driven to play by an unpleasant experience. "To the extent that the client is 'normal' and is not beyond the pleasure principle," said Ellis, "then the psychoanalytic view of play behavior does not seem helpful—particularly since it does not look forward to predict future behavior."[16]

Developmentalism Theory.   Play is caused by the way in which a child's mind develops. Thus, play is caused by the growth of the child's intellect and is conditioned by it. As a result of play, the intellect increases in complexity. Ideally, this concept should be integrated with a more precise theory of motivation and learning.

Learning Theory.   Play is caused by the normal processes that produce learning. The individual acts in such a way to maximize the likelihood of pleasant outcomes and vice versa. Thus, the child plays because he learns to play.

As the child accumulates experiences, he becomes more complex and eventually approximates adult behavior.

Fig. 1-11   THE FUN OF IT ALL. As a participant or as a spectator, recreation may involve enjoying a sack relay at a picnic, watching a stage show, playing a softball game or a game of pool. These are only a few of the wide variety of activities known as recreation.

Self-Expression Theory.   Two leading educators, Elmer Mitchell and Bernard Mason, saw play primarily as a result of the drive for self-expression. In "The Theory of Play," they wrote that man was perceived as "an active, dynamic creature, with a need to find outlets for his energies, to use his abilities, and to express his personality."[17]

The self-expression theory recognizes the nature of man, his anatomical and physiological structure, his psychological inclination, his feeling of capacity, and his desire for self-expression.

Recreation Theory.   Play is viewed as the natural change-over from work in that it refreshes, replenishes, and restores energy. Play is quite as essential as rest.

Modern Theories of Play

There are two modern theories of play: play competence and play arousal. Both theories are

[16] Ibid.

[17] Kraus, op. cit., p. 266.

concerned with the existence of surplus behaviors and try to explain why the child, adult, or animal continues to behave when apparently all his needs have been satisfied.[18]

Arousal-Seeking Theory.   Play is a class of behaviors concerned with increasing the level of arousal of the organism. Play is caused by the need to generate either interactions with the environment or interactions with the individual that elevate arousal. "There comes a time when they cease to be arousing," wrote Ellis. "Then, the need for continued stimulation causes the person, or animal, to search for and generate other interactions that are stimulating. As the process proceeds, the person becomes more complex and so do the necessary interactions."[19] The recreation professional, therefore, is involved in facilitating the delivery of opportunities for people to optimize their arousal levels.

Competence Motivation Theory.   Play is caused by a need to produce effects in the environment. Such effects demonstrate competence and produce feelings of effectiveness. Ellis believes that competence motivation is merely a subclass of arousal-seeking behaviors, but at this time, the theory does not add anything to the arousal-seeking model.[20]

Integrating the Theories

According to Ellis, only three of the above theories can be integrated: developmentalism, play as learned response, and the arousal-seeking model.

The arousal-seeking model provides us with a motive for the continuance of surplus energy. The organism has a need for optimal arousal, and arousal-elevating behaviors are not necessarily surplus or trivial.

In the case of the child, a further restraint is imposed on the interactions that can produce appropriate arousal—the cognitive complexity of the child. Early in life, a child has fewer experiences

and knowledge, and simple interactions are arousing.

In summary, theories of play are too important to us to be ignored. "We need to develop an approach to theory as professionals," stated Ellis, "so that we are constantly testing and evaluating the fundamental theoretical bases of the profession—one class of which concerns play. Play theories are legion and many are logically or empirically inadequate. It is important to evaluate them critically, to actively reject theories that are of no use to us, and accept those that are useful in our everyday practice."[21]

OBJECTIVES OF RECREATION

The field of recreation has many worthwhile objectives such as the following:

1. Satisfying basic human needs
2. Promoting total health
3. Lessening the strains and tensions of modern life
4. Encouraging abundant personal and family life
5. Developing good citizenship and a democratic society.

One of the best statements of objectives was discussed by the Commission on "Goals for American Recreation."[22] The objectives are six in number:

1. Personal fulfillment, the need for each person to become all that he is capable of becoming
2. Democratic human relations
3. Leisure skills and interests
4. Health and fitness
5. Creative expression and esthetic appreciation
6. Environment for living in a leisure society

RELATIONSHIP OF RECREATION TO OTHER AREAS

There is a close and significant interrelationship between recreation and related areas such as

---

[18] Ellis, op. cit., p. 55.

[19] Ibid.

[20] Ibid.

[21] Ibid., p. 90.

[22] The Commission on Goals for American Recreation: "Goals for American Recreation," Washington, D.C., 1964.

Fig. 1-12 THE SPIRIT OF PLAY AND COMPETITION can make a significant contribution to the physical, mental, and emotional well-being of participants. Many people do not compete enough—they give up too easily. These personality traits apply to life too.

work, education, religion, health, and social welfare.

Education. The goals of recreation and education are similar; both are working toward the enrichment of life for individuals.

Work. Activity is not recreation when its nature is money-making or prestige. Satisfaction in the activity should be the sole reward.

Physical Education. Recreation and physical education are complementary, not identical. Emphasis in physical education is on physical fitness and the development of attitudes, interests, and skills. Recreation experiences contribute to the satisfaction of such human needs as creative self-expression, personal fulfillment, and living in a leisure society.

Group Work. Group work and recreation are not synonymous. However, participation in group rec-

reation activity may be one method of achieving desired goals.

Adult Education. The goals, organization, and methods of the adult education profession closely resemble those of recreation. Generally, adult education pertains to activities used for vocational progress, while recreation relates to skills and appreciations. Classes in sewing and woodcrafts are good examples of recreational activities offered by adult education programs.

THE NEEDS OF SOCIETY

The need for recreation is affected by several conditions of social life. Attitudes have been altered significantly by various social changes, such as those that have been occurring in America and various parts of the world for the past decade. Indeed, these attitudes and factors have formed a

Fig. 1-13 THE MANY NEEDS OF SOCIETY. The enjoyment that comes from engaging in recreation activities should be experienced by individuals of all age groups.

new philosophy of the importance of leisure. Factors that have influenced the growth of recreation needs are:

Increased leisure
Increased income
Education
Industrialization and mechanization
Civil unrest
Changing home life
Population
Greater mobility
Urbanization
Environmental concerns

The joy that comes from engaging in recreation activities should be experienced by everyone. These activities must fit his needs, interests, and desires.

A doctoral study by Norvel Clark at New York University in 1962 investigated the needs and interests of junior high school students in the Bedford-Stuyvesant area of Brooklyn, New York. The purpose of the study was to develop a recreation activity program based on the identified needs and interests. According to Charles A.

Bucher, "The study revealed the rank order of needs of children as evaluated by experts in the field of education, recreation, social group work, and community education."

The needs were as follows:

1. The need to achieve
2. The need for economic security
3. The need to belong
4. The need for love and affection
5. The need for self-respect through participation
6. The need for variety as relief from boredom and ignorance
7. The need to feel free from intense feelings of guilt
8. The need to be free from fear[23]

An opportunity to have challenging work is what people really want and need in life if they are to enjoy a sense of belonging. According to Jay B. Nash, "Leisure alone is not enough to satisfy; neither is work unless it has significance. Recreation and work, together, make for fullness. To people who do not work, leisure is meaningless. To people who are overworked, leisure may become just as meaningless."[24]

THE VALUES OF RECREATION

The relationship of recreation to personality is very important. Since each individual's personality is unique and distinct, each has his own ideals, attitudes, habits, interests, and desires. However, the various elements of personality are not all present in equal degree or arranged exactly alike among all people. Since the various personal elements fit well together, the person with a well-integrated personality knows how to enjoy and make the most of new experiences.

William Menninger of the famed Menninger Clinic in Topeka, Kansas, has stated that "The happy and healthy person today is the one who has recreation pursuits. Good mental health is di-

[23] Charles A. Bucher, *Foundations of Physical Education* (St. Louis: C. V. Mosby Co., 1972), p. 245.

[24] Jay B. Nash, *Philosophy of Recreation and Leisure* (Dubuque, Iowa: William C. Brown Co., 1970), p. 106.

rectly related to the capacity and willingness of an individual to play."[25]

Personal Values In Recreation

Recreation can make three major contributions with respect to the growth and development of its participants:

Psychological Aspects of Recreation. Recreation has been recognized as an important tool in the prevention of mental illness and in the rehabilitation of mentally ill patients. Recreation can offer important outlets for frustrations, as petty worries and unnecessary concerns may be forgotten as the individual focuses his attention and interest on active as well as passive forms of recreational activity.

Recreation is recognized by leading psychiatrists as essential to the mental health of all individuals. Menninger strongly subscribes to the view that the value of recreational experience is an essential part of happy and well-balanced living. He stresses the great importance of hobbies, sports and games, and group involvement in maintaining emotional health.

Physical Aspects of Recreation. Recreation in the form of sports, games, and moderately strenuous outdoor pastimes can make an important contribution to the physical well-being of all Americans. Emphasis should be on activities involving moderately physical exercise that can be carried on through adulthood. If they are enjoyable, people will perform them willingly. There is a significant need for providing physical activities suitable for the later years. Until recently, this has not been sufficiently recognized and exploited.

Social Aspects of Recreation. Recreation can provide the opportunity for group experiences that meet fundamental human needs. According to the distinguished social work authority, Gisela Konopka, "Next to the biological necessities, man's deepest longings are to love and to be important —important to someone." Dr. Konopka points out

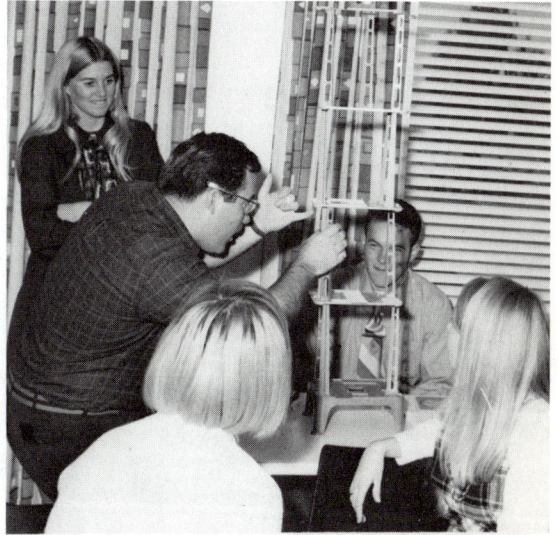

Fig. 1-14 SOCIALLY SATISFYING GROUP ACTIVITY is a fundamental human need that can be met by enjoying party games such as this one.

that this important need can be met through a healthy group life.[26]

Through recreation, an individual can develop respect and understanding for others and a recognition of one's own place in society. Even personal faults may be overcome through recreational activities.

For a growing number of people, recreation has been responsible in part for the development of character traits such as initiative, self-reliance, restraint, courage, perseverance, ingenuity, honesty, love of fair play, and consideration for others. No wonder, the various character-building organizations use recreation as a major tool for the attainment of their aims and objectives.

PSYCHOLOGICAL ASPECTS OF PLAY

According to many noted psychologists, play and recreation are decisive factors in the psychological development and maturing of man. Although psychologists wrote extensively on the role of play

[25] Bucher, op. cit., p. 244.

[26] Gisela Konopka, *Social Group Work, a Helping Process* (Englewood Cliffs, N.J.: Prentice-Hall, Inc., 1963), pp. 39–40.

Fig. 1-15 THE ROLE OF PLAY. Recreation activity is one of the best outlets for pent-up emotions. Children can also develop intelligence through play. Here, children unleash some of their excess energy in a game of "follow the leader."

during the early decades of the twentieth century, the most significant studies have come after 1940. Since World War II, play has come to be regarded as an important experience through which children can develop emotionally, psychologically, and socially. Through play, important patterns of behavior can be formed that will prove beneficial throughout their lifetime.

In 1951, Ruth Strang, a noted child-guidance authority, wrote, "The play life of a child is an index of his social maturity, and reveals his personality more clearly than any other activity."[27] According to two prominent child psychologists, Arnold Gesell and Frances Ilg, in recommending that mothers play with their children, "Deeply absorbing play seems to be essential for full mental growth."[28]

Recreation also can play a vital role in the maintenance of mental health. According to William Menninger,

Psychologically, recreation is one of the best outlets for pent-up emotions, particularly hostile feelings. This is most obvious in competitive games in which there is running, hitting, throwing. It applies equally, however, to sedentary games like chess, bridge, and poker.[29]

As psychiatrists, we heartily endorse and strongly recommend that every individual develop a hobby or an organized program of play for himself. There is much less interest in hobbies and recreation activities among psychiatric patients prior to their illness than among well-adjusted persons. Hobbies do not necessarily prevent a mental illness, but their cultivation seems to tend to the development of a more stable personality by providing even a momentary diversion from stress.[30]

---

[27] Ruth Strang, *An Introduction to Child Study* (New York: The Macmillan Co., 1951), p. 495.

[28] Arnold Gesell and Frances Ilg, *The Child from Five to Ten* (New York: Harper & Row, 1946), p. 360.

[29] William C. Menninger, *Psychiatry in a Troubled World* (New York: The Macmillan Co., 1948), p. 359.
[30] Ibid., p. 72.

Fig. 1-16 PLAY IS A CHILD'S WAY OF LEARNING. Children are shown involved in deeply absorbing play, as they enjoy their nature experiences in Sequoia National Forest, California. (Courtesy of U.S. Forest Service.)

Insufficient opportunities for active and creative play can result in nervousness and irritability of children, waste of spare time, poor imagination, aggressiveness and rowdyism of many teenagers.

> **NO ONE IS EVER TOO BIG OR TOO OLD TO PLAY.**

Social Function of Play

For many years, psychologists felt that children's play was little more than an expression of excess energy and good spirits. The importance of their activities was questioned. The primary function of play was to "let off steam" so that the child could return to the more important business of study and learning. Recently, however, studies of how intelligence develops in children have revealed that play is the way in which children develop intelligence.

According to Richard Dattner, "Play is a child's way of learning. . . . Control of children's play is one way in which a society prepares the child to participate eventually in the world of adults. Train up a child in the way he should go, and when he is old, he will not depart from it."[31]

Heredity Vs. Environment

Recent studies in developmental psychology have combined the two formerly antagonistic main schools of thought about mental development. For a long time, however, people such as Francis Galton believed that heredity was the determining factor of intelligence, while behavioral psychologists held that the environment was more important.

In 1869, Galton, the cousin of Charles Darwin, studied the biographical backgrounds of a thousand eminent men with the purpose of finding out if any unique qualities were present in their families. He found that men of great reputation in Great Britain tended to come from a small group of families. From this study, Galton concluded that genius is inherited, a conclusion heavily influenced by Darwin's conception of evolution as the survival of inherited characteristics."[32]

---

[31] From *Design for Play* by Richard Dattner, © 1969 by Reinhold Books Corporation, p. 17. Reprinted by permission of Van Nostrand Reinhold Company.

[32] Ibid., pp. 23–24.

Fig. 1-17 CREATIVE PLAY. Children should have sufficient opportunities for active and creative play such as tree climbing. These two boys enjoy the adventure and excitement of George Washington National Forest in Virginia. (Courtesy of U.S. Forest Service.)

On the other hand, behavioral psychologists maintained that environment was the primary factor in the development of intelligence. According to Jean Piaget,

... intelligence is a special form of adaptation, which consists of a continuous creative interaction between the organism and the environment. Life thus becomes the process of creating increasingly complex structures of behavior. Neither the organism nor the environment exists alone, but only as they interact and affect each other. . . . Piaget conceived of two complementary processes—assimilation and accommodation. Assimilation is the mastery of familiar or new skills by repetition and practice. It occurs when we see a new situation in terms of something familiar, or when we act in a new situation as we have acted in past situations."[33]

Accommodation, which is complementary to assimilation, occurs when variations in the environment demand a modification in man's pattern of behavior. "Accommodation occurs when a previously learned response fails to work in a new situation, and the organism modifies its response."[34] Assimilation and accommodation are the two processes by which the child gradually develops his intelligence from the primarily instructural responses of infancy to the eventual

> WHEN CHILDREN BECOME INTERESTED IN THE NATURAL AND MAN-MADE WORLD THEIR CURIOSITY IS BEST SATISFIED BY FIRST-HAND EXPERIENCE.
>
> *Richard Dattner*

---

[33] Ibid.

[34] Ibid., p. 24.

achievement of adult logical thinking. This development takes place in stages, each with its own characteristic forms of play.[35]

Understanding Human Behavior

As he understands why people behave as they do and the forces which drive them on, the leader is able to influence their behavior more effectively. Recreation people are continually involved in the conduct of activities whose outcomes are more than fun, enjoyment, and relaxation.

A boy playing softball on a playground team is having fun, but since the "whole person" is involved many other things are also happening to him. He is active, therefore physiological outcomes, either good or bad, are certain to result, and skills, either properly or improperly executed, are engaged in. His intellectual operations may involve the learning of rules and the making of intelligent decisions during play. These intellectual operations interlock with the development of social behavior as he responds to his teammates, his opponents, the officials, spectators, and to his coach, or leader. The emotions may be aroused in many of these responses. Moral and ethical choices may have to be made.[36]

The recreation leader, therefore, must directly concern himself with all of the outcomes of the activity. "If he shuts his eyes to moral and ethical values," continued Danford, "he may develop a skillful player who is also a bully, a liar, a cheat, and a thief. If he ignores social behavior, he may contribute to the development of non-cooperative, selfish individualists whose sole concern is themselves."[37]

Human beings constantly are searching for goals. People behave the way they do in order to satisfy their need for self-esteem, personal adequacy, or self-enhancement. "This is why they join groups," said Danford. "For example, a boy joins a baseball team because it enables him to have fun, satisfy the need for recognition, and the need for acceptance."[38]

Fig. 1-18 A BOY PLAYING SOFTBALL is involved with far more than mere fun and enjoyment. Social behavior, playing according to the rules, making intelligent decisions, and performing skills are additional outcomes of great importance to his growth and stability.

Developing the Personality

No one can teach what a child learns while playing. By exploring and experimenting, the child learns to live in our symbolic world of meaning and values, continually striving for goals and trying to meet his needs.

Children can develop inner strengths and learn self-control through play. As they move from the toddler age to about five or six, children shift from solitary activities to side-by-side play. Finally, they become involved in integrated, cooperative play projects.

The child explores the air, the water, the ground, he climbs, he kicks, he runs, he wades, and swims. Through all this, he practices language and manipulatory skills; he finds out about gravity, velocity, the weight and strength of objects and tools, and the way others respond to his behavior. By the time he has reached puberty, the child should have achieved, through play, a variety of interests, skills and social competencies which help him enter this difficult and challenging period of development.[39]

---

[35] Ibid.
[36] Danford and Shirley, op. cit., p. 31.
[37] Ibid.
[38] Ibid., p. 61.

---

[39] Kraus, op. cit., pp. 276–77.

Fig. 1-19 JOINING A TEAM. To satisfy their need for self-esteem, personal adequacy, and acceptance, boys and girls should be given the opportunity to join groups and teams. Teamwork, sportsmanship, discipline, and having fun are program objectives that will prove very beneficial to them.

The relationship of play and recreation to the social and emotional growth of teenagers has undergone much research by psychologists. They have found that the adolescent's self-image is closely related to participation in extracurricular activities. High school students with a high degree of self-esteem tend to take part actively in sports, musical groups, publications, and social activities. Those with a low degree of self-esteem were less involved in their involvement and participation.

Richard Kraus suggested that: ". . . extracurricular or other recreational experiences for youth can offer an opportunity for real involvement with others, and provide a sense of acceptance and security within the group, that will contribute to psychological well-being."[40]

---

[40] Ibid., p. 277.

Fig. 1-20 FREE PLAY ACTIVITIES. Children today would be better off if they played more. Here, young children enjoy backyard fun in a tree house.

Recreational activities offer other important implications for the adjustment of teenagers. They provide constructive outlets for the release of tensions and aggressions. Competition in extracurricular activities can offer meaningful preparation for living in the adult world.

Preventive Aspects of Play

The extensive research and study relative to the problems tormenting many young people today lead to an unavoidable conclusion. Psychologists and psychiatrists should focus less of their time and energy upon therapy and a great deal more upon prevention. Arthur Weider, Director of Behavioral Research of the Outdoor Game Council USA and a supervising psychologist at Roosevelt Hospital in New York City, wrote: "I am convinced that children today would be better off if they played more. Not only would they enjoy their childhood more, but, in my opinion, they would be better able to cope with the complexities of modern life."[41]

What does Dr. Weider mean by prevention? "In the case of children," he said, "I think of play activities. Play is to children what living and working is to adults. Who does not remember with fond nostalgia the free-play activities of their youth— racing around the block or hiding behind a tree in an exciting game of hide-and-seek; playing softball in the school yard, a game of jacks, or just playing one of those solitary outdoor games like not stepping on sidewalk cracks? I am convinced that our children today would be better off if they played more of these games."[42]

According to Weider, free play is good prevention against the psychological problems tormenting many young people today. "When a child is allowed to play without adult supervision," said Weider, "he is allowed to express his personality; he can release the feelings and attitudes that have been pushing to get out in the open. Free-play affords the child the opportunity to 'play out' his feeling and resolve frustrations just as the individual adult 'talks out' his difficulties."[43]

Weider pointed out numerous spin-off values of free-play:

1. Free-play encourages the development of self-reliance.
2. Free-play inspires respect for the individual.
3. Free-play offers abundant opportunity and experience for social interaction and adjustment.
4. Free-play is a training ground for coping with competition.[44]

An Opposing Point of View

Weider is one of many psychologists who argue the merits of "free" or "unstructured" play as

an aid to children's emotional growth. However, there are those in the education field who take an opposing point of view. "Simply putting a child or adult into a play situation is not the answer," asserted Frances Jellinek Myers, Professor of Physical Education, Florida Atlantic University. According to Myers, many coaches and physical educators believe that involvement in sports helps students learn behavior patterns such as good sportsmanship, aggressiveness, "good loser," "working off aggression," etc. Myers feels that research and considerable personal observation indicate that these people had these characteristics prior to their play experience. Without the personality cushion of adequate self-image and the opportunity to gain "success," competitive situations like these could be very detrimental to the individual.[45]

"The point is that 'Try, try, again' has too often resulted in 'fail, fail, again,'" wrote Dr. Myers. "The only people—any age—who can experience failure 'well' are those who already have an ego, a self-image of worth . . . free play is not a panacea . . . children need to learn skills—going from simple locomotor activities to more advanced ball handling activities—so that all of them can experience success."[46]

"I wish that the 'play cure' were a real one," concluded Dr. Myers. "But the idea of competitiveness is failing because the competitors are on terribly unequal footings. Competition only works well when both sides have a fairly equal chance."[47]

Psychological Benefits of Lifetime Sports

In addition to the recreational activities of childhood, young people should be taught how to play the lifetime sports, the kind they can play and enjoy as long as they live. To be prepared physically and psychologically for the future, children need to learn the basic skills of such sports as golf, tennis, bowling, water sports, and winter sports.

[41] Arthur Weider, "The Way Our Children Play Can Save Their Mental Health," *Family Weekly Magazine,* July 4, 1971, p. 7.
[42] Ibid.
[43] Ibid.
[44] Ibid.

[45] Frances Jellinek Myers, "Is Play Really Good for All Children?," letter of rebuttal, *Family Weekly Magazine,* October 3, 1971, p. 10.
[46] Ibid.
[47] Ibid.

Fig. 1-21   THE MANY VALUES OF SPORTS PARTICIPATION. More and more medical people believe the person who participates regularly in sports is better adjusted and has the emotional control to enjoy a fuller life.

Sports that carry over into one's lifetime can offer many psychological benefits which will help meet the stresses of our present way of living. Children must not only be taught the benefits of play, but also how to play. Too many adults are reluctant to start bowling, skiing, or golfing because they don't want to experience the embarrassment of learning. And if they fail to learn when they are young, they very likely will lose all interest in participating later in life when they really need to be active.

The value of regular activity in maintaining physical fitness is rarely questioned, but activity is equally important in the matter of psychological fitness. In psychiatric hospitals, participation in sports has aided recovery and contributed significantly to the individual's rehabilitation of himself.

More and more psychiatrists feel that sports participation can contribute to the prevention of mental illness. They believe the person who participates regularly in sports is better adjusted. In addition to having a better image of himself, he will have increased potential to cope with crisis situations. Having stronger faith in himself and those about him, he will have the emotional control so necessary to enjoy a fuller life.

If young people are not given the opportunity to play in a wholesome atmosphere, they will likely seek the same experiences in less constructive and desirable pursuits. Finding the activity satisfying is the secret to a lifetime enjoyment of participation in a sport. The individual must possess the skills to play the game well enough to want to continue playing it.

2

The Economics of Leisure

Recreation and the leisure services field has emerged as one of the world's fastest growing industries that has great economic significance. Economists estimate that the total leisure industry produces a $150 billion market per year, and that by 1980, with an anticipated easing of the current energy squeeze, this figure could reach $250 billion. Actually, this huge amount of money is the *direct* expenditure for one year by the American people; however, these direct purchases of services and goods when filtered through our complex economic system, cause a *total* effect that is much greater than the amount of the direct expenditure.

Money spent on travel, sports equipment, campers, boats, summer houses, and a host of related items reaches into almost every aspect of the nation's economy. In the last twenty-five years, public park and recreation capital improvements have soared from $5 million to $325 million. Outdoor playgrounds grew in number from 9,921 to 27,000. Tennis courts escalated from 13,188 to 22,000, and softball diamonds from 5,452 to 11,-000. Outdoor swimming pools have doubled in number; indoor recreation centers have tripled. Tax-supported park and recreation agencies hiked their spending from $31 million to over $125 million annually. This tremendous growth accounted for over $100 billion sales in 1969 and represents only a hint of what is to come. By the year 2000, the park and recreation sales market is expected to double again![1]

Employment in the field of recreation service expanded rapidly in the 1960s. By 1970, there were approximately 1.6 million full- and part-time recreation workers in the United States. Analysts were predicting that there would be a serious shortage of trained personnel in the field in the years ahead.[2] "However, in the years immediately following, the trend was sharply reversed," declared Richard Kraus. "Critical budgetary limitations have compelled severe roll-backs of personnel in a number of city and state recreation and

Fig. 2-1 TREMENDOUS GROWTH IN OUTDOOR RECREATION. Manufacturers of everything from boats to backpacking equipment are finding huge profits in the leisure-time market. Here, hikers marvel at the beauty of Pisgah National Forest in North Carolina. (Courtesy of the U.S. Forest Service.)

---

[1] *Parks and Recreation,* January 1970, p. 25.

[2] Peter Henle, "Recent Growth of Paid Leisure for U.S. Workers," *Monthly Labor Reivew,* 85, March 1972, p. 256.

Fig. 2-2 OUTDOOR ENTHUSIASTS launch their boats at Dodge State Park in Michigan. (Courtesy of Michigan Department of Conservation.)

park departments, and the support of voluntary and therapeutic agencies has also been cut."[3]

Most Americans have more leisure time than ever before, and this important economic trend will continue in the years ahead. More and more opportunities for people to recreate have been provided by such factors as labor-saving devices, the shorter work week, automation, greater mobility, increased family income, better working conditions, longer vacations, and a higher standard of living for more people.

To a large degree, the recreation opportunities in a community affect the ability of the area to attract and retain both residents and industries. The movement to the suburban areas has been favorably influenced because of the belief that recreation and cultural opportunities are greater there than in the city. However, should the present energy squeeze continue, a greater movement back to the city could occur.

RECREATION AN ECONOMIC FACTOR

Millions of people are employed in the numerous industries that produce equipment, materials, and services designed to meet our leisure needs. As it progresses, the recreation movement will provide work for more people, from laborers and clerks to skilled technicians and professional workers. The recreation field has the potential to create considerably more economic wealth in the future.

Leisure expenditures affect community growth, land values, and governmental income. Recreation, parks, and leisure services make communities more desirable places for home-owners, industrialists, and business investors and create wider markets for capital and consumer goods, for services, and for jobs. Land and property values are generally increased by park areas and recreation facilities. This is particularly true if the areas are properly maintained and operated.

Recreation is also given credit by the insurance industry for the reduction in accident and health expenses by helping to keep people alert and healthy. Similarly, if more money were spent

---

[3] Richard Kraus, "The Economics of Leisure Today," *Parks and Recreation*, August 1971, p. 62.

Fig. 2-3 AMERICA AT PLAY. Campers, travelers, boaters, fishermen, tourists, and weekenders comprise an astonishing picture of America at play. The campsite shown is located in the Deschutes National Forest in Oregon; the fishing scene was photographed in the Clark National Forest in Missouri. (Courtesy of the U.S. Forest Service.)

for wholesome and constructive recreation from childhood through adulthood, law enforcement officials believe there would be less need to spend public money to control juvenile delinquency and crime.

A sizeable portion of recreation and leisure funds is spent on goods and services for outdoor recreation, such as skiing, boating, hunting, fishing, camping, mountain climbing, sightseeing, outdoor photography, and many other outdoor activities.

Clayne R. Jensen cites the following example:

A recreationist buys a boat from a boat distributor, and that purchase represents a direct expenditure of $1,000. To know the impact of that purchase, one must recognize that the boat was made by a manufacturer. The manufacturer purchased certain parts and products from other manufacturers, who in turn purchased certain raw materials that had to be originally taken from the earth. When finally completed, the boat represents $1,000 worth of materials and services.[4]

---

[4] Reprinted by permission from *Outdoor Recreation in America*, Clayne R. Jensen, 1970, Burgess Publishing Company, Minneapolis, Minn., p. 215.

UNDERSTANDING ECONOMICS

The use or consumption of goods and services is the final purpose of all economic processes. There is little need to produce goods unless they are consumed. Unless there is production, there is no supply. If there is no consumption, there is no demand. Therefore, the economy of a society depends upon production and consumption, supply and demand.

If goods and services are to be consumed, people must want them and have the money to purchase them. They must also have the time to use them—hours available beyond the time needed to produce the goods. This is the leisure time, the consumption time, the time which becomes increasingly significant, economically, in a leisure-centered society.[5]

Income

Few aspects of life in the United States are more impressive than the tremendous amount of goods and services produced by the American people. The total annual market value of goods and services is referred to as the *gross national product* (GNP). The GNP is a good indication of the economic well-being of a nation, indicating the productivity of its people.

According to the most reliable statistics, in 1929, the first year it was calculated, the GNP was estimated to be $104 billion. In 1968 it exceeded $860 billion.[6]

Based on past trends, it appears that by the late 1970's (or by 1980) the GNP will exceed one trillion dollars.

Greater expenditure in all phases of life has been the result of this additional income per individual and per family. Although one cannot accurately predict all of the influences that will result from additional income, in all probability, people will spend more on hobbies, sports, entertainment, and other recreational activities that provide increased enjoyment. "Many will own two homes," concluded Jensen, "one of which will be in a resort area. Two-car families will become three-car families, and the cars will be used more for pleasure than necessity. Boats, ski equipment, athletic gear, hunting, and fishing supplies, and other recreational goods will appear in ever increasing amounts. People will travel more miles and spend more time in activities which require these luxury goods."[7]

RECREATION EXPENDITURES

During the past decade, there has been a tremendous upsurge in leisure spending, and from all indications, leisure will be the dynamic element in the domestic economy in the decade ahead. While the energy squeeze may force more people to stay closer to home, it is highly unlikely that Americans will want to reduce their leisure spending drastically. A leading stockbrokerage firm, Merrill, Lynch, Pierce, Fenner and Smith, described the leisure market in 1968 as rapidly approaching the $150 billion mark, and predicted that it will reach $250 by 1980. Furthermore, the firm forecasted that the leisure market will even outperform the economy.[8]

The leisure-time market has been described as the fastest growing business in America by the *U. S. News & World Report*. The September 1969 issue of the national publication stated that "Affluent Americans, with more time on their hands and money to spend than ever before, have boomed leisure into an $83-billion business this year. That figure tops the current annual outlays for national defense."[9]

[5] Harold D. Meyer, Charles K. Brightbill, and H. Douglas Sessoms, *Community Recreation—A Guide to Its Organization* (Englewood Cliffs, N.J.: Prentice-Hall, Inc., 1969), pp. 50–51.

[6] Jensen, op. cit., p. 47.

[7] Ibid., p. 50.

[8] *Leisure: Investment Opportunities in a $150-Billion Market* (New York: Securities Research Division, Merrill, Lynch, Pierce, Fenner and Smith, 1968), p. 4.

[9] *U.S. News & World Report*, September 15, 1969.

Items in the Leisure Budget

Recreation equipment—boats, motor bikes, camping vehicles, hunting and fishing equipment and supplies, color television sets, snowmobiles, surfboards, and the like—constitutes the largest item in the leisure-time budget.

Vacation Vehicles. The surge to the great outdoors has caused vacation vehicles to skyrocket in sales. Travel trailers, motor homes, truck campers, and camping trailers grossed over a billion dollars in 1970. Travel trailers continue to hold a commanding lead over the others. Production is now approaching 200,000 units annually, about 40 per cent of the recreation vehicle market.

Motor Homes. Self-powered motor homes have become a big business, with a sales volume of close to $200 million annually. They are built directly on a truck or bus chassis and offer comfort, convenience, and ease of handling. They measure up to 36 feet in length and vary in cost from $5,000 to $20,000.

Snowmobiles. Another giant in recreation vehicles are snowmobiles. Over a million snowmobiles are in use in the United States and Canada. This all-purpose snow vehicle can carry two people at speeds up to 50 miles an hour, and tow a sled behind. The average cost for a snowmobile is $1,000, although some models can be purchased for as little as $600. (Snowmobiles and other off-road vehicles have caused some serious problems (see Chapter 13), and major controls are currently being enacted by federal and state agencies.)

Tennis. Tennis is another sport enjoying an upsurge in the recreation market. Over 10 million Americans play tennis and spend more than $35 million a year on rackets, balls, and accessories.

Skiing and Surfing. The sports of snow and water skiing have boomed in popularity and in business profits. Snow skiers, now over 5 million in number, are big spenders, paying more than a billion each year in getting to the ski slopes, and for equipment, lodging, and entertainment costs. Surfers are buying over $10 million worth of surfboards annually.

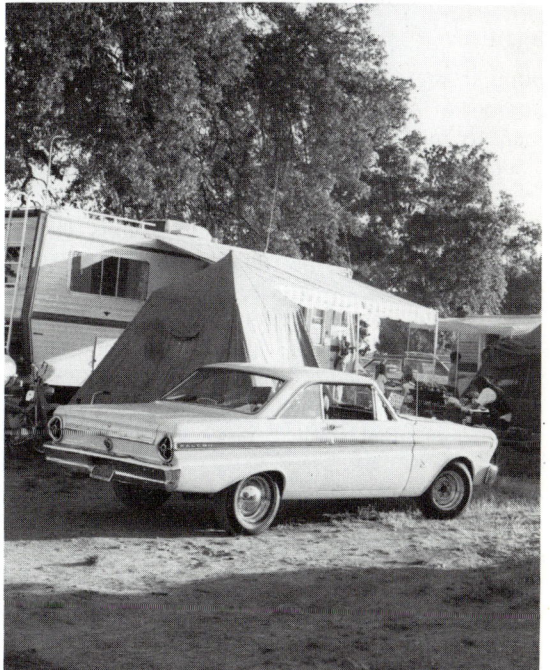

Fig. 2-4 THE LEISURE MARKET is the fastest growing business in America. Pleasure boats and motor homes are two big reasons for the tremendous upsurge in leisure spending.

Fig. 2-5 THE HOUSING MARKET has benefited from the desire to earn lucrative profits from second-homes and the urge to live in "marine living" recreation communities such as the new Porta Ballena Townhouse Condominiums in Alameda, California, which provide boating access to beautiful San Francisco Bay.

Boating. Pleasure boats continue to be a highly popular recreation activity with an increasing number of Americans. Americans now own more than 10 million boats, which are kept at some 5,500 marinas and docks throughout the nation.

Golf. There are over 12 million golfers in the United States, playing regularly on about 10,000 courses. The city of San Diego, California, alone, has over 100 courses. When one considers green fees, club memberships, sales of golf equipment, rental of electric carts, and various spin-off sales, the sport of golf is, indeed, a major business in the leisure market.

Second Homes. The housing market has profited from the vacation mania. Nearly two million American families now own second homes. Sales of recreational housing have now surpassed a billion and a half dollars annually. These vacation homes are of many kinds, including A-frames, condominium apartments, townhouses, factory-made "pre-fab" units, and standard, year-round models.

A typical second home is a single-story structure with four rooms, valued at $7,800. The average owner of the vacation house has an income in excess of $10,000 annually. He is dedicated to the idea of getting away as often as possible for the long weekend. The desire to get away for the long weekend has set off a big boom in vacation-land sales. According to government figures, there are about 1,000 land development projects in the United States. Many vacation lots start at about $1,500, and the cost can run as high as $30,000 for an exclusive shoreline site.[10]

Travel. The closest rival to outdoor recreation is travel. According to the American Automobile Association, Americans spend $60 billion annually for travel. This includes vacations, overnight trips, and pleasure jaunts of more than 100 miles. The AAA estimates that Americans drive over 225 billion miles each year, just getting to and from vacation areas. Seventy-five per cent of all domestic pleasure travel involves the automobile.

Americans like short trips. Approximately 65 per cent of all auto travel for leisure is for distances of 200 miles or less.

[10] Ibid.

Fig. 2-6 VACATION LAND SALES have resulted from the desire to get away for the long weekend. Developers usually build a swimming pool, golf course, beaches, and tennis courts for community use.

Each year, foreign travel becomes a bigger item in the leisure time budget. The Department of Commerce estimates that five million Americans go abroad each year and spend over $5 billion there annually.

Flying. Flying for pleasure, long considered a sport for the rich, is now becoming very popular with the general public. Veteran pilots report that once a person gets his first taste of handling the controls of a light plane, he becomes a solid flying prospect. Lessons to turn him into a qualified pilot will cost anywhere from $750 to $1,000. If the new pilot wants to buy his own plane, he can get a single-engine job for as little as $8,000 or as much as $50,000. In the United States, there are about 750,000 licensed pilots and 250,000 student pilots. More are joining the ranks daily.

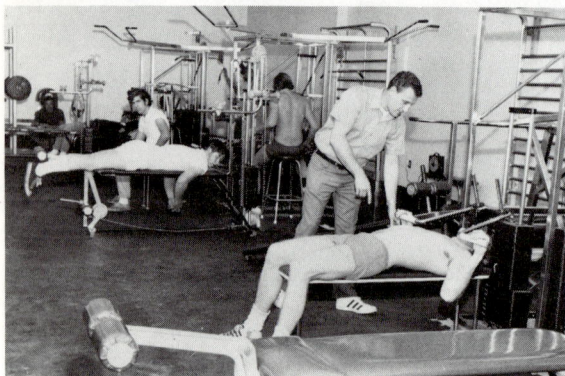

Fig. 2-7 SPORTS AND FITNESS. On every age level, sports activities of all types have been very popular. The emphasis on physical fitness has greatly increased the use of weight training and fitness equipment.

LEISURE ACTIVITY IN THE UNITED STATES

Generally, Americans engage most frequently in easily accessible activities that do not require specialized equipment, elaborate organization, or supervision. Some of the most popular leisure activities are those normally carried on at home, such as relaxation, watching television, visiting with friends and relatives, reading, and studying. Popular activities engaged in away from home include going to a racetrack, attending movies or the theatre, or spending time in a bar or night club. Arts and crafts, dancing, or active musical participation are also high on the list of popular leisure-time pursuits.

The most popular participation activities are probably the simplest and most readily available,

such as driving and walking for pleasure, swimming, playing outdoor games or sports, and bicycling. Driving and walking for pleasure have been favorite pastimes with Americans for many years. More strenuous or dangerous activities such as water skiing, canoeing, or mountain climbing have been growing in popularity.

Sports Participation

Participation in all kinds of sports activities has become a major leisure interest for great numbers of Americans. Team sports such as baseball, basketball, and football have been emphasized on the younger age levels. A variety of leagues for children and youth are operated by youth organizations, schools, or recreation departments. Intramural play at the schools has been increasing each year.

Fig. 2-8 HUGE CROWDS AT SPORTS EVENTS. Attendance at professional football, baseball, and basketball games has enjoyed a spectacular increase. Here, a capacity crowd fills Wrigley Field in Chicago.

Adults seem to prefer a more personal involvement, and participate in such sports as bowling, tennis, golf, aquatics, and winter sports. For many years, spectator interest in professional sports competition has been big business. Participation sports that have enjoyed great popularity include fishing and hunting, cycling, shuffleboard, and volleyball.

The yearbooks published by the National Recreation and Park Association offer a means of assessing the relative popularity of sports activities in the United States.[11] In the 1960s, the most popular activities for adults reported in the yearbook were softball, swimming, tennis, basketball, volleyball, and picnicking. Youth sports ranked high were baseball, basketball, swimming, tennis, volleyball, and picnicking.

During the last twenty-five years, there has been a sharp rise in the number of various sports facilities offered by local park and recreation departments. These include baseball diamonds, bathing beaches, golf courses, softball diamonds, swimming pools, and tennis courts.

[11] *Recreation and Park Yearbook, 1972* (Washington, D.C.: National Recreation and Park Association, 1973), p. 53

Activities that doubled in popularity in the ten-year period between 1960 and 1970 were golf, boating, bowling, track and field, horseback riding, regulation and touch football, synchronized swimming, water skiing, and skiing. Bowling has enjoyed phenomenal growth, as the number of bowling lanes nearly tripled from 1950 to 1970.

All in all, sports continue to make a great contribution to the national economy and no letup is in sight for the future. Statistics indicate that cash outlay for participation sports had increased 600 per cent during a fifteen-year period in the 1950s and 1960s. Indeed, the growth of active participation in sports has been a most encouraging sign. Emphasis on physical education by the schools—particularly on the carry-over types of physical activity—and the impetus given to fitness programs by the President's Council on Physical Fitness and Sports have made Americans more conscious of the value of wholesome exercise.

Spectator Sports

Another highlight of the 1960s was the greatly increased attendance at spectator sports events. Although many of them have not grown in the

Fig. 2-9 VACATION AND WEEKEND PLEASURE TRAVEL. A father enjoys a game of shuffleboard with his children at Woodlake Inn in Sacramento, California. A major portion of the travel business involves vacation trips, with an average stay of three or four weeks.

past few years as have some of the other forms of recreation, sporting events still attract big crowds and profitable gate receipts.

Major Team Sports. Baseball, football, and basketball are the three leading team sports in the United States. Based on attendance, the leading sport has been baseball, traditionally recognized as the national pastime. Attendance at both professional and collegiate football games has enjoyed a spectacular increase, with corresponding increases in gate receipts. Attendance at professional football games, for instance, has risen from 1.5 million in 1948 to 8.2 million in 1967.

Perhaps television has been the key factor in making sports big business. The major networks have enjoyed tremendous advertising revenues from sports programs.

Horse Racing. Attendance at thoroughbred and harness racing tracks throughout the nation was over 65 million in 1972, while total betting rose to nearly $6 billion. State revenues from racing in 1972 were over $400 million.[12]

Automobile Racing. Attracting a paid attendance of over 40 million people in 1972, auto racing

is the second major area of spectator sport. The Indianapolis 500 brings in perhaps 225,000 spectators. Daytona has gates of 100,000 and Riverside 80,000. Auto racing is even more popular abroad. One event alone, the Twenty-Four Hours of Le Mans, has had as many as 400,000 spectators.

Outdoor Recreation Activities

Outdoor recreation is another major area of participation for Americans. The Bureau of Outdoor Recreation of the Department of the Interior reported in 1972 that the participation of individuals in outdoor recreation had reached a total of 7.2 billion "occasions" during the year. An "occasion" is defined by the Department as a single participation in any sport by one person in a calendar year. State and national parks are overcrowded to the crisis point, with an estimated four-fold increase in visitors since 1950.

Pleasure boating has enjoyed a sharp rise, too. The National Association of Engine and Boat Manufacturers and the Boating Industry Association reported that there were a total of 8.2 million boats in the nation's pleasure-craft armada, belonging to some 7 million Americans. The total

_____

[12] *Leisure Investment Opportunities* . . . , p. 53.

fleet of pleasure craft was broken down approximately as follows: outboard boats, 4.8 million; inboards, 591,000; sailboats without power, 561,000; and rowboats, canoes, dinghies, etc., 2.3 million. The total number of people participating in recreational boating was estimated at 41.7 million.[13]

Fishing and hunting continue to be two of America's favorite outdoor recreation sports. In 1972, it was reported that the number of licensed fishermen and hunters in the United States had reached 36 million.[14]

Tourism

The recent growth of leisure time, with more holidays and longer vacations, has provided owners of hotels, motels, and restaurants with a strong market. In 1972, the gross income of hotels, motels, and restaurants was estimated at over $40 billion. Major motel chains now offer attractive recreation and entertainment facilities to encourage weekend vacations. Some of the motels provide golf, horseback riding, tennis, boating, fishing, and even hunting facilities.

Tourism has been a very big business indeed. However, the energy squeeze has had a marked effect on the industry. It is estimated that 70 per cent of all tourist travel is by automobile. With the problems of fuel shortage and inadequate transportation, the tourist industry has had to curtail its activities.

Major Entertainment Complexes

A very popular form of recreation has been the rapid expansion of "fun centers" throughout America. Of course, Disneyland (now in Florida as well as Anaheim, California) is the best example of such business ventures. A unique entertainment area presenting the past and the present, a fairyland fantasy, and a modern space sciences center as well as a huge hotel complex, Disneyland had attracted over 60 million visitors by 1970.

[13] Richard Kraus, *Recreation and Leisure in Modern Society,* © 1971 by Meredith Corporation. Reprinted by permission of Prentice-Hall, Inc., Englewood Cliffs, N.J., p. 324.

[14] Ibid.

Another example of business investment in recreational facilities has been the construction of large sports stadiums throughout America in the 1960s. A variety of entertainment and business exposition functions are housed at these huge facilities. The Astrodome in Houston, Texas, a marvel of modern technology, is a fully enclosed structure that cost $37 million to build and attracts over 4 million people annually. In addition to professional and college baseball, football, and basketball, the Astrodome schedules boxing, motorcycle racing, polo, bloodless bullfights, religious revivals, and the circus. Huge new stadiums have been built by other cities throughout the country. In Los Angeles, for example, five major sports palaces have been built within the past twelve years. The new Madison Square Garden in New York city, costing $150 million, has been described as the greatest sports and entertainment center in the world.

Another trend in the construction of entertainment centers has involved commercial recreation in suburban shopping centers. Huge new regional shopping complexes today offer restaurants, bowling alleys, and motion picture houses.

Cultural Activities

Public interest and involvement in the "cultural arts" has been another rapidly growing major area of leisure development. The performing arts include such popular activities as music, drama, and dance, while painting, sculpture, and drawing continue to attract strong participation in the plastic and graphic arts.

The "cultural explosion" in America has been evidenced by the building of cultural centers and museums, as well as the growth of personal consumption related to the arts. Musical activity in the United States since World War II has had a phenomenal growth in all forms. The number of symphony orchestras and opera companies has also increased remarkably. Record sales, musical instruments, and other forms of related expenditures have increased at a great rate.

Consumer spending on the arts increased by about 130 per cent during the period from 1953 to 1960. By the mid-1960s, Americans were

Fig. 2-10 POPULAR FUN CENTERS. Recreation and entertainment areas have expanded rapidly throughout America. The log ride at Magic Mountain in Los Angeles gives daring youngsters (and adults, too) the thrill of log riding in the style of early Californians. Nearby, Lion Country in Laguna Hills, California, enables visitors (in cars) to experience an exciting "African safari."

spending nearly $400 million a year at theatres, opera and concert performances, buying over $1 billion worth of books and spending $200 million for painting, prints, and art materials, $300 million to operate art museums, and $600 million a year for musical instruments. It was predicted that the renaissance in culture would result in an annual expenditure of $7 billion by the early 1970s.[15]

Major building programs for the performing and graphic arts have been planned and are being carried out by many cities. Lincoln Center for the Performing Arts is a magnificent $142-million building in New York City, while the National Cultural Center for the Performing Arts in Washington, D.C., has received international acclaim for its beauty and practicality.

The Television Industry

Television is probably the most important influence on the leisure time of people of all ages. Obviously, television viewing has greatly displaced other forms of leisure activity, the most notable being attendance at movie theatres.

A 1968 study revealed that the average American home with pre-school children has the television set turned on between fifty-five and sixty hours a week. Based on Nielsen survey statistics, the study concluded that "the average American adult will spend from ten to fifteen years of his life watching TV."[16]

ECONOMIC CRISIS

Recreation and park professionals are currently faced with some economic problems that affect government on all levels. The sustained inflation, a major rise in unemployment, the energy crisis, and serious social problems have added to the cost of operations on all levels of government.

On the federal level, a serious budgetary deficit can be attributed to the cost of military and foreign aid programs, the huge highway expan-

sion program, and the multi-billion dollar space program. Many states have also been forced to cut back their budgets as a result of new demands for service and programs related to education, pollution, and welfare.

The financial problem is particularly serious in the cities. As an example, the 1960 annual budget for New York City was $2.2 billion. The mayor's proposed budget for 1971–72 totaled $9.1 billion.[17] The costs of municipal government have risen steadily in cities throughout the nation. As businesses and industries have left the central cities and relocated in new suburban shopping areas or urban industrial plazas both the tax base and overall revenues have tended to decline as the financial burden of the cities has grown.

The federal government has been forced to cut back some of its programs and services related to recreation and parks. The National Park Service, for example, was forced to accept severe budgetary restrictions. Support of recreation-related programs had to be withdrawn by the federal government. Perhaps the most decisive cut involved the dropping of the "crash" summer Community Action programs by the Office of Economic Opportunity.

Budgetary cutbacks have been imposed on park, recreation, and conservation departments, youth bureaus, and programs serving the aged or physically handicapped. Local governments have had to withstand the most severe impact of the current fiscal crisis. Inner-city areas are badly deteriorated and vandalized. Many small parks and playgrounds have become "no-man's land," while various types of recreation facilities are seriously underused.

What, then, are the solutions to the economic crisis? According to Richard Kraus, the solutions fall into two areas: first, a redetermination of priorities for funding that will give fuller support to badly needed social services; and, secondly, the kinds of actions that can be taken by park and recreation administrators themselves.[18]

A fuller share of the national income should be funneled to badly needed domestic programs.

---

[15] Ibid., p. 327.

[16] *New York Times Magazine*, July 14, 1968, p. 26.

[17] Kraus, "The Economics of Leisure Today," p 327.

[18] Ibid.

Fig. 2-11   THE APPEAL OF TELEVISION. The television industry has been a major factor in making sports big business. The major networks have enjoyed tremendous advertising revenues based on programs such as National Football League action on Sunday and Monday evenings.

Clearly, the states and cities can no longer continue to permit the federal government to collect two-thirds of all the taxes in the nation, but only return them an average of 14 cents on the dollar.[19]

There is a need for the federal government to reconsider its own priorities. A number of experts believe a more flexible defense policy would lead to a substantial saving in the over $70 billion annual defense budget. The billions of dollars being spent for space exploration and the Interstate Highway System are also being challenged.

---

[19] Ibid.

Fig. 2-12   THE EFFECTS OF HIGHWAY EXPANSION PROGRAMS. In addition to causing serious budgetary deficits, the huge highway construction programs, consuming
approximately forty acres per mile, have greatly diminished valuable green belt areas.
They have forced cutbacks in some recreation and park services.

3

Social Forces that Influence Leisure

As the recreation movement moves into the decade of the 1970s, the United States is faced with the question of how its millions of citizens can best deal with the various social forces and problems that influence their leisure. The evolution of recreation as a social institution did not occur by itself. Rather, mass leisure and the rapidly growing recreation movement were shaped and influenced by a complex of conditions, developments, and determinants that have been a part of the total picture of our progressive, modern nation.

To comprehend the social forces that have influenced the development of the leisure and recreation field, one must understand the rapid advances of American civilization, particularly man's perennial struggle for enlightenment. While it is true that American technology has contributed much to create our leisure opportunities, it should also be observed that the changes in the behavior patterns of people, institutions, and communities have also been instrumental in giving "rise to recreation as a major design in contemporary society."[1]

These forces have greatly affected people, how and where they live, as well as influenced their leisure behavior. These influences include their work, greater leisure time, higher income, the energy crisis, automation, population, changes in homelife, mobility, communication, and mental stress. Other conditions have affected people's interactions with each other and their environment.

Ever since the scientific and industrial revolutions began, the recreation movement has been faced with many challenges caused by the numerous and rapid changes in our lives. According to Thomas Yukic:

> The most notable challenges have been the effects of an ever-changing technology, a broad and diverse change in urban life, and the appearance of many unique social and economic conditions affecting both individual and family. These influences have both advanced and curtailed recreation. . . .
>
> A galaxy of great social changes has buffeted society during recent history resulting in the

Fig. 3-1 MAKING THE CITIES LIVEABLE AGAIN is a task all urban residents and public officials should assume responsibility for. Once again the cities of America can be places of culture, beauty, and enjoyment.

[1] Thomas S. Yukic, *Fundamentals of Recreation* (New York: Harper & Row, 1970), p. 40.

43

Fig. 3-2 EVEN WITH THE GROWTH OF CITIES and their population and traffic problems, people can work together to keep them beautiful.

conditioning of the kind and number of leisure uses, the universal demand for recreation and its relative importance in people's lives.[2]

According to Howard Danford:

Social change generally sharpens conflicts of values. The bases for conflict exist in the facts of economic, political, and religious differences, in racial and ethnic variations, and in conflicts of interest which characterize complex societies. We have seen technology and science have a bright future, and yet if we look at our nation socially and are realistic concerning the future, there is room for some disillusionment or discouragement.[3]

LEISURE AND THE AMERICAN WORKER

Our attitudes and behavior toward work are changing, but so are the conditions of our lives. The rising levels of income, greater leisure time,

the energy shortage, the development of private pension plans, the introduction of social security, and other factors are changing the way that Americans look to the present and the future. Former Secretary of Labor J. D. Hodgson wrote: "In the past century, reduction of the average work week by about 13 hours has netted the American worker 675 hours of free time annually. Added to increased vacation time and more paid holidays, this amounts to a total gain in time free of work of nearly 800 hours annually, or roughly one month out of twelve."[4]

The four-day, forty-hour work week, which is in effect in a growing number of companies, has shown widespread appeal with Americans. Labor union leaders, however, have voiced opposition to the four-day, forty-hour work week and favor plans that would reduce the total number of hours worked. Most of American business and industry is already on a four-day week for ten per cent of the year. Hodgson believes "It is easy to envision additional Monday holidays over a period of time, possibly to a point where each month would offer a three-day weekend."[5] Already, the five Monday holidays provide new opportunities for the American worker to indulge in leisure-time pursuits. Whether his leisure-time interests lean toward sports or travel, painting or community theatre, these new unbroken blocks of leisure give the worker more time to pursue his interests.

Michael Wilkins and Richard Ragatz wrote:

With increasing work productivity, a worker may 'earn' more leisure with less time on the job; the benefit of greater efficiency may be his in the form of leisure. It is projected that American workers will continue taking part of their increased productivity in time off the job. What the new attitude toward nonwork time means is that they could use it without guilt and feel freer to use part of their leisure for recreational activities.[6]

---

[2] Ibid., p. 41.

[3] Howard G. Danford and Max Shirley, *Creative Leadership in Recreation*, 2nd ed. (Boston: Allyn and Bacon, Inc., 1970), p. 2.

[4] J. D. Hodgson, "Leisure and the American Worker," *Leisure Today*, 1972, pp. 5–6.

[5] Ibid.

[6] Michael H. Wilkins and Richard L. Ragatz, "Cultural Changes and Leisure Time," *Leisure Today*, 1972, p. 2.

Fig. 3-3 SOCIAL FORCES have had a significant influence on people and their families. In short, they have more leisure time and less work. Many Americans are using this increased leisure to picnic with their families or take a fun ride with their children. Here, a family is taking a stroll along a nature trail in Bankhead National Forest, Alabama. (Courtesy of the U.S. Forest Service.)

The sabbatical, or taking extended, paid leave from work, is another form of leisure that may become more extensive in the future. "The usefulness of a year's leisure may be greater when a worker is 50 or 55 years old than at the end of his working lifetime," said Hodgson. "It may be more useful than a reduction of one hour in the workweek throughout the working years, which is roughly equivalent to a year's leisure."[7]

Also, earlier retirement has created additional blocks of leisure for many of this nation's workers. "By 1980, it is expected that improvements in social security benefits and private pension plans will have enabled all but 22 per cent of male workers over 65 to choose retirement over work," concluded Hodgson.[8]

LEISURE—A BY-PRODUCT OF HARD WORK

Great cultural changes are occurring in America that will significantly influence our use of leisure time in the future. One change is that leisure time is gradually being accepted as a by-product of hard work. For many members of the youth subculture, work is no longer the central goal in life. They are spending much of their time traveling with no apparent guilt feelings. "Today, because of affluence and the stress we put on education," wrote Eli Ginzberg, "a lot of youngsters do not want to make work commitments prematurely. They do not want to get caught up in a bureaucracy. Youngsters want to travel and learn more about themselves."[9] This retreat from

---

[7] Hodgson, op. cit., pp. 5–6.

[8] Ibid.

[9] Eli Ginzberg, "Is Hard Work Going Out of Style?," *U.S. News & World Report,* August 23, 1971, pp. 52–53.

Fig. 3-4 CREATIVE LEISURE EXPERIENCES. With the importance of work steadily dwindling for many, people need challenges—the joy of achievement and creativity.

technocracy, however, is not generally accepted by most middle-class Americans, who are oriented to a world of work.

The average American's relationship to things, places, and people is becoming increasingly transient. In turn, this developing culture of transience has tremendous implications for the use of leisure time and the demand for outdoor recreational activities. "For an increasingly mobile, experience-seeking population not wishing to be tied to possessions or places, the need for more locations and different types of recreation activities is apparent," stated Wilkins and Ragatz. "The traditional desire for ownership of property appears to be declining—suggesting opportunity for additional entry in rented and shared types of recreation facilities."[10]

CREATIVE AND CHALLENGING WORK

The importance of work has dwindled for many of the less skilled workers in our society except as a source of income. This is particularly true of the workers on the production line whose ego involvement in work has diminished markedly. Instead, emphasis has been shifted toward leisure activities to find identity, self-satisfaction, and enrichment in their lives. In discussing what he called "the moral equivalent of work," Jay Nash stated that "Work must be viewed in the light of accomplishment and mastery, as craftsmanship work has always been, not as a curse on the brow of man. Through accomplishment, by work and craftsmanship, man's ego, small enough at best, gets a chance to expand. His work is partly himself."[11] Leisure and work, together, make for full-

[10] Wilkins and Ragatz, op. cit., p. 2.

[11] Jay B. Nash, "The Moral Equivalent of Work," *The Physical Educator*, May 1965, p. 51.

Fig. 3-5 MIGRATION TO THE COUNTRY. An increasing urban environment has caused more Americans to spend their weekends and vacation periods away from the city at nearby lakes and parks. Here, outdoor enthusiasts enjoy the beach and swimming area of Lake Russell near Cornelia, Georgia. (Courtesy of the U.S. Forest Service.)

ness in living. In Nash's words, "Work, creative, challenging, and meaningful—is one of man's significant wants and needs."[12]

EFFECT OF INCREASED LEISURE

The shift in the ratio of working hours to leisure hours has had a significant effect on the average worker. "For one thing, it has made him more conscious of the opportunities that his leisure hours present him," said Hodgson. "Such sports activities as golf, tennis, and boating have suddenly come within the economic reach of the average worker, who now happily has the time to enjoy them."[13]

With more leisure hours available and more money in his pocket, the American worker has become culture conscious. We see this in the big cities where places like New York and Washington's Lincoln and Kennedy Centers for the Performing Arts and Minneapolis' Tyrone Guthrie

Theater regularly play to sold-out houses. But we see it even more dramatically in smaller towns and cities throughout the nation where the community theatre movement has mushroomed, local light-opera companies feature talent recruited from the ranks of office and factory workers; and art supply stores find themselves selling easels, paints, and brushes to amateur artists who spend their leisure hours fulfilling their urge "to do something creative."[14]

The potential for increased leisure for the 1970s is expected to continue at about the level of the 1960s. Further reductions in working time are likely to be small, with attention centering on the reshuffling of time free of work in order to provide larger blocks of leisure.

According to Edwin Staley, the age of leisure has not and will not spread its advantages with an equal hand to all workers. ". . . those in the professional and management jobs and those owning their own businesses will continue to work as long hours as they are today. In general, the

[12] Ibid.

[13] Hodgson, op. cit., pp. 5–6.

[14] Ibid.

greater riches or prestige that a man enjoys, the less leisure he is likely to have."[15]

LEISURE PARTICIPATION

Americans differ very widely in their recreational interests, depending on their social class affiliations. The term "class" generally refers to the horizontal stratification of a population determined by such factors as family background, occupation, income, community status, group identification, and education.

As people get older, they tend to settle into the ways of the class to which they belong. As a result, they choose leisure activities congenial to their class. In recent years, however, it has been suggested by a number of sociologists that the traditional concept of social class is no longer useful in predicting leisure interests and needs. According to Max Kaplan, "The label of 'class' in the social sciences is becoming increasingly dubious. Inexpensive travel, the mass media, and common affluence have brought varied forms of leisure within the psychological and economic reach of almost everyone. In no area of American life more than leisure has the idea of social class become an outmoded concept."[16]

Another sociologist, Nels Anderson, also writes that class lines today are less strictly drawn: "All classes attend the same ball games, the same prize fights, the same night clubs, even the same opera. All listen to the radio and view the same television program. The difference is in money outlay: how much is spent for the fishing outfit, the automobile, the television set, the seat at the opera or the table at the night club."[17]

AUTOMATION

Automation will continue to present unique problems for our society, challenging our values and the ways we express them. Unemployment, re-training, re-deployment of personnel, increased leisure time, and the guaranteed minimum wage are just some of the present problems posed by the automation wave.

Automation will require a substantial alteration of our philosophy concerning: the value and necessity of work, the function and value of leisure in American Society, the kind of work suitable for human beings, the causes and cure of unemployment, the economics of abundance, and a host of other concerns. . . .
Automation is frequently confused with mechanization but the two are not the same. When machines do man's work that is mechanization but when they do man's work and control their own operation, that is automation.[18]

Increasingly, automation is freeing workers from tedious routine tasks. In turn, it has shortened working hours necessary to maintain a high standard of living, and has made goods available on an unprecedented large scale. On the other hand, as a result of automation, the number of employees in manufacturing has decreased although production has increased. In New York City, alone, automatic elevators have displaced thousands of operators.

If the process of automation continues, its ultimate effect will be to severely limit the work available to most people. Will we then be capable of developing a society that does not depend on work to give it meaning? "Obviously due for alteration are our ideas on the causes and cure of employment and unemployment," says Gray, "the social duty to work, the social right to work, the right to the fruits of one's labor, the character of human incentive, the use of leisure, the role of recreation in American life."[19]

[15] Edwin J. Staley, "The Changing Community Role of the Recreation Agency," presented to 18th Annual Conference of California Park and Recreation Society, March 8, 1966, p. 4.

[16] Max Kaplan, *Leisure in America: A Social Inquiry* (New York: John Wiley, 1960), p. 92.

[17] Nels Anderson, *Work and Leisure* (New York: Free Press, 1961), p. 34.

[18] David Gray, "The Changing Pattern of American Life," *Parks and Recreation*, March 1966, pp. 212–19.

[19] Ibid.

Gray goes on to ask, "What form will social changes take and how rapidly will they occur? Norbert Wiener, an eminent scientist in this field, has said, 'Automation is bound to devalue the human brain.' Will man have a sense of place in society? Man certainly needs to feel needed and wanted. He needs to achieve something. What will happen when automation produces a situation in which, for the first time in history, people will be spending more of their lives in leisure than in work?"[20]

WAR ON POVERTY

The rise in prosperity has not spread to all sections of the American public. With an estimated 32 million—or about 17 per cent of the population—living in poverty, society is faced with the prospect of a "poverty war" for a generation.

Approximately one out of every six persons over 65 in the United States has an income below the government-defined "poverty index." However, the number took a dramatic drop in 1972, due largely to the 20 per cent increase in Social Security payments. The Social Security Administration in 1973 defined poverty as an income of $1,980 for a single elderly person and $2,520 for a couple annually. In addition to these 3.1 million elderly Americans who are considered impoverished, an estimated 2 million would be in that category if they did not live with families whose incomes are over the poverty threshold.

WELFARE

Welfare has become a problem of great magnitude. The nation spent about $14.2 billion on welfare in 1970, more than twice the outlay of only five years ago. Yet the 13.5 million Americans or 6.3 per cent of the population who received that aid, are only half the estimated number of the needy and eligible. "Increased by the recession and the growing activism of welfare rights groups, the rolls continue to grow in every part of the country," wrote Time magazine. "After 35 years

of legislation and programs, the world's wealthiest nation seems caught in a paradoxical trap: the more the U.S. spends on its poor, the greater the need seems to be to spend more still."[21]

In the current crisis, frustration and anger have brought federal officials and the states and localities into open warfare over welfare budgets. Together, the two largest states in population, California and New York, have 3 million people receiving aid and distribute almost 37 per cent of the nation's welfare money. "Very few live better on welfare than they would with full-time jobs at adequate wages. Obviously, cheating does happen. In California, for example, a man combined a secret job and welfare for an annual income of $16,800."[22]

There are those who feel that the President should put aside his revenue-sharing plan and instead propose a full federal take-over of welfare. As a result, the states and cities would have available for other programs the $6 billion they now spend on welfare. In addition, with only the federal government financing welfare, one standard of aid and one set of rules would apply nationally.

POPULATION

There has been a dramatic decline in birthrates in the United States. The U.S. Census experts once thought we might have about 100 million more people by the year 2000 than they now project. The expectation now is that we may have under 266 million people in 2000. But even with the current projected low 1 per cent annual increase, the U.S. population will double in a little under 70 years. Experts stress the two-child family as the only way to stabilize growth. The Census Bureau says that if the average family has two children and if there is no immigration, population could stabilize at under 300 million around the year 2037.[23]

---

[20] Ibid., pp. 212–19.

[21] "Welfare: Trying to End the Nightmare," Time, February 8, 1971, pp. 14–15.

[22] Ibid.

[23] 1971 Environmental Quality Index, reprinted from National Wildlife Magazine, Oct.-Nov. 1971, pp. 14–15.

Population control is now official U. S. policy. Over $180 million has been spent for family planning assistance and research. "Our challenge is to discover ways to improve our own environmental quality in the United States," said the editors of the 1971 Environmental Quality Index, "and to help people abroad. That can be done only by developing a worldwide balance between population and resources."[24]

Unfortunately, the population boom continues around the world, and it is growing most rapidly in those areas of Asia and Latin America where people are already hungriest. An estimated 7.5 billion people will fight for existence in the year 2000. People are beginning to ask: "Can our earth ever support its 3.6 billion people at anywhere near U.S. standards?"

URBANIZATION

A significant development in our way of life has been a steady and rapid increase in the density of population in towns and cities. The movement can be attributed in part to industry and subsequent automation, a growing population, and the mass media. The energy shortage has been an important factor in a greater movement of middle-class whites back to the city.

Sixty-five per cent of Americans now live on nine per cent of the land, while 140,000,000 Americans live in the 215 metropolitan areas with central cities of fifty thousand or more and in the surrounding suburbs. The number of people living in urban areas is expected to double during the next quarter of a century. Consequently, the open spaces now surrounding cities will turn into suburban developments. The present suburbs will be built into high-rise apartments. Single family units will become very costly.

The United States is urbanizing at the rate of a million acres a year, the heaviest concentrations being on the Atlantic and Pacific seaboards and around the Great Lakes. In the past 15 years, almost 67 per cent of new land has been put to urban uses. Authorities have become con-

cerned that a severe encroachment is being made on present and potential recreational lands. Many farsighted city planners are calling for greenbelts of recreational and scenic lands of prudent size and character to surround urban centers.[25]

The trend toward urbanization has already resulted in a great migration to the country during weekends and vacation periods, as people struggle to keep in touch with nature. "Increasing numbers of Americans will own two homes," explained Clayne R. Jensen, "one in the city and one in the country. In spite of strong efforts to cling to our rural heritage, urban living will dominate the lives of a great majority of people, and urban values will strongly prevail."[26]

Recreation has also contributed immeasurably to the growth of cities. Many communities in Arizona, California, Nevada, Florida, Vermont, and Idaho became populated and thriving as a result of recreation. Today, thousands of American cities feature centers with attractive recreational and entertainment facilities that attract vacationers, hunters, skiers, retired persons, and health addicts. Many of these cities have become recognized as resort centers, cultural centers, beach towns, and art colonies.

Urban ills, such as poor housing, school problems, recreation problems, and numerous other social problems, have arisen from the movement to the city. Probably the most urgent problem facing today's cities involves the disadvantaged, who have been victimized by their race, nationality, socioeconomic status, or a combination of these factors.

The reaction to unfair and repressive city codes became increasingly evident in the 1960s. The mass media, particularly television, reported the horrible clashes between police and civil rights protesters in Birmingham, Montgomery, and Selma that contributed significantly to

---

[24] Ibid.

[25] Yukic, op. cit., p. 43.

[26] Reprinted by permission from *Outdoor Recreation in America*, Clayne R. Jensen, 1970, Burgess Publishing Company, Minneapolis, Minn., p. 40.

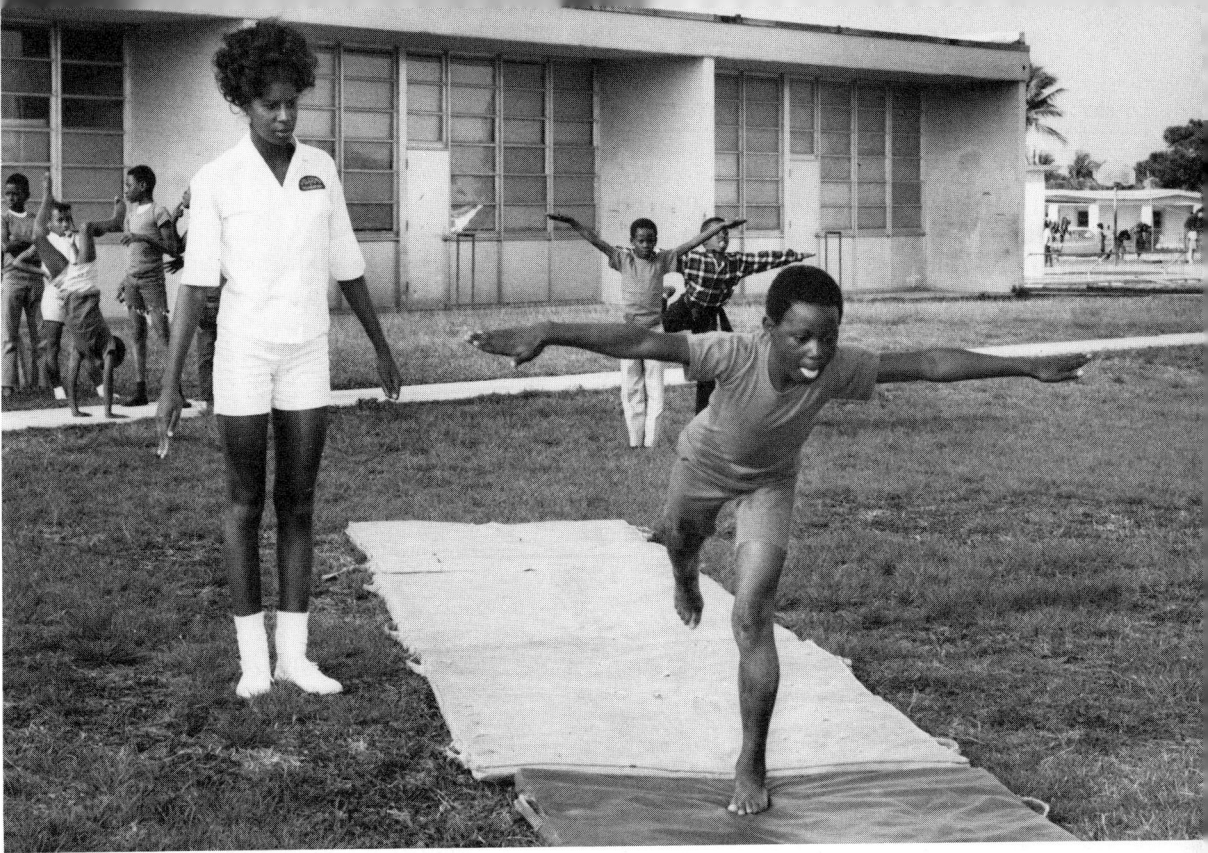

Fig. 3-6 RECREATION SERVICES FOR THE DISADVANTAGED. Deprivation in recreation and park services and facilities has been a major source of dissatisfaction among disadvantaged minorities. However, in some cities in the country, outstanding programs are offered, such as this gymnastics program sponsored by the Metro-Dade County Park and Recreation Department in Miami, Florida. (Courtesy Metro-Dade County Park and Recreation Department.)

public sentiment and anger against the outmoded and terribly dehumanizing racist laws.[27]

The anger of the black was never so fully illuminated as in 1967 with the full-scale rioting of discontented inner-city residents.

The National Commission on Civil Disorders revealed that the lack of sufficient recreation leadership and facilities was a major source of the dissatisfaction among ghetto residents that led to the worst racial encounters in the history of America. The report ranked recreation fifth as a source of grievance among ghetto residents and at the same level of intensity as the provisions for education. The report notes "that deprivation in recreation and park services

and facilities is a major source of dissatisfaction among ghetto residents."[28]

Follow-up studies continued to show that recreation services to blacks and other disadvantaged minorities are usually poorly conceived, loosely operated, and underfinanced. Professional recreation objectives to serve all people with equal quality are not met in most cases.

SUBURBIA

Intensive urbanization in America has given rise to suburbanization. During the past decade, the population of suburbia has grown by more than 15 million. According to the preliminary 1970

---

[27] James F. Murphy, *Recreation and Leisure Service for the Disadvantaged* (Philadelphia: Lea and Febiger, 1970), p. 127.

[28] Ibid., p. 128.

census reports, there are now 74.9 million people classified as suburbanites, a 25 per cent increase over 1960. This surge has made suburbanites the largest group in the land, outnumbering both city dwellers and those who live in rural areas. According to an article in *Time* magazine, the biggest single factor for moving to the suburbs is people's desire to have a home of their own. Next in order of importance came the search for a better atmosphere for their children (40 per cent), a goal that is not always realized.[29]

Even though suburbanites enjoy an increased self-sufficiency and a sense of satisfaction, many have found that suburbia shares the same problems as the cities, though possibly less severely. Whether white suburbanites like it or not, the suburban scene is being altered. Blacks are moving to the suburbs in growing numbers, although the white influx over the past decade has been so great that the percentage of blacks in suburbia has risen very little. Industry, too, has been deserting the central city for the suburbs. According to Milton Rakove, a University of Illinois urbanologist,

We are urbanizing the suburban areas to the point that many of them are coming to resemble the cities of a few generations ago. The quest for a home of one's own is increasingly frustrated. As demand goes up, supply diminishes, and prices have risen steadily. Now, half of all new suburban housing around Chicago is multiple dwellings.[30]

The cities have already been diminished by the movement of people and industry to the suburbs. If not reversed, the trend will have major consequences for urban America: declining tax bases within the cities, less incentive for the cities themselves to develop efficient mass transportation, and greater reluctance in the state capitals to provide aid for cities. In short, it could lead to the isolation of the central city. According to *Time*, however, isolation need not happen. "Planned development of new towns at the city's edge and a greater amount of regional urban-suburban cooperation could help jump the mounting barrier."[31]

New patterns of American population are now beginning to emerge. The rural population, which is diminishing, is not likely to be replaced by big-city or suburban drop-outs in search of a better life. The cities will become increasingly the habitat of singles, childless couples, blacks, and other non-white minorities.

In between the farms and the cities will be an ever growing, ever more self-sufficient suburbia expanding into one continuous blur, as it does already along the northeast corridor from Boston to Washington. In these spreading suburbs will come a further test of American democracy. The combination of civic concern with a manageable governmental unit can work very well.[32]

Suburbia may never re-create the New England town meeting, but it could succeed in allowing its citizens to re-assert some control over their lives and their governments, to create a fresh sense of community and roots across the land. According to Richard Kraus,

The task that lies ahead is to make the cities livable again, and to join them with their surrounding suburban neighbors in viable, unified, logically ordered metropolitan districts. As part of this effort, the task of recreation and parks is to help the urban areas of our nation continue to be places of culture, enjoyment, delight in the human and physical environment, centers of communication, the arts, and sports —places where people of all ages and kinds can come together for excitement and fun.

Despite the crushing financial difficulties of the present, this function cannot be ignored. It must be forcefully presented by professionals in the field, and it must be understood and supported by city planners and officials, and by the public at large.[33]

---

[29] "Suburbia: The New American Plurality," *Time*, March 15, 1971, pp. 14–20.

[30] Ibid.

[31] Ibid.

[32] Ibid.

[33] Richard Kraus, "The Economics of Leisure Today," *Parks and Recreation*, August 1971, p. 86.

Fig. 3-7 THE NEED FOR A FATHER-SON RELATIONSHIP. While changes in modern society have altered the roles of the American family, this scene will be with us for a long time to come. Rather than on a neighborhood vacant lot, it will probably take place on a public playground.

MOBILITY

One of the most distinctive features about American life has been its mobility. Comfortable and rapid means of transportation are available to the people, whether traveling long or short distances. True, the gasoline shortage has resulted in less tourist travel, but if America's energy needs can be met in the years ahead, we will continue to be known as a "land of travelers."

Development of a vast network of highways can be attributed to the rapid increase in the use of the automobile. In turn, greatly increased space is needed for parking. Until the energy crisis is over, though, tourist travel will continue to operate at a reduced level.

In addition to the automobile, other modern means of travel have become increasingly important. Passengers on airlines in the United States have increased from 25 million in 1940 to over 70 million in 1970. "Aeronautic experts claim that during the 1970s, planes traveling twice the speed of sound will become routine, and short route helicopter systems will become popular within large metropolitan areas. Automation experts pre-

dict that some of us will live to see airliners cross the continent in 90 minutes, trains travel at 200 miles per hour over an air cushion, and ships skim through the water at 75 knots."[34]

In the future, our great mobility will afford large numbers of people the opportunity to test their skills and interests against exciting leisure-time challenges in every geographic area of the world. Our highly developed system of transportation will deliver large numbers of people to the doorsteps of every outdoor recreation area. The accuracy of this promising forecast will depend on the availability of fuel to provide the needed energy for such a highly mobile society.

COMMUNICATION

While personal communication is improving very slowly, if at all, the technical means of communication are improving radically. One goal is to devise a radio-telephone that will provide full color and total sight and sound on a three-dimensional television screen. Each radio-telephone will have a personal channel and code similar to today's telephone number.

There is much to be done to improve the ability of individuals to communicate with one another. One source of violence in our society stems in part from a lack of effective communication. "Divided by prejudice, misunderstanding, exploitation, and brutality, we lack the ability to communicate our humanity. We respond with violence. We are alienated from one another."[35] In time, hopefully, people will gain the skills, the attitudes, and the desire to communicate with each other.

FAMILY AND HOME LIFE

Indeed, the impact of societal changes has altered the roles of members of American families. All aspects of recreation, the reasons, forms, and times,

---

[34] Jensen, op. cit., p. 43.

[35] Gray, op. cit., pp. 212–19.

have changed markedly. Thomas Yukic expressed the belief that "The stereotype of the stable, close-knit family is rapidly becoming outmoded since sons and daughters marry earlier, gain freedom sooner, and in most instances break away from the family unit."[36] In addition, the modern mother is no longer confined strictly to a domestic role. The American woman has become an active force in the community. It is estimated that women make up one-third of the national working force, and nearly 3 million of these women have children under 6 years of age.[37]

MENTAL STRESS

The increase in the frequency of mental disease is a result of a modern society which subjects its members to social strain, personal problems, and mental stresses. This unfortunate trend has substantiated a need for recreation. Some of the most prevalent influences in our way of living are a hurried pace of living; anxieties and stresses caused by such situations as unemployment and economic insecurity; a decline of acceptable family and neighborhood living; and a high rate of delinquency, vice, and suicide. Substandard living conditions and slums have coincided with this deterioration. Fortunately, in recent years increased emphasis and support of the national mental health movement in America has done much in achieving more favorable social situations for the young and old alike. Recreation, more than ever before, is being recognized as a strong asset to individuals, groups, and the community in maintaining favorable mental health conditions.

---

[36] Yukic, op. cit., p. 55.

[37] Ibid.

CENTRAL - PARK, WINTER

4

History of the Recreation Movement

Like other social movements of great significance, the history of municipal recreation in the United States cannot be interpreted fully in terms of a series of specific events characterized by distinct periods of development. Rather, "The recreation movement was the result of a combination of ideas, experiments, and developments," wrote George Butler, one of America's most distinguished historians on the study of play and recreation. "Some of them were closely related to each other in time, place, and influence, while others had little connection with preceding, current, or subsequent happenings."[1]

Any great social movement grows out of a pressing social need. The events of the closing years of the nineteenth century brought about the realization that there was a growing need for recreation. Although individual developments in recreation were made throughout the nineteenth century, they were relatively isolated in scope and intensity.

To generate a force of sufficient magnitude to meet the need for recreation, it remained for the pressures of a changing industrialized society to force individual leaders, municipalities, and private and public agencies to unify their efforts. Along with technological and industrial progress, the advance of science and medicine, more widespread education, and changing social attitudes were other social forces that played prominent roles in the growth of recreation in the United States.

Since the beginning of the recreation movement, recreation has, indeed, come a long way. While America has realized many significant gains, there are problems and key issues that still remain. These will be approached and discussed in Chapter 17.

ORIGIN OF THE PLAY MOVEMENT

The first evidence of any form of recreational facility for the public in the United States was the

Fig. 4-1 EARLY CENTRAL PARK, the play space for the privileged in the winter of 1862, served people from all segments of the population. (Courtesy of the Harry T. Peters Collection, Museum of the City of New York.)

[1] From *Introduction to Community Recreation* by George D. Butler. Copyright © 1967 by the National Recreation Association, Inc. Used with permission of McGraw-Hill Book Company. P. 77.

establishment of the New England town commons, which dates back to the early part of the seventeenth century. Evidence shows that these commons, established as early as 1634, were used by boys for play.[2]

Between 1821 and 1830, outdoor gymnasiums were built for the first time in the schools of New York City and the New England states. In 1821, the Salem (Massachusetts) Latin School opened an outdoor gymnasium with equipment, but did not provide for a supervisor. The Round Hill School at Northampton, Massachusetts, opened one in 1825 equipped with German gymnasium equipment, and a supervisor was provided. Harvard and Yale were the first colleges to provide outdoor gymnasiums in 1826.[3]

Although in colonial times public gardens, plazas, and public squares were set aside for the enjoyment of the people, it was not until 1853, when New York City acquired Central Park, that any city set aside land for strictly park purposes. During the latter half of the nineteenth century, many cities followed New York's example and acquired large parks. For many years, however, parks were considered primarily for rest and relaxation and not for recreation activity.

In 1872, Brookline, Massachusetts, became the first city in the United States to set aside public lands for playgrounds, purchasing two lots for such purposes. During the same year, the Young Men's Christian Association built an outdoor gymnasium in Boston, which provided for games, athletics, and a running track.

The establishment of the "sandgardens" in Boston in 1885 and 1886 has come to be accepted by many historians as the origin of the "play movement." The idea originated with Dr. Marie E. Zakresewska when she was visiting in Germany. While summering in Berlin, she observed that children were playing with heaps of sand in the public parks. The first sandpiles in America were started in the yards of the Parmenter Street Chapel and the West End Nursery in Boston. There were no regular play supervisors provided during the first years, but in 1887, several women supervisors were hired.

In 1889, the Boston Park Department converted a ten-acre tract along the Charles River in a congested neighborhood into an open-air gymnasium for boys and men; two years later, one was opened for women and girls.

The experience in playground organization in Boston had a direct influence upon the organization of similar movements in other cities. A "model" playground was opened at Hull House in Chicago in 1892. The playground provided sandboxes as well as facilities for playing handball and indoor baseball. It was much larger than the earlier sandgardens and was able to accommodate older children. New York City provided for thirty-one playgrounds in 1898 under the direction of the State Board of Education. The city moved quickly to develop a network of playgrounds that would be paid for and administered completely by the city. All schools were required to have open-air playgrounds. The demand for city playgrounds was gradually supported by prominent civic leaders, businessmen, social and church workers, reformers, educators, and newspapermen. By the close of the century, fourteen American cities had made provision for supervised play facilities. "In each case, private initiative and financial support were prominent factors in getting the first playgrounds under way, and in bringing pressure upon city governments to accept responsibility for providing play areas."[4]

The founding of settlement houses was an attempt by social workers to meet the increasing problems resulting from urban living in the 1880s. The social settlement, which grew out of the humanitarian movement to aid the poor, made a great impact on the promotion of play activity in America. The first expression of the movement in the United States was in New York in 1887, followed by the opening of the Hull House in Chicago by Jane Addams in 1889. Commonly called the community center, social settlements originally were located in slum areas but later became cen-

---

[2] Clarence E. Rainwater, *The Play Movement in the United States* (Chicago: University of Chicago Press, 1922), pp. 13–14.

[3] Ibid., pp. 14–15.

[4] Richard Kraus, *Recreation and Leisure in Modern Society,* © 1971 by Meredith Corporation. Reprinted by permission of Prentice-Hall, Inc., Englewood Cliffs, N.J. Pp. 184–85.

ters of education, recreation, and welfare activities in other areas of the community.

Commercial amusements and various forms of play equipment began to appear. The circus reached its highest peak in the last quarter of the nineteenth century. Large shows played cities and towns, "pitching the big top wherever they could hope to draw a crowd. The circus meant for the farmer the one taste of theatrical entertainment that he might ever have a chance to enjoy."[5] P. T. Barnum, William C. Coup, James A. Bailey, and the Ringling brothers were all instrumental in establishing the Greatest Show on Earth and attracting great popularity in the circus.

Adult roller skating, so popular in the 1880s, began to wane as bicycling became the most universal sport of any city and town. The 1890s became known as the golden age of the wheel. Through the bicycle, an increasing number of Americans rediscovered the outdoors. People of all walks of life took to the wheel.

Toward the end of the 19th century, with transportation more easily available, amusement parks sprang up in the outlying districts of cities. By this time the penny arcade, the traveling medicine show, and the annual visit to the circus "big top" had become popular. Band concerts in the parks, huge holiday celebrations with fireworks on the Fourth of July, "taffy pulls" in the homes, and museums were now in small and large towns across the nation.[6]

During the closing years of the nineteenth century, blacks were still largely segregated from public recreation service. However, some voluntary organizations were attempting to bridge the gap. "During the early years of the recreation movement, the northern Negro was a recipient of some YMCA and settlement house recreation programs," wrote James Murphy, "although basically

Fig. 4-2 EXCITING AMUSEMENT RIDES. Many Coney Island type amusement parks were developed in the major cities, and like today, they proved highly popular entertainment. Increasingly, they were also being seen at state fairs.

white children were the beneficiaries of organized recreation in the initial years of the movement.[7]

Meanwhile, municipal parks were being developed in areas throughout the country. The first metropolitan park system was established in Boston in 1892, while the first county system was in Essex County, New Jersey, in 1895. The New England Association of Park Superintendents, later known as the American Institute of Park Executives, was organized in 1898, bringing together park superintendents to discuss and promote their professional concerns. As a result, the playground and park movement, later to be known as the recreation movement, got under way. Now, the concern was for the needs of people of all ages and not just children.

[5] Foster Rhea Dulles, *A History of Recreation,* © 1965 by Meredith Corporation, New York. Reprinted by permission of Prentice-Hall, Inc., Englewood Cliffs, N.J., 1973, pp. 282–83.

[6] Harold D. Meyer, Charles K. Brightbill, and H. Douglas Sessoms, *Community Recreation: A Guide to Its Organization* (Englewood Cliffs, N.J.: Prentice-Hall, Inc., 1969), p. 13.

[7] John A. Nesbitt, Paul D. Brown, James F. Murphy, *Recreation and Leisure Service for the Disadvantaged* (Philadelphia: Lea & Febiger, 1970), p. 115.

A number of pioneers of the public recreation movement—men such as Joseph Lee, Henry Curtis, Clark Hetherington, and Luther Halsey Gulick—made major contributions in providing a fuller rationale for the need for public recreation. Many noted psychologists and educators provided their views and theories regarding the values of play in human growth and development.

SOCIAL REFORMS INFLUENCING THE RECREATION MOVEMENT

Toward the end of the nineteenth century, people began speaking out on the national scene deploring the breakdown in human relationships that the industrial revolution had created. Social investigators became deeply concerned by the suffering, poverty, and squalor of the masses who lived squeezed into America's large cities. Newspapers, books, and magazines all aroused the American public to support great social and civic reforms.

Social movements were beginning to stir. The YMCA, founded in Boston in 1851, grew rapidly and was soon offering basketball leagues, baseball, gymnastics, and other athletic events. Free public schools, perhaps the most notable achievement in American society, began to appear in growing numbers. New concepts in education and psychology made a more realistic approach to the needs of children. Churches took the initiative in developing recreation programs for children and families, which contributed much to social interaction.

Many of the conditions that gave rise to the recreation movement had their origins in the last half of the nineteenth century. Some of the conditions that influenced the shape of the movement included the following:

1. Effects of the Industrial Revolution
2. Modern science and technology
3. Changing work patterns
4. Urbanization
5. Increase in population
6. Rise in crime and delinquency
7. Depletion of natural resources
8. Increase in mental illness patients

9. Expansion of commercial recreation opportunities
10. Greater mobility of the population
11. Need for greater unification in recreation efforts

According to Thomas Yukic, the recreation movement in the United States was essentially a social one from its beginning. Social leaders pointed out such evils as dangerous streets, delinquency, unsanitary living conditions, child labor, congestion of cities, and lack of space for play and rest. A new psychology emerged during the movement that declared that "the child should be the center of the educational effort and that his play during leisure was acceptable and worthwhile."[8]

THE EARLY TWENTIETH CENTURY

With the exception of Boston, Chicago's South Park playground system influenced the development of playgrounds and recreation in the United States more than any other city. Indeed, the creation of small parks for an estimated $5 million made a tremendous impact on the growth of the recreation movement. The success of the planned parks was a great influence in extending the recreational use of parks in other cities. Reynold Carlson, Theodore Deppe, and Janet MacLean wrote: "With their carefully planned fieldhouses and their spacious outdoor areas, the playgrounds represented the first acceptance of public responsibility for indoor and outdoor recreation facilities, for varied interest programs, for recreation outlets for all ages, for year-round activities, and for leadership as well as facilities."[9]

In the early 1900s, small parks began to appear in many city neighborhoods. A trend began to emerge—city planning, esthetic influences, and a new concern for play habits of people. From 1900 to 1904, four cities—Chicago, Los Angeles,

[8] Thomas S. Yukic, *Fundamentals of Recreation* (New York: Harper & Row, 1970), p. 26.

[9] Reynold E. Carlson, Theodore R. Deppe, and Janet R. MacLean, *Recreation in American Life* (Belmont, Calif.: Wadsworth Publishing Co., 1972), p. 41.

Rochester, and Boston—developed recreation centers that could be open twelve months of the year to the public. In the South, however, Negroes were still denied access to most public facilities and were restricted almost entirely from recreation participation.

As industry expanded into great corporations with thousands of employees, further economic and social changes became apparent. Work patterns became more specialized. The rapid growth in population was matched by a strong move toward urbanization. The result was a serious congestion of large cities, giving rise to slums, crime, epidemics, and other social ills.

Emergence of the Playground Association of America

By 1906, the movement for municipal public recreation had grown to such a level that playground promoters meeting in Washington, D.C., founded the Playground Association of America, later to become the National Recreation and Park Association. Luther Halsey Gulick became its president, while Henry Curtis was elected its first secretary. Formation of the association was considered by many historians as the single most important event in the American recreation movement. The drive for playgrounds was given new impetus and qualified national leadership. Richard F. Knapp wrote that: "Leaders of the organization soon began to foster municipal responsibility for provision of public recreation for all people, a wider concept of recreation, and a sense of professionalism among workers in the field."[10]

Within a few years, two new leaders accepted the top positions in the PRAA and were to head it for decades. Joseph Lee, a Harvard-bred Boston philanthropist and social worker, was elected president, while social worker Howard Braucher became its executive secretary. Under the effective leadership of Lee and Braucher, the Association, as well as the playground movement, prospered and moved closer to the so-called "community

movement," which enjoyed its peak influence in America during World War I. Richard Knapp, in discussing the community movement, wrote:

> Advocates of the community movement, including such figures as Jane Addams, founder of Hull House, and sociologist Charles H. Cooley, claimed that technology and other impersonal forces operating on a national scale were destroying close-knit local groups important to the social structure. Literature on community cooperation and organization for such purposes as the constructive use of free time began to appear with increasing frequency. All of these trends with roots in institutions such as the rising numbers of school-house community centers and settlement houses, constituted the community movement, where promoters aimed to show the potential for beneficial coordination of neighborhoods and communities.[11]

By 1914, attention was centered on neighborhood and community interests. Increasing emphasis on the importance of the community received widespread acceptance by the PRAA and the recreation movement. Encouraging an attitude of community and cooperation among the users of public recreation, Braucher felt citizens should be able to develop a stronger community spirit. According to Clarence Rainwater, the period from 1915–18 was known as the "neighborhood organization" stage. Through its field secretaries and annual conventions, the PRAA promoted community spirit and was most instrumental in developing municipal recreation on a neighborhood basis. The number of municipalities with recreation centers in schools soon increased to over 150 cities.[12] The budget of the Association in 1916 surpassed $100,000, as over 400 cities reported some local provision for playgrounds and recreation. Increasingly, the yearly cost of $4,235,000 came from municipal funds.

The entrance of the United States into World War I created a need for reorganization of recreation activities and facilities. The population of camp towns increased tremendously. The War Camp Community Service allowed each commun-

---

[10] Richard F. Knapp, "The Playground and Recreation Association of America in World War I," *Parks and Recreation*, January, 1972, p. 27.

[11] Ibid., p. 27.

[12] Rainwater, op. cit., pp. 46–48.

Fig. 4-3 FATHER OF THE AMERICAN PLAYGROUND—JOSEPH LEE. As president of the Playground Association of America from 1910 to his death in 1937, Lee was instrumental in the tremendous expansion of municipal recreation during this period. (Courtesy of Miss Susan Lee.)

ity to assume the responsibility for planning and organizing recreation for service men. This was the first major effort to give unity to the various recreational programs that had grown so rapidly prior to the war. Following the war, the WCCS—now known as "Community Service Incorporated"—continued to serve and promote community recreation.

FATHER OF THE AMERICAN PLAYGROUND

Joseph Lee, known as the "father of the playground movement," was perhaps the most influ-

ential of the pioneers of the recreation movement. Born in 1862, Lee was a lawyer and a philanthropist who came from a wealthy New England family. His father instilled in young Lee a sense of social responsibility and a desire to serve mankind. His social work experience in the 1890s proved very useful in learning the importance of both governmental and private responsibility in social improvement. It also taught him the necessity for well-planned and organized campaigns of reform.

Shocked to see boys arrested for playing in the streets, Lee organized a playground for them in an open lot, which he supervised. In 1898, Lee was responsible for the creation of a model playground in Boston, which featured a play area for small children, a boys' section, a sports field, and individual gardens.

As his influence expanded, Lee was in great demand as a speaker and writer on playgrounds.

Lee recognized the great creative power of individuals, and argued that the key element in a municipal recreation system was the one man who headed it. He often lectured on the relationship of strong individuals to a healthy society. If he emphasized individualism, however, he also supported cooperation and the community of individuals. Before 1902, he wrote that "It is no longer what I can do for you, but what we can do for ourselves and our country." If people would just get together and work for the common good, all of the individuals too could benefit.[13]

Lee was the first to express, in *Play in Education* (1910), a modern interpretation of play and its meaning to society and youth. Play, Lee argued, was the serious activity in children's adjustment to life. He felt recreation had vital significance not only for children but also for everyone who wanted a meaningful life.

According to Lee, quality was more important than quantity, in both individual and community efforts. He believed in efficiency. The key to quality was through fixed goals, organization, and expertise. He emphasized education for the wise

[13] Richard F. Knapp, "Play for America: The National Recreation Association, 1906-1950," *Parks and Recreation*, October 1972, pp. 21–23.

use of leisure as the means to help people achieve happy, creative lives.

Lee was president of the Playground Association of America from 1910 until his death in 1937 and was also a leading lecturer of the National Recreation School, a one-year course for carefully selected college graduates. The tremendous expansion of municipal recreation during this period was largely due to the work of the Association under his leadership.[14]

THE SECOND DECADE OF THE TWENTIETH CENTURY

During the early part of the new century, a social and civic center movement began in the public schools to meet the needs of an adult population through social, educational, cultural, and civic activities.

Although the school building was considered taboo for recreational use, a system of social centers was initiated in Rochester, New York, in 1907, under the leadership of a former minister and athlete, E. J. Ward.

The Rochester plan was a pioneer attempt to establish the public school center as a catalyst in American social life, to help develop community interest, and to spread democratic ways. Spurred on by Rochester's successful example, other cities began to use their schools as centers for music, drama, and other cultural interests. . . . As early as 1910, pioneers such as Clarence A. Perry adopted an educational philosophy which recognized that the school plant belonged to the people and it was proper for it to be used for social purposes.[15]

The Boy Scouts of America was organized in 1910, while the Girl Scouts and Camp Fire Girls were started in 1912. The organization of these agencies emphasized the growing concern for organized recreation for youth. The camping movement received much impetus between 1910 and 1914, as many youth camps and private camps were organized.

Schools, both high schools and colleges, were placing more emphasis on athletics. Intramural sports gained a foothold about 1914 and have made steady progress since.

When America entered World War I, the recreation needs of men serving their country were soon recognized as being of great importance. In 1917, the War Department requested the PRAA to assist communities near training camps in providing recreation activities for soldiers and sailors. The War Camp Community Service was organized to entertain in homes, and musical, social, and athletic programs were developed for training camps. "Before the war ended," wrote Thomas Yukic, "WCCS had organized social and recreation resources of over 6500 communities near military camps and 50 war industry districts. As a result, a great range of local communities had, through this participation, become conscious for the first time of the power and functions of organized recreation."[16]

Service to underprivileged communities was beginning to receive stronger emphasis in organized recreation programs. A concept of recreation service for the entire community began to emerge as programs increased at playgrounds and recreation centers.

The problems and needs of black Americans were beginning to be recognized by a growing number of those in the field. In 1919, the Playground and Recreation Association of America hired Ernest T. Attwell, a black, to work for the Association. Although concerted efforts were made by Attwell and the Bureau of Colored Work to reach all citizens, still only token results were achieved in the black community. "Some Negroes found private and voluntary recreation facilities as good alternatives to public, tax-supported programs," said James Murphy. "Although blacks had difficulty in qualifying for membership in the Boy Scout and Girl Scout organizations, and only a few were touched by the YMCA, Negro membership grew rapidly in voluntary recreation agencies after the twenties."[17]

---

[14] Jay B. Nash, *Recreation: Pertinent Reading* (Dubuque: William C. Brown Co., 1965), p. 52.

[15] Yukic, op. cit., p. 28.

---

[16] Yukic, op. cit., p. 29.

[17] Nesbitt, Brown, and Murphy, op. cit., p. 121.

Fig. 4-4 AS SPECTATOR SPORTS INCREASED IN GREAT POPULARITY, many large athletic stadiums and facilities were built in the larger cities, such as County Stadium in Milwaukee.

THE DECADE AFTER WORLD WAR I

A period of prosperity followed the war and brought with it a marked increase in appreciation of the importance of recreation. Americans had more money to spend for leisure than at any previous time. Laboring classes were working shorter hours, and the population of cities was increasing. Indeed, the nation in the "Golden Twenties" had become a nation at play as well as at work. For the first time, play was beginning to be recognized as one of the major interests of life.

This decade was characterized by a growing appreciation of the importance of leisure and a marked expansion in public recreation services. The rapid increase in community recreation areas and facilities reflected the acceptance of recreation as an essential factor in city planning. Recreation programs were greatly enlarged in scope and in the number of participants as recreation budgets increased. Leadership training was emphasized, and the production of recreation literature increased markedly.[18]

Automobiles, radios, motion pictures, tourist travel, large sports events, and many other opportunities came within the reach of many people. A phenomenal upsurge of interest in both private and public recreation facilities such as new parks, community houses, swimming pools, dance halls, picnic areas, golf courses, beaches, skating rinks, and bowling establishments swept the country.

An emphasis on legislation for recreation and parks also followed World War I. New laws were

---

[18] George D. Butler, *Community Recreation* (New York: McGraw-Hill Book Co., 1940), p. 89.

passed in many states giving cities the legal authority to provide organized park and recreation services. In addition to the school board or park group, recreation commissions were created with power to expand appropriations, employ workers, and provide year-round systems. A spurt in recreation spending followed such favorable legislation.

In 1921, the National Conference of State Parks was organized to further the state park movement, preceded by the formation of the National Park Service in 1916. By 1926, the number of cities possessing parks grew from 100 in 1892 to 1620 in 1926.

Commercial recreation boomed for a population with increased purchasing power. Spectator sports increased in popularity, and women began to join in sports activities without fear of embarrassment. Interest in the development of outdoor recreation prompted President Calvin Coolidge to call a National Conference of Outdoor Recreation in 1924.

THE GREAT DEPRESSION

After the period of heavy spending and inflation in the 1920s, a great depression followed which was unequaled in history. To combat the mass unemployment, the Roosevelt Administration's New Deal started an extensive public works program that operated on the principle that any kind of work was better than none. Work projects were established including a project in the field of community public recreation. These relief programs served to stimulate mass recognition of recreation in the community.

During the third year of the depression, the Federal Emergency Relief Administration (FERA) was established with the prime purpose of providing employment. The FERA took two approaches: (1) the construction of facilities; (2) the development of recreation programs and activities under trained leadership.

The FERA, the Works Projects Administration, and the Civilian Conservation Corps all served to advance the status of recreation. They also aided in the rehabilitation of the country. Besides providing jobs, the projects were responsible for the construction and improvement of centers, parks, picnic areas, roads, trails, and similar facilities. In addition, the WPA provided one of the most intensive training programs for recreation workers ever attempted.

To supplement the work of these agencies, a demand arose for recreation leaders to supervise the new facilities and to provide direction to the programs. Thus, many recreation jobs were created in the newly constructed recreation centers. WPA leaders worked under the supervision of local tax-supported units such as recreation departments, park boards, planning boards, departments of education, recreation councils, and welfare boards.

On a national scale during the depression years, there was still little being done to meet the recreation needs of the black. However, the National Recreation Association did report increases in the facilities and leadership serving black neighborhoods.

It was not uncommon in America, particularly in the South, for a recreation department to have a separate division of service for blacks. Such divisions would usually be inferior and poorly staffed. The existence of separate provisions of recreation services was consistent with the common practice of segregation and de facto segregation of public facilities.[19]

There were numerous errors or shortcomings in the emergency programs in the 1930s, but there was no doubt of the beneficial contributions they provided the rapidly growing recreation and parks field.

RECREATION AND WORLD WAR II

The nation was slowly recovering from the depression when the United States entered World War II in December, 1941. The American people have never united and cooperated so strongly in war work as they did during World War II. Nearly total effort went into the operation of agencies and organizations which contributed directly to those in the armed forces.

---

[19] Murphy, op. cit., p. 123.

Fig. 4-5 NEW PUBLIC RECREATION AND PARK AGENCIES were created throughout the nation following World War II. Beautiful neighborhood parks like this one were built in growing numbers in large and small cities and towns.

As America went to war, so did recreation— the USO, American Red Cross, Army Special Services Division, the Welfare and Recreation section of the Bureau of Naval Personnel, and the Recreation Service of the Marine Corps. They promoted programs in training centers, close to the battle fronts, on ships, in hospitals and rest centers, in industrial centers, and in every area of the nation where people were working to produce for war. Recreation contributed to every aspect of the war effort. It was recognized as a definite "morale builder," relieving tension and lessening the worries of the millions of citizens in the thousands of communities throughout the nation.

The Special Services Division in the Army had charge of providing facilities and programs for recreation and entertainment on the various military posts. Approximately 12,000 special service officers and several times that number of enlisted men and thousands of volunteers made possible the program.

The United Service Organizations, formed in 1941, consisted of six national agencies: Salvation Army, Catholic Community Services, YMCA, YWCA, Jewish Welfare Board, and the National Travelers Aid. Their prime role was to serve the leisure needs of the armed services in community settings and to provide recreation for industrial workers engaged in the war effort.

The American Red Cross provided recreation in leave areas overseas, on posts throughout the world, and for programs in hospitals, both overseas and at home. The program offered opportunities in all fields of recreation.

Meanwhile, in American communities, many civilian programs had to be curtailed during World War II due to manpower shortage and travel restrictions. However, local recreation and park departments offered new programs to support the war effort. These included salvage drives, victory gardens, learn-to-swim programs, and many teen-canteen programs to counteract the increase of

Fig. 4-6 THE STRUGGLE FOR OPEN SPACE. Millions of dollars and acres of irreplaceable park lands slipped away from public recreation use into the path of freeways, commercial and industrial enterprises, and housing developments. Observe the encroachment conditions that have engulfed this Chicago area park. (Courtesy of Chicago Aerial Survey.)

juvenile delinquency. Youth-serving agencies made equipment and supplies for military recreation centers and sold war bonds. Many municipal recreation departments extended their facilities and services to local war plants, serving war-industry workers around the clock.

FOLLOWING WORLD WAR II

By the end of the war, the great numbers of servicemen and servicewomen who had been exposed to the variety of recreation programs and services had developed a new appreciation of this field of organized service. The many individuals who had been trained and gained experience in recreation programs were ready to assume professional jobs in civilian life.

Many communities established parks, pools, civic centers, and other recreation facilities as memorials to their war dead. Much of this activity was used to build much needed recreation facilities which supplemented existing community buildings or areas.

The establishment of new public recreation and park agencies gained impetus throughout the nation. Tax supported public recreation systems increased in number. The expansion of state participation in the recreation field was a striking postwar trend. The states increased their efforts in establishing programs to improve recreation facilities and services. New state recreation commissions and boards, state youth authorities, and state inter-agency recreation committees were established. The formation of special districts was a growing trend throughout the country.

The development of recreation programs in the hospitals was advanced significantly, particularly in Armed Forces hospitals, veterans' hospitals, state neuropsychiatric hospitals, and children's hospitals.

Public recreation had become an established part of American culture and an accepted responsibility of all levels of government. According to Knapp, "Outdoor recreation was available in national, state, and local park systems. Expenditures for public recreation by local governments exceeded by several times the combined state and federal outlay."[20]

Increase of public interest in recreation and the rise of inflation resulted in sharply increased expenditures for recreation on all fronts. As a result, more money was being spent for commercial recreation, as well as community recreation. Youth centers gained popularity as enthusiastic parents, genuinely interested in the welfare of their children, provided increased support to these and other community endeavors.

Following the war, the federal government increased recognition of blacks through various civil rights maneuvers related to higher education, Armed Forces, and employment opportunities. James Murphy wrote:

Also, the late forties and early fifties brought forward a new identifiable, improved image of the Negro, as Black people began to cross over racial barriers into the heretofore all-white sport pastimes. The increasing popularity of sport spectacles was a possible hope for propelling the Negro socially and enhancing the dignity of all Blacks.[21]

During the first half of the twentieth century, "the National Recreation Association provided significant leadership in fostering the expansion of organized municipal recreation in the United States. The Association rendered important services, such as field assistance to local proponents of public recreation, a central clearinghouse for information, training programs as well as the formulation of standards to further the establishment of a new profession on a solid footing."[22]

---

[20] Richard F. Knapp, "Play for America: Part VIII—A Trial Balance," *Parks and Recreation*, January 1974, pp. 27–28.

[21] Ibid., p. 126.

[22] Ibid., p. 55.

THE 1950s TO THE PRESENT

A tremendous expansion of recreation and leisure activity occurred in the 1950s in all areas of the field including public recreation, voluntary agency recreation, employee recreation, Armed Forces recreation, commercial recreation, and recreation for the ill and handicapped.

Leisure pursuits were changing significantly. Leisure continued to increase for many segments of the population, such as the aged person, the school dropout, the unemployed, the unemployable, and the youth who refused to accept Establishment work roles. A great many Americans found themselves with more discretionary time and money. Tremendous increases in international travel also occurred during this period.

In the late 1960s and the early 1970s, the American public has developed a great concern for the quality of the environment. The nation has become alarmingly aware of the vanishing forests, air pollution, water pollution, inner-city decay, noise pollution, and the problems of population explosion. President Nixon's first official act in 1970 was to approve the National Environmental Policy Act of 1969, which declares that it is the policy of the federal government, in cooperation with other levels of government and public and private organization, "to create and maintain conditions under which man and nature can exist in productive harmony." With more people, increased leisure, and greater mobility, public lands were being used more extensively. A new challenge involved the struggle for open space, not merely its acquisition, but its maintenance protection.

A nation-wide survey concluded in 1961 by the National Committee on Encroachment of Recreation Lands and Waters did much to alarm the nation of the scope of the encroachment threat.

The survey indicated that within a ten-year period, 2687 acres of recreation land were lost in 257 areas recording encroachment. The estimated land value in 44 of these areas alone was nearly $9 million. Millions of dollars of irreplaceable park lands and open spaces slipped away from public recreation use, into the path of highways, commercial and industrial enter-

Fig. 4-7 ENVIRONMENTAL QUALITY. The need to protect and preserve our natural resources began to receive governmental and public attention. The Wilderness Act of 1964 was designed to preserve areas in their natural form and provide a natural habitat for the diminishing wildlife population, like this scenic area in Gallatin National Forest in Montana. (Courtesy of U.S. Forest Service.)

prises, schools, community buildings, and housing developments.[23]

The National Park Service and the U.S. Forest Service both implemented new programs to improve and develop the national parks and recreation areas. The Outdoor Recreation Resources Review Commission established by Congress requested an estimate of needs for outdoor recreation space in the year 2000. Subsequently, in 1963, President John F. Kennedy created the Bureau of Outdoor Recreation in the Department of the Interior.

Recreation needs also played a part in the problems of urban planning and development. The Housing and Urban Development Department was established as an agency to serve the urban and metropolitan areas of the nation. In 1965, the Administration on Aging was established as a part of the Social and Rehabilitation Services of the Department of Health, Education, and Welfare. The Open Space Program of the Department of Housing and Urban Development was created in 1961, and through it, funds may be granted to communities for park and recreation sites. The Land and Water Conservation Fund was initiated in 1964 to provide federal aid in outdoor recreation to states and local communities.

---

[23] Meyer, Brightbill, and Sessoms, op. cit., pp. 25–26.

Fig. 4-8 DESEGREGATION OF PUBLIC RECREATION PROGRAMS AND FACILITIES. As a result of the 1954 Supreme Court decisions affecting integration, the demands of black people for equality began to spread throughout the nation.

In 1965, five different organizations within the broad field of recreation and parks merged into a single body known as the National Recreation and Park Association. Soon, other groups, such as the National Association of Recreation Therapists and the Armed Forces Section of the American Recreation Society, fully merged their interests with the newly formed organization. Today, the National Recreation and Park Association is an independent, nonprofit organization intended to promote the development of the park and recreation movement.

Other highly significant governmental actions included the establishment of a unified wilderness system in 1964; the 1966 Historic Preservation Act; and the creation of a Wild and Scenic Rivers system. Special cabinets were organized that dealt with water and air pollution, natural beauty, and recreation. The Council on Recreation and Natural Beauty was established in 1966, followed by the Environmental Quality Council in 1969.

The 1954 Supreme Court decisions affecting integration paved the way for desegregation of public recreation and amusement facilities. As a result, segregation in public recreation facilities,

public housing, and interstate travel facilities was held to be unconstitutional. The blacks' demands for equality began to spread throughout the nation. The demonstrations in the early 1960s at lunch counters and outdoor theatres were followed shortly by much stronger demands and protest demonstrations.

New concern for the physical fitness of youth and adults received strong emphasis in the 1950s. The Kraus-Weber survey showed that American youth lagged far behind young Europeans in basic levels of physical fitness. Almost 58 percent of Americans were unable to pass a series of tests; only 8.7 percent of Europeans failed. Soon after, in 1956, President Eisenhower's newly created Council on Youth Fitness called for a national conference on youth fitness which produced significant results. Programs to improve fitness were developed in most states. Many public recreation departments expanded programs involving fitness classes, conditioning, jogging, and sports for people of all ages. The President's Council on Physical Fitness, the Lifetime Sports Foundation, the American Association for Health, Physical Education, and Recreation, the National Collegiate Athletic

Fig. 4-9 NEW CONCERN FOR PHYSICAL CONDITION. With the alarming decline of the physical status of both American youth and adults, programs to improve the fitness level were initiated in many public recreation agencies and schools. Jogging classes involving both sexes are now in great demand.

Association, and the American Athletic Union spearheaded the national concern for improving the fitness level of the American people.

Additional concern for mental fitness and the role of recreation in mental health included the Washington Conference on Recreation for the Mentally Ill in 1957 by the American Association of Health, Physical Education, and Recreation.

A "cultural explosion" involving the performing arts as leisure outlets resulted in a marked expansion of cultural centers, performing organizations, museums, and art centers. Evidence of the increased national impetus is the 1958 act of Congress that made possible the National Cultural Center for the Performing Arts.

With the sharp increase in the number of elderly citizens, stronger emphasis was given programs and facilities involving the aged population. The White House Conference on the Aging in 1961 placed considerable emphasis on recreation for "senior citizens."

The growing urban crisis, civil unrest, dissent, and alienation marked the late 1960s and the early 1970s. Many problems continued to plague the nation: the needs of disadvantaged citizens, particularly members of minority groups; growing black militancy; the wave of urban riots in the 1960s; relaxation of moral standards; drug abuse; violence and a growing disregard for law and order; distrust in government; the energy crisis, and the economy.

The creation of the Urban Affairs Department by the National Recreation and Park Association in 1967 and the employment of Ira J. Hutchison, Jr., has brought increased focus and recognition to the culturally deprived. Forums, seminars, and institutes have brought together national professional and lay leaders to identify areas of need and to establish guidelines and steps for serving the urban disadvantaged.

After several years of striving to integrate recreation programs, it appears that the new vogue is to identify each ethnic group's uniqueness. Young Blacks are increasingly turning away from white-oriented recreation programs and focusing on the richness of their cultural heritage. By studying African history, wearing their

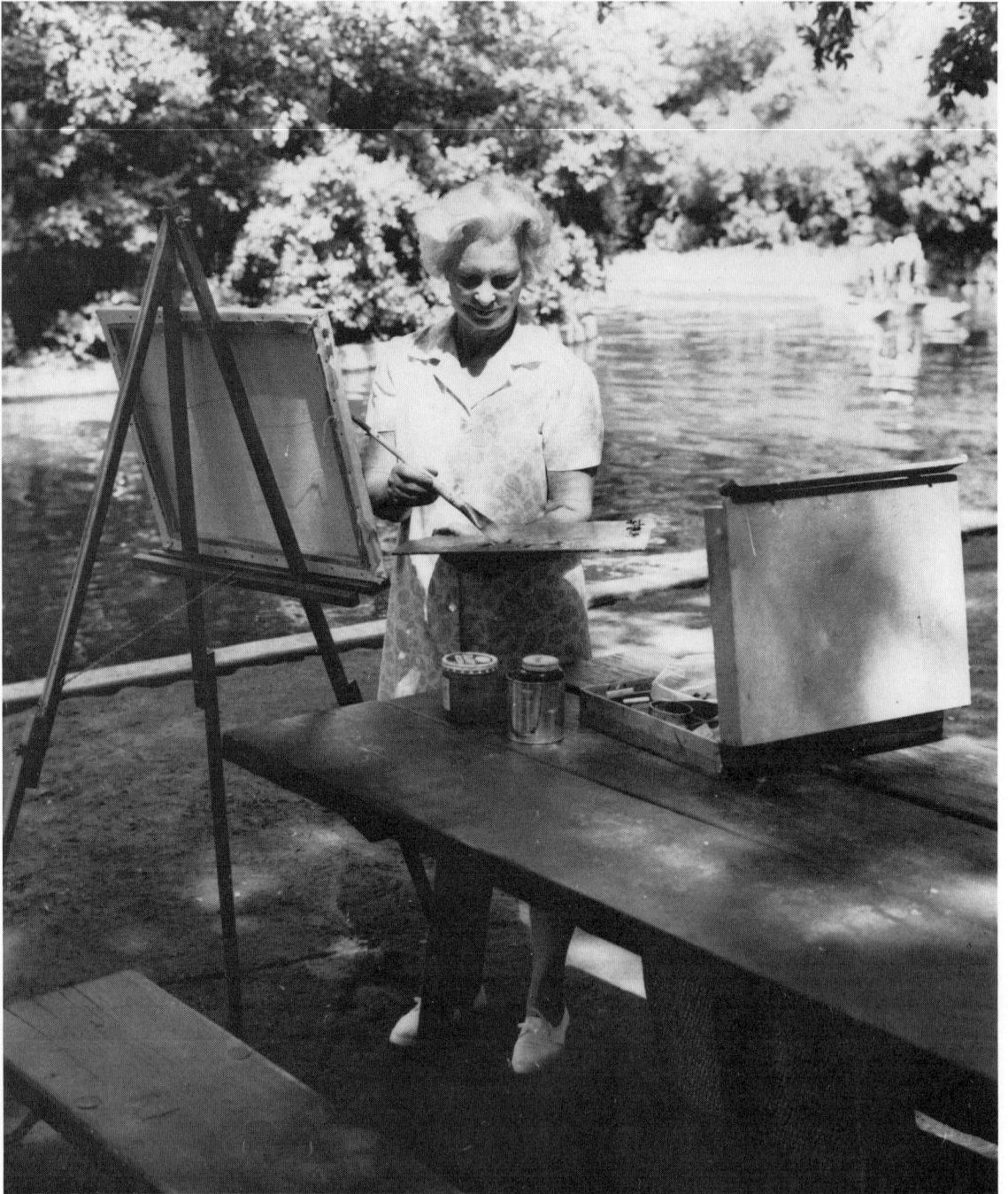

Fig. 4-10 A CULTURAL ARTS EXPLOSION resulted in a great expansion of arts centers, museums, and performing arts organizations. Art programs for the elderly received stronger emphasis, resulting in many classes and activities.

hair "natural," and proclaiming their individuality, blacks are recapturing the pride and dignity which disappeared during slavery.[24]

With the pressure of increasing social crisis in the cities, austerity budgets, and the changing roles of government, those responsible for recrea-

tion services have found it necessary to develop innovations and new approaches to program planning and to secure additional means of financial support. In meeting the needs of a new technological age and a society rapidly becoming leisure-oriented, all aspects of recreation program planning, including the underlying philosophy, have had to be revised.

---

[24] Nesbitt, Brown, and Murphy, op. cit., pp. 129–30.

II

The Role of
Government in
Recreation and Parks

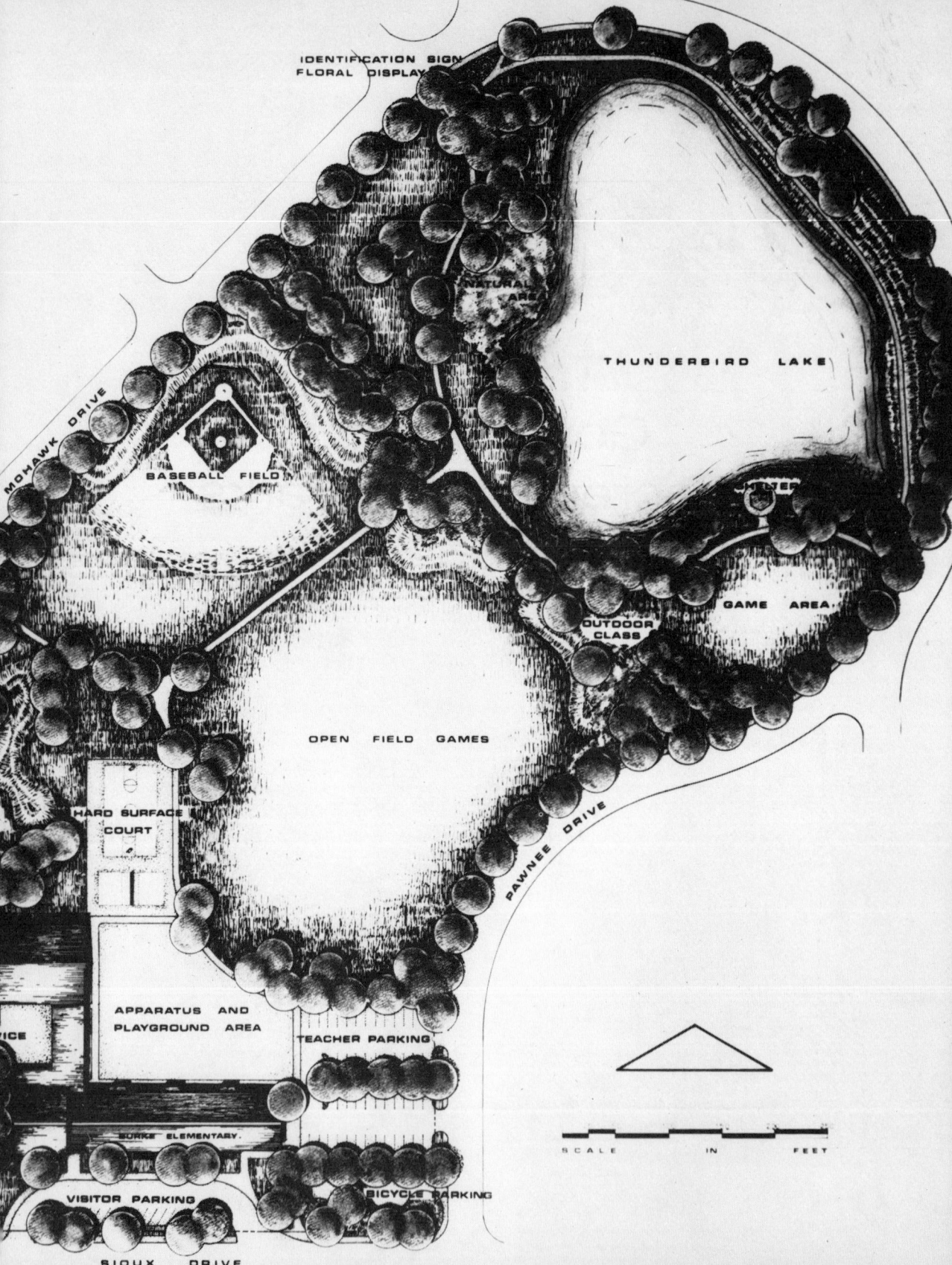

IDENTIFICATION SIGN
FLORAL DISPLAY

NATURAL AREA

THUNDERBIRD LAKE

MOHAWK DRIVE

BASEBALL FIELD

GAME AREA

OUTDOOR CLASS

OPEN FIELD GAMES

PAWNEE DRIVE

HARD SURFACE COURT

APPARATUS AND
PLAYGROUND AREA

TEACHER PARKING

OFFICE

BURKE ELEMENTARY

VISITOR PARKING

BICYCLE PARKING

SIOUX DRIVE

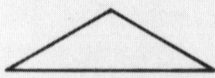

SCALE   IN   FEET

5

Local
Government

Before the twentieth century, local government was relatively simple and concerned with few functions and services. Today, however, municipal government has taken on a new dimension, the result of a growing acceptance that government should contribute to the welfare of the people. Although recreation services were once the concern of private agencies only, as their need became recognized, many have been gradually taken over by municipal authorities.

As the recreation movement grew in scope, and the facilities and services increased, there developed a need for specific legislation giving municipalities the power to appropriate funds for parks and recreation services.

Today, municipal recreation is accepted by public officials and civic leaders as an important function and responsibility of local government.

> Municipal recreation, unlike that provided by most other agencies, is for all the people. In large measure it is equally available for rich and poor, for people of all ages, racial backgrounds, social status, political opinions, and religious preferences, for boys and girls, men and women. It gives to all the opportunity to engage in activities of their choice. Municipal recreation conforms with the American spirit and way of living.[1]

To meet the urban citizen's needs, the many functions of municipal government have expanded greatly during the past half century. Increased demands have been placed on local governments to provide services (including parks and recreation) to the citizens of the community.

However, the local municipality cannot meet all the recreation and leisure needs of all the people. The needs and interests of a community are too diverse and expensive for any one municipal agency to serve. Instead, the resources and services of all recreation agencies, organizations, and institutions are needed to serve the ever growing leisure-time needs of our society. For a nation which is rapidly becoming leisure-oriented,

Fig. 5-1 THE PLANNING PROCESS. The park and recreation department, in cooperation with the local planning agency, prepares the designs for the development of parks and recreation areas. This master plan was used for Thunderbird Park in Boulder, Colorado. (Courtesy of the Boulder, Colorado, Recreation and Park Department.)

---

[1] From *Introduction to Community Recreation* by George D. Butler. Copyright © 1967 by the National Recreation Association, Inc. Used with permission of McGraw-Hill Book Company. P. 68.

77

Fig. 5-2 DRAWING THE PLANS for Thunderbird Park took a lot of hard and careful desk work. (Courtesy of the Boulder, Colorado, Recreation and Park Department.)

there is a growing demand for a great variety of recreation activities and park services.

According to George Butler, "The term 'local government' is considered applicable to any local unit of state government such as the county, city, village, borough, or township, or school, park, and recreation districts. The term 'municipal recreation' is intended to include services provided by park or school authorities as well as by other local governmental agencies."[2]

THE NEED FOR MUNICIPAL RECREATION

The recreation and park services provided by a local municipality are determined primarily by the expressed will of the people and their readiness to pay for them from tax funds. In cities throughout America, the people have indicated that they consider recreation a needed function of local government.

2 Ibid., p. 64.

Although recreation is considered an individual responsibility, the provision of areas and facilities and organized programs for everyone in the community to enjoy is not within an individual's means. Government, through municipal services, voluntary agencies, and commercial groups, has an important role in the overall community recreation program.

In meeting the needs of the community, municipalities have the resources and ability to acquire, develop, and maintain a system of areas and facilities. They also have the financial capabilities through taxation, special assessments, and bonding powers to appropriate the funds needed to fulfill their responsibilities.

George Butler gave eight reasons why recreation has become a primary concern of local government:

1. Municipal recreation affords a large percentage of the people their only opportunity for wholesome recreation involvement.
2. Only through government can adequate lands be acquired for playgrounds, parks, and other recreation areas.
3. Municipal recreation is democratic and inclusive, serving all ages, races, and creeds.
4. Municipal recreation is comparatively inexpensive.
5. The local government gives permanency to recreation, assuring both continuity and the ability to respond to the changing needs of the community.
6. The job is too large for a private agency.
7. Recreation plays an important role in the local economy.
8. The people demand recreation and are willing to be taxed for it.[3]

TYPES OF SPONSORSHIP

Within the United States many groups and agencies strive to meet the recreation and leisure needs of a community. Essentially, the following four groups contribute the greatest portion of the community recreation program:

3 Ibid., pp. 66–70.

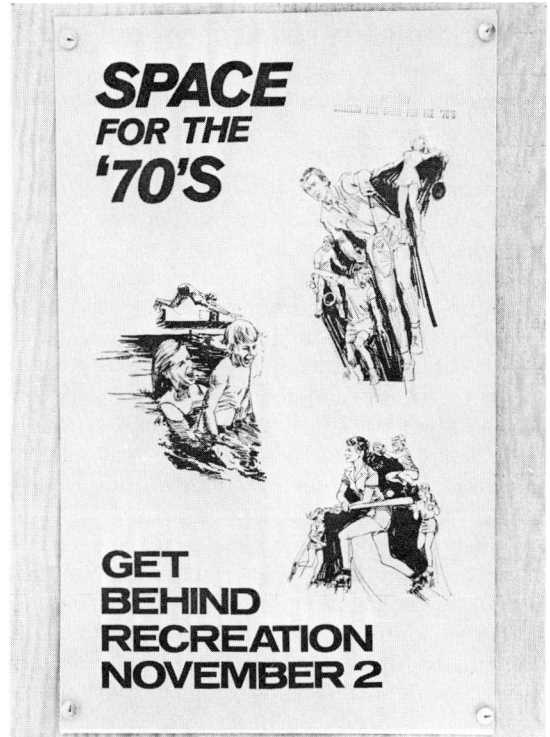

Fig. 5-3   LEISURE-TIME NEEDS. For a nation that is rapidly becoming leisure-oriented, there is a growing demand for a great variety of recreation activities and park services.

1. *Public agencies and institutions,* created and controlled by governmental bodies on local, state, and federal levels, and supported by taxes. The local municipality has a major responsibility of providing, maintaining, and operating a system of major areas and facilities, such as parks, playgrounds, recreation buildings, golf courses, athletic fields, community centers, playfields, water and winter sports facilities, and outdoor reservations. The recreation department should also provide leadership for a diversified program of sports, arts and crafts, drama, music, social recreation, outdoor recreation, special events, and other activities at the local facilities.

2. *Voluntary group work agencies,* consisting primarily of youth-serving organizations supported by membership fees and community funds. Even though the local government has taken over many of the recreation functions of the voluntary agen-

cies, these agencies will continue to meet important leisure needs of the community. The voluntary agency, however, usually restricts its primary service to a limited membership group.

3. *Private groups* such as industry, clubs, churches, armed forces, and fraternal and social groups that are supported by membership fees. Private agencies will continue to support the overall community recreation effort. Many types of private agencies offer enjoyable recreation for their members in restricted recreation groups.

4. *Commercial recreational enterprises* which are organized to gain a profit from their services and business and are designed to meet a specific leisure activity need of the people. The varied array of commercial recreation services and interests provides a strong contribution to the community and assures citizens a higher quality of service.

LEGAL AUTHORITY FOR RECREATION

To operate as a local governmental function, a municipal recreation department must receive legal authority from the state before a program can be organized. City and county types of government and the scope of their power are derived from the state constitution and statutes.

The legal bases for local government participation in the parks and recreation field and open space preservation are state enabling laws, local charters, and ordinances. They allow local governments to acquire land and buildings for park and recreation purposes by negotiated purchase, donation, bequest, or lease. Many cities may acquire land for park purposes by condemnation, which involves the right of eminent domain.

State enabling laws for recreation enable communities in the state to establish and conduct recreation programs under any type of administrative authority. Such an act means that the local community has the legal authorization of establishing the local recreation program most appropriate for its needs. Such acts also permit local governments to acquire land and spend public funds for land and buildings, and provide the authority to join with other local governments in cooperative efforts.

Many states have passed laws that have authorized county, district, or metropolitan park and recreation districts. Some state recreation and park enabling laws empower school districts, municipalities, counties, and other units of local government to join together to establish, operate, and maintain park and recreation systems.

LOCAL CHARTERS AND ORDINANCES

Operating under home-rule charters, cities and counties have the authority to establish and operate park and recreation systems under the power of such charters to promote the general welfare of citizens. Charter provisions related to recreation and parks usually provide for the creation of a park and recreation department, the appointment of an administrator, and an advisory board.

A local government that does not act under home-rule may create a park and recreation department and an administrative board by use of ordinances. Like charters, most ordinances will indicate the manner in which the park and recreation director and the administrative board are selected and will outline their duties. Ordinances provide the park and recreation agency with the permission to pass regulations and rules pertaining to the uses of parks and recreation facilities. Typical rules provided in city ordinances indicate speed limits to be observed in parks, closing hours of facilities, and types of conduct allowed.

Two recent ordinances passed by the City Council in Los Angeles will provide the Recreation and Parks Department with an estimated $4.5 million to be used exclusively for capital improvements and land acquisition. In 1971, the Council approved the Quimby Ordinance, which requires a developer to dedicate land or pay a fee for park purposes as part of the fee procedure in obtaining tract map approval. In 1972, the City Council of Los Angeles passed a Dwelling Unit Construction Tax that required a payment of $200 for each new dwelling unit constructed in the city.

ORGANIZING A RECREATION DEPARTMENT

After identifying and clarifying its need for establishing a municipal recreation program, a community must determine the administrative authority that is best suited to administer its recreation program. In addition to the type of authority, it should also consider the best use of tax funds and offer the best possible services and program.

No one authority is best suited to administer the recreation program. In the past, recreation has been administered by: (1) the park department, (2) a separate recreation authority, (3) the school administration, and (4) a combined department of parks and recreation, which has gained strong popularity in recent years.

Since community conditions vary, a number of factors must be considered that will determine the type of administrative authority. First, the existing state statutes should be examined to determine how such legislation will affect the local government in establishing a new department. Since the ability to obtain funds is an important

Fig. 5-4 A WELL-ROUNDED COMMUNITY RECREATION PROGRAM is the result of all agencies and organizations working together for the best interest of the people. Voluntary agencies, private clubs and organizations, and commercial recreation enterprises all have an important role in providing recreation services in the community.

consideration, the organizing committee must determine under what agency the most adequate funds can be provided. In order to secure the most widespread community support, the committee should determine the public's attitude toward the various types of organizations. The logical authority to direct the recreation program is the agency that can develop policies, coordinate plans, and secure the close cooperation with other organizations in the community.

Many large cities maintain separate park and recreation departments, each with its own director and some degree of autonomy. A large park department usually has a general manager, superintendents for both parks and recreation and special assistants for each. However, small to medium-sized cities tend to maintain a combined department of parks and recreation with one director and a separate supervisor of parks as well as a supervisor of recreation.

In a small community, the director or administrator usually is responsible for both parks and recreation. Under the combined department system, the administrator is apt to be a person trained in recreation with an experienced park foreman to handle the park work.

Some metropolitan areas have formed park districts that have elected commissioners as the primary decision-making body. San Francisco combines a city and county recreation and park department which operates under a general manager. The general manager has both a superintendent of parks and a superintendent of recreation.

TYPES OF ADMINISTRATIVE AUTHORITY

Although there are various types of managing authorities, administering recreation as a separate function has been the most practiced approach in America. However, there is a continuing shift in management from separate departments to a combined park and recreation authority. The main types of administrative patterns are as follows:

1. *Administration of recreation as a separate function.* Those who advocate this approach feel that more prompt and efficient management occurs with a separate department directly under the mayor or city manager. By centralizing all re-

sources in a separate recreation authority, greater concentration on the responsibility for recreation can be attained.

Establishing recreation under a board or commission is advocated by the majority of recreation professionals. The general feeling is that a board provides for more opportunities for greater citizen involvement, better continuity of policy and programs, and more effective use of public opinion.

Major disadvantages of separate departments are that they generally compete for budgetary appropriations, and the respective leaders are often unwilling or unable to coordinate the efforts of the two departments. Also, duplication of equipment and personnel often leads to a more expensive operation.

2. *Park administration of recreation.* In its early developments, recreation joined forces with park departments. However, those who argued against having park departments administer recreation programs stated that park administrators were more concerned with administration of areas and equipment. They contended that park officials were more involved with maintaining beautiful lawns, trees, and plants than with getting more people to use the recreation areas. Fortunately, park directors today are more oriented toward recreation and people. They realize that, essentially, public parks have one primary function—to help people enjoy their leisure time.

3. *School administration of recreation.* School administrators are becoming more aware of the need in the community for recreation services. For many years, many professional recreation and park planners have strongly encouraged recreational use of school facilities and school use of recreation facilities. Since the school board and administrative officials have the respect from parents and the public, backers of this type of authority feel that the public would respond favorably to the schools' direction of recreation programs. Indeed, the schools have the facilities, such as buildings and playgrounds, to contribute significantly to an overall community recreation program.

Many school recreation programs emerged from the community center movement. Today, the "community school" theory has been effective in promoting recreational uses of the school plant. The "community school" is a modern concept of community education in which the school is considered an agency that makes maximum use of its facilities and other resources to serve both the educational and recreational needs of the community.

However, school districts are usually not in a position to operate an adequate total park and recreation system. A large portion of the public recreation demand is for golf courses, swimming areas, hiking trails, boat-launching facilities, and shaded picnic areas, which for the most part are outside the range of a school district's interest, jurisdiction, and financial capacity. Still, the school district can make a significant contribution to the park and recreation program and should cooperate to the fullest in the planning and use of local areas and facilities.

4. *Combined department of parks and recreation.* In recent years, considerable attention has been given to the consolidation of parks and recreation into a single department. In fact, where new departments are now being established, nearly 100 per cent are combined departments of parks and recreation.

The combined department of parks and recreation often results in a more effective integration of maintenance and program which benefits from greater centralization of control and direction. In addition, the combined agency results in financial savings, improved services, and better perspective with which to balance program needs.

5. *District or regional park department.* The establishment of district, county, or metropolitan park and recreation departments has been a recent trend in recreation administration. They are often formed under the terms of enabling state legislation to meet certain local needs not satisfied by existing governments. Special districts have been accepted by the state as regional complements to both local and state park systems. They are allowed to levy taxes and issue bonds with voter approval.

FINANCE

No agency or department can operate effectively without adequate financial support. While there

Fig. 5-5 RECREATION — A PRIMARY CONCERN OF LOCAL GOVERNMENT. Adequate lands and facilities can best be acquired through government for parks, marinas, playgrounds, sports arenas, and other recreation areas

are still many individuals who feel that recreation is a personal concern, most communities in America have accepted recreation as a vital governmental function. Finding a consistent and effective source of financing for recreation and parkland acquisition and improvements still remains a problem in most American cities.

Money is needed to acquire areas and facilities, to provide qualified leaders, to purchase supplies and equipment, and to maintain the parks, playgrounds, community centers, and other facilities that are essential for a well-rounded program. A steady flow of funds, therefore, is required to finance a strong park and recreation system. Money may come from such sources as the general fund, special tax levies, bond issues, fees and charges, federal and state grants, donations, gifts, and concessions.

METHODS OF FINANCING RECREATION

Financing municipal recreation is normally divided into two categories of funds: current operating funds, and funds for capital outlay.

Current Operating Funds

The following are considered to be the prime sources of current operating funds:

1. *Appropriations from the general fund.* A widely used method of securing money for recreation is for the recreation department to submit a budget to the appropriating body. Following approval by the reviewing boards, the money is drawn from the city's general fund. The general fund is created and maintained to finance the many functions of municipal government. Along with such departments as police, fire, and public works, the recreation department strives to obtain its fair share of the city's tax funds, which come primarily by property assessments.

2. *Special recreation tax.* Authorized in many states, a special tax levy for recreation involves a special revenue fund. Created through statutory provisions, this type of fund provides definite revenue for parks, recreation, and schools. The special tax is usually expressed in terms of a certain number of mills on each dollar of assessed valuation, or so many cents per hundred dollars of assessed valuation.

3. *Fees and charges.* Fees charged for certain services or use of facilities are another means of supporting municipal recreation. They are often charged where certain facilities or services have a high initial cost and have limitations as to the number of people they accommodate. Two of the most common examples of facilities for which fees are normally charged are swimming pools and golf courses. Playgrounds, parks, and community centers that serve large numbers of people in the community are free to the public. Recreation activities for children are often made available at no cost.

Funds for Capital Outlay

Some of the principal sources of funds for capital outlay are as follows:

1. *Bond issues.* In order for large and costly projects to be funded, such as the construction of community buildings, swimming pools, or golf courses, the issuance of bonds involves borrowing for capital acquisitions and major improvements. Voters must approve a bond issue authorizing the governing body to borrow money and pay it back over a specified period of years. Bonds are a supplement to taxation and should not be considered actual revenue, since they create a liability that must be paid from future taxes.

2. *Special assessments.* Special assessments are commonly used to finance permanent improvements, which are paid for in whole or in part by the property owners in the area who benefit from the services. In essence, the cost of services is placed on those who benefit and are willing to pay. An example of a special assessment is when a community charges for the cost of a particular recreation or park project against the specific neighborhood which will receive much of its benefit.

3. *Grant-in-aid assistance.* Many communities have received financial assistance from federal and state governments. Not all states have grant-in-aid programs, however. The six classes or general types of state grant-in-aid programs include specific activities, specific situations, funds to complement federal matching grants, acquisition, acquisition and development, and revenue sharing.

Several states have matching grant programs that provide funds when used in conjunction with federal matching grant programs, primarily the Land and Water Conservation Fund. However, there is an indication that matching grant-in-aid programs for acquisition and development are not sufficient to provide needed park and recreation opportunities at the local level. Political subdivisions, particularly the poorer ones, often have to forego needed projects because they cannot raise matching funds or provide the needed maintenance, operating, and planning funds. The growing feeling is that what is needed are grant programs for both comprehensive planning-maintenance-operations and for acquisition-development.

4. *Donations and gifts.* Gifts from philanthropic organizations and civic-minded individuals have been a prime source of funds for capital

Fig. 5-6 CLUSTER-ZONING. A unique example of cluster- or density-zoning is this development in Alameda, California, in which single family and apartment units are grouped around lakes and waterways, recreation areas, courts, and plazas.

outlay for many of the semi-public agencies. Valuable gifts have been presented to municipal park and recreation departments as well.

PARK AND RECREATION PLANNING

The local planning agency or the park and recreation department normally has the responsibility for the development of a park and open space plan for the community. Most master plans are drawn up by the park and recreation agency in cooperation with the local planning commission.

In some cities and counties, the park and recreation department draws up the master plan and submits it to the planning department. The plan is then coordinated with other segments of the total community plan. It is often advisable for the local planning agency to prepare the master plan with assistance from the recreation department. Officials of the park and recreation agency can propose acquisition of particular sites and prepare designs for their development.

Generally, the procedure of planning can be separated into three major phases:

1. Collection of information and data on present recreation supply and demand, such as population and existing areas, facilities, and programs
2. Analysis of future recreation and park needs of the people
3. Formulation of proposals to meet present needs

Before the first phase of the planning process is undertaken, a list of basic principles should be developed.

ZONING

Cluster or density-zoning ordinances have been enacted in some communities to preserve open spaces in new residential areas. Essentially, a cluster-zoning ordinance establishes an overall density for the area, usually in terms of acreage for each dwelling unit. However, it allows the developer to reduce the lot sizes and group the homes as long as the overall density is maintained.

An increasing number of local municipalities have found that cluster developments are a practical way to preserve adequate open space. According to Clayne Jensen, "One section of the tract may be developed at a high density with the remaining portions developed at a lower density, or all development may be centered in one section with the remaining open space preserved for park and recreation purposes."[4]

The more recent new communities of the United States have been built in response to burgeoning population expansion and to relieve the crushing strain on the over-burdened urban centers where two-thirds of American people are now concentrated.

Miami Lakes was the first such new town to be built in Florida. An essential feature of all new towns is that they take their form, stage by stage, from a comprehensive master plan which determines from the start the patterns of traffic movement and land use. John O. Simonds wrote:

> Traffic studies determine the location of the community entrance ways or portals, the distribution roads and cul-de-sacs, loops, motor courts, and local frontage streets. A distinguishing feature of the Miami Lakes plan is the great spiral "lakeway" which sweeps all traffic inward along a lineal scenic park route as it moves to and around the site of the future town center.[5]

New techniques of grouping single-family and apartment units around lakes, recreation areas, and garden-like courts and plazas are being developed in other areas of the country. In Alameda, California, a sizeable portion of the land was set aside by the developers for a planned community. Lakes, golf courses, swimming pools, parks, woods, tennis courts, and other recreation facilities were constructed on the land.

Cluster-zoning ordinances should clearly indicate whether open space is to be retained and maintained by private organizations or by the local government.

LAND ACQUISITION

An increasing challenge to all city and county officials is the acquisition of adequate park, recreation, and open-space acreage to meet the needs of a growing population. Indeed, land is being consumed for subdivisions at an alarming rate. Bigger shopping centers surrounded by large parking spaces are becoming commonplace. Additional land is needed for residential purposes, wider highways, and larger industrial establishments.

Rising spectacularly is the price of land, particularly sites suitable for parks. Many public officials fear a crisis is developing. Land values generally are rising throughout the country at the rate of 5 to 10 per cent annually, and the value of land for recreation purposes is increasing at an even higher rate. The most successful and widely used method of obtaining land is negotiation with the owner on price and then cash purchase. Some departments have been able to acquire much of their park land by donation.

By European standards, American cities are park poor and getting worse. The growth in park acreage is nowhere near proportional to the growth in area of our cities, particularly the faster growing cities such as Phoenix, Houston, Dallas, and Los Angeles. For a city of over three million people, Los Angeles has only two well-located parks of respectable size.

One of the major problems facing local governments is the chronic shortage of funds for acquisition and development of parks and outdoor recreation areas. In 1965, the federal government took a big step toward meeting this need when it established the Land and Water Conservation Fund Act. Still, many political subdivisions find that funding is a big problem.

---

[4] Reprinted by permission from *Outdoor Recreation in America*, Clayne R. Jensen, 1970, Burgess Publishing Company, Minneapolis, Minn., pp. 150–51.

[5] John O. Simonds, "Miami Lakes New Town," *Parks and Recreation*, October 1970, pp. 29–33.

Fig. 5-7 PARK FACILITIES that will bring the most recreational pleasure and satisfaction to the greatest number of visitors should be provided.

AREAS AND FACILITIES

To provide attractively developed recreation areas that meet the leisure needs of its citizens is a major concern of the modern city. Properly spaced and creatively developed land is essential if a well-balanced recreation program is to be achieved in the community.

If adequate recreation areas and facilities are to be provided, a city or county must perform several functions, including the following:

1. Acquire, develop, and maintain sufficient land for the needs of the community
2. Provide an organized program with supervision
3. Develop immediate and long-range plans and goals
4. Coordinate the use of areas and facilities
5. Curb the danger of encroachment

Types of Areas and Facilities

The following is a list of some of the main types of recreation areas:

1. Neighborhood playground
2. Tot-lot or play lot
3. The park-school
4. Playfield
5. Neighborhood park

6. Large city park
7. Reservation—forest preserves

PROFILES OF CITY DEPARTMENTS

Hutchinson City (Kansas)

Both choral groups and sports program are an integral part of the well-rounded schedule of activities and services now offered to the area residents of Hutchinson. Strong leadership, increased finances, and construction of new athletic and cultural facilities have contributed to the Hutchinson Recreation Commission's success.

In 1969, the recreation staff numbered thirteen full-time professionals, 167 part-time personnel, and 325 volunteers. Professional specialists include a men's sports supervisor, a women's and girls' activities supervisor, a cultural arts coordinator, and a senior citizens' center director.

Total unit participation in athletic activities alone has soared to almost 750,000. Women now enjoy softball, gymnastics, and cycling. The city now boasts a new Leisure Arts Center which offers classes in more than thirty arts and crafts skills. A new swimming pool and a variety of lighted baseball fields, tennis and horseshoe courts attract residents both for informal play and for tournament competition.

The cultural arts program is directed by a formerly retired music teacher. Thus far, he has developed a 100-voice oratorio society, a 40-voice adult chorus, a 30-voice boys choir, and a music appreciation course for children.

Since 1960, the recreation department's total budget more than tripled from $76,304 to $238,624, while the Park's Public Buildings budget grew from $124,908 to $209,630. But the city has gained valuable additional funds from federal grants, tax monies, and contributions from private citizens and groups.

Englewood City (Colorado)

Each of Englewood's main parks has a special theme for play apparatus, which is designed, constructed, and installed by department personnel.

"Gold Discovery Days"—a park at the campsite location of the Russell Party, who first discovered gold in Colorado—features swings with supports shaped like gun holsters, a mule-drawn gold ore cart, and a large 45-colt revolver. The "Space Age" park boasts rockets, an airplane-shaped sandbox, and an old 1903 Wright-model type plane, while the "Sports" park contains playground equipment in the form of oversized footballs, baseball bats, etc.

Englewood's fifth and sixth graders get a further opportunity to enjoy the department's creative ideas through the "Junior American" sports program offered at the schools. Boys can choose from football, basketball, wrestling, and track, while for girls the choices are volleyball, track, soccer, and pep club. The sports program is highlighted by an annual "Circus Day" for which the department provides all equipment.

Los Angeles (California)

The ability to look inward has enabled the city of Los Angeles to develop park and recreation programs that have met many of the crucial needs of inner-city residents. Through imaginative programming, the Department of Recreation and Parks has succeeded in helping to transform what might have been potentially explosive summers within the inner-city into new and positive outlets for residents' energy.

While conducting a diversified program that served the needs of all its citizens, the main thrust of the Los Angeles plan was directed toward the inner-city and ghetto youths who did not have ready access to park district facilities, programs, and instruction.

The department carried out its goals by providing unique mobile playground units equipped with slides, basketball, tetherball, volleyball, and similar recreational equipment. New play lots were built in open inner-city areas. Children were bused to other locations where they could participate in barge fishing, beach programs, and rock music concerts. Trips were arranged to Disneyland, Marineland, and other Southern California attractions. In order to reach young people who were reluctant to attend any sponsored activities, the department established a Street Council Unit

Fig. 5-8 THE NEIGHBORHOOD PLAYGROUND. This city-wide system of playgrounds is perhaps the heart of any community recreation program. Many smaller communities operate their playgrounds only during the summer months, but most large cities conduct programs throughout the year. This well-conducted playground is sponsored by the city of Roseville, California, a department twice selected for National Gold Medal honors.

which went out and made personal contact with hard-to-reach youths in their own neighborhoods.

Other successful activities staged by Los Angeles for residents have included the annual Festival of Friendship, a joint effort between the department and the local Chamber of Commerce, which encourages people to perpetuate their own ethnic, cultural, and racial heritage, and the "Summer Soul Caravan" in which well-known jazz and rock recording stars give live performances on a mobile outdoor stage that is moved from location to location around the city.

A COORDINATED APPROACH TO COMMUNITY RECREATION

For the entire community to be effectively served, there is a strong need for the activities of com-

munity recreation agencies to be coordinated. Otherwise, the special interests of individual agencies are considered of greater importance than the over-all good of the community. The end result is often duplication or overlapping of programs, services, and facilities. And, too, competition for the leisure interests of the young people becomes a severe problem.

In spite of the wide range of programs and facilities offered, recreation and leisure opportunities are still inadequate in many American cities and towns. Only through an integrated and coordinated approach can the best interests of an entire community be achieved. A well-rounded community recreation program is the result of all agencies and organizations working together for the best interests of the people.

Most recreation agencies have the same major

Fig. 5-9 PARK-SCHOOL COOPERATION. Park and school districts have found joint-use agreements to be an intelligent means of using each other's resources. This neighborhood park operated by the Alameda (California) Park Department is located adjacent to a school.

purpose and goal: to provide services for community and individual betterment. Although their objectives are much the same, agencies do differ in the scope of their organizational methods and the manner in which they achieve their goals. While the Boy Scouts, Girl Scouts, and the 4-H Clubs are concerned with specific age groups, other agencies, such as the municipal recreation and park departments, are involved with the total population. Recreation is considered as a secondary function by such organizations as the church, school, and industrial companies. Private clubs limit their program and activities exclusively to their members. Then again, some organizations accept members from the entire community.

A varied and comprehensive community recreation program demands a unified total effort involving public, private, semi-public, and commercial agencies. It also requires the coordinated efforts of the home, the church, the school, and other social and civic institutions that offer recreation activities. Each agency and organization must determine its role and function, and how it can best contribute to the total community effort.

COORDINATING COUNCILS

First organized with the prime purpose of preventing juvenile delinquency, the interests and functions of coordinating councils have expanded to cover all phases of community service. In large cities, coordinating councils are operated on a neighborhood basis; in small communities, these councils are usually organized on a community basis.

Community Councils

Community councils have proven very effective in improving life in the community. In approaching existing needs and problems, a council is often instituted to survey, plan, and initiate action to improve the existing conditions. Health, schools, government, welfare, and recreation are some of the needs to which community councils give their attention.

To be successful, the council should represent all groups in the community, such as youth-serving agencies, churches, governmental agencies, women's groups, service clubs, lodges, business organizations, health organizations, recreation clubs, and special interest groups. If a coordinated effort is to be achieved, both lay and professional leaders of representative agencies should participate on the council.

Councils of Social Agencies

Comprised of a federation of social agencies, various councils of social agencies have provided distinguished service to communities throughout the United States. Councils of this type attempt to coordinate the work of all agencies, serve as a center of information, and provide a medium by which to promote progressive plans and innovations.

Relationships among Local Governmental Agencies

Closer relationships must be developed among the various public agencies providing recreation services in the community. Cooperation must exist among these agencies such as the schools, park departments, recreation commissions or boards, libraries, museums, and housing agencies.

Close working relationships must not only be maintained among these agencies but among governmental divisions such as purchasing, planning, personnel, and finance. Cooperation from all areas of government must be realized if the best interests of the taxpayers are to be served and the maximum recreation opportunities are to be provided.

6

County and District Government

During the last two decades, interest in county-wide park and recreation services has grown steadily, and it appears that county government in the United States is headed for a much greater role in our system of government. Indeed, a most promising trend is towards the urban county, which arose when counties began to provide new services not offered by state government.

Since the early years of the twentieth century, a most significant change in the functions of county government has been the growth of new services more closely related to local government. County libraries, airports, hospitals, health services, utility systems, and park and recreation services are prime examples of the new functions of county government.

With interest in recreation growing at a rapid rate, boards of county commissioners are beginning to accept recreation and leisure services as a major responsibility of county government. Increasingly, county park and recreation units are being developed to meet the needs and interests of all the people.

James Arles cited several factors as being responsible for creating a stronger demand for county services:

1. Since much of the available land lies outside the city boundaries, the counties have the resources to plan area-wide park systems.
2. More outdoor recreation facilities closer to home are being demanded by urban residents.
3. County government offers a broad tax base which can finance major land acquisition and the development of specialized facilities.
4. Superior transportation today provides the mobility for urban people to use facilities and resources farther from home.
5. Federal and state grants-in-aid programs have had an accelerating effect on county governments.[1]

For a large portion of the country, county parks are a relatively new development. However, some counties in New York, Michigan, and California have enjoyed county-developed facilities for

Fig. 6-1 MOBILE UNITS such as this show wagon have been a great asset to the Naperville Park District, which covers a large area of suburban Chicago. This evening drama show can be presented to many neighborhoods spread throughout the district. (Courtesy of the Naperville Park District.)

[1] James Arles, "County Government," *Parks and Recreation,* August 1969, pp. 30–31.

Figs. 6-2 and 6-3 RECREATION AND PARK SERVICES have become a major responsibility of county government. More outdoor recreation facilities closer to home are being demanded by urban residents. Here, a spirited group of teen-agers enjoys

many years. The greatest deterrent to park and open space development by counties has been a lack of funds.

Today many counties throughout America are acquiring and developing sites for camping, boating, picnicking, and other activities. Like most rural park or outdoor recreation areas, these sites provide the space, facilities, and services to meet the vacationing and camping needs of both local residents and tourists.

HISTORICAL DEVELOPMENT OF COUNTY GOVERNMENT

County government has evolved largely since World War I when significant changes occurred in its functions and structure. Rather than operating as an administrative arm of the state, county departments today operate more independently as units of local governments. Most state enabling

laws permit counties, or districts, to function for recreation.

The first county park was established in Essex County, New Jersey, in 1895, with the expressed desire to develop a system of parks. During the 1920s, a significant increase in county park acquisitions took place.

By 1930 the number of county parks increased from 22 to 415, and the acreage expanded from 2,169 to 108,485. Today, we find 358 counties reporting the operation of a park and recreation system with a total of 4,149 park areas totaling 691,042 acres. Total county expenditures for parks and recreation gradually increased from its meager beginning of $410,000 in 1913, to $7.6 million in 1957, to $195 million in 1965.[2]

_____
[2] Ibid.

a hot summer day in the Sacramento County pool at Elk Grove; meanwhile, a Sacramento family visits a newly developed island area located in the Elk Grove park.

GROWTH OF COUNTY PARK AND RECREATION SYSTEMS

According to a study conducted by the National Recreation and Park Association, there is a definite trend towards the establishment of more county-wide park and recreation systems throughout the United States. A comparison of the results of the Recreation and Park Yearbook published in 1966 with those of an earlier study in 1961, indicates quite conclusively that there has been a substantial increase in county government's involvement in providing park and recreation services.

There was a substantial increase in combined park and recreation departments from 38 in 1960 to 173 in 1965, and the trend is expected to continue. Since 1960, the majority of county agencies established have operated as combined park and recreation departments.

One very promising trend is the trend toward the urban county. Where metropolitan areas lie within a single county, it is possible for county government to become the main unit of local government. Norman Beckman pointed out that:

Excepting New England, county government is on the move in urban sections of the country; and it will ride the wave of the future with regard to metropolitan governmental organization and political power. The reason for this is that county government has a priceless asset which many municipalities do not have: adequate area jurisdiction or space. In addition to "space," it has high political feasibility. It is directly accountable to an electorate that, under recent court decisions, will be reasonably representative. Finally, it has a broad tax base and well established working relations with the state and federal governments on the one hand and cities on the other.[3]

---

[3] Norman Beckman, "Taking Account of Urban Counties," *American County Government*, 30, no. 68 (October 1965).

RESPONSIBILITY OF THE COUNTY

Essentially, county responsibility for the provision of park and recreation services rests somewhat between that of the municipality and the state. Although most counties are more involved with meeting the needs for regional recreation areas and facilities, some county authorities also provide a local recreation service to people in the unincorporated areas.

A wide divergence of operational procedures and departmental objectives characterizes the administration of parks and recreation in the counties. In serving the recreation needs of the people, counties have taken different approaches in the provision of resources and programs.

County park units, such as San Mateo County in central California, are similar to some medium-sized urban departments. The county park and recreation department is headed by a director, who is aided by an assistant director. The director is responsible to the county manager, a board of park supervisors, and a board of county commissioners. Several special divisions such as buildings and grounds, recreational services, fiscal and clerical, supplies and equipment, and environment interpretation are headed by chiefs. Each park is controlled by a park superintendent with three levels of rangers as assistants.

Early in the 1960s, the County Supervisors Association of California adopted an overall recreation policy designed to serve as a guide for individual counties. The policy not only set forth responsibilities for the county but suggested the roles and responsibilities of local, state, and federal government for recreation planning, acquisition, development, and management of recreation areas. The report as officially adopted listed, in part, the following recreation responsibilities for the counties of California:

1. Encourage the provision of neighborhood and community recreation facilities and activities through planning, consultation, and other services.
2. Assist and recommend the means of financing unsatisfied community and neighborhood recreation and park needs.
3. Provide day-use regional recreation facilities within the county.

4. Investigate the feasibility of utilizing the "user-pay" concept in meeting public demands for recreation.
5. Should not offer property tax inducements to private recreation suppliers.
6. Voluntary inter-county cooperative agreements are strongly recommended when day-use recreation demand crosses county boundaries.
7. Local agencies requesting recreation services for unsatisfied community and neighborhood recreation and park needs should first make such requests to the county.

CREATION OF A BOARD

County commissioners have the authority to prepare an ordinance creating a park and recreation board. In addition, the commissioners can appoint a recreation advisory council of twenty-five to thirty members with county-wide representation. As a general practice, the county planning commission serves as the executive committee for such an advisory council. The park and recreation board has the initial responsibility of hiring the most qualified personnel available to serve on the park and recreation staff.

Facilities

A basic essential for the implementation of a recreation program is the acquisition and development of park and recreation facilities. To a large extent, the extent of the facilities serves as an indication of the importance a county regards its park and recreation services.

During the period of 1961–66, the study indicated that the areas acquired by county agencies doubled in number, while three and a half times more acreage was acquired than was realized in the previous five-year period.

Personnel

Like the programs offered by municipal agencies, the key to a successful county recreation program lies in the quality of its leadership. The serious concern that county agencies have for the admin-

Fig. 6-4 REGIONAL AREAS AND FACILITIES. Many counties throughout America are acquiring and developing sites for camping, boating, golf, and other recreation activities. The county's primary role is to meet the regional needs; it also provides local recreation services.

istration of its park and recreation functions can be reflected by the employment of competent, qualified professional personnel.

Professional leadership within the ranks of county agencies gained substantially during the period of 1960–65. In 1965, a total of 11,912 professionals were employed by county park and recreation agencies. This represented an increase of 3,922 over those reported in 1960. The most noticeable gain was in the area of full-time, year-round employment, an increase of 2,273 or approximately 400 per cent.[4]

Expenditures

The expenditures of county agencies also increased significantly during the period of 1960–65. "In 1965, 344 of the county agencies reported a total expenditure of $195,711,383 compared with $95,589,079 by 268 agencies in 1960, or an increase of 105 per cent. The operating budget expenditure increased by 76 per cent, while that spent on lands, buildings, and improvements jumped by 147 per cent."[5]

[4] Arles, op. cit., pp. 30–31.

[5] Ibid.

NATIONAL POLICY FOR COUNTY PARKS

Since the role of county government in providing park and recreation services was unclear, a committee of the National Association of Counties was formed in 1962 to develop a more meaningful national policy for county parks and recreation. After two years of study, in 1964 NACO published its "National Policy for County Parks and Recreation." A condensed statement of this policy follows:

> The special role of the county is to acquire, develop, and maintain parks and to administer public recreation programs that will serve the needs of communities broader than the local neighborhood or municipality, but less than statewide or national in scope.
>
> In addition, the county should plan and coordinate local neighborhood and community facilities with the cooperation of the cities, townships, and other intra-county units, and should itself cooperate in state and federal planning and coordinative activities.[6]

Where there is no existing unit of local government except the county to provide needed local neighborhood or municipal facilities and programs, the county should provide such facilities and programs, utilizing county service districts, local assessments, and other methods by which those benefited will pay the cost.

Internal Organization

Counties have an obligation to create organizational structures for meeting their park and recreation responsibilities. Internally, such organizational structures should fix responsibility for the county park and recreation program clearly with the elected county governing body.

External Organization

Park and recreation facilities and programs serving a community larger than an individual county,

---

[6] "Policy For County Parks and Recreation," *Recreation*, June 1964, pp. 271–72.

but of less than a statewide scope, should be administered jointly through cooperative arrangements between two or more counties.

Financing County Programs

County park and recreation programs should be financed principally through general taxation. This may be supplemented by such sources as general obligation and revenue bonding, donations of money, land and services from private individuals and groups, and fees.

County governments have strongly supported the concept that users of certain kinds of public park and recreation facilities and programs should pay for such use. Revenue from this source should be applied toward the acquisition, development, maintenance, and administration of parks and recreation programs.

Planning Responsibility

Parks and recreation should be an integral element of all county land use planning and zoning. Such planning and zoning should embrace not only areas to be acquired for the county park or recreation system, but maximum use should also be made of zoning and other regulatory powers to preserve open space, protect scenic values, and otherwise enhance recreational opportunities in private developments.

Counties should encourage, through planning, consultation and other services, the providing of adequate, local neighborhood and community facilities and programs by municipalities, townships, and other intra-county units of government.

THE COUNTY AND STATE GOVERNMENTS

Every state should acquire, develop, maintain, and administer park and recreation facilities and programs that provide values for the benefit of the entire state. In addition, every state should authorize appropriate enabling legislation so that coun-

Fig. 6-5 PROGRAM SERVICES. There has been a substantial increase in county government's involvement in providing recreation programs and services such as art shows, Special Olympics, and workshops.

ties and other local governments will have full authority to provide a balanced program of park and recreation services and to finance it adequately.

THE COUNTY AND THE FEDERAL GOVERNMENT

In 1962, the Outdoor Recreation Resources Review Commission presented to Congress an excellent report, entitled "Outdoor Recreation for America." The report recommended that county government endorse the basic recommendation of the commission that the primary responsibility for adequately meeting the nation's recreation and park demands lies with "private enterprise, the states, and local government" and that the role of the federal government should not be one of domination, but of cooperation and assistance in meeting the nation's park and recreation challenge.

THE COUNTY AND THE PRIVATE SECTOR

Some two-thirds of the nation's land is privately owned. Collectively, these lands have an enor-

mous potential for park and recreation development, at private expense, which has been only partially realized. Counties should seek opportunities to stimulate such development. County cooperation should include the provision of access roads, where feasible and where traffic volume will justify, to permit the park and recreation development of private lands.

Counties should cooperate with and support in every way possible the efforts of private businesses and of charitable, service and civic organizations to acquire and appropriately manage recreation and park sites that serve public needs.

PROFILES OF COUNTY DEPARTMENTS

Santa Barbara County (California)

Santa Barbara County has scattered 26 parks throughout the county since the first acquisition in 1913; these parks are situated so that interesting, scenic drives form a connecting link.

Taking advantage of the state bond money and oil royalties collected from beach park operation, together with matching federal funds, a program was launched two years ago with strong support from the park commission and the board of supervisors. This program has resulted in the acquisition of two beach parks with over a mile of beach frontage; two inland parks, with negotiations under way for one more inland park; and one more beach park, as well as a development program for several parks.

The Santa Barbara County Park Commission, a seven-member advisory board to the board of supervisors, was created in 1953 with the advent of Cachuma Lake. This commission not only serves the residents well in their role as commissions, but practices what it preaches—use of park facilities.

Nassau County (New York)

The year 1970 marked the twenty-fifth anniversary of the creation of park services in Nassau County, located on Long Island just east of New York City. The county offers a typical case study of the problems besetting an area being engulfed by the urban sprawl of a major city. Nassau's 1940 population of 406,748 reached 672,765 by 1950, and practically doubled in the next decade. By 1960, Nassau's population was over 1,300,000.

Established in 1945 at Salisbury, the first Nassau County park was a major facility larger than Central Park in New York City, with three eighteen-hole golf courses, a myriad of ball fields, tennis courts, picnic tables, playgrounds and play facilities, and open meadows. Through the years before and after the creation of Salisbury Park, the county had acquired for other purposes excess plots of land which were kept as green spots when the public-works developments on them had been completed.

In the early 1960s, progress began on acquisition of new park sites. In 1965, with the opening of Cantiague Park near Hicksville and Christopher Morley Park in North Hills, both a hundred acres or more in area, the county had the beginnings of its own park system. In the summer of 1963 the county opened its first boat-launching ramp at Milburn Creek, an example of cooperation between a drainage project and recreation. In 1965, the county completed the new Natural History Museum at Seaford adjoining Tackapausha Pre-

serve, began the filling of North Woodmere Park and the construction of the million-dollar reception center for the Old Bethpage Restored Village. Planning also began for the development of Storyland Park which now consists of many smaller parks each drawn around a theme based on children's stories such as *Robinson Crusoe, Alice in Wonderland,* and others.

Other significant developments in 1965 included construction of the first county swimming pool in Cantiague Park. Construction also began on the first three artificial ice-skating rinks.

San Mateo County (California)

One of the leaders in county-provided outdoor recreation sites, facilities, and services is the county of San Mateo in California. The San Mateo system features beautiful Memorial Park with over 300 acres of redwood forest on a stream near the Pacific Ocean. Memorial Park is open all year and offers camping, picnicking, swimming, hiking, and other outdoor activities. San Mateo County owns and operates 2,200 acres of park recreation lands of both an urban and rural nature, including historic sites and hiking and riding trails.

The director of the San Mateo County Park and Recreation Department is responsible to the county manager, a board of park supervisors, and a board of county commissioners. This form of organization has worked well in San Mateo, and their versatile park system is recognized among the finest in the nation. The county has received some excellent grants from the Open Space monies which have enabled some of its communities to acquire and develop new parks.

Los Angeles County (California)

Although golf courses are among the most essential recreation areas sought by this county's burgeoning populace, the quest to preserve nature has also produced some singular acquisitions. The Devil's Punchbowl, a geological masterpiece that took nature some 60 million years to develop, is one of the newer county regional park areas in the Antelope Valley. Also maintained by the department is Vasquez Rocks regional park in Saugus, a 334-acre park which provides extensive picnic and overnight camping facilities for families and organized groups.

When silent movie star William S. Hart died in 1946, he left his Horseshoe Ranch, his home, and a large sum of money to the people of Los Angeles. His estate, valued at almost $1 million, was set aside by Hart in his will for public recreation. The late actor stipulated the ranch be maintained by the county exclusively as a public park and pleasure grounds.

A short 45-minute trip from the Los Angeles civic center are Puddingstone Dam, the water capital of the county, and San Dimas Park, a rugged wilderness area. Both offer much to families in search of weekend diversions. Puddingstone Dam is a 225-acre inland lake in LaVerne where boating, fishing, water skiing, and swimming are popular year round. The Puddingstone area possesses a giant four-pool swim park, nature museum, archery range, equestrian trails, overnight campsites, and picnic facilities and shelters.

The Los Angeles County Department of Parks and Recreation also maintains twelve beach properties, about twenty regional developed parks and areas, three wildlife sanctuaries, two wildflower sanctuaries, and six roadside rests. The department also operates some 200 miles of riding and hiking trails. The world-famous Hollywood Bowl and the Pilgrimage Theater are also department jurisdictional areas.

Sacramento County (California)

Rapid urbanization of the unincorporated areas of Sacramento after World War II created a need for recreational facilities that were not being supplied at a rate comparable to the urban growth. In 1956, a twelve-member committee on parks and recreation appointed by the County Board of Supervisors recommended that a county-wide plan be prepared for a system of regional park and recreation facilities, and in 1959, the County of Sacramento Parks and Recreation Department was established.

The department's major objectives were: (1) to institute an aggressive acquisition program to provide regional park and recreation facilities; (2) to acquire this land as close to the expanding urban core as was economically feasible; and (3) to defer funding of developments, if necessary, in order to preserve funds for acquisition of the choicest possible recreation lands.

Since the department was established in 1959, the county has been successful in providing regional day-use recreation opportunities. In addition to the regional functions of the department, the county has been able to meet the need for neighborhood facilities within a given community. Sacramento County applied provisions of the state law that authorized the county to create special tax assessment districts, called county service areas.

The Sacramento Department of Parks and Recreation today has four major areas of concern:

1. the park maintenance division.
2. the program services division.
3. the planning and design division.
4. the administrative section.

The American River Parkway has received extensive development as a recreational and natural open space green belt. The idea of protecting the American River for its recreational qualities, while still retaining its natural beauty, can be attributed to the vision and foresight of various local conservation and recreation groups.

The parkway features a system of bike-hike-horse trails extending, uninterrupted, from the mouth of the American River to Nimbus Dam, a distance of twenty-three miles through the heart of the populated area of Sacramento. Within this parkway area are three county-owned regional parks, Discovery Park, Ancil Hoffman Park, and C. M. Goethe Park, which were acquired jointly through local funds and federal open space funds.

Among the recreation activities enjoyed along both shores of the American River are rowing, rafting, water skiing, fishing, hiking, bicycling, motorcycling, picnicking, and motor boating.

Gibson Ranch is a historic ranch preserved and maintained by Sacramento County to revive the atmosphere of early life on the farm or ranch. Owned and operated by the county, the park is a working ranch which provides the public

Fig. 6-6 EVENING CAMPFIRE PROGRAMS. Accompanied by the guitar playing of two county park rangers, this group of family campers enjoys singing and eating marshmallows around the campfire.

an opportunity to learn about present-day ranch operations. The Gibson facility also offers unusual opportunities for hiking, camping, and fishing that are rare in urban America.

Metro-Dade County (Florida)

The Metro-Dade County Park and Recreation Department provides and operates a county-wide system of parks and recreation areas for public use. During the past forty years, over 8,000 acres of planned and developed park and recreation areas have been created in Dade County, a county the size of Delaware.

The Dade park system is considered one of the top ten in the nation. Annually, it serves more than 18 million visitors and year around residents who like to swim, boat, fish, camp, shoot, take a nature walk, play tennis or golf, or inspect rare plants.

The county also maintains "Vizcaya," a seventy-room mansion built on Biscayne Bay by industrialist James Deering. The Dade County Auditorium features New York stage shows, opera, concerts and ballet, while the Crandon Park Zoo boasts a collection of 1,200 mammals, birds, and reptiles exhibited in tropical outdoor settings.

Recreation programs are varied and coordinated in forty-two neighborhood areas. Tot lots, playgrounds, tennis, learn-to-swim programs and crafts are offered in every section of the county.

The Dade park system is water-oriented since most people come to Florida primarily for sunny beaches, fishing and year-round outdoor living. Dade County offers four miles of ocean beaches at its Crandon and Haulover Beach parks. There are sixteen swimming pools with twin atoll pools on Biscayne Bay. The county's five marinas offer wet or dry-land dockage.

Somerset County (New Jersey)

In the five-year period between 1965 and 1970, the Somerset County Park Commission has in-

Fig. 6-7 REGIONAL PARK DISTRICTS continue to grow and provide more leisure-time facilities and activities for their residents. The Auburn Area Recreation and Park District has combined a versatile system of parks and recreation areas with a varied program of year-round services.

creased the number of its cultural activities by more than 800 per cent. This same type of impressive progress has been evident in the growth of park and recreation facilities in the Somerville, New Jersey, area.

The commission's present land acquisitions include more than 2,300 acres. A major corporation donated an 800-acre site to be preserved as a natural geologic phenomenon. Projections call for an additional 1,000 acres to be acquired that will be developed to include a major winter sports complex, family camping, and day camp sites.

In response to recognized needs by the community, a number of special facilities were developed by the commission. Among these was a riding stable of thirty-four horses that were used in instructional classes for youth and adults. During the winter, the horses are also employed for riding, hay rides, and sleigh rides.

Another project now under development is Somerville's new Environmental Education Center. The project involves a natural area of 350 acres with a $750,000 building program. The commission has also expanded the use of its present facilities by lighting many recreation areas to allow for night-time activities such as tennis, golf, ice skating, and football.

REGIONAL PARK DISTRICTS

The regional park concept is still relatively new in America. Essentially, regional parks do not differ from county parks except they can involve more than one county and therefore cross political boundaries. Regional parks are funded by a regional park district that has the legal power to levy taxes for the establishment, development, and maintenance of outdoor recreation sites.

Perhaps the pioneer in the regional park concept is the East Bay Regional Park District, located among the East Bay cities of Berkeley, Oakland, and Hayward, California. Presently, over fourteen parks with a total of over 20,000 acres are open to the public in Alameda and Contra Costa Counties. The taxation rate through 1975 will be ten cents per $100 of assessed valuation. The East

Bay regional parks provide outdoor recreation facilities and service to thousands of people throughout the San Francisco Bay—Oakland area. They offer picnic and campgrounds, bridle trails, a botanical garden, a large heated swimming pool, and a park for motorcyclists.

Regional parks are usually operated under a district structure with their own officers, employees, and equipment. They have the power to tax within the two or more counties that constitute the district's boundaries. Since the system offers greater potential in park resources at a lower tax rate, more counties throughout the nation will probably form regional park districts.

Just as a large county organization, each separate division of the regional park district has its chief and lesser officials, who are responsible to the chief administrator. All clerical and fiscal work for budgets, purchasing, and salaries is carried on entirely within the district framework.

Some metropolitan areas have formed park districts which have elected commissioners as the primary decision-making body. Chicago operates under this system and its major administrative officers are a general superintendent and his assistant.

SPECIAL DISTRICTS

The park or recreation district has performed an important service to those areas of the country where county government does not exist or is inadequate to meet the needs of the people. In many instances, the special district has provided park and recreation services in a most efficient manner. In recent years, there has been a significant increase in the formation of special recreation taxing districts in suburban and rural areas.

Recreation districts, or a combination of recreation and park districts, often include all incorporated areas in the county. The creation of special districts is particularly prevalent in smaller counties, or when two or more districts operate in larger counties. Typically, a district board, similar to municipal recreation boards, is responsible for administering the recreation and park functions.

Depending on their specific purpose, special districts may be responsible for recreation programming or for park land open space acquisition and development, or both. The district is governed by an elected five-member policy-making board of directors.

Special taxing districts have made it possible for small communities to provide collectively for recreation and park services that individually they would be unable to give their residents. Communities located in adjacent counties have been successful in pooling their facilities, money, and leadership in the operation of a special district.

The creation of park districts, in some instances, has resulted from default. A frequent reason is a lack of adequate services by the local governments because of insufficient funds. Although special districts have sometimes proven responsive to the needs of people, they have caused numerous problems to existing governmental units. Conflicts arise because special districts are superimposed upon existing governmental units. Jensen wrote, "Generally, special districts are not recommended, but in a few instances they seem to be the best solution to the local problem."[7]

Hayward Area Park and Recreation District (California)

Hayward's recreation district has proved successful because of a blend of strong leadership, sound financing, and community participation. More than sixty-four square miles of Alameda County, California, are included in the district. The general manager and board of directors guide policy and planning functions of the area and are assisted by a Citizens' Advisory Committee and a Youth Citizens' Advisory Committee.

To reach the goals set forth, district officials have developed sound new methods of program financing. One is to sponsor state legislation permitting authorized credit for lending institutions and permits borrowing of funds at a reduced interest rate.

---

[7] Reprinted by permission from *Outdoor Recreation in America*, Clayne R. Jensen, 1970, Burgess Publishing Company, Minneapolis, Minn., pp. 142–43.

Better funding has meant better facilities. Hayward's parks have expanded from 30 sites with 136 acres in 1959–60 to 59 sites with 447 acres in 1969–70. Simultaneously, recreation facilities have increased from 70 to 192. Sports groups for both adults and children have more than tripled in enrollment.

Hayward's softball association has made a hit with adults and youth alike. Recreation leaders helped interested residents form a softball association, provided a sports director and playing fields, and authorized the association to operate concessions on park grounds. Profits are used to improve the facilities and expand the leagues.

The recreation department is responsible for promoting, organizing, and coordinating a balanced year-round recreation program for all ages. The parks department oversees park maintenance which is coordinated with community needs and recreation activities.

The district operates on a budget supported principally by property taxes. The approximate $2.9 million budget is reflected in the balance of acquisition, development, programs, and maintenance, to provide maximum leisure facilities and services for the people of the Hayward area. To date, the district has received over $670,000 in federal funds for programs and facilities.

Stiles Park District (St. Clair County, Illinois)

Brooklyn, situated just south of East St. Louis, Illinois, and National City, Illinois, are two municipalities that have been very successful in jointly creating a special recreation park district. The action of this all-black, disadvantaged area of the United States should inspire other areas of the country with similar problems to follow the same path. The Stiles success story is all the more remarkable in that it was realized in an economic crunch period when bond issues and money available for recreation and park improvements were difficult to obtain.

After a dedicated three-year effort, Stiles Park District passed a $660,000 bond issue to build an indoor swimming pool complex. "Someone seeing this area of the county might well remark, 'This seems impossible!' Yet, it did happen, and the efforts of the park district board are stimulating the entire community for more action programs for a better life."[8]

Stiles Park District is located in St. Clair County, Illinois, which has a population of about 300,000 people. The county contains 22 townships, 31 municipalities, and 68 special districts. The total population of the district itself is about 2,000. The district is surrounded on the east, north, and west by railroad lines, on the south by stockyards.

After establishing their special district, the park district board contacted the University of Illinois at Urbana-Champaign for technical assistance. Tom Brown, a student in recreation and park administration, volunteered to help the park district establish a recreation program. He not only served as part-time director for the agency, but was an enthusiastic teacher for the members of the park district board.

Brown coordinated the new recreation program with the Equal Opportunity Commission program. The two agencies jointly utilize a multipurpose room and offices in the basement of the Brooklyn city building. "After the board hired a part-time recreation supervisor, from the Neighborhood Opportunity Corps as their director, interagency cooperation became automatic."[9]

The progress of Stiles Park District has been the result of cooperation and understanding of not only the board and staff but the residents of the community. In emphasizing the importance of his experience with the people of the district, Brown said, "It cannot be overemphasized how important it is to become aware of the lifestyle of the people with whom you are working. People have traditional ways and ideas about how to do things, and the leader should be receptive to their ideas."[10]

---

[8] Charles W. Pezoldt, "They Didn't Give Up," *Park and Recreation,* October 1972, pp. 35–36.

[9] Ibid.

[10] Ibid.

Fig. 6-8 BRINGING PARKS TO THE PEOPLE will continue to be the major objective of county and regional recreation and park agencies. More outdoor recreation facilities will be developed closer to home to meet the growing needs of the people, such as Auburn Regional Park which includes this multi-use athletic field.

COUNTY SERVICE AREAS AND PRIVATE RECREATION SERVICES

The county-applied provisions of many state laws authorize a county to create special tax assessment districts, called county service areas. The service areas are designed to fill the void left in portions of the county not covered by the city or special district services. Although administered by the county department of parks and recreation, the expense of this total service is borne by the residents of the service area. The programs provided by county service areas include land acquisitions, maintenance, and park and recreation master planning.

A new concept in local and county recreation and parks services is a system under which private firms provide recreation services. In Sacramento, the concept has been employed in County Service Area No. 7, covering the Mission-Oaks area, where a local consulting firm, Creative Planning & Management, Inc., has had a contractual agreement with the county of Sacramento.

LOOKING AHEAD

County government has made rapid strides in park and recreation administration over the past half century; continued progress will require further changes based on a study and understanding.

A deeper understanding must be gained of the patterns of organization by which county parks and recreation now function. James Arles mentions several questions that must be considered. "Why did the governing authorities select the type of administrative pattern under which they now operate? Has there been a thorough examination of the relationships between governmental units and have they set their responsibilities? What are the factors which help determine the pattern of organization best suited for the particular situation?"[11]

Arles believes that:

The rapidity with which counties can adjust to changing needs will depend, in part, on the realistic answers to the above questions. It will also depend upon the flexibility given to it by the state legislature. It will depend in part on the willingness of county officials to support necessary changes in functions, organization, and intergovernmental relationships. It will depend also on a better public understanding of the achievements and potentialities of county government in providing park and recreation services.[12]

---

[11] Arles, op. cit., p. 31.

[12] Ibid.

7

State Government

State park and recreation services are a rapidly developing aspect of state government. Perhaps the most significant development of state government in recent years has been the multiplication of public services. Today, a multitude of state departments and agencies provide park and recreation areas and services. They are responsible for such areas as parks, forests, wayside picnic areas, winter sports facilities, game preserves, monuments, historical sites, museums, and waterways.

According to the United States Constitution, the states have a responsibility to authorize the establishment of local services. The Tenth Amendment to the Constitution gives the individual states authority to provide recreation services as the need for such services becomes evident.

All powers not delegated to the nation reside in the states. In addition, statewide services that are beyond the scope of the subdivisions of the state are often rendered by state agencies.

Through divisions, commissions, councils, and many other political administrative units, the fifty state park systems are striving to meet the "on-slaught by leisure," estimated at 400 million visits to state parks annually.

Many states, particularly the western ones, own a considerable amount of land which is being used increasingly for recreational purposes. However, the states hold approximately one-fourth as much parkland designated for outdoor recreation as does the federal government and one-tenth as much forest agency land. The fifty state park systems administer a combined total of more than 3,200 areas, covering 7.4 million acres.

State parks vary considerably in size and significance. They range from large natural lands with vast acreage to small parks of only a few acres. Approximately one-third of all areas have fewer than fifty acres each.

BACKGROUND OF STATE PARKS

State park systems today have evolved from a late nineteenth-century tradition. "A state is responsible for the preservation of outstanding natural and historical resources," wrote Barry Tindall, "and a system of lands and waters for public

Fig. 7-1 A YOUNG VISITOR to Sutter's Fort, in Sacramento, is supplied with a set of automated sound track earphones that provides a self-conducted tour of the facilities.

recreation. California, with Yosemite State Park, in 1865 (now Yosemite National Park); Michigan's Mackinac Island State Park in 1895; and New York and New Jersey's Palisades Interstate Park in 1900, helped set a pattern and stimulate action for the future."[1]

According to Elvin R. Johnson,

The state park concept is believed to have started in California, although other states, such as New York and Michigan, founded early systems. In 1864, Abraham Lincoln signed an act of Congress whereby the world-famous Yosemite Valley and the Mariposa Grove of giant sequoia trees were granted to the state of California to be held for public use for all time. The Yosemite land grant formed the first state park in the nation. In 1902, the California Redwoods State Park, now known as Big Basin Redwoods State Park, was set aside as the first California State Park.[2]

As early as 1921 when the National Conference on State Parks was formed, Stephen T. Mather, founder and the first director of the National Park Service, believed that state and local support for the federal government to take over large and small scenic areas had to be redirected. Mather's well-defined concept of national parks stated that they be areas of some magnitude, distinguished by scenic attractions, natural wonders and beauty, and distinctly national in interest. He also felt that there were many scenic areas of importance to individual states that should be preserved. It was his feeling that in many instances, the states were in danger of having their natural landscapes vanish forever. In 1920, Mather's strong belief in the need for state parks resulted in the start of serious discussions on the possibilities of a conference to organize the states.

A number of decades later in 1964, the National Conference on State Parks recommended the following classifications:

1. *Parks*—relatively spacious areas of outstanding scenic or wilderness character, often-

times containing significant historical, archeological, ecological, geological, and other scientific values, preserved as nearly as possible in their original or natural conditions and providing opportunity for recreation which will not destroy or impair the features and values to be preserved.

2. *Monuments and historic sites*—areas, usually limited in size, established to preserve objects of historic and scientific interest and places commemorating important persons or historical events.

3. *Recreational areas*—areas selected and developed primarily to provide non-urban outdoor recreation opportunities to meet other than purely local needs and still having the best available scenic qualities.

The conference also classified but did not define: wayside rests and campgrounds, wilderness, nature preserves, beaches, parkways, scenic roads, trails, free flowing streams, forests, and underwater parks.

At a meeting in Ontario, Canada, in 1965, the National Conference on State Parks voted to join the National Recreation and Park Association.

TYPES OF STATE PARK ADMINISTRATION

There are three common patterns of administration of parks used in the various states. Most of the states operate within one of the following types of structure:

1. Administration within a department that administers all natural resources.
2. Administration within a department that also administers forests.
3. Administration by a separate department.

In some states the state park agency is a separate department of state government as in Arizona, Georgia, Idaho, and Kentucky, where the park system is administered by the State Park Department. In several states, the park system is a division within a larger department. For instance, in Alabama, New York, Illinois, Iowa, and several other states, it is a division within the Department of Conservation. In Alaska, California, Hawaii, Indiana, Utah, Michigan, and

[1] Barry S. Tindall, "Land for All Seasons," *Parks and Recreation*, December 1970, p. 25.

[2] Elvin R. Johnson, *Park Resources for Recreation* (Columbus: Charles Merrill, 1972), p. 109.

Fig. 7-2 A SCENE OF NATURAL BEAUTY. Some of America's great tourist attractions are the many beautiful beachlands along Oregon's 400-mile Pacific Ocean seashore. These impressive coastal seascapes are located at Ecola State Park on U.S. Highway 101. (Courtesy of the Oregon State Highway Department.)

other states, the park system is within the Department of Natural Resources. In Oregon, it is a division of the Highway Department.[3]

STATE RECREATION COMMISSIONS OR BOARDS

The basic responsibility of state commissions and boards is not to operate recreation programs themselves but to advise local communities, sponsor training institutes, organize conferences, and make surveys. Although they have performed ably as a separate function of state government, few states have established separate commissions or boards.

CLASSIFICATION OF AREAS

A prerequisite of the establishment of a good state park system is the classification of areas. The task of classifying areas is made easier when the agency has some criteria on which to base its selection.

According to Clayne Jensen:

State parks vary considerably in type, depending on the geographic features in the state and the philosophy and purpose on which the particular state park system is based. They are primarily intermediate type areas, usually being more remote than municipal areas but closer to the using population than national parks and forests. Typically, they contain considerable wild features along with man-made improvements in the form of picnic and camp sites, boating accommodations, and various sports facilities.[4]

[3] Reprinted by permission from *Outdoor Recreation in America*, Clayne R. Jensen, 1970, Burgess Publishing Company, Minneapolis, Minn., p. 122.

[4] Ibid., p. 121.

Fig. 7-3 PRESERVATION OF NATURAL RESOURCES. The state park systems of America are responsible for the preservation of outstanding natural and historical resources. One of Florida's outstanding seaside parks, St. Joseph Peninsula State Park has twenty miles of sand-duned beaches stretching along the Gulf and bay in northwest Florida. (Courtesy of the Florida Development Commission.)

Units in the State of California Parks and Recreation Department, for example, are classified into the following seven areas:

1. Parks
2. Recreation areas
3. Reserves
4. Beaches
5. Roadside campgrounds
6. Wayside rests
7. Underwater parks

PURPOSES OF STATE PARKS

Until only recently, state park systems have had two main purposes: the preservation of significant features, and the provision of outdoor recreation for the public. The State of California Parks and Recreation Department, under the direction of William Penn Mott, Jr., has added a third concern, education. In addition to managing the natural and cultural resources, Mott believes his department has the further responsibility of managing people. Park ranger positions are not only being filled by people trained in resource management but those who are trained in the social sciences,

in order to combine both resource management and people management.

"Unless we understand people, their motivations, and teach them to enjoy and appreciate the resources," said Mott, "we are convinced that people can destroy the very resources that they want us to preserve. Therefore, we are now broadening our entire management concept in this field of people management with resource management, in a totally combined management program."[5]

FUNCTIONS OF THE STATES

Over 225 different state agencies throughout America play a vital role in park and recreation development. Although their role has centered largely on the provision of outdoor recreation opportunities, increased emphasis is being given to

_____

[5] William Penn Mott, Jr., taken from a tape recorded speech, "The Role of the California State Park System," American River College, Sacramento, Calif., November 18, 1971.

special services for youth and for aging persons, to disadvantaged urban areas, and to similar programs.

In providing recreation facilities and services, each of the fifty states has operated within the following eight functions:

1. *Promote outdoor natural resources and recreation opportunities.* Each state operates a comprehensive network of parks and other outdoor recreation areas to meet the needs of both its citizens and visiting tourists. Special emphasis has been the preservation of the state's cultural, historic, and natural heritage, as well as scenic landscape.

2. *Promote conservation and open space.* State agencies have the responsibility for promoting conservation and educational programs and supporting open-space and beautification efforts by local municipalities.

3. *Enabling legislation.* Enabling laws enacted by the states authorize local authorities to operate recreation and park facilities and programs.

4. *Assist local governments.* State agencies provide varied assistance to local authorities, such as technical guidance or consultation, subsidies for special programs for youth and the aging.

5. *Serve special populations.* State governmental agencies operate a variety of recreation programs that serve the special population, such as aging persons, those in penal or corrective centers, the mentally ill, and the retarded.

6. *Develop and enforce standards and regulations.* The states serve an important function in screening personnel by establishing standards and regulations for personnel. Employment procedures are established, and a growing number of states have set up certification and registration programs in the field.

7. *Promote professional advancement in recreation and parks.* State colleges and universities provide higher education in recreation and park administration. They sponsor conferences, workshops, and research in recreation.

8. *Promote leisure and recreation involvement as good economy.* A wide range of leisure activities have received strong promotional support by state agencies, such as tourism, vacationing, and a wide array of outdoor recreation activities.

ENABLING LEGISLATION

The legal authority for the operation of public programs is granted to the local communities by the states. Through its own enabling laws, each state designates the means by which counties and municipalities may operate recreation programs, whether by schools, parks, or separate recreation agencies. Local government authorities are permitted by the states to conduct recreation programs under the type of administrative organization considered most effective.

Today, each of the fifty states has legislative codes that empower local government to acquire land, develop recreation and park facilities, tax the people for recreation purposes, and provide direct program services.

OUTDOOR RECREATION SERVICES

Traditionally, state parks have provided outdoor recreation opportunities for those who desire this type of leisure-time experience. Some state parks have been primarily historical and featured a diversity of unusual natural areas to be preserved; other parks have offered a variety of recreation activities and facilities.

State parks have a definite advantage in providing opportunities in outdoor recreation. There is considerable more flexibility of location when servicing the people of an entire state than there is in city and local parks. There are also many more potential sites available for selection by the state park system.

State parks are potentially more capable of meeting the needs for mass outdoor recreation in the future than in any other kind of public or private areas. The expansion of the state park system in the post-war generation is only a prelude to what will happen, to what must happen, in the next generation or two.[6]

According to a report in 1964 by the Outdoor Recreation Resources Review Commission,

---

[6] Marion Clawson, "State Parks," *Parks and Recreation,* December 1970, p. 35.

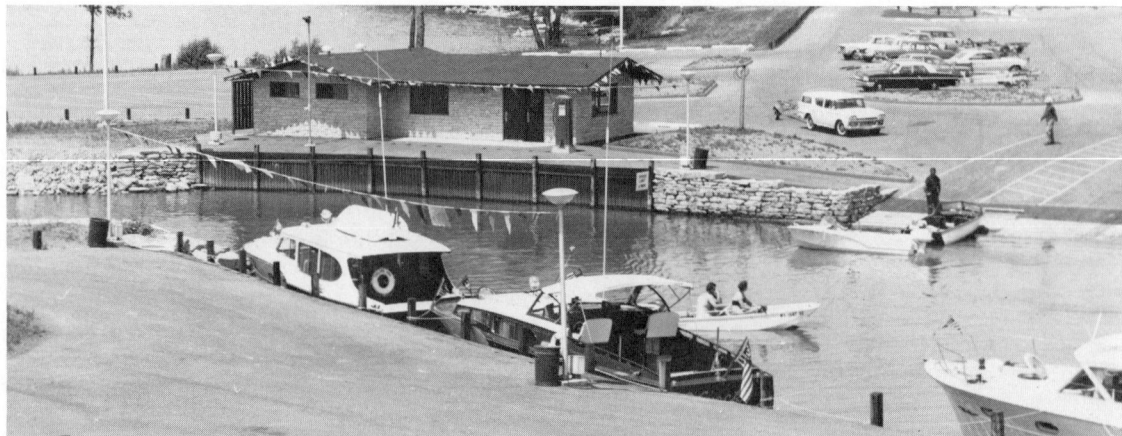

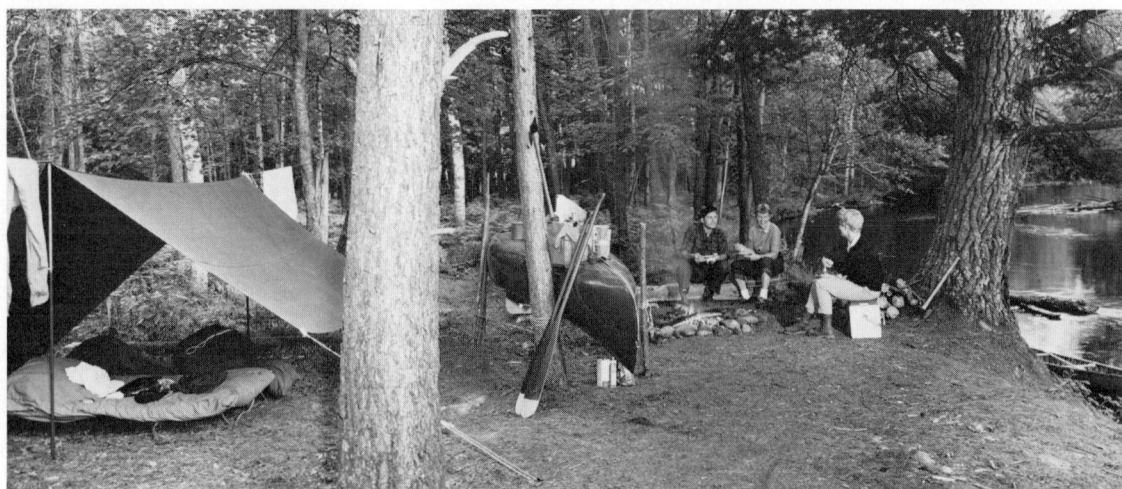

Figs. 7-4 and 7-5   PUBLIC OUTDOOR RECREATION. State park systems also have a major responsibility of providing outdoor recreation opportunities for the public. These attractive boating facilities are located at High Cliff State Park in Wisconsin, while the camp scene depicts the beauty of Michigan's Mackinac Island Park. (Courtesy of the Wisconsin Natural Resources Department and Michigan Tourist Council.)

The states should pay the pivotal role in providing outdoor recreation opportunities for their citizens since other responsibilities that affect outdoor recreation opportunities such as highway construction and the management of forest, wildlife and water resources, are also generally focused at this level; thereby, the state governments can make sure that these programs are in harmony with recreation objectives.[7]

State government can be particularly effective in stimulating counties and municipalities to take separate and joint action. They also provide the best means through which Federal aid can be channeled to meet varying needs.

HISTORICAL SITES

A major dimension closely related to state park and recreation services is historical events and

[7] Outdoor Recreation Resources Review Commission, "Action for Outdoor Recreation for America" (Washington, D.C.: Citizens Committee for the ORRRC Report, 1964), p. 27.

the people and sites associated with them. Considerable resources in many states are being devoted to this type of program. For instance, the park program of New Hampshire is being shifted from the acquisition of large, natural tracts to acquisition of unusual and historic sites.

STATE FORESTS

Most of the fifty states have a state forest system which is usually administered by a separate state forestry agency. In a few states, however, state forests are administered in combination with other state-owned lands. State forests, considerably more extensive in area than state parks, have always received good use for recreation purposes. Unlike state parks, state forests are usually open to hunting and fishing.

Camping areas for families and resident youth camps are available on state forest lands. Sites for summer homes are often leased in state forests. State forests also accommodate such popular outdoor activities as hiking, horseback riding, sailing, swimming, canoeing, boating, sightseeing, and skiing.

FISH AND WILDLIFE

A separate department or a major division within a department has been created by each of the fifty states to administer a program of fish and wildlife management. Essentially, the responsibilities of a state fish and wildlife agency are to propagate, manage, and distribute game animals, fur-bearing animals, game birds, and game fish. The department manages game land and fisheries and issues licenses for hunting, fishing, and trapping.

A variety of wildlife areas, such as reserves, sanctuaries, game farms, fish hatcheries, and special shooting grounds, are administered by state fish and wildlife departments. Most states provide broad programs for regulating and improving hunting and fishing. The departments work very closely with the Bureau of Sports, Fisheries and

Fig. 7-6 AN HISTORIC MONUMENT commemorates important people. This monument of Abraham Lincoln, one of America's great presidents, appears on the campus of Milliken University at Decatur, Illinois. (Courtesy of State of Illinois Department of Conservation.)

Wildlife at the federal level, and with several other federal and state agencies.

More than 25 million people participate annually in hunting and fishing in the United States. Many nonhunters and nonfishermen, such as photographers, nature hikers, and sightseers, also reap enjoyment from the effects of the State Fish and Game Departments.[8]

A major wildlife problem in many states is that private lands have been increasingly unavail-

---

[8] Jensen, op. cit., p. 125.

able to the majority of sportsmen. Much of the good land and water areas is under private ownership, in the form of hunting and fishing clubs. Steps have been taken by state fish and game authorities, however, to open private lands to the public and to make them more productive to wildlife.

The states provide programs to improve wildlife habitats and to propagate and distribute fish or game. Distribution of forest tree seedlings is a typical service of state-maintained nurseries.

TENT AND TRAILER CAMP SITES

The most significant increase in state park usage has been in tent and trailer camping. State parks throughout America have been overwhelmed with demands for campsites. In fact, since World War II the use of state parks has expanded about eight times as fast as the population.

To help meet expenses and finance improvements, many state park systems have had to charge fees. Although fees should be kept to a minimum, many authorities believe at least fifty per cent of the cost should be borne by the park users. Typical sources of funds are gate and parking fees, admission charges for the use of special facilities, and returns from concession operations.

RESORT AND LODGE FACILITIES

An increasing number of states are providing resort and lodge facilities for both state residents and the traveling public. Lake Barkely Lodge and Resort Park in Kentucky is highly regarded for its functional beauty as well as its services, resources, and facilities.

TOURISM

Tourism and recreation have been one of the states' largest income-producing activities. In

> THE TRUE SPORTSMAN IS MORE INTERESTED IN THE CHANCE TO GET AWAY, TO COMMUNE WITH NATURE, TO PIT HIMSELF AGAINST THE ELEMENTS.
>
> *Ray Arnett, Director, State of California Department of Fish and Game*

Michigan, for example, visitors during 1969 spent over $1.3 billion in recreation-related activities. Estimated statistics show that park visitors alone spent over $63 million in grocery stores, gas stations, and other businesses.

Tourists spend substantial sums of money while traveling, for such items as food, drinks, and various other leisure or resort expenses. From the economic standpoint, this money is turned over many times on various levels of the local economy which provides substantial employment.

HIGHWAYS AND ACCESS ROADS

The state highway departments are charged with the responsibility to construct roads into certain areas of recreational value. They also participate in maintaining such roads and often keep roads open to certain winter sports areas. Many recreation areas would receive much less use if they were not readily accessible by good roads.

Roadside parks and historic markers are often the responsibility of state highway departments. Roads inside state-owned recreation lands, such as state parks and state forests, are usually constructed under the authority of this department.

COOPERATION WITH FEDERAL AGENCIES

Intergovernmental efforts have contributed to the growth of state park systems. Through the National Park Service, the federal government has long supported and assisted state park development across the nation. Planning and technical assistance provided by the Park Service to state parks has involved training situations and technical publications. With Land and Water Conservation Fund monies, the Bureau of Outdoor Recreation has also been a catalyst for accelerated state park action in recent years. The Corps of Engineers and the Tennessee Valley Authority have also been instrumental in furthering development.

PARK INTERPRETATION PROGRAMS

State park systems today provide much needed "Park Interpretation Programs." In addition to the park situation, these programs attempt to teach visitors the basic facts about the natural environment and its management. Many innovative programs have been introduced in the state park systems that have helped people to re-evaluate their own role in the natural world.

Many states have developed interpretive services programs designed to provide visitors with a deeper understanding and appreciation of the natural or historical features in or near the area visited. Services of this type make the park experiences more meaningful and enjoyable. In addition to various publications and personally conducted programs, wayside exhibits, interpretive buildings, and self-guiding trails are offered.

Utilization of resources for environmental awareness programs is an area experiencing greatly increased attention among state park agencies. Environmental education programs with local school systems, vocational school programs, and inner-city youth work projects are another area which has provided another dimension to state parks. Wolde Forest State Park, a 664-acre state facility in populated southeastern Pennsylvania, is devoted entirely to environmental awareness activities. The park provides resident student accommodations, instruction centers, special observation facilities, and other related services.

In California, the State Parks and Recreation Department has changed their management philosophy considerably. The department started with the concept of preserving the redwoods in California, but found the job much broader than the problem of preservation. In addition to the responsibilities of preservation and recreation, the department is deeply involved in an educational program of interpreting to the public the natural and cultural values that exist in the various units of the state park system.

PUBLIC EDUCATION

Education for leisure has now become recognized as an important function of the public schools. Modern education provides valuable skills, attitudes, and abilities in various recreation activities.

Professional preparation programs for recreation leaders are now offered by many state colleges and universities. An increasing number offer specialization in outdoor recreation. Nearly one hundred educational institutions in the United States now offer majors in recreation and forty offer graduate degrees in recreation.

Many institutions serve an important function by providing recreation and park field service, which involves teaching, research, and service. The field service programs are administered through the various departments of recreation and municipal park administration.

The purpose of field service is (1) to assist communities and their organizations by helping them to develop their park resources and opportunities for recreation, (2) to strengthen the university's teaching efforts in recreation and parks through staff participation in research and practical field work problems, and (3) to share the findings and results with all who may have an interest in them.[9]

STATE ORGANIZATIONAL PLANS

California

The majority of the state of California's responsibility for outdoor recreation is centered in the Resources Agency, one of the major divisions of the state government. The three departments within the Resources Agency that have principal

[9] Harold D. Meyer, Charles K. Brightbill, and H. Douglas Sessoms, *Community Recreation* (Englewood Cliffs, N.J.: Prentice-Hall, Inc., 1969), p. 134.

Fig. 7-7 CALIFORNIA HISTORY. Sutter's Fort and Coloma Park, located in the Sacramento area, are two of California's most popular historic sites. Tourists are able to relive the "Gold Rush Days" of 1849. One of the rooms shows General John Sutter giving James Marshall instructions to build a mill at Coloma along the American River. While constructing the facility, Marshall discovered some gold particles in the water and the Rush was on. Although he died penniless, he is still remembered by a monument located at the famous historic site.

outdoor-recreation responsibilities are the Department of Parks and Recreation, the Department of Harbors and Watercraft, and the Department of Fish and Game. Also making a significant contribution to outdoor recreation are the Department of Conservation, the Department of Water Resources, and the State Water Resources Control Boards.

Acting under the authority of the governor, the head of the Resources Agency is responsible to the governor for the efficient operation of the various departments, boards, and commissions within the agency. Formulation of policy and long-range programs is also under the governor's jurisdiction. Within the agency, the administrators of the various departments are directly responsible to the administrator of the Resources Agency.

The units in the California state park system are classified into seven different classifications. Each classification has its own maintenance, operation, and management policy. The state park and recreation commission has the responsibility for classifying units in the state park system. In California, the commission consists of nine people on a staggered term and appointed for four years. They determine the policy for the director to carry out the responsibilities of administering the park system for California.

1. *The state parks.* These are areas set aside to preserve a unique natural resource in California within nine landscape provinces. The state has been divided into specific provinces; the redwood province, for example, consists of the coastal belt where the redwoods grow that extends from the Oregon border down to San Simeon.

2. *State recreation areas.* These are areas

set aside not because of any landscape value but to provide for the recreational needs for the people of California. The Point Mugu recreation area, perhaps the most talked of area, was set aside to provide for the recreation needs of the people living in the Los Angeles metropolitan area.

3. *State reserves.* These areas preserve a specific and unique cultural or natural resource. They are set aside for that purpose alone. They have limited or no development and are basically for scientific and cultural research and investigative purposes. The most prominent area is the Point Lobos preserve that was set aside to preserve the unique groves of Monterey cypress and the unique relationship of the ocean and the land in that particular area.

4. *State beaches.* The beach areas along the Pacific Ocean are set aside for the preservation and the utilization of the beaches of California.

5. *State roadside campgrounds.* This is a new classification established by the California legislature in 1969. The purpose of wayside campgrounds is to set aside land adjacent to major highways for overnight stops by people traveling up and down the highways of California.

6. *Wayside rests.* These are areas set aside by the highway department for daytime rest purposes of travelers along the freeways and highways. The park and recreation department and the highway department are trying to pool their efforts so as to combine roadside rests with wayside campgrounds and eliminate duplication of facilities.

7. *Underwater parks.* This is a new classification, established by the legislature in 1970. The state of California is setting aside four such underwater parks along the coast. These areas are unique because of their underwater topography, the existing flora, and the quality of the underwater environment.

Underwater exploration by divers for photography, fishing, and exploring has become a very popular activity. This sport is expected to become even more popular in the future as equipment becomes less expensive. In California alone, there are over 300,000 divers using the four underwater areas. The most exciting area is probably the La Jolla Canyon near San Diego, where the canyon comes almost to the shore and then continues into

the ocean to great depths that provide exciting archeological study of underwater areas.

Michigan

Michigan's state park system has long been recognized as one of the finest in America. Indeed, it has come a long way since 1895 when Mackinac Island State Park was created to take over military lands and buildings previously controlled by the federal government.

In Michigan, the principal state agency involved in the administration of outdoor recreation is the Department of Natural Resources. Other agencies involved on a more limited basis include the State Waterways Commission, the Huron-Clinton Metropolitan Authority, the State Highway Department, state universities and colleges, and the Department of Public Instruction.

The Department of Natural Resources is headed by a seven-member commission appointed by the governor with the consent of the senate. The commission annually appoints a director and a secretary. The various functions of the departments are organized into divisions, whose heads are directly responsible to the director.

Within the parks division, the development and operation of the State of Michigan Park System revolves around three major sections:

1. *Park design.* The division's physical planning unit is headed by a landscape architect in charge of park planning and design. The acquisition of aesthetically unique or historically significant areas is a major goal of the state park system. Historic restoration and preservation programs comprise another major activity. The ghost town of Fayette State Park is an outstanding example.

2. *Policies, procedures, and special services.* This section has established guidelines for planning that aid the design section in its large-scale task of park planning.

3. *Programming.* Given the responsibility for land acquisition and development funding, this section is an important part of the planning process. "Like many states, Michigan has developed an interpretive services program," wrote Robert O. Dodge, "designed to provide visitors with a

Fig. 7-8 WILDLIFE MANAGEMENT. One of the responsibilities of state fish and wildlife departments is to propagate, manage, and distribute game animals such as deer. This doe and buck were photographed in Colorado. (Courtesy of the State of Colorado Division of Wildlife.)

deeper understanding and appreciation of the natural or historical features in or near the area visited, thus making the experience more meaningful and enjoyable."[10]

Utah

Utah has three governmental units primarily concerned with outdoor recreation at the state level. They are the Division of Parks and Recreation, the Division of Fish and Game, and the Outdoor Recreation Assistance Agency. These units function as divisions of the State Department of Natural Resources. State agencies that make a secondary contribution in outdoor recreation are the Utah Outdoor Recreation Assistance Agency, the Division of State Lands, the State Division of Travel Development, the State Road Commission, and the Utah National Guard.

The Division of State Parks and Recreation functions under the direction of the Board of Parks and Recreation. The division has responsibility for acquisition, planning, protection, development, operation, and maintenance of park areas and facilities in such manner as may be authorized by the policies and rules and regulations of the board.

The board receives its income from user and entrance fees to state park facilities and from state appropriations.

NEW DEVELOPMENTS IN STATE PARKS

The most interesting developments taking place in state parks in America are related to a number of new recreational activities.

Snowmobiles and Other Winter Vehicles

The fastest growing recreation activity involves the use of snowmobiles and snow sleds in the

[10] Robert O. Dodge, "Michigan," *Park and Recreation,* December 1970, p. 44.

Fig. 7-9 INTERPRETATION PROGRAMS. State park systems today provide much needed park interpretation programs. These programs attempt to teach visitors the basic facts about the natural environment and its management.

snow country of such popular outdoor areas as the Sierras, the Rockies, the midwest, and New England.

While recreation vehicles have been an exciting and exhilarating activity, they have created many problems for park and recreation departments. Hazardous areas and unfamiliarity with the snow country have presented numerous problems for those who use such recreational vehicles. In addition, many drivers have been guilty of driving irresponsibly through private and public areas destroying natural resources and often scattering and disrupting deer herds and other wildlife.

Motor Bikes and Other Recreation Vehicles

A rapidly growing activity involves recreation vehicles such as sand or dune buggies, motorcycles, four-wheel jeeps, and various other motor bikes or cars. As a result, an increasing number of state parks and recreation departments have set aside and planned special areas and facilities for this

kind of recreation activity. In California, for example, the state parks department is setting aside a 300-acre canyon area at Pt. Mugu recreation area near Los Angeles where the noise will not be disruptive to others.

Underwater Exploration

Another area which is growing very rapidly is underwater exploration. In addition to setting aside and preserving underwater areas along the Pacific Coast, the State of California designed and built an underwater park on the land and then filled in the reservoir. Underwater divers are using these man-made developments to explore and observe the various fish and plant life underwater.

Bringing Parks to the People

A greater number of state parks are being built that are within a two-hour drive of major cities. While the unique and scenic state park far from the city is accessible only to the long weekender,

Fig. 7-10 UNDERWATER EXPLORATION. This underwater scene was photographed at Pennekamp Coral Reef State Park in Key Largo, Florida. (Courtesy of Florida News Bureau, Department of Commerce.)

increased effort is being made to provide nearby areas that are accessible to those who prefer a one-day outing.

Current Problems

Because of changing economic conditions, equipment, and recreation trends, flexibility is required to meet the changing demands for public recreation. State park administrators have had to cope with increased pressure from recreation vehicle and other motorized equipment owners. In addition to dune buggies, hundreds of thousands of snowmobiles have been registered in the United States since their inception. Increasing pressures have been felt toward the permissive use of such equipment on state parklands. Through zoning, and research, hundreds of miles of snowmobile trails are now available in state parks across the country during the winter months.

"The greatly accelerated growth of recreation during the 1950s made it readily apparent that a development program was needed to narrow the widening gap between demands and facilities," said Clawson. "And the state legislature, in 1960, enacted legislation through which the commission could finance expansion and improvement in the state park system."[11]

---

[11] Clawson, op. cit., p. 45.

Fig. 7-11 A SUNDAY DRIVE. Off-road vehicle enthusiasts enjoy the thrills and adventure of a drive with their four-wheel jeeps through the Sierra Nevada mountains. (Courtesy of California Association of 4-WD Clubs.)

Wisconsin's Bureau of Parks and Recreation has expressed concern for land acquisition. Al Ehly, director of the bureau, believes their most serious problem is the inability to acquire key parcels of land at a rapid enough rate to consolidate state park projects and stay ahead of the subdivider. He has proposed that the Bureau of State Planning impose a "freeze" on private lands within state park project boundaries in order to buy time for orderly acquisition.

With open space land becoming increasingly scarce, many state agencies have adhered to the philosophy of acquiring as much needed land as possible now. Increased service costs and inflation have hit state parks, requiring revisions and restructuring of fee schedules.

U.S.D.A. FOREST SERVICE
INYO NATIONAL FOREST

MT. WHITNEY TRAIL

DISTANCES FROM WHITNEY PORTAL

LONE PINE LAKE	2½ MI
OUTPOST CAMP	3½ MI.
MIRROR LAKE	4 MI.
CONSULT___ ___AKE	5 MI.
___ ___ANYON	8 MI.

8

The Federal Government

The federal government did not become interested in providing for the recreational needs of the people until the period of the Civil War. Originally, the recreational activities of the federal government centered around the use of federal land and water areas for recreation. Steadily, the government expanded its involvements in recreation-related activities, until today nearly every major division of federal government contributes in some measure to outdoor recreation.

FEDERAL AGENCIES INVOLVED IN OUTDOOR RECREATION

The federal government first became involved in outdoor recreation chiefly because of its position as custodian of public lands. The types of federal land-administering agencies are divided into two groups:

1. Those administering natural lands, such as the National Park Service, the Bureau of Land Management, the Bureau of Indian Affairs, and the Fish and Wildlife Service
2. Water-resource developing agencies that acquired lands for the purpose of developing dams and reservoirs, such as the Corps of Engineers, the Bureau of Reclamation, and the Tennessee Valley Authority

The National Park Service

From the establishment of the first national park, Yellowstone, in 1872, national parks have evolved through Congressional enactments into a system containing more than 250 parks in the fifty states, Puerto Rico, and the Virgin Islands.

The national parks were set aside in 1916 "to conserve the scenery and the natural and historic objects and the wildlife therein, and to provide for the enjoyment of the same in such manner and by such means as will leave them unimpaired for the enjoyment of future generations."[1]

Fig. 8-1 QUALIFYING FOR THE PRESIDENTIAL SPORTS AWARD are these two backpackers enroute to the Mt. Whitney area in California's Inyo National Forest. (Courtesy of the U.S. Forest Service.)

[1] Organization and Functions, Document No. 0-274-118 (Washington, D.C.: United States Department of the Interior, 1967), p. 16.

Fig. 8-2 OUR AMERICAN HERITAGE. The awesome beauty and splendor of Grand Canyon National Park and many other truly great scenic attractions were set aside in 1916 as national parks to be preserved in their natural condition. Today, the need for preserving natural and historic areas is even more critical, while still encouraging their use by the people. In this picture, visitors view the south rim of the Canyon from Mather Point. (Courtesy of the National Park Service.)

The National Park Service developed rapidly under the aggressive leadership of its first director, Stephen T. Mather, a young industrialist and outdoorsman from California. A great organizer, Mather set the pattern for the park service as it is today—career service with outstanding **esprit de corps**, and an agency without partisan politics.

In 1933, all national parks and monuments, national military parks, national battlefield parks and sites, the national capital parks, national memorials, and certain national cemeteries were consolidated under the administration of the park service.

The National Park Service, in administering America's vast park system, officially acts as a national recreation consulting agency for federal, state, and local governments. This responsibility was given to the park service in the Park, Parkway, and Recreation Area Study Act of 1936. The act provides that the National Park Service make comprehensive studies and develop plans to provide adequate public park, parkway, and recreational area facilities for the people of the United States.

As a bureau of the Department of the Inter-

ior, the national park system is composed of three categories of areas: natural, historical, and recreational.

1. *Natural areas*—the great scenic wonderlands: unspoiled mountains, lakes, forests, desert canyons, and glaciers.
2. *Historical and archeological areas*—examples of ancient Indian cultures, as well as buildings, sites, and objects that have been witness to great events of American history.
3. *Recreational areas*—together with recreation areas administered by other agencies, provide healthful outdoor recreational opportunities for a population which today is increasingly urban.

Each national park has some distinctive feature that justifies its inclusion in the system. Mt. Rainier contains over fifty square miles of glacial ice; while the park at Carlsbad protects one of the largest known natural caverns in the world. The Grand Canyon National Park features the timeless erosion and canyon construction of the Colorado River, which has excavated over one vertical mile of the ancient rocks of

Fig. 8-3 FATHER OF THE NATIONAL PARKS. Stephen T. Mather was the first director of the National Park Service, serving from May 16, 1917 to January 8, 1929. He believed that "Only those areas of truly great scenic, scientific or historical value and of unquestioned significance should be added to the Park System." (Courtesy of the National Park Service.)

the Kaibab Plateau. In the east, Acadia National Park in Maine protects a portion of the most rugged and rocky wave-pounded coastline of the Atlantic Ocean.[2]

Mission 66.   In the years following World War II, neglect and abuse were threatening our national parks. During the past fifty years, industrial expansion, technological progress, urbanization, and population growth have changed American life from what it was when the National Park Service came into being. In 1956, Conrad L. Wirth, Di-

rector of the National Park Service, launched Mission 66, an imaginative ten-year plan designed to upgrade the quality of parks and expand the national park system. In ten years, Congress appropriated over a billion dollars for facilities, management, and training.

The 1960s resulted in record expansion of the National Park System, with emphasis on historical, recreational, camping, and wilderness areas, and broad environmental education programs stressing the ecological approach and innovative use of parks for urban residents. National parks today comprise a total area of 29.5 million acres.

"The national park system is a system of the

---

[2] Elvin R. Johnson, *Park Resources for Recreation* (Columbus: Charles E. Merrill Co., 1972), p. 118.

greatest diversity," said George B. Hartzog, Jr., "offering the widest possible variations for recreation—the experience of absorbing nature's beauty and seeing wildlife existing in a natural environment in a national park or sharing memories of the past such as at Fort Laramie, Wyoming, or spiritedly enjoying the broad waters of the several national recreation areas and national seashores."[3]

The Preservation-Use Concept.   The basic idea of the National Park Service is to preserve in their natural condition areas of national significance, in order that these areas will be available for the enjoyment of people in the future as well as the present. The preservation concept must be balanced with the use concept, since the primary justification for preservation is the use the areas serve for the people. However, the use must be controlled in such a manner that the areas are preserved in their natural condition for future use.

Although the National Park Service has been criticized by some preservationists for being too recreation-oriented, some recreationists and resource-user groups have objected to the strong preservation concept employed by the park service. Clayne Jensen explained the current philosophy, "The essence of the whole preservation-use idea seems to be 'Eat as much of the cake as we can, but be sure we still have it to eat in the future.' "[4]

Visitor numbers for the national parks increased from slightly over 1 million in 1920 to around 20 million just prior to World War II; from a low of 7 million during the war to over 70 million in 1960; to 140 million in 1965, and in 1969 the number reported was 179.6 million. Today, there are approximately 200 million visits annually to the parks, and forecasts indicate that this figure will reach 300 million in the 1980s.[5]

The pressure of increasing visitor numbers

on these unique areas is creating a severe problem for long-term maintenance. According to Robinson Gregory, "It remains to be seen whether the organization can devise a management system that will permit 'enjoyment' of these parks, in such manner and by such means as will leave them unimpaired for the enjoyment of future generations."[6]

Today, we must preserve the irreplaceable feature, natural and historic, of the great national parks while encouraging their use by the people. Although the principles may be the same as those Stephen Mather faced over fifty years ago, we must introduce new management techniques in all areas of the system to enable our fellow Americans to enjoy more fully their parks.[7]

In 1973, for the first time, campsites could be reserved at six of America's top national parks: Acadia, Everglades, Grand Canyon, Grand Teton, Yellowstone, and Yosemite National Parks. A check or money order payable to American Express Reservations, Inc., should be mailed with a self-addressed, stamped envelope to: National Parks Campsite Reservations Center, P.O. Box 13802, Phoenix, Arizona 85002.

Park Ranger Training Center. Located in Grand Canyon National Park, the Horace M. Albright Training Center is designed to train National Park Service employees to help people enjoy and understand their national parks. The most important feature of the training program is its course for national park rangers entering the service. The park ranger's principal job is to deal with people, primarily park visitors. The course, entitled "Introduction to Park Operation," seeks "to develop an understanding of the history, philosophy, and goals of the Department of the Interior and the National Park Service, knowledge essential to the park ranger if he is to carry out his responsibilities adequately."[8]

[3] George B. Hartzog, Jr., "Parkscape U.S.A.," *Parks and Recreation*, August 1966, pp. 617–18.

[4] Reprinted by permission from *Outdoor Recreation in America*, Clayne R. Jensen, 1970, Burgess Publishing Company, Minneapolis, Minn., p. 62.

[5] G. Robinson Gregory, *Forest Resource Economics* (New York: The Ronald Press Co., 1972), p. 456.

[6] Ibid.

[7] Hartzog, op. cit., p. 618.

[8] Wayne Cone, "Preparing the Park Ranger for His Job," *Parks and Recreation*, December 1969, p. 31.

Fig. 8-4 CAMPING IN THE BACK COUNTRY. This family cooks an early morning meal at a wilderness trail rider camp in Montana's Flathead National Forest. Millions of Americans find enjoyment in their national parks and forests each year—refreshment of mind, body, and spirit. (Courtesy of the U.S. Forest Service.)

United States Forest Service

Indeed, with the tremendous public demand for recreational use of the land, the Forest Service is presently very much in the recreation business. During 1968, the national forests attracted 165 million visitors for recreational purposes. This figure represents a great increase over the 46 million visitors in 1955.

Administered under the Department of Agriculture, national forests are based fundamentally upon the Act of March 3, 1891, which authorized the President to reserve, by proclamation, certain lands from the public domain and to designate such lands as forest reserves.

Created in 1905, the United States Forest Service "found itself attempting to manage recreation in order to minimize fire hazards, stream pollution, and hazards to the recreationists themselves. Once having become involved, the Forest Service personnel apparently adapted themselves to the situation. In so doing, they caused the official policy of the U.S. Forest Service to become one of encouraging recreational use of the forests."[9]

The United States Forest Service administers 186 million acres of outdoor land within the 154 national forests and 19 national grassland areas.

---

[9] Jensen, op. cit., p. 68.

129

Fig. 8-5 THE PRESSURE OF INCREASING VISITOR NUMBERS is creating a severe problem for many national parks and forests. In recent years, visitor use has taxed our natural areas to such an extent that the preservation concept has been severely tested. Here, swimmers frolic in a cool creek in Arizona's Coconino National Forest. (Courtesy of the U.S. Forest Service.)

The many types of resources are protected and managed under a system of multiple use and sustained yield. "On a given square mile of national forest land there may be a ski area, or a campground on a stream or lake, or a dam providing flood control and hydroelectric power, or a controlled logging operation."[10]

As a bureau of the Department of Agriculture, the administration of the forest service begins with the Secretary of Agriculture, with the service staff headed by the chief forester and operated in Washington, D.C. Regional offices administer the forests from headquarters across the nation.

Each national forest has a forest supervisor as its head. In turn, he has a staff of specialists in timber and range management, protection, public relations, recreational activities, and engineering.

Forest recreation was defined by Robinson Gregory as "leisure-time activity voluntarily undertaken in a forest environment for the primary pur-

pose of enjoyment."[11] The scope of forest recreation covers a wide range of outdoor activities: hunting, fishing, hiking, horseback riding, camping, mountain climbing, snowmobiling, skiing, canoeing, swimming, automobile riding, and many others.

Bureau of Reclamation

Another agency in the Department of Interior is the Bureau of Reclamation which has a primary responsibility for water resource development, primarily for irrigation and power in the seventeen western states.

For many years, the bureau has permitted boating, fishing, picnicking, swimming, hiking, and other recreation activities on its reservoir areas. Rather than develop and administer the recreation resources of its areas, however, the bureau's policy has been to transfer them to other appro-

[10] Johnson, op. cit., p. 114.

[11] Gregory, op. cit., p. 453.

Fig. 8-6 A RECREATION BUSINESS. While preservation is still the major responsibility of federal outdoor agencies, both the Park Service and Forest Service are encouraging their use by the people. Here, outdoor enthusiasts enjoy speedboating on Stanley Lake in Idaho's Challis National Forest. (Courtesy of U.S. Forest Service.)

Summary of Activities in National Forests, 1969 [12]

Activity	Visitor Day Use	Per Cent of Total
Viewing	55,427	3.3
Auto driving	342,962	21.0
Hiking	48,570	2.9
Horseback riding	21,705	1.3
Other riding and looking	65,471	4.1
Canoeing; sailing; other water team sports and games	12,566	.7
Team sports and games	5,855	.3
Swimming, skin diving, water-skiing	35,367	2.1
Fishing	148,682	9.1
Individual camping	416,297	25.5
Organization camping	43,240	2.6
Picnicking	68,377	4.1
Resorts	40,332	2.4
Recreation residence	80,152	4.9
Skiing	47,774	2.9
Other winter sports	11,212	.7
Hunting	141,479	8.6
Nature study, programs, tours, etc.	42,919	2.5
Total	1,628,387	

[12] Data supplied by Bureau of Outdoor Recreation.

priate federal, state, or local governmental agencies.

The recreation use of the bureau has soared. In 1951, there were 6.5 million recorded visitor-days. By 1970, this figure had increased to over 54 million. This sharp growth can be attributed largely to the great popularity of boating activities.

Bureau of Land Management

Operating under the Department of the Interior, the Bureau of Land Management is another agency that is concerned with maintaining and strengthening the quality of our natural resources. Created in 1946, the bureau has jurisdiction over federally owned public lands that have not been incorporated into specific national forests, parks, or other recreation areas. This land includes a total of about one-fifth of the United States, or approximately 470 million acres located chiefly in Alaska and the western states.

Although its recreation efforts are not in the same scope as those of the National Park Service and the National Forest Service, the bureau is growing in importance, and its facilities and services should help to relieve the pressures on the more prominent areas. Properties of the Bureau of Land Management are being used increasingly for camp and picnic sites, trailer areas, swimming beaches, and boat launching ramps.

The Fish and Wildlife Service

The U.S. Fish and Wildlife Service consists of two separate bureaus: the Bureau of Sports Fisheries and Wildlife and the Bureau of Commercial Fisheries. Within the Department of the Interior, the Fish and Wildlife Service has the responsibility for the protection of fish and wildlife on federal properties throughout the United States.

The Bureau of Sports Fisheries and Wildlife uses public land only for wildlife refuge areas, fish hatcheries, and waterfowl production areas. Much of its work is advisory and involves research on fish, game animals, and game birds.

Many of its 300 national wildlife refuges covering over 28 million acres afford not only havens for game but facilities for boating, camping, picnicking, and nature study.

Corps of Engineers

Organized in 1775, the Corps of Engineers of the U.S. Department of the Army, is responsible for the improvement and maintenance of rivers and other waterways to facilitate navigation and flood control. In doing so, this agency affects recreation by constructing and operating reservoirs, protecting and improving beaches, and providing harbors and waterways used by recreation craft.

The agency operates about 350 reservoirs in 44 states covering approximately 8 million acres. These facilities are used for such outdoor recreation activities as camping, swimming, picnicking, hunting, boating, and water skiing. Like other federal agencies, the corps cooperates fully with local government and private interests in many aspects concerning the betterment of water resources.

Land and Water Conservation Fund Program

Enacted into law by Congress in 1965, this fund was created to provide urgently needed public outdoor recreation areas and facilities to states and local governments. In order to be eligible for funding assistance, each state is required to prepare a comprehensive outdoor recreation plan, analyzing the needs of the various cities.

The Tennessee Valley Authority

Created by act of Congress in 1933, the original purpose of the Tennessee Valley Authority was to develop the Tennessee River for navigation, flood control, and electric power. While recreation was not specified as a major purpose of TVA programs, it soon became apparent "that the construction of a water control system for the Tennessee River would create a whole new range of recreation opportunities unfamiliar to this inland region of great natural beauty."[13]

[13] Jack H. Hendrix, "Recreation in the Tennessee Valley," *Parks and Recreation*, April 1973, p. 41.

Fig. 8-7 FUTURE DAM SITE. Construction of the world's longest concrete arch dam is scheduled for completion in 1981, providing northern California with a tremendous source of power and irrigation. The Bureau of Reclamation has a primary responsibility for water resource development and flood control.

The TVA has brought a new spectrum of recreation opportunities to the Tennessee Valley. Wildlife refuges and management areas cover 190,000 acres of land and waterways. Extensive boating and camping facilities attract growing numbers of visitors to lands which once offered nothing to the public in the way of recreation.

Recreation use has grown rapidly in the Tennessee Valley Authority, both in number of participants and in kinds of activities. Backpacking, canoeing, hiking, and nature study have grown tremendously in popularity.

Bureau of Indian Affairs

The primary responsibility of the bureau is to provide service to American Indian tribes in health, education, economic development, and land management. Created in 1824 within the control of the War Department, the bureau was transferred to civilian control with the creation of the Department of the Interior.

The various tribes develop and manage recreation facilities on their reservations, including campgrounds, museums, restaurants, hunting and fishing areas, lodges, and ski resorts. The bureau provides technical assistance to tribesmen in operating these facilities and programs, which attracted over 10 million visitors in 1970.

Tourist travel to Indian reservations stems from the keen interest in the ceremonials, arts and crafts, architecture, and the life of the Indian. The cultural heritage of the American Indian is of special interest to many visitors. Most Indian ceremonials are held during the summer and early fall, when visitors are most numerous.

Bureau of Public Roads

Operating within the Department of Transportation, the Bureau of Public Roads has three basic functions:

1. Highway research
2. Road-building on federal domain
3. The administration of federal aid to the state for highway construction.

"It would be difficult to overemphasize the importance of the relationship between outdoor recreation and the functions of the bureau," wrote Clayne Jensen. "Not only are good roads to the recreation sites indispensable, but roads within the areas determine in considerable degree the demand for, and the capacity of, the recreation areas."[14]

OTHER FEDERAL AGENCIES

In addition to the resource-management agencies, a number of federal agencies have made a significant contribution to outdoor recreation by providing technical and financial assistance. Many programs of the federal government provide services to special groups or purposes.

Programs for military personnel, veterans, and federal employees have been effective in meeting their needs and demands. While there has been an increase in services for the disadvantaged, the recreation needs and living conditions for disadvantaged segments of the population are still alarmingly acute. Greatly expanded programs will

[14] Jensen, op. cit., pp. 91–92.

be needed to meet the expanding demands of a growing public.

The newly created Committee on Recreation and Leisure is part of the President's Committee on Employment of the Handicapped and offers important services to those handicapped or disabled. The Bureau of Education for the handicapped provides for training programs in recreation.

Various special committees, councils, boards, and commissions have been established from time to time to perform duties or services not provided by federal agencies.

Bureau of Outdoor Recreation

Established in 1962 by executive order of President John F. Kennedy, the bureau has the responsibility of promoting coordination of the outdoor recreation programs of the various federal agencies and working with states in developing state and local outdoor recreation programs.

To provide financial support for the bureau and for the expansion of outdoor recreation opportunities, the Land and Water Conservation Fund Act of 1965 was enacted. This act provides that funds be derived from the federal tax on marine gasoline, the sale of federal real property, and admission charges at federal recreation sites.

The bureau is a planning, research, and advisory agency for all levels of government and does not manage any areas or facilities of its own. It has devoted special attention to the natural beauty of outdoor recreation resources and has helped to stimulate state and local efforts to meet the needs of urban populations.

Department of Health, Education and Welfare

This department administers many federal programs related to recreation. The Office of Education provides recreation services to state and local school systems, colleges, universities, and professional organizations. Working through state and national agencies and organizations, the Children's Bureau has shown a continuing interest in providing recreation opportunities for all children and youth.

The Public Health Service assists other federal agencies in planning sanitary developments in parks, camps, bathing and boating areas, picnic areas, and trailer parks. Working chiefly through the states, it assists in planning standards and inspection programs for bathing sanitation, food handling, disposal of refuse and sewage, and various problems in camps and parks.

The Rehabilitation Services Administration administers the federal law authorizing vocational rehabilitation programs designed to help the physically and mentally disabled. A number of college programs training therapeutic recreation specialists are receiving grants for curriculum development and scholarships by the Vocational Services Administration.

The Administration on Aging is concerned with problems of older persons in society. In promoting programs for aging persons, the federal agency provides grants for training of professional personnel and demonstration projects intended to prepare professional staffs for work with older people. The largest number of local projects have involved recreation and leisure time activities, with particular emphasis on senior centers.

Department of Housing and Urban Development

The federal government has been very active in promoting slum clearance and assisting housing programs in America's cities. Established in 1965, the Department of Housing and Urban Development has been effective in encouraging the provision of recreation areas and facilities to meet the needs of the residents of housing projects. The department is responsible for a wide range of federally assisted programs, including public housing, mass transit, urban renewal and planning, community facilities, and open space.

The federal government has provided increasing support for parks and recreation in urban areas. The 1966 Demonstration Cities and Metropolitan Development Act provides up to 80 per cent of the cost of projects, improving the physical environment of cities, such as preserving his-

Fig. 8-8 FISHING IN THE ROCKIES. A fisherman from New York tries his luck at Maroon Lake in Colorado's White River National Forest. Protection of fish and wildlife on federal properties is the responsibility of the Fish and Wildlife Service. (Courtesy of the U.S. Forest Service.)

toric structures and acquiring and developing parks, playgrounds, community centers, and other facilities.

Soil Conservation Service

Established in 1935, the Soil Conservation Service carries out its activities chiefly by providing technical and financial assistance to local soil and water conservation districts formed under state laws.

The service has promoted the improvement of recreation resources by urging the conservation of soil and water on privately owned land.

United States Travel Service

In 1961, Congress established the U.S. Travel Service, authorized to operate branch offices in foreign countries in order to encourage residents of other countries to travel in the United States. Since it was initiated, this service has proven to be of strong economic value to the nation.

The Armed Forces

Recreation first became recognized as an important need of the U.S. military forces in World War I. At this time, a number of national agencies, including the YMCA, the Salvation Army, the American Red Cross, and others undertook the responsibility of providing recreation and social services for uniformed personnel in state-side posts and overseas.

When it became apparent that organized social and recreation programs were helpful in maintaining morale, counteracting fatigue, and reducing other service problems, special services divisions were established to meet the need. Today, each branch of the service has its own pattern of recreation sponsorship and administration.

Fig. 8-9 RIDING THE TRAIL. Tall saguaro cactuses and taller crags make a rugged backdrop for horseback riding in Arizona's Coronado National Forest. (Courtesy of the U.S. Forest Service.)

Prior to World War II, the Special Services recreation program tended to be extremely decentralized and lacking in both uniformity and professional leadership. Often, programs depended on the personal whims of base commanders and on many posts tended to be limited to sports competition. However, during and after World War II, armed forces programs expanded greatly, to meet the needs of the rapidly growing branches of the service.

As the nature of military assignments and personnel changed, so the content of recreational programs in the armed forces has changed as well. Today, there is a greater stress on variety of activity and on direct participation, rather than on spectator events.

Army Special Services. In 1970, 10,092 full-time military and civilian employees helped to make Army Special Services one of the largest recreation programs in the world with a multi-million dollar annual operating budget.

Army Special Services has positions for the following types of personnel: civilian employees, enlisted men and women, commissioned officers, military and civilian volunteers, part-time employees, and reservists.

A high turnover rate in personnel is characteristic of the U.S. Army, and Special Services is no exception. Military personnel seldom serve more than three years in an Army Special Services assignment. Also, many of the civilians are under contracts that cover three years or less. As a result, there is a continuous requirement for new personnel.

The soldier who desires an assignment in Special Services should insure that his qualifications are adequately described on his records. Whether a particular soldier is assigned to Special Services will depend on the vacancies that exist and the strength of his credentials compared with those of other applicants.

The 6,500 civilian full-time employees in Special Services embrace a wide range of experience and training. They include many women recreation graduates who serve as Service Club activities specialists. After their interview by a Special Services recruiter who visits their college, they report to Washington, D.C., for a three-day orientation at

Headquarters, Department of the Army, where they depart for their assignment, such as a three-year stint in Europe. Army service club personnel are serving today from Berlin to Tokyo, from the Panama Canal Zone to Alaska, in the islands of the Pacific, as well as in Korea and Vietnam. Around the world, there are 285 Army service clubs, staffed by more than 750 of the "ladies in blue."

The Department of the Army Overseas Recruitment Center maintains a staff of five full-time civilian recruiters whose job it is to find qualified personnel to fill Special Services professional positions in all overseas areas. The address: Special Services Section, Department of the Army Overseas Recruitment Center, 12th and Pennsylvania Avenue, N.W., Washington, D.C. 20315.

Information concerning civil service examinations may be obtained from the United States Civil Service Commission, 1900 E. Street, N.W., Washington, D.C. 20415; or from one of the regional offices of the United States Civil Service Commission.

Air Force Special Services. The Special Services program "fulfills the recreation needs and interests of Air Force personnel and their families by providing maximum opportunities for them to participate in leisure-time activities that help to stimulate, develop, and maintain their mental, physical and social well-being."[15]

The United States Air Force Special Services program consists of sports, service clubs and entertainment, crafts and hobbies, motion pictures, youth activities, rest centers and recreation areas, library service, special interest groups, and a variety of other recreational services and activities.

Primarily, the Special Services program operates at base or installation level. While the service club or gymnasium is often the focal point for many activities, the Air Force also has been effective in coordinating its program with communities near its bases.

Navy Special Services. The commanding officers have the responsibility of providing adequate recreation programs for their personnel. The Special

Services programs are conducted and administered under the direction of the Special Services Officer and his staff. "Because of a less professional philosophy of recreation service and the fluctuation of personnel who are assigned to afloat units, the Navy's program of Special Services is less developed than that of the Army or Air Force. Recreation on board ship is difficult to standardize because of limited space."[16]

Most naval installations ashore have swimming pools, hobby shops, gymnasiums, golf courses, athletic fields, tennis courts, and movie theatres.

A navy warship, at sea for weeks at a time, is not an ideal setting for a recreation program. Life at sea can be quite different from that on shore. Still, there is an important need for a recreation program for those who serve aboard the ship.

> Recreation activities on Kitty Hawk, the world's largest conventionally powered warship, for example, are supervised by the ship's Special Services Office. One officer and a staff of nine enlisted men organize and conduct the various athletic, social, craft, and special activities that make up Kitty Hawk's recreation program. The Special Services officer and his staff work full time on recreation programming except when involved on watches or other ship evolutions such as battle drills. . . .
>
> . . . the necessity for a comprehensive recreation program for men in the military at sea is as obvious as it is great. Loneliness, restlessness, and boredom have adverse effects on a ship's crew after long periods away from home when the men on a ship like Kitty Hawk are enclosed in a steel box that can be completely encircled in a ten-minute walk.[17]

Marine Corps Special Services. Special Services in the Marine Corps are those services or activities provided each marine and his dependents. The Marine Corps places strong emphasis on physical fitness, particularly programs provided in war

[15] *Air Force Special Programs,* Air Force Regulation no. 215-1 (Washington, D.C.: Department of the Air Force, 1966), p. 1.

[16] Richard Kraus, *Recreation and Leisure in Modern Society,* © 1971 by Meredith Corporation. Reprinted by permission of Prentice-Hall, Inc., Englewood Cliffs, N.J. Pp. 43–44.

[17] Ronald C. Hallberg, "Recreation Afloat," *Parks and Recreation,* November 1965, pp. 439, 442.

zones, as a rest-and-recuperation service for fighting personnel.

Similar to the Navy, the responsibility for the conduct of a Special Services program unit rests with each local commander. Special Services for the Marine Corps include such programs as recreation, athletics, education and information, personal affairs, and post exchanges.

Veterans Administration

Through its recreation section in the Physical Medicine and Rehabilitation Service, the Veterans Administration operates a program at each V.A. hospital and home. Its program has three aspects: medical care, insurance, and financial assistance for veterans.

Under professional leadership, the recreation program is considered part of the medical treatment and rehabilitation. Activities include sports, music, arts, crafts, entertainment, motion pictures, hospitality services, special events, and hobbies.

Federal Anti-Poverty Programs

During the early 1960s under the Johnson Administration, a number of anti-poverty programs were initiated by the federal government which gave significant support to the provisions of recreation services for economically disadvantaged urban populations. The Office of Economic Opportunity was created to coordinate all anti-poverty programs on the federal level. Among others, the OEO sponsored such recreation-related programs as Job Corps, the Neighborhood Youth Corps, and Vista.

A major factor in the federal government's "war on poverty" was the community action program involving a large number of separate projects in local communities which were sponsored by various governmental or voluntary groups.

While the scope of the Job Corps and other anti-poverty programs has been reduced, it is apparent that the federal government will continue to provide increasing services and facilities to the economically disadvantaged urban populations.

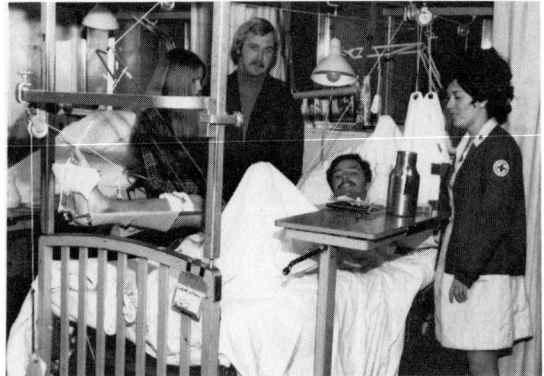

Fig. 8-10   VETERANS' HOSPITAL. Under professional leadership, Veterans Administration hospitals provide a well-balanced range of recreation activities to meet the needs and interests of patients. Recreation majors from American River College visit Vietnam wounded at the Travis A.F.B. hospital near San Francisco.

President's Council on Recreation and Natural Beauty

Established in 1966, the Council has been effective in helping to restore and maintain the quality of the environment. The Council has studied extensively ways in which federal property can be used to increase outdoor recreation services and help to alleviate the increasing visitor pressures at recreation areas and sites.

President's Council on Physical Fitness and Sports

Created in 1956 to stimulate the physical fitness of the nation's youth, the President's Council has played a key role in improving the fitness level of both youth and adults. Today, after steady progress and reorganization, the council should prove a potent force in continuing to upgrade the physical fitness status of America.

When President Kennedy came into office in 1962, he appointed Charles "Bud" Wilkinson, highly successful football coach of the University of Oklahoma, his special presidential consultant and placed the council under Wilkinson's direction. With the cooperation and assistance of nineteen leading school and medical organizations, the

Fig. 8-11 THE PRESIDENT'S COUNCIL ON PHYSICAL FITNESS AND SPORTS. President Richard M. Nixon discussed the reorganization of the national program of physical fitness and sports with Chairman Captain James Lovell, former astronaut, and C. Carson Conrad, Executive Director. (Courtesy of the President's Council on Physical Fitness.)

council developed and organized a suggested program of physical fitness for the nation's schools.

Soon after taking office in 1968, President Richard M. Nixon reorganized the council and directed it to study the status of school physical education, physical fitness programs, and the fitness of America's adults. Under the aggressive administrative leadership of C. Carson "Casey" Conrad, Executive Director, the council has succeeded in developing effective fitness programs for the young and old alike.

The President's Council has been very successful in promoting a school-centered program for physical fitness. It has also been effective in developing special working relationships with colleges and universities, community groups, voluntary agencies, and other organizations.

The council has been able to mobilize mass media to communicate the need to be fit to the general public. In conducting a nationwide promotional campaign, it has effectively utilized radio, television, newspapers, movies, and articles in prominent national magazines.

Many regional physical fitness clinics have been conducted by the President's Council featuring some of the nation's physical fitness leaders and the council staff. Several fitness films have been produced, and publications have been printed and made available both to the communication media and to all segments of the population.

The President's Council on Physical Fitness and Sports is also concerned with summer programs in recreation and physical education. In conjunction with the National Collegiate Athletic Association, it has established the National Summer Youth Sports Program. This program provides disadvantaged youth of cities opportunities to participate in planned physical activities.

One of the most successful programs to be developed and conducted by the council is the Presidential Sports Award Program. Men and women aged eighteen years and older can win the Presidential Sports Award, including a certificate bearing the President's signature, simply by participating regularly in their favorite sports. During the first year, over 20,000 men and women received awards in the program.

The object of the new program is to encourage more adults to become active participants in sports, rather than being content with a spectator's role. The council believes that the physical and mental benefits resulting from vigorous exercise contribute significantly to personal health, appearance, and performance.

Standards for the Presidential Sports Award program were developed by the council in cooperation with forty-five major sports governing bodies and coaches' associations. The award is being offered in thirty-eight sports, ranging from archery to water skiing. Bowling has been the most popular award sport, followed by jogging, swimming, tennis, bicycling, karate, riding, softball, golf, and skiing. The basic principle governing qualification for the new award is a minimum of fifty hours of participation, spread over at least fifty activity sessions, within a four-month period.

Anyone may obtain a free personal log book and a set of qualifying standards for all the sports by writing to: Presidential Sports Award, P.O. Box 129, Radio City Station, New York, N.Y. 10019.

9

International Recreation

The park and recreation movement is making a strong impact throughout the world. Indeed, play speaks a universal language. Whatever the differences in their languages and customs may be, people of all nations have responded to the multitude of opportunities for recreation and leisure.

In a growing number of countries, dedicated leaders are discovering how beneficial a well-rounded program in parks and recreation can be toward life enrichment. They have found that people who play together are relaxed and understanding. Even though they speak different languages and have different customs, people from different nations can communicate effectively through recreation. Still, the people of the world have yet to create the type of effective international exchange capable of achieving more positive understanding among each other. Hopefully, future cultural and recreational contacts and changes among nations will contribute significantly toward a better world. Representing a "power for peace," they have the potential to help bring people together in mutual understanding and respect.

RECREATION IN EUROPE

Many American forms of recreation originated in Europe. As a field of professional service, though, recreation has not developed as fully in Europe as it has in the United States. However, in some forms of recreational involvement, European nations have surpassed similar activities found in the United States. "Typically, they have achieved a higher level of sports participation for the masses of people," said Richard Kraus, "and have promoted the arts and folk culture far more vigorously than in the United States."[1]

Generally, leisure and recreation services in Europe are viewed as a governmental responsibility. Both the states and the large cities own ex-

Fig. 9-1 THE GREAT POPULARITY OF RACING. Track and road bicycle races take place in Europe's largest cities. (Courtesy of Bundesbildstelle, Bonn.)

[1] Richard Kraus, *Recreation and Leisure in Modern Society,* © 1971 by Meredith Corporation. Reprinted by permission of Prentice-Hall, Inc., Englewood Cliffs, N.J. P. 211.

tensive acreage in many municipal and national forests which are open to the public for recreation. In addition, a large number of voluntary organizations have been active for many decades in promoting sports, outdoor activities, folklore, and the arts. With strong government support, numerous sports and gymnastic organizations have developed large networks of play fields, sports arenas, and stadiums.

Europeans are very sports-minded, both as participants and as spectators. Soccer, handball, and other popular sports often draw huge crowds. Bicycle and motor races are extremely popular. Private sports clubs are numerous in Europe, particularly in the northernmost countries.

The origin of many European municipal parks which have been in existence for many years can be traced to gardens and hunting grounds owned by royalty. Comprehensive systems of large and small parks have been developed, particularly those in German cities such as Cologne, Munich, and Wiesbaden.

In 1909, Sweden became the first European country to pass laws regarding the establishment of national parks. Since then, many European nations have set aside areas for national parks, although they are not the natural areas found in the United States.

Interest in the theatre, music, and arts has been widespread. Opportunities in the performing arts have been provided by many private associations. Opera, ballet, and symphony groups have been supported by various government subsidies. Still, in many European cities, theatres, opera houses, and museums are publicly owned and operated.

Camping, hiking, canoeing, mountain climbing, and other forms of outdoor recreation have strong appeal in Europe. Low-cost travel for European youth has been made possible by youth hostels. Europeans enjoy camping with their families or with small groups at camp sites close to large cities and in natural areas farther away.

Many voluntary youth-membership organizations similar to those found in the United States, such as the Boy Scouts, Girl Guides, and YMCA, are also found in Europe. The practice of supporting youth services through voluntary donations, however, has not been established in Europe to the extent enjoyed in America. Public funds are

Fig. 9-2 MOTOR RACING EVENTS in Europe attract hundreds of thousands of spectators. The Nuerburg Ring is acclaimed as the most beautifully situated and trickiest racing track in the world. (Courtesy of Bundesbildstelle, Bonn.)

available to youth organizations. Soccer betting pools provide income which is distributed to youth organizations, sports groups, and youth hostels.

People in the Scandinavian countries enjoy gymnastics and vigorous outdoor sports. They like to ski and skate in the winter season, and swim and go boating in the summer months. Feasts, festivals, and celebrations of all types are very popular in Scandinavia.

Germany

For many decades, the German people have been known for their participation in all forms of indoor and outdoor sports. The young and old alike enjoy hiking into the hills and forests, swimming in the lakes, and enjoying the outdoors. Camps, inns, and hostels are located in all areas of the country. Interest in tourism is at an all-time high.

Fig. 9-3 IN RECENT YEARS IN EUROPE, there has been an increase in the development of park and recreation facilities such as play courts and areas, swimming pools, and athletic stadiums. This crowded swimming pool in Königswinter is a typical summer scene in Germany. (Courtesy of Bundesbildstelle, Bonn.)

During the nineteenth century, Germany was one of the first nations to develop a strong gymnastics and physical education movement as well as establish many parks and outdoor activity areas. This interest has grown steadily through the years, and today the traditional sports and games are enjoyed by the very young, men and women, families, and older citizens.

Much emphasis in the past has been placed upon drill, calisthenics, and Turnverein type of physical recreation involving precision, skill, and agility. Today, however, team games, such as soccer, handball, and track and field, enjoy great popularity among the Germans, while swimming, skating, and skiing are also highly popular. Soccer (fussball) is one of the most popular sports, with more and more young people joining the country's soccer clubs.

Many German cities have developed comprehensive, well-planned systems of small and large parks, which provide park sites throughout the city. Many of the sports and play areas are controlled by amateur sports organizations and clubs. The German Sports Federation is responsible for the physical fitness program of West Germany. The number of sportswomen and their associations, particularly in soccer, is increasing rapidly in the country.

In 1959, the "Second Way" to sports was organized to encourage all citizens who had not taken part in sports to take up a sport in their leisure time. "Sports are essential to occupy one's free time and to keep one's health." This is what prompted the German Sports Confederation to start its "Get Trim through Sports" campaign in 1970. According to a survey, over nine million

143

Fig. 9-4 FITNESS FOR LIVING. Germany was one of the first nations to develop a strong physical education movement, an interest which has become traditional for a nation of sports enthusiasts. Arranged by the schools, the Federal Youth Games are the biggest annual sports festival in the world — with five million participants. (Courtesy of Bundesbildstelle, Bonn.)

people were spurred into taking an interest in keeping fit, including the federal president, Dr. Gustav Heinemann, who kept fit by going for a swim each morning.[2]

The TRIM campaign was adopted to continue the work of the "Second Way" on a larger scale with improved programs. A small sum of $28,000 was allotted by the federal government. The balance of a $2 million budget is donated by private and public sponsors and participants.

The federation has been successful in getting cooperation from trade unions, churches, schools, industries, business promotions, and the news media. Newspapers, trade journals, sports programs, radio and TV networks are all actively committed and dedicated to the promotion of the TRIM campaign.

The "German Sports Emblem" is the undisputed highest award for sports in the Federal Republic of Germany. Each year more than 300,000 citizens prove their prowess in sports by gaining

the award. The various performance requirements allow youngsters and men and women of all ages to win their own "Olympic medal."

The German people are also very fond of music and dancing. Their traditional restaurants and open-air gardens are internationally famous for singing, good eating, merrymaking, and dancing. Popular festivals and fairs are held the year around.

New leisure-time groups are being formed in which men and women practice sports regularly. In Bonn, for example, around thirty members, mostly married couples between twenty-five and sixty years of age, meet every Monday for gymnastics and volleyball.

In addition to the parks and playgrounds, much of the organized play in Germany takes place in and around the schools. During the Nazi regime, recreation was regimented and directed toward the glorification of the state. After World War II, however, the Germans reverted to many of the activities they had experienced traditionally, and, influenced by the allied democracies, patterns of public recreation such as those practiced in America began to take hold in Germany. Rec-

---

[2] Woodrow M. Hutchison, "A Survey of Physical Fitness and Sports in European Countries" (Project on behalf of the President's Council on Physical Fitness and Sports, 1971), pp. 22–26.

Fig. 9-5 RHYTHMIC GYMNASTICS has strongly influenced physical education in schools. The Medan School in Coburg is one of the best known finishing schools for modern gymnastics in Germany. Competitive gymnastics appeals very strongly to young European girls. (Courtesy of Bundesbildstelle, Bonn.)

reation centers, especially for children and youth, were an example of the interest which was first generated by the United States Army and the State Department.

German health spas are discovering that fitness training is a useful therapy. More and more spa doctors are prescribing walking, dancing, gymnastics, and rowing.

Increasingly, vacation centers such as the Marina Wendtorf in northern Germany are being built. Described as a "maritime vacation harbor with a club character," this German vacation port provides fun and festivities for the old and young alike. Elaborate apartment complexes for living accommodations are reasonably priced. Leisure-time activities include swimming, sailing, bicycling, tennis, bowling, golf, and volleyball.

Denmark

The Danish people take great pride in all of their sports programs. The young children start at an early age in gymnastic programs, and as a result, Denmark has developed outstanding gymnastic teams over the years. Schools and sports clubs place much emphasis on physical conditioning programs. There are many programs offered in physical fitness and sports for all age levels. The

Fig. 9-6 THE 1972 OLYMPIC TRACK AND FIELD CHAMPIONSHIPS were held in the ultramodern velodrome in Munich, built by the great German architect Schürmann.

Fig. 9-7 EUROPEANS ARE VERY SPORTS-MINDED. In a recreation field in the heart of Oslo, a group of Norwegian youths engage in a fast-moving game of soccer. Playgrounds and playfields of various sizes and forms can be found in most European cities. (Courtesy of Norges Idrettsforbund.)

objective of the national leaders in sports is to promote participation in physical activity by as many people as possible.

Many of the recreation activity programs are sponsored by business organizations. One newspaper, for example, sponsors a 50-kilometer bicycle event. The bicycle, Denmark's national vehicle, provides many possibilities for inexpensive touring. Organized seven-day cycle tours in different areas of the country are priced from $69 to $75, including bike rental, youth hostel accommodations, and meals.

Norway

Designed to meet the sports and recreational needs of everyone in Norway, the Norwegian TRIM program is financed by the Norwegian Sports Federations, the municipalities, and fees from the participants.

Norway has one central sports organization, the National Sports Association, which is responsible for the coordination and guidance of the sports policy for the country. To perform these tasks, there are thirty-eight special sports federations representing the different branches and twenty-four sports districts which cover roughly the county divisions. The sports clubs (5,200) form the active base of the entire organization.[3]

The TRIM program receives approximately $100,000 per year from the National Sports Federation. Soccer pools are the chief sources of revenue. Participants, too, pay small fees for various programs. Popular activities include "orienteering" (with map and compass), organized town hikes, night-time skiing, and use of home gymnasiums.

Norway has eleven national parks and six more are being established. The nation's first national park was set aside in 1962 by royal decree.

One of Norway's biggest summer attractions is its International Jazz Festival in Molde on the fjord-filled west coast. Along with jazz musicians from the United States and Europe, the festival features poetry readings, folk and ballad singers, classical music and theatre performances.

Sweden

The physical fitness program of Sweden includes all the activities in competitive and other physical

---

[3] Ibid., p. 6.

146

ways in which people get exercise or active recreation for their general well-being. The program is financed through state allocations, regional and club memberships.

The Swedish Sports Federation is a union of special associations and groups or clubs. The aim of the federation is to increase the physiological and physical strength of Swedish citizens by recreation, sports, and competition. The federation is trying to spread the idea of sports and physical activity to as many people as possible by different campaigns, with cooperation from many special associations.[4]

In 1966, the federation was granted money from the state to employ a secretary to handle "Sports for All." The secretary's prime job has been to induce all the sports associations and clubs to add programs that will add to the "Sports for All" movement.

Regional organizations of the federation encourage the organization of local physical activity groups for women, encourage communities to improve sports facilities, and offer courses for leaders in the "Sports for All" activities.

All new buildings, schools, clubs, and cities are making provisions for "Sports for All." Big companies and industries are developing TRIM centers to encourage their employees to participate. There are exercise breaks in the mornings and afternoons for short gymnastics. Companies sponsor teams and sports programs.[5]

The Netherlands

The Dutch Sports Federation also operates a TRIM, "Sports for All" program. Starting on an experimental basis, the federation urged each person at TRIM pilot centers to take up two activities. Upon completion, he or she would receive a badge or emblem.

The sports clubs have joined the program in large numbers, organizing several activities and maintaining "open house" (for nonmembers to

Fig. 9-8 WINTER SPORTS HAVEN. Norway is blessed with ideal winter conditions for skiing and ice skating. Here, two Norwegian women enjoy a leisurely journey on a cross-country ski-track. (Courtesy of Norges Idrettsforbund.)

acquire new skills in sports). As a result, people became more interested in the sports awards, especially the TRIM and sport-passport awards.[6]

Baseball in Holland is enjoying increasing popularity, as the new training facilities, instructional clinics, and competitive leagues will indicate.

[4] Ibid., p. 13.

[5] Ibid., p. 18.

[6] Harold Meyer, Charles Brightbill, and Douglas Sessoms, *Community Recreation—A Guide to Its Organization* (Englewood Cliffs, N.J.: Prentice-Hall, Inc., 1969), pp. 173–74.

Fig. 9-9 ORIENTEERING IS A SPORT that originated in Sweden and still flourishes in many European countries. Orienteering games provide fun and valuable experience with map and compass for the young and old alike. (Courtesy of Sports Council, London.)

England

Traditionally, the English people have always been great sports enthusiasts who enjoy a variety of leisure-time pursuits. Among the favorite traditional sports are cricket, rugby football, soccer, boxing, tennis, badminton, golf, horse racing, and boat racing. Hunting and fishing are also very popular.

The English, in large numbers, have taken advantage of many opportunities to pursue the arts—music, drama, literature—and to attend the great art centers in England.

The appointment of the Albemarle Committee on Youth Service by Parliament was the result of increasing interest in recreation and leisure. The committee recommended the following: A National Youth Council with grant-aiding powers charged with the provision of an adequate supply of qualified youth leaders, coordination and development of youth service, and supervision of research to explore new ways of reaching hard-to-get young people.[7]

The British "Sports for All" program is under the direction of the Central Council of Physical Recreation. The council consists of about 300 members, representing various branches of physical recreation. The function of the CCPR is to encourage all forms of physical recreation. This organization works with governing bodies of sports to sponsor instructional courses, lectures, and other public events.

In the five-star program, involving five levels of awards for each age group, the pentathlon and

[7] Ibid.

Fig. 9-10 NATIONAL SPORTS CENTERS in England have been a major influence on the development of the "Sports for All" program, including facilities for almost all sporting activities. (Courtesy of the Sports Council, London.)

the decathlon events are of a physical fitness nature. Other sports programs, such as skiing and swimming, are administered by federations. In general, most sports and recreation activities originate at local levels in the clubs, schools, industries, and with voluntary organizations.

The Youth Services cater to young people, ages fourteen through eighteen. All local authorities are required to provide facilities and opportunities for this group. Youth centers and clubs are available and under the direction of youth leaders.[8]

The national sports centers in England give a strong impetus to the growth of a comprehensive range of sports—a philosophy suggesting that a voluntary enterprise should be supplemented by government resources. There are ten national centers that include facilities for almost all sporting activities.

Bisham Abbey, located in the rolling green countryside of Buckinghamshire just six miles from London, is one of seven national sports centers in the British Isles, established to train recreation leaders and provide opportunities for the devel-

opment of skills in all types of sports and outdoor activities.

Much of the work of the CCPR is carried out in direct association with specialist organizations concerned with sports, outdoor activities, dancing, and other forms of recreation, and with local education authorities and voluntary youth organizations. From CCPR headquarters extends a network of regional councils and local sports authorities that dispense services to all parts of the country.

France

Essentially, the promotion and implementation of the French sports and recreational programs are the responsibilities of the schools, federations, unions of organizations, industry, and private clubs. Emphasis is on youth programs.

Most of the sports programs in France are handled by the Olympic clubs, non-Olympic clubs, federation groups, and the university clubs. The French government concentrates on physical activities for youth. Many programs are planned for skiing, swimming, tennis, and group games. France

---

[8] Hutchison, op. cit., p. 37.

Fig. 9-11 RIDING HUNTS are a great tradition in Europe. Spacious grounds like this park are ideally suited for riding hunts in which outstanding skills of horsemanship are required. (Courtesy of the Sports Council, London.)

In recent years, family camping has undergone a substantial expansion in France. The support of youth hostels enables thousands of French young people to vacation independently or in groups or to take tours which include bicycling, hiking, and camping.

Belgium

Sportbiennale, "Sports for All," in Belgium features programs of physical recreation for all people. The motto of *Sportbiennale* is "Don't sit down and think of your troubles, join us!"

Gezinssport is sports for the family. The motto for this program is "Stay young with your family." Family nights are planned at sports centers for family games in volleyball, basketball, tennis, and swimming.[9]

Switzerland

The Federal School of Gymnastics and Sports has the responsibility of administering sports programs for all of Switzerland. The facilities at the sports school are excellent, and through efficient leadership and organization, the facilities receive maximum usage. The sports associations are not controlled by the state, but some receive limited financial grants from the federal government.[10]

Spain

The Federal Sports Association is in charge of all sports programs in Spain, and it offers financial assistance to all provinces to build sports facilities. The sports association works in cooperation with town councils, each assuming 50 per cent of the cost for providing sports facilities.

Madrid has some twenty sports facilities in operation. These sports centers are a complete sports complex with adequate acreage. The National Institute for Sports in Madrid is also one of the most modern institutes in Europe. This insti-

depends upon several agencies to help train its young people in outdoor activities.

The European physical fitness test, administered by the Minister of Youth Sports, is very popular with young people. This test is comprised of six events: one short race, shot-put, high jump, rope climbing, swimming, and a 1,000-meter run. A certificate is awarded to participants meeting established standards.

The French government has encouraged industry to build sports facilities and to sponsor amateur athletic teams. Some of the larger companies have built sports facilities and later donated them to the city.

[9] Ibid., p. 55.

[10] Ibid., p. 59.

Fig. 9-12 MOUNTAINEERING IN THE ALPS. Mountain climbing is a sport that demands physical fitness, technical knowledge, experience, and perfect equipment. There are numerous mountaineering clubs in Switzerland, Germany, and throughout Europe. (Courtesy of Bundesbildstelle, Bonn.)

tute has provided the leadership in the "Sports for All" campaign. Young married couples and families are encouraged to take part in the sports programs, with the motto: "Start together and grow together."[11]

Greece

In Greece, the International Olympic Committee provides the impetus for the planning and organization of physical fitness and sports. The Committee is responsible for the twenty-four sports federations, each of which has its own programs. The committee oversees the football lottery program and makes decisions for the disbursement of these funds. One of the aims of the committee is to build sports centers in all cities with populations of 1,500 or more.[12]

"The Greeks emphasize culture along with sport, perhaps more than any other country. Therefore, there is a cultural building in each sports center which consists of a library for sport, conference rooms, dining facilities, and living quarters."[13]

Greece has some private sports clubs for tennis, swimming, and gymnastics. Some adults participate in volleyball and gymnastics, but most prefer to take advantage of the environmental opportunities for sailing, swimming, fishing, hunting, or hiking.

Italy

The National Olympic Committee and the National Sports Federation are the two primary organizations working with physical fitness and sports in Italy. The National Sports Federation now supervises thirty-two sports federations, and two new federations in archery and handball. The most popular sports for adults are swimming, tennis, hunting, and fishing.[14]

Soviet Union

Rather extensive recreation services have been developed in the Union of Soviet Socialist Republics. Although leisure was enjoyed by only a small group for centuries, the Soviet Union today provides recreational opportunities for all age levels.

---

[11] Ibid., p. 64.
[12] Ibid., p. 66.
[13] Ibid., p. 66.

[14] Ibid., p. 69.

According to Richard Kraus, "Every aspect of Soviet life is regarded as part of a collective scheme to build national morale, improve health, and increase national productivity. The concept of leisure within the Soviet Union has been closely linked to the promotion of 'socialist discipline' and the development of communal solidarity and morality. Economic expansion in the Russian system has required stringent controls over all aspects of life, including the use of leisure time."[15]

Parks and play centers of rest and culture are located throughout the country, and during the past decade, there has been a building boom in parks for mass sports. The government has been very active in establishing vacation centers for families; for many of the Soviet people, vacations away from home are becoming a reality.

There are more than 100 state parks and hunting and game preserves in the Soviet Union, with a combined area of 17 million acres.

Directly adjoining the outskirts of Moscow is a 695-square-mile forest park belt, which serves as a place of recreation and helps keep the capital's air fresh. In zones like these, nature is carefully protected, even though there are such elements of civilization as sports facilities, beaches, and cafes. The forest park belt has many old mansions turned into museums, as well as places in which major historical events took place, the Borodino battlefield, for example.[16]

The recreation areas near Moscow have very diversified landscapes, much like those of Russia's temperate zone generally. As a result, Moscow citizens who go away for the weekend have a wide choice of activity even in winter. They can downhill or cross-country ski or adventure into the wilderness.

The choice is even more varied during the summer season—fishing, hikes, canoe trips, berry and mushroom-picking excursions. The local bodies of water in Moscow's forest park zone have about fifty varieties of fish. There is also excellent hunting, with hunting seasons and quotas observed very strictly, however.

Moscovites use their own cars, electric trains and buses for weekend travel. The network of suburban transport routes is very good. Large enterprises regularly organize group excursions using chartered city buses. On weekends, about four million people, half of the capital's population, travel out to the forests near Moscow.[17]

An extensive youth movement (for ages from seven to twenty-five) is under state direction. Children belong to the Pioneers organization which offers numerous recreation activities but its primary purpose is political indoctrination. Along with thousands of camps for children and youth, there are over 3,000 Pioneer Youth Palaces or centers. When the Soviet youth reach their teens, they join the *Komsomol,* or party cell.

Characteristically, the Soviet Union is known for its excellence in cultural activities. State-sponsored activity in the arts includes opera, ballet, concerts, legitimate theatre, and circuses. The extremely popular Bolshoi Ballet receives a large annual grant from the government for millions of rubles.

The primary emphasis of the Soviet government regarding leisure and recreation is in the field of sports and physical culture. Russians view physical education and sports as a necessity in "developing national strength, unity, and prestige."[18]

When the work day is over, industrial and office workers by the thousands join students, engineers, farmers, and other sports lovers in crowding the country's gymnasiums, stadiums, courts, and water-sports areas.

RECREATION IN ASIA AND THE FAR EAST

Traditionally, recreation in Asia has come through the home, religion, private clubs, and great national festivals. With the exception of Japan, organized recreation as a governmental responsibility has had to cope with numerous problems. Overpopulation, poverty, and various industrial weak-

[15] Kraus, op. cit., p. 217.

[16] Kraus, "Queries from Readers," *Soviet Life,* April 1973, no. 4, p. 17.

[17] Ibid.

[18] Kraus, op. cit., p. 219.

nesses are some of the serious problems that have prevented many nations from developing their full recreation and leisure potential. Still, significant progress is taking place as the various countries strive for social betterment and international prestige.

Japan

A powerful economy and a high standard of living, along with a reduction in working hours for many of its people, have resulted in a recreation boom in Japan. The traditional combative sports activities of the ancient *samurai* still enjoy strong popularity, such as *kendo* (fencing), *judo,* and *sumo.* Along with baseball, *sumo*—a form of wrestling involving athletes with immense weight—is today the most popular spectator sport in Japan. Boxing and wrestling are other combative sports which have been popular. Baseball has grown to such an extent that the Japanese are now providing strong competition with major league teams in America.

There has been a phenomenal market for baseball and other sports equipment in Japan. The sporting goods sections of Japanese stores provide a great variety of equipment and gadgets for use in games and sports.

Golf in Japan, with its 500 courses, now ranks fifth in the world, although only a small per cent of the facilities are public.

Extensive travel and the use of the out-of-doors for hiking, sightseeing, skiing, and boating can be attributed to the excellent transportation system in Japan.

The cultural arts of music, drama, crafts, and arts have tremendous interest among the Japanese. Avid lovers of beauty, the Japanese have a tremendous interest in such arts and crafts as sculpture, painting, ivory carving, and metal work. Music in Japan is a combination of oriental and western melodies.

Numerous cultural recreation activities are still practiced in Japan, largely developed in connection with Buddhism and the native Japanese religions. The Japanese people have a great interest in festivals that are held either at Shinto or Buddhist temples. These festivals have been popular religious events from earliest times and people

Fig. 9-13 COMBATIVE SPORTS. The traditional sports activities of the ancient *samurai*, such as *judo, kendo,* and *sumo,* are tremendously popular in Japan. Japanese judoists are among the best in the world. Judo has grown to be a very popular international recreational sport.

have also used the occasions as a form of recreation.

National Sport Day is celebrated as a holiday on October 10 when huge demonstrations are conducted in stadiums and schools throughout the country. "Children play with bales, hoops, and wands; oldsters in white perform gymnastic skills; and kimono-clad ladies fluttering their fans move with grace through beautifully rhythmical dance patterns."[19]

India

Much of the present recreation services in India are still provided by private or voluntary organiza-

[19] Marjorie A. Potter, "Recreation in Asia," *Parks and Recreation,* November 1970, pp. 45–46.

tions, such as the Boy Scouts or YMCA. Festivals and village fairs have in the past been enthusiastically supported in the smaller communities, with local citizens enjoying dancing, music, and traditional games and events. Industrialization and urbanization, however, have resulted in a general decline of these local forms of play, and many have been replaced with large stadiums and other facilities involving mass sports and cultural activities.

There has been a trend toward the establishment of a number of recreation centers in Indian cities under national subsidy. Eventually, the Indian government intends to "provide sports and recreation centers in towns and villages throughout the country. These will include libraries and cultural programs to maintain interest in traditional Indian customs and folkways."[20]

For many years, Balkan-ji-Bara, the all-India children's organization, has been active in the promotion of playground programs and other leisure opportunities for children and youth. In addition, an Indian Recreation Association has been created to promote recreational development and train leadership, with particular emphasis on industrial and urban populations.[21]

Republic of China (Taiwan)

There is a growing need in the Republic of China today for the nation "to balance the lives of its people by promoting recreation to offset the exhausting demands of a society striving to progress."[22]

The major responsibility for recreation rests with the Recreation Activity Society of the Republic of China. The Chinese Youth Anti-Communists and National Salvation Corps is a dominant youth organization that is popular with young people. "In addition to its nationalistic endeavor, recreation is a primary aim of the Corps which organizes clubs and activities during vacations,

such as horseback riding, car driving, explorations, art, camping, and physical training."[23]

Recreation is on the increase all through Taiwan, and major recreation centers are in the planning stages.

As tourism grows in popularity, the Tourism Bureau has taken the responsibility for cleaning scenic spots and building structures and attractions. There are many beautiful parks and fountains in Taipei, the capital city. Many of these parks feature rest pavilions of striking Oriental design.[24]

People's Republic of China

Like those of Soviet Russia, all forms of recreational and sports activity in Communist China has been used to promote national propaganda and social control.

The Chinese have made strong progress in the field of sports since it began a sports build-up in the 1950s.

> The government has subsidized the entire project, spending billions of dollars for schools, facilities, stadiums, training, and equipment. And China has become sports-minded, with 65 million athletes, huge crowds jamming the big new arenas for athletic events and a widespread eagerness for physical fitness.[25]

The major sports in the People's Republic of China include track and field, table tennis, swimming, soccer, speed skating, and weightlifting. Similar to Soviet Russia, Communist China's approach to leisure is that all forms of recreation must contribute to national goals and be under the direct control of the Republic.

Thailand

National sports such as Thai boxing, kite flying, *takraw* (played with a hollow woven rattan ball

---

[20] Kraus, op. cit., p. 229.

[21] Ibid.

[22] Potter, op. cit., pp. 50–51.

[23] Ibid.

[24] Ibid.

[25] Wolf Lyberg, "Communist China Bidding for Athletic Supremacy," *New York Times*, 16 January, 1966.

Fig. 9-14 SING-OUT ASIA. An enthusiastic group of young men and women from Asia express by song their dreams and hopes for the future. Sing-out groups from the Far West and America made extensive world tours during the 1960s and early 1970s.

kept aloft), and sword fighting are still highly popular in Thailand. Western types of recreational sports also have developed to such a degree that the Thais won the 1968 U.S. Open Badminton Championships.

Bowling has gained strong popularity over the past decade as have hunting and aquatic sports. Sightseeing is another leisure-time activity which has enjoyed increasing interest among the Thai people.

Interschool track and field competition on all levels takes place at local playgrounds and stadiums. The programs have achieved such national prominence that the King is present at the opening day of these competitions.

Hong Kong

Patterns of leisure have changed to a remarkable degree in Hong Kong. More than 1,200 acres of land now provide a series of attractive parks and playgrounds, swimming pools, and safe bathing beaches where many thousands of the colony's dense population may relax. Each year, over a million people use the public swimming facilities which have been bolstered by the development of elaborate swimming complexes in some of Hong Kong's congested urban areas.

The range of facilities has been broadened to include more tennis courts, boating pools, running tracks, putting greens, and outdoor television, in addition to conventional facilities for soccer, basketball, and volleyball.

RECREATION IN SOUTH AMERICA

Recreation and parks have introduced whole new industries in South America, in addition to enhancing the quality and enjoyment of life. In recent years, there has been a considerable development of sports arenas and playgrounds throughout South America. Argentina, Brazil, Ecuador, and Peru are four Latin American countries that have established national recreation associations.

> In the smallest village in South American countries, one can always find the playfield crowded on Saturday afternoons and Sundays with the local teams competing in their brilliantly collored uniforms. Every boy has a try at soccer, some dreaming of joining the big professional teams that play at the great city stadiums, like the world's largest in Rio de Janeiro (capacity of 200,000) or those in Sao Paulo and Porto Alegre.
>
> Next to soccer, music is, perhaps, the most popular leisure pastime in South America, either in songs, usually gay and at a fast tempo, or from a variety of instruments. Radio is among the major sources of recreation, especially since the appearance of the small portable transistorized sets which are owned by even the poorest workers.[26]

Basketball, volleyball, hiking, rowing, and table tennis are also well-liked. And in the last ten years, tourism has enjoyed a great boost due to the extraordinary growth of the automobile industry, a trend that resulted in the development of modern highways.

Brazil

The people of Brazil and other South American countries go to modern stadiums to watch the popular soccer games and other sports attractions, view television, attend the movies, become members of sports and cultural clubs, and visit the national parks.

To a great many of its citizens, leisure time in Brazil means endless hours of playing cards or talking around a coffee or bar table. There is also fishing, singing at open-air parties, dancing, and swimming in the rivers, artificial lakes, and at the coastal beaches. There is also the rodeo, the country fair, and the circus for entertainment. And, of course, there is Carnival, a four-day festival of masquerade balls, parades, singing, and samba demonstration schools.

Argentina

Generally, Argentinians patronize their parks and support conservation. The Argentine National Park Service receives 7.5 per cent of the revenue from the new national lottery.

Argentina's Nahuel Huapi, the world's first privately donated national park, protects nearly two million acres of trout-filled lakes, dense forests, and vaulting Andean mountains. Granted 25,000 acres by Argentina for settling a border dispute, Moreno dedicated the land in 1903 as the nucleus of today's public park. "The forests of Nahuel Huapi are fascinating," wrote Mary and Lawrence Rockefeller. "Curious orange-barked arrayan trees reminded me of the setting for Walt Disney's motion picture Bambi. Nearby stands a plantation of California coast redwoods, now grown thirty to forty-five feet high since their introduction here some seventy years ago."[27] In recent years, Nahuel Huapi, with its excellent skiing, has begun to become an international winter tourist attraction.

With its 150 parks and public gardens, Buenos Aires offers more open space than any other city. "Palermo Park brings lakes and an elaborate rose plantation to the heart of Argentina's vibrant capital and port city. Ardent park users flock to bridle paths, outdoor theater, race track, polo fields, and a golf course in Palermo's 1,100 acres lining the Rio de la Plata."[28]

The Buenos Aires YWCA, oldest in South America, was founded in 1890 as a hostel for English working girls, then became firmly established for local citizens. Today, the YWCA trains volunteers in social work, holds classes in adult education that range from volleyball to flower arranging, and works actively with children in redevelopment areas.

---

[26] Ethel Bauzer Mederiros, "Brazil, Land of Contrasts," *Parks and Recreation*, April 1970, pp. 36–37.

[27] Mary and Lawrence Rockefeller, "Parks, Plans, and People," *National Geographic,* 131, no. 1 (January 1967): 91–93.

[28] Ibid., p. 99.

Fig. 9-15 THE BEAUTY OF CANADIAN PARKS. As parks in Canada continue to enjoy unparalleled growth and popularity, all levels of government are placing greater emphasis on recreation and leisure time services. This magnificent scene is Maligne Lake in Jasper National Park, Alberta. (Courtesy of Canadian Parks/ Recreation Association.)

Uruguay

In proportion to size, Uruguay has more area (300,000 acres) of planted forests than any other South American country. Every tree was planted by private concerns, with no government subsidy of any kind.

The Uruguayan Government has set aside a fifty-two-square-mile area in Cabo Polonio as a wildlife preserve and park. The rocks offshore are a natural habitat for sea lions.

Almost half the 2,500,000 Uruguayans live in Montevideo, the capital, which claims the largest YWCA membership of any city in South America.

RECREATION IN CANADA

The rapidly growing recreation and park developments of Canada are following a pattern similar to the recreation movement in the United States. As Canadian parks enjoy increasing use, the local, provincial, and national governments of Canada continue to place greater emphasis on recreation and leisure-time services.

The national park system in Canada has been expanded through the addition of ten new national parks during the last six years, an addition of 18,500 square miles, bringing the total to twenty-nine national parks.

The city of Edmonton is unique in Canada and North America. With a population in excess of 400,000, it has 6,600 acres of parkland—better than 15 acres for every 1,000 citizens.

The creative playground movement is quickly becoming established in Canada. Similar to the adventure playgrounds in Europe and the United States, these new play environments are built with cheap, easily available materials and are being developed with increasing emphasis in metropolitan areas such as Toronto.

157

Fig. 9-16 ICE FISHING. The annual Ottawa Winter Carnival Ice Fishing Derby is held in February at Britannia Bay. Ice fishing is extremely popular in Canada. (Courtesy of Canadian Parks/Recreation Association.)

Bicycling has proven extremely popular as commuters both bicycle to work and participate in recreational cycling on weekends. Over thirty miles of bike trails were created in 1971 and 1972 throughout the national capital region around Ottawa.

The Canadian Symposium of Recreation held in 1967 helped to create an awareness and interest in the importance of leisure. One of the most important conclusions of the symposium was that a national approach to leisure cannot be achieved by the piecemeal efforts of hundreds of organizations and agencies working in their own limited and isolated way. Instead, there is a need for a strong cooperative effort by all groups involved in recreation, both public and private.

Significant developments are taking place in Canada which are steering this rapidly growing nation on a new and positive course in the recreation field. The Montmorency Conference in 1969 established basic principles and objectives to serve as a basis for designing policies and programs.

According to Louis J. D'Amore, president of Leisure Consultants, Ltd., "Organizational integration is taking shape with four provinces now having a sports federation which includes all the sports governing bodies of these respective provinces. There is a strong possibility that "Sports Canada" will be formed in the not too distant future. And hopefully there will be a Department of Leisure in the federal government by the end of this decade."[29]

The Canadian Parks and Recreation Association has been a major force in encouraging and stimulating dialogue and communications. The association sponsors conferences and seminars, encourages the development of research programs, and acts as an information center for data and studies related to parks and recreation. *Recreation Canada,* featuring many articles on "the growing recreation movement in Canada," is published bi-monthly by the association. Subscriptions may be obtained by writing Art Drysdale, Editor, 40 Hopedale Avenue, Toronto, 355, Ontario, Canada.

RECREATION IN MEXICO

A traditional spectacle in Mexican life, bullfighting continues to maintain its popular appeal. Nevertheless, the new generation is turning more and

---

[29] Louis J. D'Amore, "Recreation in Other Lands," *Parks and Recreation,* April 1970, pp. 46–47.

more to football (called soccer in the United States), baseball, and basketball as recreational outlets.

Contrary to the general trend in the United States, the emphasis in Mexican sports is primarily on the amateur. In many Mexican cities, a Sunday morning finds thousands of people engaging in ball games.

On the professional level, *jai alai*, a court game of Basque origin, has an almost fanatical following at the Fronton Mexico in Mexico City. There is great interest among the spectators for betting.

The carnival in Mazatlan is one of the biggest pre-Lenten celebrations in Mexico, with a fireworks display, three parades, two grand balls, and a bullfight.

Mexico City's racetrack, Hipodromo de las Americas, is one of the most lavish in the world, with races held almost the year-round.

RECREATION IN AUSTRALIA AND NEW ZEALAND

The governments of Australia and New Zealand offer many opportunities for the enjoyment of parks and recreation activities.

Australia

The people of Australia enjoy abundant health and vigor; with ample leisure and increasing affluence, recreation and leisure time are increasing in scope and participation.

The recreation horizon in recent years has been broadened and enriched by parks, camping facilities, playgrounds, and youth and adult services. The community use of physical education school sportsgrounds and gymnasiums by approved community groups is an indication of this enlightened approach to community recreation.

The Australian Institute of Parks and Recreation has played a very effective role in creating public interest in the development and use of Australian parklands for public recreation. The institute publishes *The Australian Parks Journal*, conducts conferences and seminars for park administrators, and keeps the public aware of the importance of parks.

Fig. 9-17 AN ANIMAL HABITAT IN NEW ZEALAND. The trail up the Reis Valley makes an excellent walk for a family "to the old mine." Virginian deer were liberated in this valley. (Courtesy of the New Zealand Forest Service.)

New Zealand

With an English sporting heritage, New Zealand offers abundant recreational opportunities. The people of New Zealand are more likely to be participants than spectators in sports and strenuous exercise. Sports participation is heavy, and local playfields are available to nearly everyone. Bowls and cricket are popular choices for the young and old. Television viewing is minimal in New Zealand.

During the last two decades, recreation in New Zealand has made rapid strides as a form of public service. Technologically advanced, with a small population, New Zealand's high standard of living has afforded its citizens an increasing number of recreation and leisure-time opportunities.

Much effort had been made in New Zealand to help promote participation in recreation. Involvement in recreation has become the active concern of many, including government, local governments, and non-government agencies in the field of recreation.

Annual grants from government funds for national schemes are made through the Department of Internal Affairs to such organizations as the National YMCA and YWCA, the National Youth Council, National Council of Churches, and

159

Fig. 9-18 ADVENTURE PLAYGROUND. Play facilities like these are being built at elementary school sites and parks throughout New Zealand. (Courtesy of the Auckland Regional Authority.)

other groups. Other government departments which do or can contribute directly or indirectly to the recreational scene are Education, Lands and Survey, Maori and Island Affairs, Tourist, Forestry, and the Ministry of Defense. Legislation allows local authorities to raise loans and spend money to provide recreation facilities.[30]

Through the schools of New Zealand, the Education Department is responsible for educating people to use their leisure wisely and thus contribute to their own individual growth.

RECREATION IN AFRICA

Starting in the early 1960s, a large-scale organization of sports development has taken place in many countries in Africa, particularly those blessed with oil and rich natural resources.

In Libya, for example, both Tripoli and Benghazi provide regional and international sports programs involving basketball, volleyball, handball, football, swimming, wrestling, tennis, golf, sailing, and other facilities. However, there has been less progress at the lower end of the sports scale. According to Don Anthony, "There is a need for a stronger effort to improve teaching and facilities. The pre-school conditions for play must also be revolutionized, for there is an absence of playgrounds for infants and juniors."[31]

Sports clubs are in need of improvement in Africa. The "multi-activity" club is most appropriate to the people of Africa. This kind of club provides for the whole family and includes lectures on health, literacy, social problems, and the arts, as well as sports activities.

Some of the most magnificent national parks in the world have been preserved by African countries. These include the world-famous Kruger National Park in the Union of South Africa, and Victoria Falls in Rhodesia. Kenya, Uganda, Algeria, the Congo, Tanzania, and other African countries today maintain national parks.

[30] John G. Hutchinson, "Government Involvement in Recreation," *Recreation in New Zealand* (Auckland, New Zealand: Auckland Regional Authority, 1971), pp. 11–12.

[31] Don Anthony, "Libya, the Role of Sports," *Parks and Recreation*, April 1970, p. 38.

Whatever the style, most countries find that, indirectly, parks more than pay for themselves. In Kenya, where game reserves are emphasized, tourists attracted by the lions and elephants spend about $25 million there each year. Annual park maintenance costs only $420,000.

UNITED ARAB REPUBLIC

Perhaps the most significant development of recreation facilities in Egypt has been the emphasis on centers for physical activity and sports, as well as social service clubs. In these centers, leadership and instruction is provided in gymnastic skills, swimming rhythms, weight lifting, and other physical activities. In addition, programs in music and dramatics are offered to help people improve their skills and to provide wholesome use of leisure time.

One of the most dramatic features of the Higher Physical Training Institute at Abukir, near Alexandria, is the art studio and music and drama center. Outside the large cities, however, recreational and cultural facilities such as television, cinema, theatre, libraries, museums, music halls, and other entertainment media are very meager.

ISRAEL

Much of the public recreation in Israel is provided by the Sports and Physical Education Authority in the Ministry of Education and Culture. The Israeli government has encouraged strong emphasis on mass sports and activities rather than spectator sports. The physical vigor of the nation has been well maintained, undoubtedly an asset in the nation's crises with Arab countries.

Israeli athletes have distinguished themselves ably in sports competition internationally. They have been aided by strong promotion efforts from the Maccabi Sport Organization, the Hapoel Association, and other athletic groups.

Popular recreation activities in Israel include folk dancing, sports and games, gymnastics, mountain climbing, sharp shooting, wrestling, boxing, and other combative sports.

While some parks and youth activities are sponsored by local government agencies, most of the recreational activities appear to be conducted by the schools.

ETHIOPIA

In the past centuries, many games have found their way into the cultural lives of the Ethiopian people. Most of these old games are played during the religious holidays. The most popular of these games is *genna,* a form of field hockey played during the Christmas season.

In recent years, many new sports have been introduced in Ethiopia. During the Italian occupation in World War II, soccer was played and is now the most popular organized sport in the country. Today, there are over 4,000 soccer players from nearly 200 soccer clubs registered with the federation.

The National Ethiopian Sports Federation is responsible for the coordination and promotion of sports. Since 1949 when it was chartered, the confederation has formed federations in many sports, starting with soccer in 1961 and followed by cycling, basketball, boxing, track and field, and most recently, volleyball. Most of the sport federations hold national championships. The weekend brings Saturday league volleyball or Sunday federation soccer at Haile Selassie I Stadium in the capital city.

IRAN

Generally, sports participation in Iran is through affiliation with a sports club. Separate sports clubs exist for boys and for girls, and members tend to specialize in one activity.

Even in remote rural areas or disadvantaged areas of Iranian cities and villages, young people are enthusiastic about sports. Typically, children and youth in these areas engage in spirited contests of volleyball and soccer with meager equipment such as sticks for goals or a rope for a net, and an improvised ball.

The backbone of the organization of sports in Iran is interclub competition. Athletes display extreme loyalty to their sports clubs, and competition is held between clubs located within a city or in neighboring localities.

Sports in which competition is sponsored in Iran include: basketball, cycling, fencing, gymnastics, skiing, soccer, swimming, tennis and table tennis, track and field, volleyball, weight lifting, and wrestling.

INTERNATIONAL VOLUNTARY ORGANIZATIONS

Many voluntary organizations, national and international, have made significant contributions to improving international relations and goodwill through recreation.

Where When
International Recreation Association

The work of the International Recreation Association has been outstanding in the world of international recreation cooperative efforts. Since the period after World War II, the IRA has been "the only agency solely concerned with the problems and potentials of a truly world-wide recreation service."[32]

Among the objectives of the association are to:

• Serve as a central clearing house for the exchange of information and experience among recreation agencies of the world.
• Aid countries to establish central recreation service agencies upon request.
• Forward the development of a world recreation movement designed to enrich the human spirit through wholesome use of leisure.
• Encourage the provision of land and facilities, training of leaders, development of varied programs, and public interpretation of the values of play for children, recreation for youth, and creative use of leisure for all ages.

• Provide a medium through which the recreation authorities of the world may work in unity on one of the common problems of man.[33]

The IRA, in its first years of existence, was given financial assistance by the National Recreation Association. Today, contributions and memberships are its chief source of funds. Through its consultive services and the IRA Bulletin, it has promoted recreation in over 100 countries.

International Youth Hostel Federation

Youth hostel associations in nearly forty countries are affiliated with the International Youth Hostel Federation. For many young people, hostels have provided the opportunity to see a country and get acquainted with its people.

A youth hostel provides low-cost dormitory and cooking accommodations, primarily for members who walk, cycle, or canoe from place to place. The hostels are centers not only for overnight stays but for making friends, singing songs, exchanging experiences, and learning about the customs, history, and scenic attractions of a country.

The youth hostel movement originated in Germany in 1910, when Richard Schirrmann, a German school teacher, began taking his students on walking trips. Although the early hostels were used primarily by school children, today older youth and young adults on vacation also enjoy hosteling.

Indeed, youth hosteling has been a significant force for the development of international understanding, giving youth from many countries the opportunity to mingle and exchange points of view.

Other Voluntary Organizations

The major youth-serving organizations are affiliated internationally. The Boy Scouts World Bureau, the World Association of Girl Guides and

---

[32] Meyer, Brightbill, and Sessoms, op. cit., pp. 165–66.

[33] Thomas E. Rivers, "The Launching of the International Recreation Association," *Recreation*, January 1957, p. 21.

Girl Scouts, the World Alliance of YMCA's, and the World YWCA are outstanding examples of world affiliation. International conferences, camps, training courses, and workshops are attended by the members of these organizations. These exchanges of information and discussions lead to better understandings and thus strengthen the respective organizations.

The American Red Cross is affiliated with the International Red Cross, and settlement houses in America are members of the International Federation of Settlements. Some service clubs and civic organizations are affiliated internationally, such as Rotary International, which has clubs in 120 countries. In addition, there are international organizations for all major sports, including basketball, bowling, boxing, golf, tennis, skiing, and archery.

INTERNATIONAL GAMES AND CONTESTS

International competition in sports and games has been enthusiastically received in nations throughout the world. The Olympic Games, of course, have drawn the greatest acclaim among international events, with athletes from all over the world living and competing in a setting designed to improve international understanding and respect. Although the Olympics have produced many positive and rewarding aspects, in recent years a growing number of problems have threatened the games' existence.

There are, however, other ways in which athletes can participate in international competition. Touring teams move from country to country, while special tournaments, exhibitions, and demonstrations enable athletes of various countries to compete against each other.

UNITED NATIONS

Many agencies of the United Nations have been placing greater emphasis on the leisure needs of their people. The United Nations Educational, Scientific, and Cultural Organization (UNESCO) has held many international meetings relative to youth services and recreation. Through international visits and exchange of ideas, UNESCO has been effective in fostering mutual appreciation of cultural values.

The European Centre for Leisure and Education was established in 1968 on the initiative of UNESCO and the Czechoslovak Academy of Sciences as a coordination and documentation center for the research and theoretical study of leisure in European countries. In connection with the general direction of its work given by the resolution of the conference of UNESCO held in Prague in 1966, the European Centre gives special attention to the possibility of educational utilization of leisure and qualitative aspects of leisure.

In the United States, professional training of leaders has been an important factor in the growth of public park and recreation services. Acceptance of this concept in other countries, however, has been relatively recent. Australia, Belgium, Canada, Germany, Great Britain, India, Japan, New Zealand, Singapore, Thailand, and Vietnam, among others, have established training programs.

III

Serving the Community

10

Recreation and the Community

As American life becomes more and more leisure-oriented, the number of settings that provide recreation opportunities and services continue to increase. While each setting or surrounding is involved with its own unique contribution, all exist primarily to meet the needs of the public at large. As the use of leisure time becomes more diverse, society cannot expect governmental and tax-supported agencies to provide all the recreational needs of a community.

Although government is involved with functions that are of broad concern to the entire population, there are many other groups and agencies that are meeting the needs of a particular segment of the population. The home, church, school, industry, voluntary, and private organizations are assuming a greater role in a rapidly growing society.

Indeed, more and more agencies are making valuable contributions to the organized recreation movement—contributions that have resulted in higher goals and standards in our use of leisure time. Although voluntary organizations may have more specialized purposes and a somewhat more independent policy, they also have a strong sense of values and social purpose.

The purposes of private and commercial recreation agencies are not as unselfish. Private organizations are primarily concerned with the recreational and social wishes of their members; commercial enterprises are essentially out to make a profit. By establishing cooperative relationships with these agencies, however, the public recreation authorities can help raise the standards of commercial recreation, thus assuring a higher quality of service for their citizens.

Although many opportunities may be found in commercial recreation settings, it is usually only the public recreation and park department or the comprehensive voluntary agency that offers a full range of opportunities at a cost reasonable enough for all to pay.

Quite often, recreational opportunities will involve an interlocking of more than one setting or form of recreation service. For example, a single form of leisure participation may cut across several types of sponsorship. An enthusiast of recreation vehicles can be involved with several types of sponsors:

Fig. 10-1 SCHOOL RECREATION . The school is playing an increasing role in providing recreation services and opportunities. Here, a community-school–sponsored after-school program offers team competition for these young fifth- and sixth-grade boys.

Fig. 10-2 VACATION PARADISE. An increasing number of groups and settings are making valuable contributions to the organized recreation movement. Many companies and labor unions are providing vacation and resort sites for their employees and families, like Konocti Harbor Inn at beautiful Clear Lake in northern California.

1. *Commercial*—Purchase a four-wheel drive jeep.
2. *Voluntary*—Be a member of the California Association of 4-WD Clubs.
3. *Private*—Belong to a private club and use its facilities.
4. *Government*—Use publicly owned desert and wasteland.

A variety of other types of sponsors provide recreation programs in the community. These include Boys Clubs, settlement houses, industrial recreation agencies, religiously affiliated agencies, anti-poverty groups, and many local and national organizations serving the handicapped.

In the years ahead, the resources of all kinds of recreation agencies and settings will be needed to serve the increasing leisure-time needs and the growing demand for challenging recreation activities and programs.

THE FAMILY

Traditionally, the home has been the center of entertainment for the family. However, during the

> ALL ORGANIZATIONS—PRIVATE, VOLUNTARY, AND PUBLIC—MUST BECOME VIABLE AND PARTICIPATING FORCES IN THE LEISURE MOVEMENT TO MEET THE BURGEONING RECREATION NEEDS OF OUR PEOPLE.
>
> Editorial, *Parks and Recreation*

past quarter of a century, there has been a definite tendency for the family to be drawn away from the home. In many American homes, in fact, there are few meals when all members of the family are present.

Parents who seldom or never play with their children rarely know them completely. Joy and happiness are basic needs that should be satisfied in childhood if the child is to grow normally and become a well-adjusted adult. Consequently, new ways are urgently needed to re-establish the authority and importance of the family. There should be a strong emphasis on services that will strengthen parents and aid the family as a whole. Giving families a chance to perform as families, to mingle with other families, and to learn from

Fig. 10-3 PLAY AND RECREATION involving children and their parents can contribute immeasurably to better family relationships and happiness. Here, a mother and her daughters enjoy a "Game of Life."

them should be one of the major goals of organizations and agencies in the community. "One of the greatest potentials for involving adults with children lies in play and recreation," stated Ruth Tefferteller. "Arousing parental interest in the children's activities through mutual participation in dances, outings, and parties helped a child to build a community of parents and families around these children. This has contributed enormously to the improved behavior of the individual children and of their groups."[1]

Modern living has tended to take people away from their homes, but the home is still the chief recreation center of millions of American families. The sharp increase in the sale of recreational equipment and products has brought about a growing trend to make the home a family recreational center.

Activities at Home

Many activities can be conducted at home, in a game room or in the yard. Table tennis, badminton, and shuffleboard are popular sports suitable for the backyard or driveway. Basketball hoops can be attached easily to a garage. Children can learn to catch and throw baseballs and footballs in the yard or at a nearby playground. A multiple sports area in an ordinary backyard can include a basketball hoop, a solid wall for throwing or hitting against, an open area for croquet, a portable Ping Pong table, and badminton posts.

Family recreation does not mean that the entire family must participate in each activity. However, there should be a proper balance of activity and participation in the family recreation program.

With its many skills for developing programs and techniques that can build group strength and solidarity, the recreation and parks field is in a position to design new types of family-oriented programs to help strengthen family life.

Family Home Evening

There are many people who declare that the family is passé. Groups such as the Church of Jesus Christ of Latter-Day Saints, however, have strengthened family solidarity through such activities as the Monday night get-together in members' homes called "Family Home Evenings." These are times when Mormon families pray, sing, play games together, and share refreshments.

[1] Ruth S. Tefferteller, "Recreation and Family Needs," *Recreation*, November 1963, p. 423.

Family Recreation Scoresheet

To determine their day-by-day recreation needs, families can use the following checklist to promote better family relationships through recreation. Mark an item your family participates in together "plus"; mark items your family does not do together "minus." If you marked more items "minus," you are missing a lot in life. If you had a greater number of "plus" items you are building up a family reserve of happiness.

1. Some form of social recreation, such as playing games together, visiting friends, going on a picnic, etc.
2. Some form of physical recreation, such as playing any active game, walking or hiking, romping with the children, etc.
3. Art, such as painting, wood carving, visiting a museum, etc.
4. Handcrafts
5. Music
6. Dance
7. Drama
8. Storytelling and reading
9. Hobbies
10. Nature and science

THE SCHOOL

The importance and value of school recreation are becoming more apparent as the need for well organized and diversified recreational programs becomes greater. Vast social and economic changes have had a significant effect on the school and on other community agencies. Our constantly changing society has had to cope with a multitude of new problems, including those created by increased leisure. As a result, schools today are faced with how to prepare people to live in a society in which their leisure hours may surpass their work hours.

Shorter working hours, automation, earlier retirements, and longevity of life are among the trends that make education for wise use of leisure time a priority need if we are to remain a strong and prosperous nation. "In a nation where leisure constitutes more than half of the waking hours of its citizens," said Howard Danford, "there can be no possible justification for the failure of the schools to prepare young people for the creative use of their leisure time."[2]

Education for Leisure

The ability of every citizen to make wise leisure choices is most essential in a society becoming steadily leisure-oriented. The school joins with the home, church, and other agencies in assuming this very important role.

The education for leisure process should include:
1. The development of a sound philosophy of leisure.
2. The development of skills and knowledges that lead to the enjoyment of leisure activities.
3. The creation of desirable attitudes, interests, and habits toward recreation activities and enjoyment.
4. The development of wholesome personalized traits through recreation experiences.
5. Counseling in the wise use of leisure time.

The School's Responsibilities

The major responsibility of the school in the area of recreation is to educate students to the best use of their leisure time.

The school has the important task of helping students acquire lifelong interests, appreciations, and skills in a broad range of recreational activities. Opportunities should then be provided for them to use these acquired recreation skills. The schools have an important role of joining with other agencies in the community to provide a well-rounded community recreation program. "Education consists primarily of awakening and stimulating their creative faculties and providing opportunities for creative expression," wrote Howard Danford. "Whenever leisure is available, peo-

[2] Howard G. Danford and Max Shirley, *Creative Leadership in Recreation,* 2nd ed. (Boston: Allyn and Bacon, Inc., 1970), p. 23.

Fig. 10-4 EDUCATING FOR LEISURE. The development of skills and interests such as swimming can lead to the enjoyment of leisure activities. The advanced swimming class shown here was sponsored by the physical education division of the Los Angeles City Schools.

ple will choose for themselves those activities that are eminently satisfying to the nature of man."[3]

The school has the additional responsibility to provide opportunities in which the various recreation activities taught can be practiced, interests deepened, and skills perfected. Participation in intramural sports, club organizaton, and the provision of recreational equipment and facilities can provide further enjoyment of these interests.

School recreation involves a great many teachers who teach subjects in the areas of the recreation program. With all of its resources, therefore, the school can play and should play an ever increasing role in providing recreation services and opportunities. In carrying out this function, however, the school should not attempt to duplicate the efforts of other established recreation agencies. Instead, they should seek to coordinate the school's programs with those of other agencies in the community.

Schools can make available their valuable areas and facilities to the total community. School personnel represent some of the strongest sources of community leadership. Teachers can provide

valuable resources of skills and leadership that can be utilized in community recreation programs. If need exists, school authorities should take the initiative in developing a municipal recreation program.

The Community School Movement

The community education concept is one of the most significant developments in our educational system in the last decade. Because of it, schools have accepted a much broader sense of responsibility to the people of the community

Community education seeks to extend the role of the school from one of the traditional concept of teaching children to one of identifying the wants, needs, and problems of the community and assisting in the development of facilities, programs, and leadership toward the end of improving the entire community.[4]

---

[3] Ibid.

[4] Taken from a brochure of the California Center for Community School Development, a joint project of the California State University and the Charles Stewart Mott Foundation.

The concept of community education is based on the belief that given the opportunity to make fuller use of their schools, people will work together to improve themselves, their homes, and their community.

In meeting the needs and wants of people, the community school:

1. Makes its facilities and resources available to all age groups in the neighborhood community, both day and night and year round.
2. Mobilizes available human and financial resources of the community to meet the wants and needs of the people.
3. Provides the opportunity for people to come together to resolve their community problems.

History of the Community School

Known as the father of the community school concept, Frank J. Manley planted the seeds for many programs of community and human betterment in the areas of adult education, health, recreation, and job training.

His theory that school facilities should be used on a twenty-four-hour basis for the benefit of the entire community inspired philanthropist Charles Stewart Mott in 1935 to sponsor a summer recreation project which has grown into a concept of community education copied throughout the world.

"Those who knew him best say Manley's greatest talent was leadership, an almost indefinable combination of conviction and personality which inspired his staff and often the rest of the community to try things never tried before."[5]

For many years, the Mott Foundation has allotted funds to educational, health, and charitable projects. Before his death in 1973, Mr. Mott had given away more than $230 million, not counting his allocation of funds to the Mott Foundation.

Through workshops and a large intern program, Flint, Michigan, was made a laboratory for training educators to establish and operate community school programs throughout the nation.

Many universities in Michigan and other parts of the country are involved in training community school leaders and setting up community education programs in their areas.

Starting a New Community School

In order to start a new program, the community school director should:

- Know the philosophy of community schools as it is known and practiced in your community.
- Become acquainted with the city in general and the local school community in particular. Talk with community members at every opportunity, giving time to listen to their viewpoints.
- Arrange conferences with the superintendent, the principal and the custodians to establish schedules, room use, and programs. Attend meetings of the community school directors. Define particular duties and learn how each person fits into the whole plan.
- Know by name the school staff, both instructional and maintenance.
- Become acquainted with the children in the school district.
- Form an advisory or community council. Its duty is to advise the principal and community school director concerning desired programs and activities.
- Become familiar with both sides of any controversial issue that may arise.
- Set up the first program offerings carefully, basing them upon the needs and desires of those participating. Start with a small program and have it running successfully before expanding it.
- Plan with the directors, consultants, coordinators, and special staff assistants of each program division before setting up activities.
- Keep a building calendar and bulletin board showing date, time, and place of each activity.
- Assign rooms and provide equipment and supplies.
- Publicize the program through newspaper articles, television, and radio, via the communications department, as well as through notes carried home by children, school bulletins, personal contacts, and telephone calls.

---

[5] *The Flint Journal*, Booth Newspapers, Inc., Flint, Michigan, June 8, 1972, p. 1.

• Plan to greet the participants of the new program with friendliness and interest and be available for advice or help when needed.[6]

Concepts of Park-School Planning Program

The park-school concept involves cooperation between school and municipal authorities in the acquisition, development, and operation of properties designated for both school and municipal recreation use. Where cities have committed themselves to the park-school concept, development is usually done by one of the following methods:

1. Establishing a park area adjacent to an existing school and developing it for use by either agency.
2. Constructing a school near or even adjacent to an existing park to take advantage of the existing park land.
3. Making adjustments in building design.
4. Eliminating fences that divide parks and adjacent schools.
5. Master-planning school development and park development together, so that when a school is built, adjacent parkland is also purchased.

INDUSTRIAL RECREATION

Most industrial firms in the United States have recognized that company-sponsored recreation programs are good business. Industry discovered many years ago that involving the worker and his family in recreation activities can be an advantage to employees, the company, and the community.

Although employee recreation began during the nineteenth century, it was not until after World War II that rapid expansion of industrial programs actually took place. The leading organization in this field, the National Industrial Recreation Association, today serves over 875 major

companies that provide extensive recreation programs for their employees.

Organized by industry to assist in the development of employee recreation, the NIRA in 1967 estimated that "there were 1,000 full-time industrial recreation directors and 500 park and recreation center managers employed by industries throughout the United States."[7]

Industrial recreation programs should meet the needs and interests of the employees, their families, and even retired employees.

Participation helps the employee consume surplus energy, relieve pressure and emotions, fulfill instinctive drives and reflexes, compensate for frustration and escape from reality. Industrial recreation is of special significance as a means of dealing with specific problems of boredom, monotony, and morale, particularly with today's desk-bound employees.[8]

Values and Benefits

There are numerous values and benefits of a well organized employee recreation program, including the following:

1. Promoting employee efficiency.
2. Improving employer-employee relations.
3. Helping employees consume surplus energy and relieve pressure and emotions.
4. Boosting morale of both labor and management.
5. Providing incentive for employment, recruitment appeal.
6. Promoting greater employee stability and motivation.
7. Establishing good community relations and cooperation.

---

[6] Taken from the Community School Director's *Training Guide*, Flint, Michigan.

[7] Richard Kraus, *Recreation and Leisure in Modern Society* (New York: Appleton-Century-Crofts, 1971), p. 97.

[8] Sal J. Prezioso, "Industrial Recreation in America," address before Industrial Recreation Directors Association Luncheon, New York, April 25, 1968.

Program Administration

There are a number of ways in which the industrial recreation program is administered. Companies are continuing to place responsibility for managing recreation programs in the hands of employee associations.

In about three-fifths of the companies, the recreation program is administered by the employees themselves. Where activities are chiefly company-administered, the personnel department coordinates this function. Employee associations, with and without the assistance of recreation directors, administer nearly half the programs. Other company programs are administered by committees, mutual benefit associations, a community recreation program, a branch of the YMCA, a foundation, or a union.[9]

Only one-fourth of the companies employ a full-time recreation director, and another sixth have part-time directors who usually report to the personnel director or industrial relations director. The programs are financed by company and employee contributions as well as vending machine profits, fees and charges, and other revenue sources.

Program Activities

The present trend in industrial recreation appears to be toward programs involving active physical participation. There is an increasing interest in sports participation, even to such expensive activities as golf, boating, and skiing.

Most of the new activities emphasize wide participation for the workers and their families with emphasis on participating rather than being a spectator. Companies are now concentrating on overall employee physical fitness through weight control programs, sports, informal gymnasium activities, and health clubs.

Although sports of all kinds are very popular, music, dramatics, and social activities are also an important part of a well-conceived pro-

gram. Camping, outings, hunting, fishing, and trap and skeet shooting are popular activities.

A growing number of companies and labor unions are providing outdoor vacation and resort sites for their employees and families. Konocti Harbor Inn, located on the shores of beautiful Clear Lake in Northern California, is owned and operated by Local 38, a plumbers' union in the San Francisco area. In addition to the elaborate living, entertainment, and recreation facilities at Konocti Harbor Inn, a well-rounded activities program is offered. During the summer, many recreation activities are provided for all age groups. The regular day-time activities include sailing, swimming lessons, tennis instruction, arts and crafts, horseback riding, and fishing excursions. Evening activities feature bingo, movies, volleyball, minature golf, and boat cruises. The Lockheed Employees Recreation Club of Sunnyvale, California, provides one of the most outstanding industrial recreation programs in America. Club activities run almost around the clock, with schedules geared for both day and night shift members.

The lunch hour is an excellent time for recreational programs. A short but satisfying recreation period can refresh employees for the afternoon. Typical activities suitable for the lunch hour program include horseshoes, chess, pool, billiards, table tennis, volleyball, shuffleboard, craft projects, card games, music, movies, and variety shows. A library, reading room, and record listening room should also be available.

Camp programs for employees and their families are growing in popularity. The camp may be available for family use on a reservation basis, for weekend use, and, in some instances, for vacations. Travel clubs are exceedingly popular for ski trips, sports excursions, weekend tours, and vacations.

Industrial recreation leaders should encourage employees to choose their recreational activities wisely and to develop healthy attitudes toward the place of leisure in our society. Opportunities should be provided to learn and practice recreational skills.

A successful industrial recreation program requires stimulating ideas, dedication, and the ability to get employees involved. Above all, success lies in outstanding leadership. Qualified recrea-

---

[9] Ibid.

Fig. 10-5 CAMP LIFE GROWING IN POPULARITY. Many churches, youth organizations, industrial companies, and labor unions are operating camp sites for summer vacation and weekend use. Camp Konocti, on the shores of beautiful Clear Lake in northern California, offers a ten-week program.

tion directors are essential ingredients to any employee recreation program.

THE CHURCH

Recreation is assuming an increasingly important role in the programs of the American churches and religion institutions. Many are presently conducting well-rounded recreation programs for their members, and indications are that many more will be placing more emphasis on recreation services in the future.

Indeed, recreation under religious sponsorship has undergone dramatic changes during the last three decades. As a result, progressive religious leaders are recognizing that man's spiritual life cannot be separated from his physical, mental, and social life. Play and recreation can be a social force of great potential value for community life.

"Churches have in no way attempted to take the place of public recreation," explained J. Robert Ward, Minister of Christian Recreation for Second Ponce de Leon Baptist Church in Atlanta. "It would be folly to think that they could. They are attempting to supplement public recreation by bringing the Christian influence into all of recreational life. Neither the public nor the private sector of society can meet the demands of recreation opportunities now being required." [10]

In addition to having its own recreation program, the religious institution has responsibility to further the community recreation program. In doing so, it should cooperate with other community agencies in providing meaningful recreation opportunities of the quality and variety to meet community needs. Whenever possible, church facilities and equipment should be made available for community recreation activities.

The time has come for all churches and religious organizations to become directly involved with recreation and leisure services. "To achieve this goal, the church hierarchy should employ

---

[10] J. Robert Ward, "Recreation—The Church's Foreign Mission," *Georgian Recreator*, 1, no. 3 (June 1972): 11–19.

experienced recreation leaders, recruit trained volunteers and seek the counsel and guidance of the professional and lay organizations that are the spearheads of the leisure revolution."[11]

The Challenge of the Church

The majority of Americans are having increasing amounts of time available for leisure. According to Burt L. Anderson, "Leisure today may be a challenge or a threat, a hazard or an opportunity, a vice or a virtue, a bane or a blessing. Therefore, it is the challenge of the church to help individuals decide which it will be for them."[12]

One of the tasks of religious organizations is to develop a theology for leisure. "The church has a theology for the Word and just about everything else," explained Anderson, "but it does not yet have a seasonal and time-tested theology for leisure."[13]

Benefits.   The provision of meaningful leisure opportunities for church members and their families can be extremely beneficial to their well-being. Some of the specific benefits derived include:

1. Creating a stronger church fellowship.
2. Enlistment of new members.
3. Revitalizing church members not previously active.
4. Building character in the areas of cooperation, good sportsmanship, acceptance of responsibility.

Staff.   Large churches may be able to afford the services of a professionally qualified recreation director, but small churches may have to use part-time leadership and/or services of volunteers. In some communities, the municipal recreation department might employ a qualified leader to work with religious institutions.

---

[11] Editorial, "Recreation and the Church," *Parks and Recreation*, December 1969, p. 11.

[12] Burt L. Anderson, "The Church and Leisure," *California Parks and Recreation*, December 1971, p. 29.

[13] Ibid.

> THE KEY TO CHURCH RECREATION IS THE PROGRAM AND NOT THE FACILITY.

Ideally, each church should have a recreation committee to coordinate the recreation activities with the overall church program. The chairman of this committee could join with chairmen from other church recreation committees to create a central church recreation committee. This larger committee would represent the various churches in community recreation affairs.

Whenever necessary, the church might employ recreation leaders of its own, or join other churches in securing someone to organize and coordinate recreation activities for those churches represented on the committee. In providing a well-rounded program to the church groups involved, the leader should also train and use the services of volunteers. Training opportunities for volunteers should be provided by the church and should include sending representatives to recreation conferences and workshops.

Program.   The church program should be varied enough to meet the needs and interests of the entire congregation. Essentially, the number and types of activities offered in various faiths and denominations vary with the philosophy of the church, the leadership and facilities available, and the culture and mores of the community.

The following is a list of activities sponsored by religious groups:

1. Social recreation such as picnics, family nights, potluck suppers, game nights, banquets, bazaars, and dances.
2. Vacation Bible schools.
3. Fellowship groups, youth clubs, Scout programs, and adult interest clubs.
4. Sports activities such as softball, basketball, bowling, and volleyball.
5. Arts, crafts, and hobby workshops.
6. Camping, nature study, and other outdoor activities.
7. Study and discussion groups.
8. Volunteer community services.
9. Coffee houses for youth.
10. Cultural activities such as literature, music, and travel.

Fig. 10-6 COMMERCIAL VENTURES, such as this "fun center," are making important contributions to the worthwhile use of leisure. Exciting new rides like these are now popular attractions at America's many state fairs.

Many churches operate camp sites. An excellent example of one of California's finest church camps is Calvin Crest, a Presbyterian Conference Center managed jointly by the Presbyteries of San Joaquin and Stockton. Combining Christian education with an attractive outdoor setting and imaginative programming, Calvin Crest offers children from grades 4 through 8 such popular activities as horseback riding, log rafts, log rolling, swimming, nature crafts, fishing, climbing trees, archery, barbecues, and moonlight hikes.

Finance. The financial support for the recreation program usually comes from the church budget. Ideally, it should be the practice of the church to set aside funds and plan a budget for recreation.

The cost of church recreation activities in terms of personal effort and financial support, however, is more than repaid in terms of the spiritual values for which the church stands.

Financing might be done through the following methods:

1. The church budget.
2. Contributions through drives, campaigns, and pledges.
3. Collections, donations, and admission for special events.
4. Sponsorship by the men's club or a church society.

5. Fund-raising sales through such events as arts and crafts, drama, and musical programs.

COMMERCIAL RECREATION

Commercial recreation has made a major contribution in meeting the mass leisure needs of modern society. With more time on their hands and money to spend than ever before, Americans have been responsible for inflating the recreation and leisure industry into a business estimated at well over $140 billion annually. Unquestionably, commercial recreation is one of the most important and growing aspects of American culture today.

A recreation facility owned and operated for profit is classified as commercial recreation. Constituting one of the major areas of the recreation movement, commercial recreation involves a system of private enterprise in which the participant pays and the purveyor, hopefully, makes a profit.

Like other products and services in business, commercial recreation depends upon public demand. "If there is no demand, if there is no market, if there are no sales, there will be no profit and hence, eventually, no commercial recreation," explained Meyer, Brightbill, and Sessoms. "When the profit disappears, so does the commercial recreation enterprise."[14]

Commercial ventures of all kinds are making strong contributions to the worthwhile uses of leisure. Popular commercial recreation, businesses, and enterprises include theaters, concert halls, amusement parks, night clubs, billiard rooms, bowling establishments, spectator sports, and summer resorts. Sporting activities, outdoor recreation areas such as day camps and riding areas, recreational vehicles, and drama and music performances are additional examples of organized commercial enterprises that also offer constructive uses of leisure time.

In recent years, travel, private clubs, radio and television, and such professional sports as football, baseball, basketball, and racing have grown significantly as popular forms of commercial recreation.

The Scope of Commercial Recreation

Almost every activity and program in the recreation and leisure market has been commercialized. The areas listed below comprise a large portion of the leisure economy, but it should be noted that there are many other items in the commercial recreation field that will not be mentioned.

Recreation Equipment. The largest item in the leisure budget is recreational equipment, such as boats, camping vehicles, motor bikes, color television sets, snowmobiles, and surfboards. The purchase of products used in the pursuit of pleasure or relaxation has had a spectacular effect on the nation's economy.

Travel. Domestic pleasure travel is the second largest component of the leisure budget and includes vacation trips and overnight journeys. Travel abroad is attracting more and more Americans. In 1972, over six million Americans traveled abroad, spending $7.5 billion on their travels. Tourism has become a steadily rising business in countries throughout the world.

Outdoor Recreation. The rapidly increasing interest in camping has triggered a boom of its own. There are well over four million camping vehicles in the United States. The surge to the great outdoors has resulted in a huge market for travel trailers, motor homes, truck campers, and camping trailers. Self-powered motor homes have also been in great demand.

Vacation Homes. The desire to get away for long weekends has created a boom in vacation-land sales. Interest in vacation and holiday homes has resulted in a flourishing market for land. According to the American Land Development Association, a trade group, there are now 9,000 vacation-land-development firms in the United States. The ALDA estimates that the industry sold 650,000 lots in 1971, valued at $5.5 billion. "The cost is high because more and more developers are offering

---

[14] Harold D. Meyer, Charles K. Brightbill, and H. Douglas Sessoms, *Community Recreation* (Englewood Cliffs, N.J.: Prentice-Hall, Inc., 1969), p. 282.

special amenities for community use, such as club-houses, riding stables, tennis courts, marinas, swimming pools, private beaches, and ski slopes."[15]

Sales of recreational housing were expected to surpass $1.8 billion in 1972. These vacation homes are of many kinds: A-frames, condominium apartments, town houses, factory-made prefab units, and standard year-round models.

New Towns. The organization and building of new towns has improved the quality of life for millions of the nation's citizens. Private enterprise, assisted by federal agencies, has injected new vigor and productivity into the growing nation-wide program of new town development.

Many developers are setting aside 25 per cent or more of the total public land within new towns for open space and the development of park and recreation areas and facilities.

Recreation Vehicles. The leisure boom has given rise to many types of recreation vehicles, such as snowmobiles, dune buggies, minibikes, and four-wheel drive vehicles. The snowmobile, for instance, has many uses. Ski lodges maintain fleets of them for nonskiers. The comeback of the bicycle continues to delight bike manufacturers, and the urge for fun on wheels has led to a mini-bike vogue.

Sports Participation. Similar to their European counterparts, Americans increasingly are participating in a wide variety of sports.

There are some twelve million golfers in the U.S., playing regularly on about 10,000 courses. "When one considers the greens fees, club memberships, sales of golf equipment, rental of electric carts and spin-off sales of sprinklers, fairway mowers and ball retrievers, golf stands out as a king-size business."[16]

More people than ever before are playing tennis. The ten million tennis players who now enjoy that game buy $50 million worth of rackets, balls, and accessories every year.

The millions of fishermen, hunters, archers, mountain climbers, and joggers contribute to the burgeoning numbers of Americans involved in leisure participation.

Flying for pleasure is also making a significant headway with the general public. "Discover Flying," a promotion sponsored by dealers and airports across the nation, is proving highly successful.

Resort Areas. The phenomenal growth and popularity of the resort industry has created a vast array of recreation services and multi-million-dollar hotel facilities and marinas. Resort recreation, whether provided by hotels or operated independently, is providing an increasing number of job opportunities for professional recreators.

The kind of resort belt found at Miami Beach, Waikiki, Acapulco, and the Grand Bahamas is predominant in the current growth of the resort industry. Outdoor-camper resort areas also provide pleasure and enjoyment to campers, fishermen, and outdoor enthusiasts. As long as the U.S. economy moves in the direction of travel and tourism, the hotel-resort business will provide an increasing array of outstanding specialty services and leisure entertainment.

Television and Radio. Radio and television as media of news and communication continue to increase in appeal and overall market. Millions of people have an opportunity to be entertained, informed, and enriched by a wide variety of programs. Portable transistor radios are owned by millions of people in the U.S. as well as in countries of low income.

Contributions to Community Recreation

Properly regulated, commercial recreation can play a highly important role in helping to satisfy the leisure demands and interests of the public. Despite the strong progress by public and private agencies to provide pleasurable and wholesome recreation, the demand for commercial recreation continues to grow.

Commercial enterprises of wide variety have been responsible for stimulating unprecedented interest in many forms of sports and entertainment. They have had a tremendous influence on

---

[15] "Leisure Boom," *U.S. News & World Report,* April 17, 1972, p. 45.

[16] "83 Billion Dollars for Leisure," *U.S. News & World Report,* September 15, 1969.

Fig. 10-7 THE RESORT INDUSTRY. The seaside resort town with a marina is a unique form of urban landscape and economic base. Resort settlements have expanded rapidly along both seacoasts.

such sport as golf, bowling, skiing, football, baseball, and basketball. The cultural arts area has also benefited greatly by the favorable influence of commercial recreation.

Private enterprise is often able to offer a service at less cost to the taxpayer. Furthermore, it may be able to do the job on a more professional and efficient basis. "As public demand for certain kinds of recreation increases, so does the commercialization of the activity, for the people of the United States have demonstrated both their willingness and their ability to pay for their recreation."[17]

Negative Aspects of Commercial Recreation

In addition to the many advantages and positive aspects, there are a number of negative factors in commercial amusements. Perhaps the most serious argument against the commercial businesses is that of "passivity," the objection that commercial recreation emphasizes the place of the spectator and tends to minimize the place of the participant.

Another accusation is that certain forms of commercial amusement have led to dishonesty, vice, gambling, crime, poverty, and sexual delinquency. Commercial recreation interests are often guilty of exploitation, being only concerned with gate receipts. Too often, the emotions of children and adults are exploited for financial gain.

THE NEED FOR COORDINATION

Coordination between public, private, and commercial recreation services would be in the best interest of the public and a society rapidly becoming leisure-oriented.

A significant step toward such cooperation would be for the community to adopt a constructive attitude toward commercial recreation. A study should be made of commercial recreation resources in the community, and based upon the survey results, commercial recreation services and facilities should be planned where needed. Undesirable forms of commercial recreation should be

[17] Meyer, Brightbill, and Sessoms, op. cit., p. 284.

condemned and controls established. Commercial recreation interests could be effectively represented by a community recreation council.

Although public or non-profit agencies and organizations will continue to advance in scope and popularity, commercial recreation likewise has a bright future. As our society becomes more and more leisure-oriented, people will have both the time and money to purchase recreation commodities, services and experiences.

Commercial amusements, however, must be regulated in the best interests of the public. Meyer, Brightbill, and Sessoms presented some ways to exercise such control:

1. By public opinion and interest of civic groups.
2. By legislation, regulation, police control, license, and supervisions.
3. By trade control.
4. By providing higher forms of amusements.
5. By censorship.
6. By actual elimination.[18]

VOLUNTARY AGENCIES

Voluntary agencies in America, both national and local, have traditionally played an important role in serving the recreation needs of the community. These include youth-serving organizations, special interest organizations, religious affiliated agencies, settlement houses, community centers, anti-poverty organizations, and similar other groups. Their programs and services often reach special groups and provide many opportunities for experimentation and innovation.

Youth-Serving Organizations

Recreation has played an important role in the programs of most voluntary youth-serving organizations. In most cases, they have been very active in the provision of recreational services (Fig. 10–10).

Boy Scouts of America.
As the nation's largest youth movement (with over three million boys), the Boy Scouts of America is located in every area

18 Ibid., pp. 294–95.

in the country. Its national council operates through an extensive system of regional councils and local units. Although programs of community service are promoted, the scouting program is based chiefly on the appeal of the outdoors and organized camping. The development of character and citizenship training are two of the primary objectives of scouting.

Sponsored by committees of influential citizens, each troop is led by a volunteer adult scout master. Approximately 150,000 units are sponsored by religious institutions. A wide range of activities are provided under trained volunteer leadership.

The Boy Scouts program is comprised of the following age groups:

Cub Scouting—a program centered in the home for boys from eight through ten years of age.
Boy Scouting—an outdoor program for boys eleven years of age and older.
Exploring—activities adapted to boys fourteen years of age and older.

Girl Scouts of the U.S.A.
As the largest girls' youth-membership organization, the Girl Scouts program is dedicated to the purpose of helping girls prepare for responsibilities both in the home and in the community. The program emphasizes such qualities as initiative, self-control, self-reliance, and service to others.

The Girl Scouts program is adapted to the needs and interests of four age groupings:

Brownie Scouts—for girls of ages seven and eight. Brownies meet weekly with their leaders, usually at schools, homes, or churches for parties, games, crafts, trips, and camping.
Junior Girl Scouts—a program for girls of ages nine, ten, and eleven. Junior Scouts are organized into groups of from twenty to thirty-two girls. Troops are divided into patrols of six to eight members each, with a patrol leader in charge.
Cadette Girl Scouts—for girls of ages twelve to fourteen. Cadettes face four challenges that test their performances in real-life situations: (1) social dependability; (2) emergency preparedness; (3) active citizenship; (4) Girl Scout promise.

Fig. 10-8 VOLUNTARY YOUTH-SERVING ORGANIZATIONS have been very active in the provision of recreational services. The Camp Fire Girls, like other scouting programs, place a strong emphasis on good citizenship.

Senior Girl Scouts—Senior Scouts, for high school girls between ages fifteen and seventeen. Senior Scouts concentrate on special interests and name their troops accordingly, such as the Mariners, Trail Blazers, and Explorers. Service to others and vocational exploration are two of the primary purposes of the Senior Scouts program.

Camp Fire Girls. Camp Fire Girls are primarily concerned with character-building through outdoor activities, community service, and various educational activities. The junior organization, the Blue Birds, provides creative play activities for girls eight and nine years old. The majority of Camp Fire Girls are in the ten- to fifteen-year-old bracket, and the oldest girls are members of the Horizon Club, ages fifteen to eighteen.

The Camp Fire Girls program is centered around Indian lore and legend, and is related to colorful honor, symbolism, and ritual. In addition, a wide range of activities is found in their community-oriented programs. Similar to other scouting programs, the Camp Fire Girls offer a system of awards and a strong emphasis on good citizenship.

Boys' Clubs of America. The purpose of the Boys' Clubs of America is to promote the social, educational, physical, health, vocational, and character development of boys. The special concern of the Boys' Clubs is city-dwelling boys, aged seven to seventeen, from low-income families, inadequate homes, and poor neighborhoods.

Typical Boys' Clubs facilities include gamerooms, libraries, gymnasiums, shops, classrooms, and group rooms. Playgrounds, athletic fields, and craftrooms are also desirable.

Girls' Clubs of America. Designed for girls from six years of age through high school, Girls' Clubs offer training in the fundamental requisites of homemaking and citizenship. Girls' Clubs are concerned with children from low-income families and crowded neighborhoods. A complete well-balanced personality is a major goal sought for members.

Fig. 10-9 HEADING FOR SUMMER CAMP! Hi-Y day camp and summer camping programs have enabled the YMCA to gain popular support in the community.

Girls' Clubs provide daily programs of varied activities, including homecraft, music, art, games, good grooming, co-recreation, health, community service, camping, and outdoor summer programs.

Young Men's Christian Association. Established in 1851, the Young Men's Christian Association is the oldest youth-serving agency of a national scope. Dedicated to Christian ideals, it is concerned with citizenship training, promotion of physical fitness and health, world peace, community welfare, wholesome social life, and recreation.

There are approximately 1,500 associations serving communities, institutions, and colleges, with a total membership of over two million members and associates. Each local YMCA is a self-governing unit affiliated with other YMCA's throughout the nation through the National Council.

Physical education and recreation are deeply rooted in the YMCA program. The program also stresses social activities, informal education programs such as crafts and dramatics, forums, public affairs groups, occupational guidance services, and seminars on preparation for marriage and adult life. Featuring Hi-Y Clubs for boys through high school age, their programs include numerous banquets, sports, and craft events for appropriate age groups.

Much of the YMCA's youth work involves the following clubs:

Y-Indian Guides—primarily for boys six through eight years old and their fathers, the program includes handicraft, storytelling, team games, hikes, trips, and camping.

Gra-Y and Tri-Gra-Y—for boys nine through twelve years of age, each Gra-Y club is comprised of at least eight boys with an approved adult leader and a sponsoring committee. Tri-Gra-Y Clubs offer similar programs for girls.

Junior Hi-Y, Junior Tri-Hi-Y, Hi-Y, and Tri-Hi-Y—Junior Hi-Y is intended for boys in the seventh, eighth, and ninth grades; the Junior-Tri-Hi-Y, for girls of the same age; the Hi-Y, for boys in the upper three grades of high school; and the Tri-Hi-Y, for girls of the same age.

Young Women's Christian Association. Although not affiliated with the YMCA, the Young Women's Christian Association provides similar programs and services. The YWCA's informal group work with girls and women has involved a variety of educational, religious, and social activities.

Primarily, the program serves high school girls in Y-Teens, women in industry clubs, and groups for women in various business and professions. Membership in the YWCA is open to any female over twelve years of age.

Various social, cultural, and recreation programs are carried on by community associations. The wide range of YWCA classes feature homemaking, shorthand, typing, and Bible study. Recreation activities include arts and crafts, swimming, volleyball, bowling, dramatics, and music. Outdoor activities such as camping are very popular.

4-H Clubs. Though subsidized by public funds, 4-H is a voluntary membership organization composed of nearly 100,000 clubs and guided by 500,000 leaders trained by professional county extension agents. 4-H members come from farms and rural areas as well as from the suburbs and the inner city.

4-H Clubs are conducted by the Agriculture Extension Service of the United States Department of Agriculture through state agricultural colleges and county agricultural agents. Founded in 1907, 4-H Clubs are known for their slogan "Head, Heart, Hands, and Health." Any girl or boy age nine through nineteen may join by agreeing to try to live up to 4-H standards and ideals.

The primary purpose of the 4-H Club organization is to promote better living in primarily agricultural and rural areas and cities. Under volunteer adult leaders, each local club develops activities such as demonstrations, judging events, exhibits, and recreational events. The members of each club plan their own program, elect officers, conduct meetings, and carry out their projects under the guidance of adult and teen leaders. In agricultural activities, a 4-H member may raise a calf or grow an acre of crops. In homemaking, a club member may learn to sew a dress or make a family meal.

American Junior Red Cross. Located in more than forty-five countries, the Junior Red Cross is an international organization of elementary and secondary school students. The aim of the Junior Red Cross is to develop a spirit of service and

friendship among young people throughout the world. The program features such community activities as service to veterans and local institutions, the National Children's Fund, and international correspondence.

The Police Athletic League. Sponsored by law enforcement agencies, Police Athletic Leagues provide extensive recreation programming, indoor centers, and summer play-streets, with a strong emphasis on sports and games. Police Athletic Leagues are located in more than one hundred communities in the United States.

Operating chiefly in poverty areas, they also maintain placement and counseling services which provide job training and assist school dropouts. Much of their funding assistance comes from voluntary contributions, although technical assistance and cooperation is rendered by various municipal police departments.

Catholic Youth Organization. Providing spiritual, social, and recreational services, the Catholic Youth Organization is the leading Catholic agency for young people in the United States.

Through participation in CYO activities, Catholic youth are involved in retreats, religious education, and other activities to strengthen and enrich their faith. Leisure and the creative recreational involvement of young people is recognized by CYO leaders as having strong potential for both social and spiritual growth.

Many of the recreational programs are sponsored directly by the CYO at various centers or administered and financed by diocesan headquarters. Other activities take place at specific parishes under the direction of parish priests.

Group Work Agencies

Many voluntary organizations depend upon group work to achieve their primary goal of community betterment. Generally thought of as "character building" agencies, they draw their chief support from philanthropic sources or the Community Chest. Most group work agencies hold membership in their local Community Chest.

Primarily concerned with religious, moral, and social objectives, group work agencies have provided society with many opportunities for participation in a variety of programs.

The Settlement House or Community Center is another type of group work agency that has provided extensive recreational services. These agencies are involved with such responsibilities as counseling, health services, education, recreation, and cultural enrichment.

Special-Interest Organizations

These organizations comprise another major type of voluntary agency which promotes activities and public support for a particular type of recreation. Many special-interest organizations are developed on a national basis with full-time staff members who handle promotional efforts and press for favorable legislation and public action. Organizations of this type are often found in athletics, the arts, music, drama, and theatre.

There are numerous examples of special-interest organizations with a special concern for outdoor recreation and conservation. The Sierra Club has become well known for its work in protecting major natural resources such as the Grand Canyon and the upper Colorado River. The Appalachian Mountain Club has promoted such sports as skiing, mountain climbing, snowshoeing, and canoeing. Founded on a regional basis in the East, the Club is primarily concerned with practical conservation.

The American Youth Hostels is a non-profit organization which gained much of its impetus from the European Hostel movement. The primary purpose of the Youth Hostels is to help all, especially young people, gain a greater understanding of the world and its people, through outdoor activities, educational and recreational travel, and related programs. The Youth Hostels maintain centers that provide simple overnight accommodations in scenic, historical, and cultural areas.

Meeting the needs of individuals with special limitations is another important category of voluntary organizations in American communities today. Organizations such as the American Cerebral Palsy Association or the National Association for Re-

tarded Children have been effective in providing special services for the disabled. There has been a large expansion of Golden Age Clubs and social centers for aging persons, many of them established by churches, local service organizations and other voluntary agencies.

Keep America Beautiful, Inc., has been effective as a national public service organization for the prevention of litter.

Adult Organizations Interested in Youth

Many community and national civic organizations have provided noteworthy services and active support of youth agencies and organizations. Some of the typical groups are as follows: Kiwanis, Rotary, Lions, and Optimist clubs; the Junior Chamber of Commerce, the National Congress of Parents and Teachers, the American Legion, American Farm Bureau Federation, Federation of Women's Clubs, Police Athletic Leagues, National Grange, and Business and Professional Women's Clubs.

Private Organizations

A significant portion of recreation opportunities and services today is provided by private membership organizations. There are many club organizations which provide facilities and organized services for golf, tennis, skiing, hunting and fishing, and boating. Such private organizations are often able to provide more extensive services than public or voluntary agencies can. They are also more expensive. In general, private agencies are established as nonprofit organizations and often limited to a select clientele. Governed by elected officers, their programs are usually self-sustaining and rely on their own income-producing powers rather than tax money or contributions. A good example of private recreation organizations are the well over 3,000 country clubs in the United States. Many clubs have become more family-oriented rather than relying solely on golf.

There are numerous private camps operated as business ventures by individuals or corporations whose fees limit patronage to those who

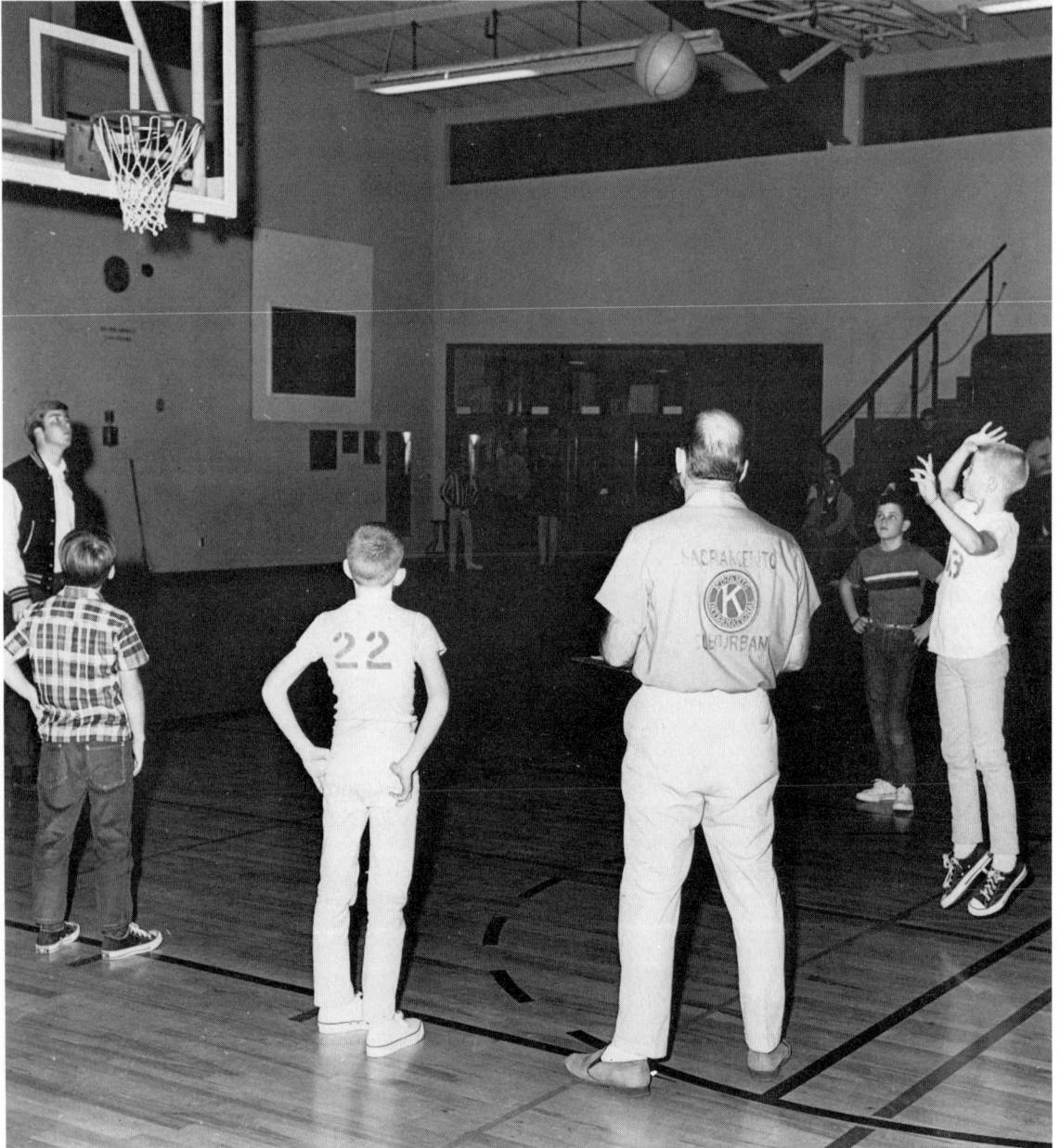

Fig. 10-10 COMMUNITY SERVICE. Many civic and service clubs in the community sponsor and support numerous youth programs and activities, like the Free Throw Shooting Championships sponsored annually by the Kiwanis Club of Suburban Sacramento, California.

can afford to pay. There are also many agency camps composed of private organizations which are of a semipublic nature. Other agencies identified with the private recreation field include condominiums, new towns, private communities, and attractive resort areas.

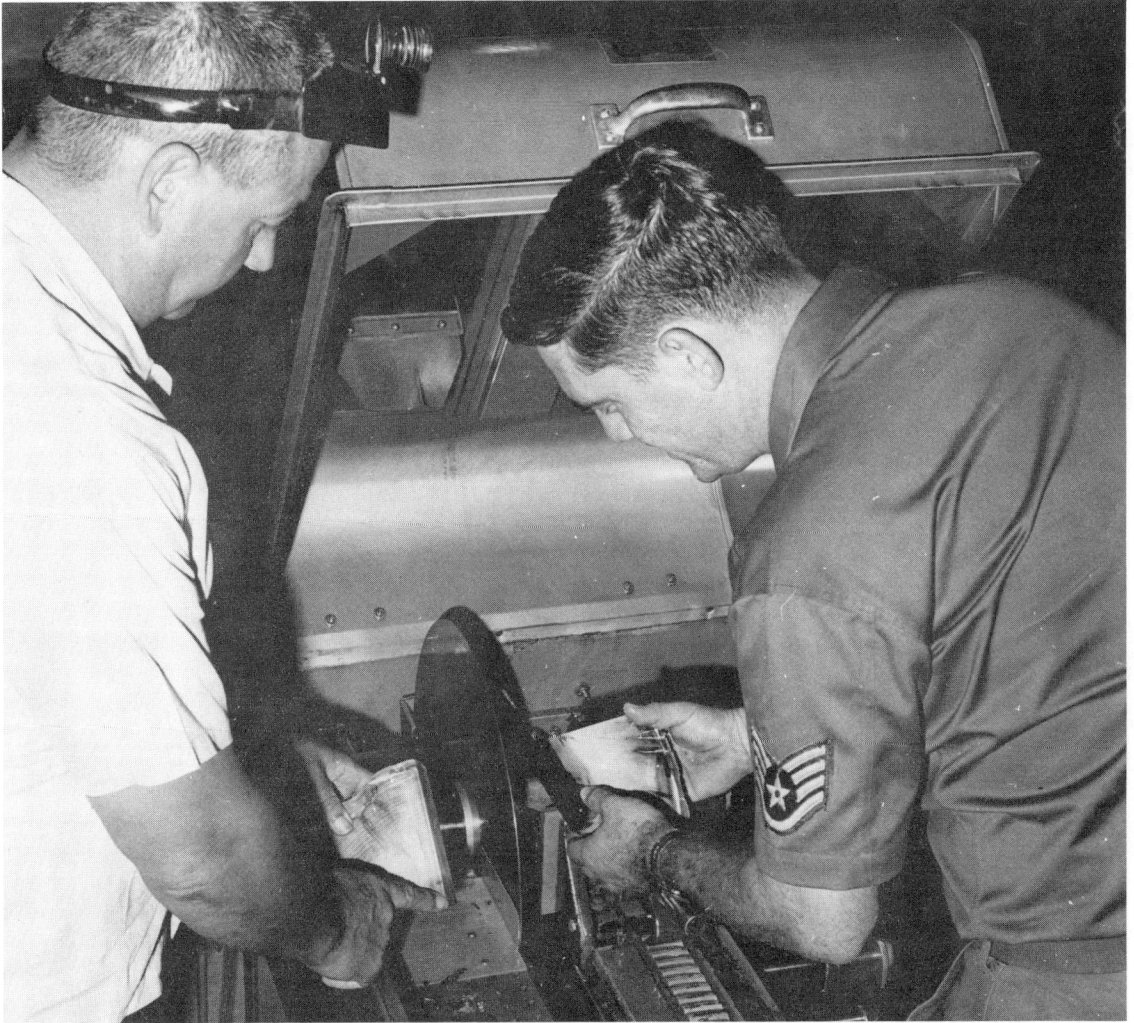

Fig. 10-11 RECREATION FOR MILITARY PERSONNEL. Each branch of the Armed Forces provides programs and services for its personnel and families. In this scene, undor skilled supervision, an Air Force man completes slabbing a piece of petrified palm tree wood to make into bookends.

Armed Forces

Today, each branch of the armed forces has a special services division which provides a variety of programs, facilities, and services at the various installations (see Chapter 8). In addition, a great number of military personnel visit nearby communities and have an opportunity to benefit from the programs and facilities.

Typical programs include sports, arts and crafts, library services, musical and theatrical programs, and many activities and services which take place at the local service club or post exchange. Both military and civilian personnel conduct the programs.

Departments of the Armed Forces have provided important assistance in strengthening community relationships so that sharing of community recreation resources is possible.

11

Recreation for Special Groups

There is a growing sensitivity and concern among professional recreators for people who are socially, culturally, or economically disadvantaged. Only within the past decade have those in the recreation and leisure services field taken a serious approach to meeting the needs and interests of these special segments of our society.

Misunderstanding or lack of knowledge about disadvantaged individuals has been a major reason for the profession's overall lack of service to special groups. In minimizing programs designed for special populations, recreation agencies have stated apologetically that they have neither an understanding of the problems of these groups nor the resources to provide these services. Progressively, however, organized recreation is beginning to provide more comprehensive programs, involving stronger leadership and financial support, for such disadvantaged groups as the physically ill and handicapped, the mentally ill and retarded, the aged, the economically deprived, and youthful and adult offenders.

Community recreators, in growing numbers, are beginning to recognize both their responsibility to provide services to special populations and the fundamental right of handicapped individuals to receive the services. Indeed, a major challenge of professional recreators during the next quarter of this century will be dealing with the leisure behavior of special populations.

THERAPEUTIC RECREATION

One of the most rapidly expanding forms of organized recreation service today is found in hospitals or other treatment centers that provide rehabilitation for the ill and handicapped. As a specialized field within the recreation profession, therapeutic recreation generally refers to "the specific use of recreational activity in care, treatment, and rehabilitation of ill, handicapped, and aged persons with a directed program."[1]

In explaining the meaning of therapeutic recreation, Edith L. Ball wrote of two concepts. She

Fig. 11-1 FUN AND GAMES IN THE HOSPITAL. Whether at home or ill in the hospital, children have a need for wholesome recreational activity. In supporting other treatment measures, recreation therapy can contribute toward a speedier recovery.

[1] *Health Resource Statistics, 1968* (Washington, D.C.: Public Health Service, 1968), p. 185.

Fig. 11-2 THERAPEUTIC RECREATION SERVICES. Through their involvement in recreation activities, patients can receive a big emotional and social lift. The recreation therapist assists the patients in their personal adjustment and progress.

referred to recreation as "refreshment or revitalization," while she defined therapeutic as "the art of healing, remedial." Thus, "Therapeutic recreation is 'pleasing refreshment that is remedial.' "[2]

Originally termed "hospital recreation," the therapeutic recreation movement has expanded its scope considerably. Initially, the field was geared primarily to the needs of psychiatric or other long-term patients in federal, or large, state hospitals. Today, however, the movement provides rehabilitation-oriented services in treatment centers to the physically disabled, the mentally retarded, psychiatric patients, the socially disabled, and dependent aging persons. From the institutionally based program, the trend has been toward a community based one.

The ill or handicapped present new challenges for society as their numbers continue to grow at an alarming rate. Although there has been a tremendous growth in the numbers of recreation professionals and services in this field, great numbers of disabled individuals are still unserved. According to Richard Kraus, "The total number of all persons who are chronically ill or disabled, or who suffer from emotional problems which prevent their successful functioning, has been calculated in excess of 40 million."[3] In addition, there are many other people who are seriously disabled, either physically or socially, and who have a need for specially planned recreation programs. Many of those suffering from alcoholism (6.5 million) and arthritis (11 million) are among the unserved.[4]

Leading psychiatrists have given strong support to recreation as a form of rehabilitative service. The late Dr. William C. Menninger, former director of the famed Menninger Clinic in Topeka, Kansas, once stated: "It has been the privilege of

---

[2] Edith L. Ball, "The Meaning of Therapeutic Recreation," *Therapeutic Recreation Journal*, IV, no. 1 (Washington, D.C.: 1970).

[3] Richard Kraus, *Therapeutic Recreation Service* (Philadelphia: W. B. Saunders Company, 1973), p. 7.

[4] Ibid.

Fig. 11-3 HANDICAPPED INDIVIDUALS who want to play games can. The activities are just done in a different way. This youngster enjoys a game of pool at the State Hospital for Crippled Children in Elizabethtown, Pennsylvania. (Courtesy of John Snyder.)

> RECREATION HAS NOT ONLY PLAYED AN IMPORTANT PART IN THE TREATMENT PROGRAM OF MANY MENTAL ILLNESSES, BUT IT HAS BEEN A CONSIDERABLE FACTOR IN ENABLING FORMER PATIENTS TO REMAIN WELL.
>
> *Dr. William C. Menninger*

many of us practicing medicine in psychiatry to have had some very rewarding experiences in the use of recreation as an adjunctive method of treatment."[5]

Dr. Menninger outlined three basic psychological needs that can be met through recreation:

1. Competitive games as an outlet for instinctive aggressive drives.
2. Creative activities in art, music, or literature as a release.
3. Entertainment activities as a means of providing relaxation and vicarious involvement.

> THE ILL AND THE HANDICAPPED STILL HAVE THE SAME NEED TO BELONG, TO CREATE, TO FEEL SECURE, TO LOVE AND BE LOVED, TO FEEL SIGNIFICANT AND TO EXPERIENCE NEW ADVENTURE.
>
> *Reynold Carlson, Theodore Deppe, and Janet MacLean*

Purpose

Like all health services, therapeutic recreation has a specific purpose: to promote health and prevent increased disability, to treat impairment, and to provide rehabilitation through a number of services.

According to H. Dan Corbin, "Therapeutic recreation makes use of play media to provide the mentally and (or) physically ill with satisfactory interests and outlets in conjunction with the other therapeutic means at hand. It is suited for all age groups and is used as adjunctive therapy to promote general well-being and develop social skills as therapy progresses."[6]

In serving the patient, therapeutic recreation services have the following specific objectives:

1. Instill morale.
2. Encourage the formation of proper habits and attitudes.
3. Channel aggressive drives into constructive outlets.
4. Encourage desire to overcome physical or mental barriers.
5. Stimulate new or dormant interests and talents.

Scope of Therapeutic Recreation Service

There are several major settings in which therapeutic recreation service is provided:

Hospitals of varied sponsorship—Veterans Administration, military, voluntary, state, county, municipal, public health, and others.

---

[5] William C. Menninger, "Recreation and Mental Health," *Recreation*, November 1948, p. 340.

[6] H. Dan Corbin, *Recreation Leadership* (Englewood Cliffs, N.J.: Prentice-Hall, Inc., 1970), p. 261.

Nursing Homes—generally regarded as extended-care facilities for ill or disabled aging persons.

Schools or Residential Centers for Specific Disabilities—offer services to the physically disabled, mentally retarded, or emotionally disturbed.

Special Schools for Treatment Centers for the Socially Deviant—include adult penal institutions and reformatories and special schools for youth.

Homes for Aged Persons—residential centers provide therapeutic services to aged persons.

Centers for Physical Medicine and Rehabilitation—treat those with serious physical disabilities.

Public Recreation and Park Department Programs—have initiated a number of new programs to serve the disabled.

After-Care Centers and Sheltered Workshops—geared particularly to the problems of mental illness, mental retardation, and drug addiction.

Role of the Therapeutic Recreation Specialist

The primary role of the recreational therapist is to plan, organize, and direct the therapeutic recreational activities in the hospital or community, in accordance with the treatment goals for the individual patients. The therapist works in a medically approved program of varied activities that assist the patients in their personal adjustment and progress.

The therapeutic recreation specialist serves as a counselor to patients or clients, an educator in the community, an organizer, researcher, or as a consultant. The diverse tasks that a typical therapeutic recreation specialist might be involved with were described by Dr. John A. Nesbitt:

Therapeutic recreation specialists perform many roles and functions in the course of a week, during a work day, within any given hour. They move quickly and easily from role to role. In a short period of time a therapeutic recreation specialist will set up a day room for the evening . . . arrange for a large group of patients to participate in a community recreation program—set up a special party for a small group of patients not yet ready to go into the community or act on their own . . . and sit down

for one-to-one counseling with a patient having problems socializing with other people. . . . The therapeutic recreation specialist performs many roles—therapist, administrator, supervisor, leader, and consultant among others.[7]

Program

The patient can receive a tremendous emotional and social lift through involvement in recreation activities. Effective recreation programs have proven highly effective in bolstering a patient's morale. Making the patient happier and more cooperative will support the other treatment measures and lead toward a speedier recovery.

Recreation activities for the ill and disabled must be planned in terms of the patient's interests, needs, and capabilities. His leisure experiences should be related to the treatment aims, which vary with the illness, disability and patient.

The following are some of the typical categories of activities in therapeutic recreation service:

1. Social activities
2. Entertainment
3. Sports and active games
4. Hobbies
5. Arts and crafts
6. Performing arts
7. Service activities
8. Outdoor recreation
9. Motor activities
10. Special events

In "prescribing" a recreation activity for a patient, the activity should never be approached in a compulsory manner. The activity is introduced to a patient who can be encouraged to participate and given assistance but should not be forced to take part. Thus, the therapist has an important role to help motivate patients to take part in a variety of wholesome activities that will give them satisfaction.

Leisure Counseling

In addition to therapeutic recreation services, the need for leisure counseling has been receiving growing attention. Experience has shown that such

[7] John A. Nesbitt, "The Mission of Therapeutic Recreation Specialists: To Help and to Champion the Handicapped," *Therapeutic Recreation Journal*, 4th quarter, 1970, pp. 2–4, 41–42.

counseling has contributed to the rehabilitation process by helping individuals deal more effectively with their free time.

With professional guidance and counseling, withdrawn patients in the hospital environment can begin to participate in social-recreational activities. Many rehospitalized patients tend to lapse into solitary ways on discharge; this behavior can reactivate old patterns of pathological behavior. This observation suggests the need for individual guidance through a leisure counseling service.

The primary objectives of a leisure counseling service are to help patients:

1. Maintain the level of social contact they attained while hospitalized.
2. Develop further social-recreational skills and experience.
3. Help them experience success in their leisure time.

A Stronger Profession

The profession of therapeutic recreation has been slow in developing a positive image for acceptance by both its professional peers and the general public. The following steps need to be taken to improve the therapeutic recreation service:

1. The entire field needs a sharper focus and a clearer identity.
2. Professional preparation curricula should be improved.
3. Public concern should be aroused.
4. More effective programs should be offered.
5. Stronger processes of selection should be developed.
6. The working relationships between therapeutic and community recreation personnel should be strengthened.
7. Governmental support of therapeutic recreation service should be expanded.

RECREATION FOR THE HANDICAPPED

One of the most significant social trends of the past two decades has been the changing attitude of the public toward handicapped or disabled

Fig. 11-4 SWIMMING PROVIDES a handicapped child with the type of exercise and a freedom of movement he cannot enjoy out of water. This aquatic activity took place at a local Easter Seal Society facility.

persons. While indifference and rejection once characterized the public's attitude, today it is giving way to a genuine concern and positive action by a more responsive society.

In the past, the needs of the handicapped were often overlooked by recreation programs in the community. In far too many communities in America, there has been a serious lack of year-round social, cultural, and educational opportunities for children whose physical and mental disabilities have prevented them from taking part in various activities with others of like interests.

With imagination and creativity, recreational activities and facilities can be effectively adapted to the needs of handicapped persons. In providing increasing services to the disabled, recreation programs have had to provide transportation for participants, including buses with lifts, buildings with stairs, ramps, and various other adaptations. Groups involving the disabled need not be stereotyped into selected activities. The more accepted practice is one of adapting any activity to meet the individual's needs, regardless of the disability.

Types of Handicaps

There are many types of handicaps or disabilities for which an increasing number of recreation programs are providing services. They include the blind or partially sighted; the deaf; the cardiac, the diabetic, and the tubercular; the orthopedically and neurologically handicapped; the physically disabled, including amputees, paraplegics, and post-polio patients; the mentally retarded and mentally ill; and those with physical illnesses of short- or long-term duration who may be home-bound or hospitalized. Other conditions that involve a degree of disability include arthritis, cerebral palsy, multiple sclerosis, and muscular dystrophy.

Definition

In 1960 at the White House Conference on Children and Youth, a handicapped child was defined as "one who cannot play, learn, work, or do the things other children of his age can do; or is hindered in achieving his full physical, mental, and social potentialities, whether by disability which is initially mild but potentially handicapping or by a serious disability involving several areas of functions with the probability of life-long impairment."[8]

While "handicapped" still refers to people with disabilities, its meaning has changed to describe individuals with degrees of difference physically, mentally, psychologically, and socially. "It no longer refers to the extent of the disability except as that disability limits that person competitively or in reaching a particular objective."[9]

Needs of the Handicapped

Handicapped individuals have the same needs as normal persons in our society. In addition, they have special needs stemming from their particular handicap. The ill and the disabled have the same need to belong, to create, to feel secure, to love and be loved, to feel significant, and to experience new adventure.

---

[8] Janet Pomeroy, *Recreation for the Physically Handicapped* (New York: The Macmillan Company, 1964), p. 20.

[9] Thomas Stein and H. Douglas Sessoms, *Recreation and Special Populations* (Boston: Holbrook Press, Inc., 1973), p. 200

The Need for Education

There are seven million handicapped or disabled children in the United States. Nearly 60 per cent of these children are denied the educational programs they need to have full equality of opportunity. Unquestionably, the education that they are likely to receive will not prepare them for a life of independence.

Unfortunately, 4.3 million mentally and physically handicapped youngsters are being deprived of learning because their schools are short of funds.

> Angela Coleman, a 9-year-old partially blind girl from Augusta, Georgia, is grades behind in reading because her school can't afford special books with large type. . . . Twenty-two educable but autistic children in the Tidewater area of Virginia were turned away from schools because the added costs of teaching them were too much for their community to bear.[10]

Benefits

Satisfying recreation activities can help relieve tensions, create substitute experiences for meeting basic needs, and serve as a therapeutic aid to mental health. Wholesome recreation opportunities can help make the patient more receptive to treatment through a happier environment. For the physically ill or disabled, recreation activities can provide the needed stimulus to do physical exercise that will improve their health. The patient may gain confidence and self-respect and develop an ability to interrelate with people again.

Physically handicapped and mentally retarded children who are too severely handicapped to be included in special schools, benefit greatly by attending daily programs where they learn to play together. For the first time they experience companionship, self-expression, and achievement. Timid and withdrawn children have responded favorably to group play by laughing and singing.

---

[10] Henry Gottlieb, "Handicapped Children are Denied Special Education," Associated Press story appearing in the *Sacramento Bee*, June 10, 1973.

Guiding Principles

The following principles were suggested by Pomeroy in providing recreation for the physically handicapped:

1. The handicapped have the same basic needs, desires, and rights as all other people.
2. The physically handicapped should have the opportunity to participate in recreation activities with the non-handicapped whenever this is possible.
3. Activities should be as nearly like those for the non-handicapped as possible.[11]

Centers for the Handicapped

An increasing number of recreation centers for the handicapped are being patterned after the original center, the famed Recreation Center for the Handicapped in San Francisco. Under its founder and director, Janet Pomeroy, the Center has pioneered in recreation for the handicapped and retarded for the past seventeen years. It provides year-round recreation and camping programs for children, teenagers, and adults with mental and physical limitations. Through their experience at the Center, participants are helped to adjust to community life with the nonhandicapped.

Staff Personnel.   Headed by a director, the professional recreation staff at centers for the handicapped includes three program supervisors; a co-ordinator of volunteer services; a social worker; a recreation counselor; recreation leaders; specialists in physical fitness, arts and crafts, drama, and music; assistants; aides; and program helpers.

The business staff consists of the business manager, secretaries and clerical workers, coordinator of transportation, drivers, housekeeper, and cook. Over 200 volunteers supplement the regular staff at the Center in San Francisco.

Program.   A recreation program for the handicapped should contribute positively to the mental, physical, social, and emotional growth and development of severely handicapped and mentally re-

tarded persons through healthful and constructive activities.

Typical activities include music and rhythms, story telling, swimming, golf, bowling, and other sports activities, physical exercise programs, singing, arts and crafts, drama, dance, club groups, summer day camp (including overnight campouts), resident camping, and trips and excursions into the community.

Handicapped children can learn to swim, and even those who cannot master swimming can learn to enjoy being in the water. Basketball, bowling, and skiing are also favorite activities for the handicapped. Experienced instructors of the National Inconvenienced Skiers Association teach one-legged skiers both to ski and race.

Classes and instructions are given in reading, writing, and basic grammar for children and adults. Many centers have library facilities, and books are available for all participants to take home. Special programs for integrating even the most severely handicapped with the nonhandicapped children, teens, and adults should be part of the program.

Adapting Activities.   Under the direction of trained and skilled recreation leaders, activities should be adapted so that all persons, even those who are bedridden, may participate to their fullest capacity. For example, handicapped persons who could not use their hands have learned to print and sketch with their toes. People in wheelchairs have learned to rock dance and play basketball from their chairs. Through adaption of activities, the severely handicapped and mentally retarded learn to use their limited physical abilities to a fuller capacity.

Finance.   Generally, recreation centers for the handicapped have several sources of financial support with which to operate. For example, the San Francisco Recreation and Park Department, the Community Mental Health Service, and the Department of Social Services subsidize a portion of the San Francisco Center's budget on a contractual basis. The Center is also financed through some federal grants for previously institutionalized retarded, for day care children, and for a physical fitness program for all participants.

---

[11] Pomeroy, op. cit., p. 20.

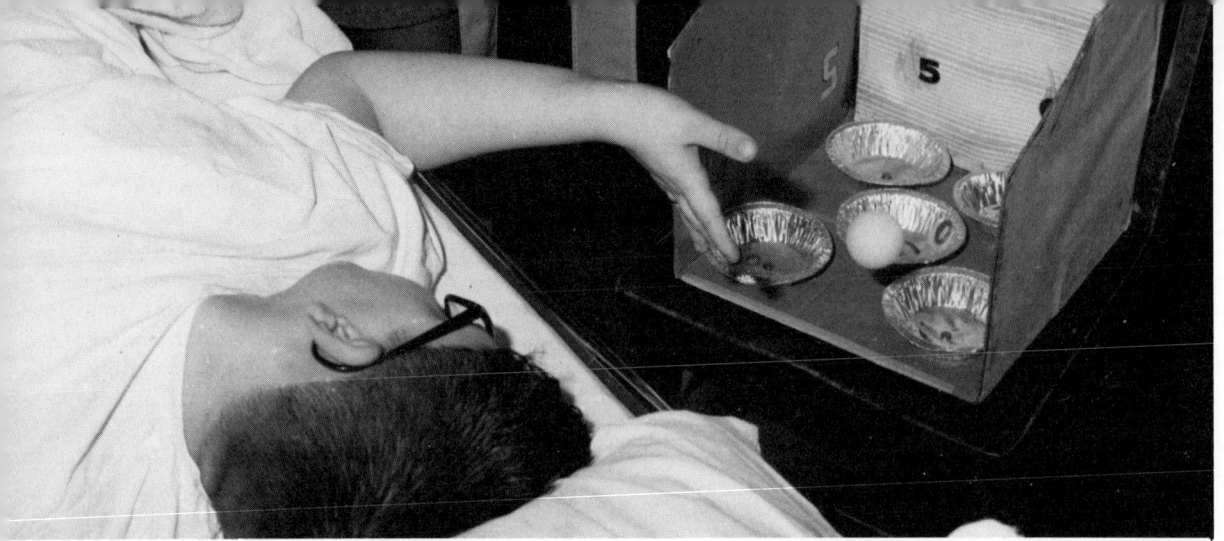

Fig. 11-5 BY ADAPTING ACTIVITIES, the severely handicapped can learn to use their limited physical abilities to a fuller capacity. This crippled boy enjoys a bedside ball game at the State Hospital in Elizabethtown, Pennsylvania. (Courtesy of John Snyder.)

A large proportion of the San Francisco Center's operating budget is raised by the board of directors through personal solicitation of individuals, service clubs, and groups; by letters of solicitation; and by such annual fund-raising events as horse shows, luncheons, bazaars, and rummage sales.

If able to do so, participants in the Center pay a nominal fee for each program attended. However, no one is deprived of the opportunity to participate, and the Center absorbs the cost of those unable to pay fees.

Facilities. In recent years, there have been increasing efforts to provide effective access to recreation facilities for individuals with limited mobility such as those with wheelchairs, crutches, and braces. Many federal, state, and local authorities have made significant efforts to make recreation and park facilities accessible to the physically handicapped. The newly created Committee on Recreation and Leisure is part of the President's Committee on Employment of the Handicapped.

Federal and state standards are being established that must be observed by municipalities wishing to qualify for assistance in the development of park and recreation facilities. Under these standards, facilities of various types are becoming more accessible, safe, and convenient for the disabled.

> HOPE AND LOVE GIVE
> THE RETARDED A CHANCE.

RECREATION FOR THE MENTALLY RETARDED

Only within the past ten years have organized recreation services for the mentally retarded emerged as a major contributing factor to the well-being of this long neglected special group. The recreational and social needs of the retarded had received very little attention until the early 1960s. In 1962, the President's Panel on Mental Retardation, instituted by President John F. Kennedy, recommended that local communities, in cooperation with federal and state agencies, provide expanded services for retarded children and youth. This was the first large-scale effort to cope with the problem of mental retardation nationally.

A growing number of communities and counties have since successfully initiated recreation programs and services for the retarded. Many programs have become a reality through financial aid from the Joseph P. Kennedy Foundation; the National Association for Retarded Children; the American Association for Health, Physical Education, and Recreation; and the Federal Department of Health, Education, and Welfare.

State and municipal organizations have promoted a variety of services and programs, including vocational rehabilitation, sheltered workshops, education, recreation, and, very important, legislation to serve the needs of the retarded.

Still, in many communities, there is a definite lack of agencies and programs. While there are signs of increasing activity on the part of public and private recreation agencies, there has been inadequate implementation. Many of the organizations and agencies responsible for developing such programs have demonstrated an unsure approach as to how to implement them. Their reluctance, perhaps, can be attributed to the fact that they have felt unqualified to serve the needs of this special group.

What Is Mental Retardation?

As defined by the President's panel on mental retardation, "The mentally retarded are children and adults who, as a result of inadequately developed intelligence, are significantly impaired in their ability to learn and to adapt to the demands of society."[12]

The American Association on Mental Deficiency defined mental retardation as: ". . . subaverage intellectual functioning which originates during the developmental period, and is associated with impairment or inadaptive behavior."[13] Unfortunately, mental retardation has an organic cause which is incurable. However, mild forms of retardation are curable, in the sense that such individuals can participate in community life, hold jobs, and live as responsible citizens.

From early childhood, the mentally retarded person has experienced marked delay and a difficulty in learning and has been relatively ineffective in applying whatever he has learned to the problems of ordinary living. He needs special training and guidance to make the most of his· capacities, whatever they may be.

AAMP

Level	IQ Range
Borderline	68–83
Mild	52–67
Moderate	36–51
Severe	20–35
Profound	0–20

Some of the characteristics of the retarded person are short attention span, immature interests, lack of imagination, deficiencies in the higher mental powers, inadequate learning, and disruptive group behavior. Others may express their insecurity and fear of failure and reproof by withdrawing. They may refuse to be drawn into group activities or participate in any way.

Extent of Retardation

Gene A. Hayes estimated that three per cent of the population of the United States are mentally retarded and that approximately 126,000 children born each year are retarded at birth. This means that there are at least 5 million retarded persons in the United States. According to Hayes, "twice as many individuals are afflicted by mental retardation as by blindness, polio, cerebral palsy, and rheumatic heart disease combined."[14]

Classification

The American Association on Mental Deficiency has developed a system of classifying the retarded in five different groups or categories.[15] This system does not reflect the same intelligence quotient guidelines as those utilized or advocated by Ingram and other educators.[16]

The five classes and the IQ range of each, as compared with the levels advocated by Ingram and others, are listed below:

Ingram et al.

Level	IQ Range
Dull-normal	75–89
Educable retarded	50–75
Trainable retarded	25–49
Custodial	0–24

[12] Rick F. Heber, "A Manual on Terminology and Classification in Mental Retardation," monograph supplement to *American Journal of Mental Deficiency,* Ind. ed., 1959, p. 3.

[13] Ibid.

[14] Thomas Stein and Douglas Sessoms, *Recreation and Special Populations* (Boston: Holbrook Press, Inc., 1973), pp. 67–68.

[15] Op. cit.

[16] Christine P. Ingram, *Education for the Slow-Learning Child* (New York: The Ronald Press, Inc., 1960), p. 7.

Causes of Mental Retardation

The causes include the following: problems incurred during pregnancy or in childbirth; genetic or hereditary factors; illness; disease or accident; and social or environmental deprivation.

Needs

Those who have served the mentally retarded have discovered that their needs and aspirations are no different from the normal population. And they have a strong need for love, affection, and understanding. They must have food, shelter, and, hopefully, a job.

The mentally retarded person is unique, however, in that some of his needs appear exaggerated. Most retarded persons are slow in learning new skills simply because they do not have the mental ability to do them. Quite often, they must be taught activities by different methods than those used with normal individuals.

Achievement and acceptance stimulate the retarded child in learning to do things for himself. As he experiences success through play, he will gain confidence in himself and in his ability. He will feel more desire, drive, and motivation to take part in a variety of activities.

The majority of mentally retarded children and youth live with their families. Only the more severely retarded children are institutionalized. "The retarded child living at home has little recreation opportunity," wrote Joan Ramm. "He may make friends with the children in his special class at school, but unlike the normal children who can play with their school chums in the neighborhood after school hours, retarded children are transported from their homes in different parts of town and have few friends in their own neighborhoods. Many just sit and watch television." [17]

---

[17] Joan Ramm, "Challenge: Recreation and Fitness for the Mentally Retarded," *Journal for American Association for Health, Physical Education and Recreation*, September 1966, p. 1.

Objectives

The following are some of the desirable objectives in meeting the psychosocial needs of the mentally retarded that can be attained through recreation activity programs:

Physical Development

1. Physical health and appearance
2. Balanced growth
3. Improved posture, body mechanics, and control of movement

Social Development

1. Better self-care skills
2. Participation with the family
3. Respect for the rights of others
4. Become more sociable, outgoing and friendly

Emotional Development

1. Improved self-confidence and courage
2. Self-image and self-respect
3. Fun and enjoyment
4. Become more independent
5. Greater security in different situations

Staff

Ideally, the recreation program should be directed by a recreation leader who has had direct experience with the mentally retarded and professional training in the field of therapeutic services. If the leader has not had specialized training, the program may be directed by a qualified recreation leader, assisted by consultants or representatives of community organizations who have sufficient expertise in the field of mental retardation.

The use of a sufficient number of volunteers is highly important to the success of the program. In working with the retarded, the ratio of staff to participants must be high. Therefore, volunteers should be recruited from colleges and high schools, civic groups, women's auxiliaries, religious groups, fraternal orders, or service clubs. In particular, recreation students from colleges and universities are an excellent source of leaders and aides for programs involving the retarded.

Parents can be involved in planning the program and providing a limited amount of leader-

Fig. 11-6 AS THE RETARDED CHILD experiences success through play, he will gain confidence in himself and in his ability. This Saturday morning softball program at American River College in Sacramento gives retarded boys and girls the opportunity to play on a team under trained leadership.

ship and services. In-service training, orientation, and on-the-job supervision should be provided for all workers, professional and volunteer alike.

Program Development

Programs for the retarded should include a wide variety of activities, as well as counseling and personal guidance for participants. Activities should involve ones that need only casual and unstructured participation as well as those that demand careful leadership and instruction. Whenever possible, activities should be integrated, giving retardates an opportunity to mix with the non-disabled. Educable retardates, particularly, can function quite effectively socially on a higher level.

Programs for the mentally retarded should help the individual gain confidence in what he can accomplish. Activities should be meaningful and geared to the person's needs and capabilities. Programs should be regarded as a means, never an end.

Generally, the scheduling of the program should follow the guidelines of the scheduling for "normals." Social groups usually function well with eight to twelve members.

A number of alternative programs exist for serving the mentally retarded. They may be sponsored by separate public recreation departments or voluntary organizations, or by joint sponsorship. When no program exists in the community, interested parents and leaders may initiate.

Grouping Participants

People generally have a desire and need to be with other people of relatively the same age. Therefore, participants in activities are often separated by

Fig. 11-7 MOST RETARDED PERSONS are slow in learning new skills. Therefore, the leader must be patient and understanding. The retarded have a strong need for love and affection.

chronological age. Typical age groups are usually broken down as: 8–12, 13–16, and 17 years and over. Adult groups can be broken down 17–30, and 30 and over, if the size of the group is large enough. Recreation services for the mentally retarded may also be classified in terms of functional performance levels.

Activities for the Retarded

Typically, recreation programs for the mentally retarded have emphasized the following areas of activity:

1. Sports and physical fitness activities
2. Low organized games and contests
3. Creative arts (arts, crafts, music, drama, and dance)
4. Special events and trips
5. Training in living skills
6. Camping

Bowling. Bowling has been one of the most successful sports activities for the mentally retarded. Bowling provides much needed physical activity in a desirable social setting. Participants are taught to keep score, as well as keep track of bowling order.

Special Olympics. This sports program involves national competition for retarded children and youth throughout U.S. cities. They compete in track and field events, swimming, and fitness events; and ultimately national champions are selected. Funded by the Kennedy Foundation and other public and private sources, the Special Olympics have been sponsored by major cities and have involved thousands of participants.

Diners Club. Dining outside the home in a restaurant provides important opportunities to learn and to practice social skills. On his visit to a restaurant with a leader, the retardate can practice ordering, conversing, and conducting himself in a socially acceptable manner. In acquiring the necessary skills and security, he will be able to dine out on his own and with his family.

Trips. Trips for the mentally retarded can provide many new and satisfying experiences. A trip to some area or site in the community can be an enriching adventure in everyday living.

Patients can be escorted to baseball and football games and wrestling matches. Visits to zoos and museums are also popular. Visits to department stores, recreation facilities, and food stores are typical excursions for the retarded. They can be taught how to purchase items at various stores.

Music. Singing and other musical activities are usually included in programs for mentally handicapped children to provide relaxing, entertaining, and enjoyable activities for the participants.

Scouting. The objectives of scouting are character building, citizenship training, and physical fitness. To the handicapped child scouting can provide a sense of belonging, accomplishment, and association with others.

Goals

Recreation services for the mentally retarded should involve more than fun and physical exercise. Of equal importance are such goals as meaningful social living and social enhancement. Since they are usually unaware of the expectations of various social situations, retarded people need assistance and direction in dealing with such experiences.

Retarded youth and adults need to be counseled about recreational resources in the community and how to become involved. Recreation department staff can also act as a liaison between the community and the retarded individual to ensure his acceptance in community programs and facilities.

RECREATION FOR LATER MATURITY

Recreation for the aging is one of the most vital areas of concern in the American society today and represents a major challenge for the organized recreation field. During the past two decades, major changes have taken place in the family structure that have caused the isolation of the aged.

Today, the smaller, two-generation family unit provides the aged person little room and little sense of personal contribution. As a result, an increasing number of older persons are living alone in small apartments or single-room units. Often, they are unable to take care of themselves properly. Consequently, more and more older people are experiencing difficulty adjusting to their new status in life. An increasing number are choosing withdrawal or disengagement from society.

There are approximately 20 million Americans today who are 65 or older, or about ten per cent

Fig. 11-8 MUSICAL ACTIVITIES involving dancing and singing provide the retarded with relaxing and entertaining activities. This group of children enjoys its monthly dance, which features a live band.

of the entire population. Richard Kraus estimates that the number of Americans over 65 will be 32 million by the year 2000. "The average life span may be extended to the age of 96 in the United States and other nations, at some time in the decades ahead. If this occurs, or even if a more modest gain in the life span occurs, the problem of the aging in society will become even more acute."[18]

As millions of people join the aging society, the concerns of this group must become the interest and concern of the community. The elderly person must be given a fairer share of the recreation tax dollar if his increasing needs are to be served. If older people are to be physically and emotionally healthy, they must continue to have a full range of social and recreational opportunities, which can help fulfill their need for friendship, social involvement, and creative activity.

Following retirement, many older persons tend to decline both physically and emotionally if they do not have social and recreation opportunities. The result is loneliness, alcoholism, mental illness, and even suicide. Social isolation is even more prevalent among aging persons with special disabilities, and is perhaps the most serious prob-

---

[18] Kraus, op. cit., pp. 142 and 161.

> WE DO NOT CEASE PLAYING BECAUSE WE
> ARE OLD; WE GROW OLD BECAUSE WE
> CEASE PLAYING.
>
> *Joseph Lee*

> MAKING THE LIVES OF AGING PERSONS
> AS REWARDING AND HAPPY AS POSSIBLE
> IS A CHALLENGE THAT SOCIETY MUST
> NOT FAIL TO MEET.

lem confronting the older visually handicapped person.

Indeed, a major challenge for recreational professionals is how to provide their expertise to the aging. The 1961 White House Conference on the Aging adopted a policy statement which stated that: "Recreation is a basic human need; together with work, education, and religion it makes up the full life. Stimulating programs of activities must be provided to make constructive the leisure hours of older adults."

The recreation and park profession must develop a stronger sense of responsibility by greatly expanding its programs in this area. Many millions of aged persons are still unserved, providing the field with a challenge it cannot ignore.

Definitions

Gerontology—The study of the aging process and of aged persons in society.

Geriatrics—The branch of medicine dealing with medical problems of the aged.

Needs of the Aging

The basic needs of aged persons are the same as for anyone at any age: new experiences, security, recognition, response, participation, self-expression, and creativity.

The elderly person's psychological needs are affection, understanding, appreciation, and a sense of worth and usefulness. The aging person's feelings of inferiority and inadequacy stem primarily from loss of status and the various disabilities of old age.

Upon retirement, the working person is faced with a big increase of free time and a decrease in income. With earlier retirement policies and medical advances, the average person will soon be spending twenty to twenty-five years in retirement.

Helping middle age adults prepare for retirement should be of prime concern to society. Mid-career clinics can examine the goals of their working life, consider possible changes, and suggest added interests and involvements outside of work.

In helping the aging adjust to social, psychological, economic, or physiological changes, the following programs and assistance should be provided by governmental and community agencies and organizations:

1. Health assistance and hospital medical care
2. Economic security
3. Housing and maintenance assistance
4. Opportunity for meaningful social relationships
5. A sense of importance and contribution to society
6. Challenging physical and mental activities
7. A position of respect and dignity
8. Helping those who are unable to live independently

The Contribution of Recreation

Increasingly, recreation is playing a greater role in the lives of aging persons. To fill their leisure hours and meet some of their personal needs, interesting and challenging recreation opportunities can make a major contribution in the following areas:

1. Improve physical health
2. Re-awaken creative impulses
3. Encourage social involvement
4. Play meaningful roles in society
5. Have positive outlook on life
6. Other social services

Programs for the Aging

The majority of activities sponsored by recreation agencies is carried on in meetings of clubs, commonly called "Golden Age" clubs. Members en-

Fig. 11-9 A PICNIC IN THE PARK. This very active Senior Citizen club enjoys an "old-fashioned" group picnic together. The most popular activities for the aging are those that involve fun, companionship, and belonging.

joy the responsibility of planning their meetings and preparing for their special events and activities, assisted by recreation leaders.

Other recreation services provided for aging persons in institutional or community settings include senior citizens' centers and clubs, special residential centers, hospitals or nursing homes, and homebound programs.

Developing the Program. The development and implementation of an activities program for the aged depends primarily on what the individuals themselves want to do. Learning an individual's interests is the basis for planning the start

of the program, and it is the key to keeping the program continually effective. Any organizational plan, however, should take into consideration existing facilities and programs in the community. Before initiating the program, a survey should be made to determine the leisure needs of the group to be served.

If given the opportunity to share in the program's organization themselves, the elderly who participate will display considerably more interest and spirit. Some activities should be provided that will extend over a considerable period of time and challenge the continued interest and dedication of the participants. Activities with long-term appeal may serve psychologically as work substitutes.

Program Activities. The most popular recreation activities for the aging are those of a social nature in which such qualities as fun, sociability, companionship, and belonging are given prime emphasis. Generally, activities for the aging are broken down into the following areas:

1. Arts and crafts
2. Music
3. Games and contests
4. Dramatics
5. Dance
6. Religious services
7. Films
8. Hobbies
9. Social programs
10. Trips and outings
11. Community service

A typical summer program at Sacramento, California's Senior Citizen Center offers equipment and space for such card games as bridge, canasta, and pinochle. There are chess and checkers. Outside, are shuffleboard and croquet grounds. Dances are scheduled regularly. Instruction is offered in oil painting, mosaic, and ceramics. "The Center opens at 10 in the morning," wrote Bob Forsyth, "and as it nears 10 at night, the sounds of dancing and talking drift through the summer evening. And on a wall is a clock which no one seems to notice."[19]

The Sacramento Center offers chartered air flights to Europe, Hawaii, and Alaska at greatly reduced prices. Regular bus tours are scheduled to Lake Tahoe, San Francisco, and the Pacific coast.

Programs in Nursing Homes.   Recreation in nursing homes is a significant part of the total concept of patient care and treatment program that includes medicine, nursing, physical therapy, religion, occupational therapy, social work services, and recreation. According to Dulcy Miller, "The administration of a progressive nursing home is committed to the encouragement and development of the imaginative recreation service."[20]

Recreation activities for the aging should be scheduled at hours of greatest leisure and should avoid conflict with nursing care or medical treatment. While some activities can be offered in the morning, the afternoons usually provide the largest segment of free time. Most group activities are scheduled after lunch. Individual activities or special events can be planned for the early evening hours. Programs should be geared to serve the needs of patients who are bedridden or limited in mobility as well as those who are able to move around easily.

Leadership Guidelines

Effective supervision and leadership are essential to a successful recreation program for the aged. It has been said that working with this age group requires more skill and ability than with any other. Perhaps the most challenging part of a leader's job is to encourage people to get involved. Therefore, the job is to provide activities that present a challenge and make people want to participate and to achieve.

In selecting activities certain physical and emotional criteria must be considered. In scheduling the activities, the leader must determine which persons will require individual attention, on what days, for how long, and who will supervise the activities.

The following are some important leadership guidelines for supervision of the aged:

1. Provide a broad and varied program for all.
2. Encourage participants to take an active role in planning. The professional leader should not attempt to dominate the group.
3. Create a friendly environment in which everyone will feel secure, accepted, and liked.
4. Consider the unique limitations of old age.
5. Consider individual education, economic status, recreational experience, and skills.
6. Do not allow the more aggressive members to dominate the others.
7. Provide the type of facilities appropriate to the particular group.
8. Emphasize enjoyment, fun, and companionship.
9. Provide instruction whenever desirable.

[19] Bob Forsyth, "It's Never too Late," *Sacramento Union,* July 26, 1970.

[20] Dulcy B. Miller, "Nursing Home Setting," *Parks and Recreation,* January 1967, p. 38.

10. Do not make sudden changes in the program or procedures unless approved by the group.
11. Encourage members to participate but don't pressure them.
12. Play no favorites and avoid controversy.

Research on Aging

Gerontologists are convinced that "the lack of social integration is a vital causative factor in mental disorders of the aging."[21] A number of recent studies support their belief that the types of social relations experienced by the aged are a crucial factor in their mental health.

Much of the research on the aging has dealt with the problems of geriatric patients in institutional settings. Such research has substantiated the views of earlier studies that much of the deterioration of older persons results from the circumstances under which they live and is not organic in nature. Dr. William C. Menninger stated that: "People who stay young despite their years, do so because of an active interest that provides satisfaction through participation."[22]

Many experimental projects have suggested that confused, deteriorated, and withdrawn geriatric patients have made significant improvements as a result of recreation activities designed to promote social interaction.

Universities and major industries are preparing older persons for retirement and for an effective adjustment to aging. With greater intensity, research and investigation studies are trying to find better ways of meeting the recreation needs of the aged.

A recent development is the growing number of retirement communities in this country. According to Peter J. Verhoven, "Older persons who reside in these communities represent a rather homogeneous group of more affluent and higher educated individuals who, contrary to the majority of the elderly population, have found self-gratification in non-occupational roles."[23]

National Organization

The National Council on the Aging is a private, nonprofit, voluntary agency that provides leadership and assistance to organizations and individuals concerned with the field of aging. The programs and activities of NCOA are centered on research and information, advocacy of a better quality of life for the elderly, training, technical assistance, and consultation. Further information can be obtained by writing to the National Council on the Aging, 1828 L Street, N.W., Washington, D.C. 20036.

Governmental Assistance

For several decades, the federal government and various state programs have provided varied forms of assistance for aging Americans. Social Security has provided retirement income, and the Medicare program has relieved the burden of medical costs for the aged by helping to pay for hospital bills, stays in extended-care facilities, and medical bills for those who live at home. Many research programs and demonstration projects have been funded. Yet, governmental assistance, at best, has been insufficient to meet the growing needs of the aging.

A number of states are providing recreation programs and services for aging persons, such as Michigan's special Commission on Aging. Hopefully, other states will adopt similar legislation, and together all the states will move to meet the many unserved needs of the elderly.

RECREATION FOR THE DISADVANTAGED

Although millions of affluent Americans have accumulated both wealth and leisure-time oppor-

---

[21] Howard G. Danford and Max Shirley, *Creative Leadership in Recreation,* 2nd Ed. (Boston: Allyn and Bacon, Inc., 1970), p. 323.

[22] Carol Lucas, *Recreational Activity Development for the Aging* (Springfield, Illinois: Charles C. Thomas, Publisher, 1962), p. 3.

---

[23] Stein and Sessoms, op. cit., p. 394.

tunities, the disadvantaged, however, have been deprived of sufficient facilities and services to lead a normal life. Wretched housing, overcrowding, lack of food and clothing, and insufficient income have made life miserable for the poor. In addition, they have lacked sufficient recreation facilities, leadership, and opportunities for satisfying leisure-time experiences. It is little wonder that people of low income feel detached from the rest of American society.

Following an unprecedented growth in the world's population over the last twenty-five years, many people predict this enormous growth in human numbers will lead to mass starvation and a breakdown of society. This pessimistic viewpoint, however, is not shared by Roger Revelle of the Harvard Center for Population Studies. "The real problem is not the danger of over-population but the wide and growing gap between the nations with two-thirds of humanity living in poverty, ill health, and ignorance, and one-third living in affluence and experiencing well-fed lives."[24]

THE NATURE AND EXTENT OF POVERTY

The poor or economically deprived were defined by James Murphy ". . . as people who are not now maintaining a decent standard of living and whose basic needs exceed their means to satisfy them."[25]

Poor people and various disadvantaged groups are the most in need of recreation services in the community. This is particularly true because they have the least financial resources available.

According to the Office of Economic Opportunity, the number of poor Americans is approximately 30 million people, many of whom are members of racial minority groups. This figure is based on a flexible "poverty line" of about $3,500 per family per annum. "Living chiefly in cities, the poor suffer from poor municipal services, deteri-

orated housing, inferior schools, higher prices, and inadequate food," declared Richard Kraus.[26]

Although poverty in America has decreased somewhat, there is still an ever-widening gap between the rich and the poor.

The deterioration of many of America's cities, where some 20 percent of the urban residents earn less than the amount necessary for a minimum decent standard of living, is compounded when skilled people move out and are replaced by new migrants from the South. The new urban dwellers add to the already poor situation existing in the central cities which consist primarily of low-income families, unemployed people, the aged, and fatherless families.[27]

Needs of the Disadvantaged

Efforts to meet the special needs of disadvantaged people have increased, but there are still great numbers of poor Americans without organized recreational opportunities.

The general feeling among those in social service is that special assistance is needed to get the poor involved and participating in leisure-service programs. "The economically deprived person often lacks the basic knowledge, attitude, skills, and habits necessary for voluntary participation in recreation programs," stated Murphy. "The middle and upper classes are usually more capable of satisfying their leisure desires independently and interests are ordinarily quite different from the poor."[28]

In America, the amount of money spent on commercial recreation opportunities is beyond the means of poor people who on the average, live on less than $3,600 a year for an urban family of four. Generally, public tax-supported park and recreation programs have been meager or nonexistent.

Since many commercial recreation opportunities are unavailable to the poor, greater services should be offered by local, state, and federal government recreation agencies, as well as by voluntary social organizations.

[24] Roger Revelle, "The Next Billion Years—The Population Bloom," *San Francisco Examiner*, July 20, 1973.

[25] Stein and Sessoms, op. cit., p. 285.

[26] Kraus, op. cit., p. 387.

[27] Stein and Sessoms, op. cit., p. 283.

[28] Ibid., p. 309.

Fig. 11-10 GREATER SERVICES should be offered the poor and disadvantaged groups by local, state, and federal recreation agencies. Here, children living in the Chicago Park District are treated to an animal demonstration at the playground.

The Role of Recreation

Recreation and leisure service has a vital role to play in efforts to improve the lives of the disadvantaged. Sociologists are convinced that a lack of recreation and leisure is a major feature of disadvantagement and a major source of discontent.

The recreation profession did not begin to take an active interest in meeting the leisure needs of the poor—particularly the non-white poor—until the 1960s.

According to Richard Kraus:

This came about as a consequence of the federal antipoverty program, which provided special funding to serve the disadvantaged; it did not gain full impetus until urban rioting erupted throughout the nation in 1964 and 1965

and brought the needs of inner-city residents forcefully to the attention of the public. In city after city where serious riots had occurred in recent summers, one of the angry complaints of ghetto residents had been about the lack of adequate parks, swimming pools, recreation programs, and leadership. The lack of adequate recreation and parks was more frequently cited as a grievance by Negro residents than the discriminatory administration of justice, inadequate welfare programs, or poor municipal services.[29]

In an effort to head off rioting in big cities in 1967, the U.S. Senate appropriated an additional

[29] Richard Kraus, *Recreation and Leisure in Modern Society,* © 1971 by Meredith Corporation. Reprinted by permission of Prentice-Hall, Inc., Englewood Cliffs, N.J. Pp. 388–89.

$78 million in anti-poverty funds. The money was to be used to provide new jobs, supervise recreation, light playgrounds, and provide swimming pools, with priority emphasis on areas that needed it immediately.

Program Guidelines

In approaching the leisure problems of the disadvantaged, recreation agencies should implement the following program guidelines:

1. Recognizing ethnic and cultural differences in program offerings.
2. Providing services in public housing developments.
3. Creating much-needed jobs in the economically depressed areas.
4. Coping with social ills in community life with positive action programs.
5. Instilling a sense of purpose in the lives of disadvantaged people.
6. Establishing mutual trust between the department staff and the public being served.
7. Establishing a compensatory recreation program, in which disadvantaged areas are often given more funds than the city as a whole.
8. Providing a decentralized recreation program that can serve various geographic areas.
9. Recruiting, training, and employing indigenous leaders and encouraging them to broaden their education.
10. Personalizing recreation and bringing it down to the neighborhood level.

Examples of New Programs

The city of Richmond, Virginia, has instituted a highly successful work-study-recreation program. The program provides poor youth with a weekly schedule of one day of work in business, one day in community service, two days in special school classes, and one day in recreation.

The Boston Recreation Department has participated in a cooperative program which provides daily bus travel for impoverished youths to the 1,000-acre Hale Reservation area for fishing.

Operating with both public and private funds, the state of Vermont and the City of New York offer programs at several sites in Vermont for 500 Harlem youths and 500 Vermont youths to live, work, learn, and play together.

A Summer Youth Sports program for disadvantaged intercity youth is sponsored by the President's Council on Physical Fitness and Sports.

Trained Leadership Needed

In providing recreation and leisure services for the economically disadvantaged, recreation workers are needed who have a deep concern for people. In addition to being skilled in recreation leadership and program development, leaders must accept the underprivileged as they are and deal honestly with them.

In recruiting, the recreation profession must offer opportunities to potential leaders to provide meaningful and satisfying service. Competitive salaries and benefits will provide the incentive necessary to attract high-level leadership. Greater effort should be made by the profession to recruit and hire disadvantaged and minority group members.

A lack of qualified personnel to work with the disadvantaged is a critical problem. Colleges and universities should provide appropriate courses and field work within the recreation curriculum, and in-service training programs, institutes, and workshops should be offered.

The Roving Leader Approach

A number of cities in America have assigned special youth workers the job of making contact with unaffiliated youth. According to this approach, roving leaders go out into the street or neighborhood hangouts where problem youth may be located.

Roving leaders have the following tasks:

1. To help gang youth make use of available community resources.
2. To encourage drop-outs to return to school.
3. To intervene on their behalf with school authorities.

4. To make court appearances in support of the youth, and provide assistance in hearing or correctional procedures.
5. To help boys and girls develop a more favorable understanding of adults and the total society.
6. To help them understand the consequences of their anti-social acts.[30]

The project was assigned to the Recreation Department, rather than as a social work function because the recreation program has the broadest basis for reaching the largest number of young people in the community.

The roving leader approach is now being successfully practiced in an increasing number of large U.S. cities, the result of encouragement and financial support by the U.S. Office of Education's Division of Manpower Development and Training. The division, in cooperation with the National Recreation and Park Association, funded the Office of Recreation and Park Resources at the University of Illinois to promote and research the roving leader concept.

The Future

As American society changes, there are indications that the general economic and social condition of the disadvantaged individual will continue to improve. In the opinion of John Nesbitt, "The disadvantaged will demand more and get more—of schools, social assistance, health care, jobs and recreation. The recreation and leisure service professions can perform a major role in overcoming disadvantagement. They can make a major contribution to the nation by making the lives of the disadvantaged as rich as possible in terms of recreation and leisure."[31]

Undeniably, man's universal problem is to provide sufficient intellectual and mechanical energy to uplift living standards throughout the world. "Yet

if we can solve the current energy crisis and spread our technology to improve the lot of the world's underprivileged," said Dr. Revelle, "we can help the world arrive at a steady state of economic and social well-being for the foreseeable future."[32]

RECREATION IN CORRECTIONAL INSTITUTIONS

Despite a growing awareness of the value of recreation, the provision of recreation services in correctional institutions is quite limited. "Prison recreation services are still seen in an administrative context rather than in a strict rehabilitative context," according to Larry Neal, "as a privilege with deprivation used as punishment, or as a means of reducing riots, or as an aid in inmate adjustment to prison life."[33]

While recreation services are endorsed highly by many prison administrators, others feel the role of recreation is primarily to relieve custodial pressures. "Unfortunately, recreation is seldom viewed as a treatment tool by correctional personnel," said Garland Wollard, Director of Education for the U.S. Bureau of Prisons. "This has resulted in a potentially significant treatment program being relegated to a minor treatment position."[34]

In the past, recreation in prisons has experienced a low priority because of other needs considered more important. In many institutions, appropriations for recreation amount to what's left after everything else has been taken care of. With minimal facilities and equipment, correctional institutions often are so understaffed and overcrowded, that they are unable to provide the type of recreation activities needed. "Of the over $1.5 billion spent annually on correction, it is estimated that 95 per cent goes for custodial costs: facilities, housekeeping services, and guards. Only five per

[30] Roving Leader Program, manual of Washington, D.C. Recreation Department, 1970, pp. 4–5.

[31] John A. Nesbitt, Paul D. Brown, and James F. Murphy, *Recreation and Leisure Service for the Disadvantaged* (Philadelphia: Lea and Febiger, 1970), p. 528.

[32] Revelle, op. cit., p. 37.

[33] Larry L. Neal, "Prison Reform—A Historical Glimpse at Recreation's Role," *Therapeutic Recreation Journal*, 6, no. 3, 1972, p. 113.

[34] Garland Wollard, "Recreation in a Prison Environment," *Therapeutic Recreation Journal*, 6, no. 3, 1972, p. 115.

cent is dedicated to rehabilitation: education, recreation, job training, and health services."[35]

Inadequate Recreation Programs

Planned, professionally conducted programs are lacking in correctional institutions, and the findings of a Recreational Planning Study for the Oregon State Division of Corrections indicate why such programs are inadequate:

1. The role and values of recreation are not emphasized.
2. There is no professional staff member trained in recreation.
3. The emphasis is on custodial care and security.
4. Professional guidance and assistance in recreation services are not readily available to the staff.
5. Recreation programs are often instituted with little planning.
6. The administrative climate is not conducive to evaluation and change.
7. The professional recreator's efforts have not been directed toward explaining and increasing the role of recreation in the institutional setting.[36]

A Need for Reform

Turmoil in penal institutions is neither new nor unique, but the increasing number of disturbances and violence have alarmed the American public. In addition to the general discontent with the methods and facilities used in treating inmates, penal institutions have failed to rehabilitate and assist them in their readjustment to society.

According to Marion and Carroll Hormachea, "Corrections is the means whereby society punishes those who violate its laws. In addition, the system of corrections has as its charge the prepara-

tion of the offender to return to society as a productive member."[37]

Unfortunately, statistics concerning America's penal institutions have indicated that rehabilitation is not working. "Over 60 per cent of the inmates released from U.S. prisons will return to a penal institution within five years of their release," according to Vance Hartke, U.S. senator from Indiana. "Nearly 70 per cent of all crimes are committed by former inmates. Consequently, there can be little doubt that we are failing to rehabilitate those we incarcerate."[38]

The Role of Recreation

Recreation can play an important role in the total treatment and rehabilitation process of those institutionalized. Skills, interests, and knowledge learned in professionally planned recreation programs can have a strong carry-over value when inmates return to society.

A comprehensive recreation program should be developed to offer the inmate a choice of leisure-time activities. The program should offer a variety of activities to serve his needs and interests as well as lessen the frustrations and tensions of prison life. Above all, the program must be geared to sustain morale and to assist in the rehabilitative process.

Staff

To derive the greatest impact, recreation programs must be professionally planned and conducted. Qualified leadership in recreation activities will provide the necessary continuity and program progression.

There should be one full-time leader in each correctional institution, assisted by part-time and volunteer workers. "The full-time leader, or director, should be a professionally trained, skilled recreation worker with understanding of the appli-

[35] Larry L. Neal, "Manpower Needs in the Correctional Field," *Therapeutic Recreation Journal*, 6, no. 3, 1972, p. 125.

[36] Larry E. Decker, "Recreation in Correctional Institutions," *Parks and Recreation*, April 1969, pp. 31–32.

[37] Stein and Sessoms, op. cit., p. 105.

[38] Vance Hartke, "An Approach to a National Problem," *Therapeutic Recreation Journal*, 6, no. 3, 1972, p. 99.

Fig. 11-11 HANDICRAFTS OF ALL TYPES have proven highly popular to inmates at Folsom State Prison in California. Many of the outstanding pieces are sold to the public at this store outside the prison gates.

cation of the leisure-time program of inmates to their morale, social, mental, and physical rehabilitation, their adjustment to the institution and their preparation for release."[39]

In addition to planning and organization, the recreation director should handle such items as funds and physical facilities. Included in the institution's recreation budget should be funds for equipment, facilities, supplies, and personnel. The director should be assisted by various recreation leaders who will actually conduct the program. Leaders should be trained in music, physical education, and arts and crafts.

Security of the program is a major concern, since many recreational items can be converted to use as weapons. Therefore, equipment should be given a regular inspection by the prison security officer to determine the danger of these items. Because of tight security measures, correctional authorities have found it difficult to use volunteer workers. Such leadership assistance could make a significant contribution to the conduct of the various activities by providing important services and ideas.

Program

Good recreation programming should be a part of the daily life of any institution. Actually, recreation in a correctional institution does not vary a great deal from the types found in other settings of society. Regimentation of the individual and the limitations of the institution are the major differences.

In satisfying the various needs of inmates, the recreation director should provide as much program variety as conditions and resources will allow. Among the activities that have proven popular are:

1. Team sports
2. Individual sports
3. Combative sports
4. Attending outside sports events
5. Movies
6. Musical performances
7. Cultural activities
    (art, crafts, drama, music)
8. Literary events
    (reading and writing)
9. Discussion groups
10. Radio and television
11. Photography

According to a nationwide survey of federal and state prison recreation service, softball ranked highest in popularity for active participation. Over fifty per cent of all the inmates in the surveyed prisons took an active part in sports. All prisons had intramural sports events. Of the social games, checkers, chess, and dominoes were the most popular.[40]

---

[39] Neal, op. cit., p. 110.

[40] T. D. Haggard, "A Survey of Recreation in Selected Federal and State Penitentiaries of the U.S." Unpublished Master's Thesis, University of Wyoming, 1963.

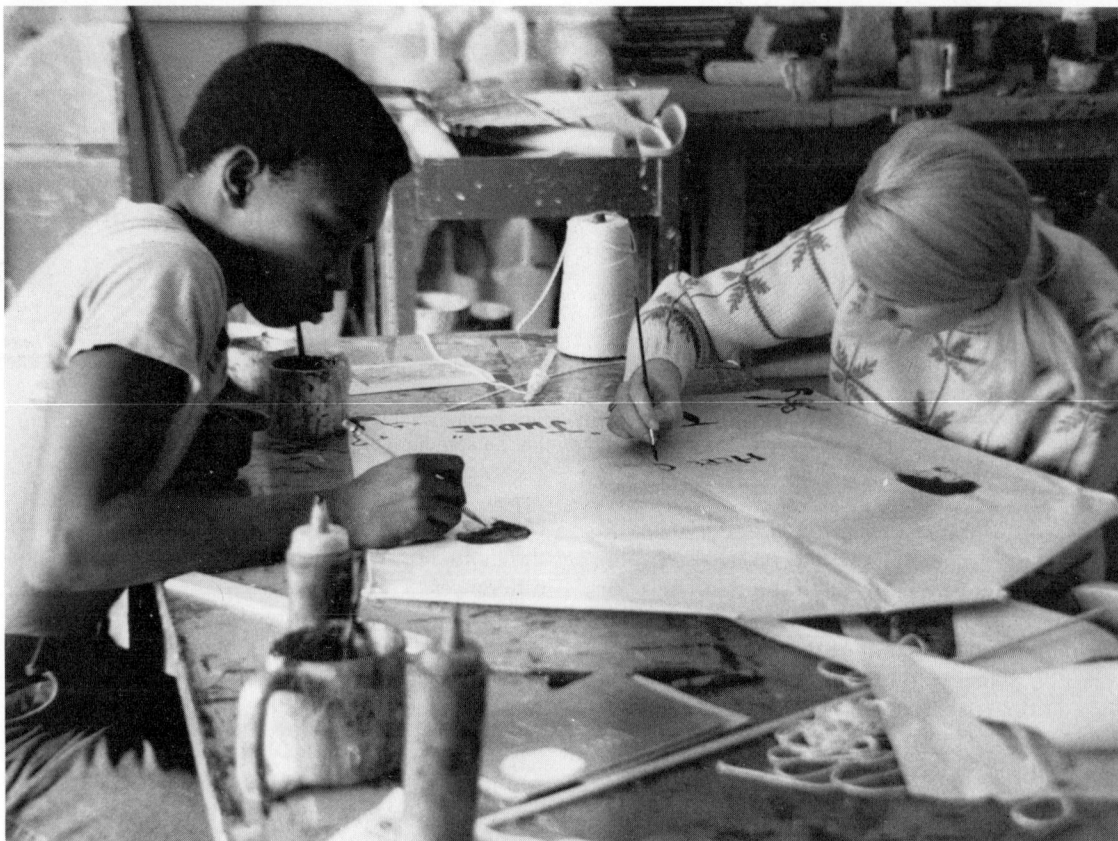

Fig. 11-12 TRAINED RECREATION SPECIALISTS, in greater numbers, are being used by youth correctional institutions in their training and treatment centers. Here, a volunteer leader helps one of the boys prepare for a kite contest at a California Youth Authority facility in Sacramento.

Art Program

The first art show held at Folsom Prison (California) in 1956 displayed thirty-five paintings. Today, the paintings submitted for judging and display have increased to over 1,000. The men do most of their art work in their cells, or in the long corridors which run in front of the cells. Handicrafts of every sort are often a mental and physical lifesaver to men who seek relief from their surroundings.

"Most men come to prison because they are failures," said Donald Moore, supervisor of academic education at Folsom prison. "Failure has become a way of life. At Folsom we try to help them achieve a measure of success so that they know what it feels like."

The Rehabilitation Program

In recent years, pre-release centers and halfway houses have been established to assist the offender in his return to the outside. A prisoner spends the last few months of his sentence in a special area of the prison or outside the institution where he receives orientation for his return to society. In addition to receiving assistance in seeking employment and a place to live, he is given help in using his leisure time constructively.

Recreation in Youth Institutions

Increasingly, recreation is playing a significant role in serving socially deviant children and youth in correctional institutions. Among the many different types of institutions are both public and private residential treatment centers. Known in the past as reform schools, they are now called training schools or residential treatment centers. In addition, many special homes are operated by voluntary and religious organizations.

Generally, the provision of recreation services in youth institutions has been very limited. However, there are a number of outstanding programs of recreation in youth institutions throughout the United States. Cherokee Lodge, a housing unit for drug abusers at the Northern Reception Center-Clinic of the California Youth Authority in Sacramento, has successfully conducted a well-rounded recreation program. The program has given its wards a sense of individual accomplishment, achievement, and has helped establish rapport between them and their counselors.

"We run one or two big evening functions each week, like Casino Night, Co-ed parties, and movies," said William Scanlon, Senior Counselor, "but we offer our fellows many low organized games such as ping pong, pool, cards, checkers, and chess." Aggression-reducing activities are given major emphasis in CYA dorms. This "controlled-violence" provides for the frustrations to be relieved through aggressive action.

Elsewhere in California, an in-depth recreation demonstration project was carried out by the California Youth Authority at two schools in Stockton. An eighteen-month project was conducted at the O. H. Close and Karl Holton Schools for Boys from January 1968 to June 1969. Under the direction of the Institute for the Study of Crime and Delinquency in Sacramento, the project had the following aims:

1. To organize and implement an in-service training program in recreation leadership for Youth Counselors.
2. To experiment in the use of Youth Authority wards as "Recreation Staff Aides."
3. To develop a community "Recreation Volunteer" program.
4. To evaluate the desirability of employing a professionally trained recreation specialist in all Youth Authority institutions.
5. To develop a recreation intern program by providing recreation field work placements in

Youth Authority institutions for undergraduate majors.
6. To test and evaluate various recreation equipment and supplies.
7. To produce a recreation handbook for use primarily by the institution line worker.
8. To develop a standardized recreation budget.[41]

Two trained recreation specialists were placed in the Close and Holton Schools as consultants. Volunteer programs were coordinated by the recreation consultant, with many volunteers recruited from nearby high schools, a college, civic clubs, churches, and other organizations. The consultants conducted training sessions for staff, wards, and volunteers. Hall recreation committees were formed. Among the projects developed were co-ed swim parties, sports nights, intramural sports leagues, and club activities.

Some of the project findings were listed by Kraus:

1. The project had a significant impact on the attitudes of the wards in residence at both schools.
2. The shifting of program emphasis to weekends meant that many hours of "dead" time were now being filled with meaningful activity.
3. Trained leadership was essential to the planning of successful recreation activities.
4. Regular staff members had "neither the time nor the ability to consistently plan and carry out imaginative programs."
5. Recreation programs are most successful when community resources and volunteers are used.
6. The interest of wards in recreation programs was stimulated when given the chance to plan them.
7. Since facilities were quite inadequate for a well-rounded program, much improvisation was needed.[42]

The project report concluded that the best programs were those that were carefully planned and conducted. Ward aides and college recreation interns were described as extremely valuable in carrying out a total recreation program.

[41] Robert E. Myers, Jr. and Cleveland Williams, "Operation Recreation," a demonstration project at two California Youth Authority Institutions, Sacramento, California Youth Authority, 1970.
[42] Kraus, *Therapeutic Recreation Service*, p. 178.

IV
The Recreation Program

12

Program Planning

The recreation program of a department or organization consists of the activities or experiences available to the participant. Recreation agencies serve people through program activities and services. In the words of George Butler, "The total experiences of a community recreation program represent a wide range of activities, planned and spontaneous, organized and informal, supervised and undirected."[1]

Essentially, programs differ according to the breadth of services offered and the concentration of interests of the participants. Programs vary with financial support, facilities available, leadership qualifications, and administrative policies. Hence, the program emphasis in one city may be on sports, in another, on the performing arts.

THE PLANNING PROCESS

Planning is the process of arranging the various elements of a program in a manner designed to obtain constructive and worthwhile results. Effective planning and organization can help attain immediate goals and determine long-range objectives. Participants at the first National Workshop on Recreation agreed that "The objective of program planning is to provide those experiences that will bring to the participant the most satisfying values and that in addition will have desirable social effects."[2]

Recreation leaders must organize and conduct activities in a manner that will accomplish this major objective. In planning a successful program, the agency or individual must understand the essential elements in providing wholesome and satisfying recreation experiences. Many factors that can determine the success or failure of the program must be considered and thoroughly analyzed.

Fig. 12-1 EFFECTIVE LEADERSHIP. The leader, the most important element of the program, sets the pace and spirit and influences the quality of involvement of the participants. Here, a young leader directs the action at one of the many neighborhood playgrounds operated by the Sacramento Parks and Recreation Department.

[1] From *Introduction to Community Recreation* by George D. Butler. Copyright © 1967 by the National Recreation Association, Inc. Used with permission of McGraw-Hill Book Company. P. 259.

[2] Committee at National Workshop on Recreation, *Recreation for Community Living* (Chicago: The Athletic Institute, 1952), p. 139.

217

Fig. 12-2 SATISFYING RECREATION EXPERIENCES. Providing experiences that bring participants the most satisfaction is a major objective in program planning. Here, children at the playground enjoy a snow cone treat on a hot summer day.

MEETING NEEDS AND INTERESTS

A program of recreation activities should be determined by the needs, interests, and desires of the people to be served. Unfortunately, many programs in the past have developed from various biases and individual interests or for the mere convenience of the administrative staff.

Through participation in activities, a person has an opportunity to realize personal objectives, as well as the objectives of the group. Although the needs of the participants are foremost in determining program objectives, the aims of any program should be in line with a sound and wholesome educational and cultural philosophy. In addition, the overall objectives of the agency should have a direct bearing on program offerings and priorities.

In planning recreation programs, it is essential to determine the specific needs of each neighborhood or area within a community. In conducting such a comprehensive inventory, a detailed study of all facilities and services should be carried out by the recreation and park department. Indicating what is available and what is missing, the study should include departmental programs as well as programs offered by private, voluntary, and commercial agencies.

The study should involve a systematic survey of the expressed wishes of the residents of the neighborhood to be served. This can be done through public meetings or hearings of such community groups as Parent-Teacher Associations, advisory groups, councils, or civic committees. Interest checklists or surveys have proven effective in securing a representative sampling of all age groups.

The capability of the community to afford the program must be carefully considered. Various

Fig. 12-3 THE SETTING AND ENVIRONMENT have an important effect on the participants and the activity. These indoor courts at the Northbrook Tennis Club in suburban Chicago offer the latest in uniform, high-level, glare-free lighting. (Courtesy of the Appleton Electric Company, Chicago.)

neighborhoods in the community often demand specific or individual programs. Programs that involve expensive equipment and supplies normally require special fees or charges. In disadvantaged areas those who wish to participate often cannot afford program fees. Therefore, it must be determined whether the residents are able to pay such charges. If they cannot, certain programs may have to be subsidized more heavily by the overall departmental budget.

THE MAJOR AGE GROUPS

Children—Preschool, 6 to 8-year-olds, and 9 to 12-year-olds.

Teenagers—Younger adolescents, 13 to 15-year-olds, and older, 16 to 19.

Adults—Young, single, younger married couples, and middle-aged group in 40s and 50s.

Aging—Minimum age of 55 or 60, those who are retired, also called senior citizens, the elderly.

MAJOR ELEMENTS IN PROGRAM PLANNING

The following elements can influence significantly the process of planning recreation programs:

The people. The basic recreation needs and interests of the people to be served must be thoroughly understood. Variations in recreation interests must be considered in relation to "different age groups, both sexes, and of people with varying racial and cultural backgrounds and in different environments."[3]

---

[3] Second National Workshop in Recreation, *The Recreation Program* (Chicago: The Athletic Institute, 1963), p. 6.

Leadership. The leader is the most important element in the recreation program. Through the leader's expertise and guidance, the participants can gain experiences that are both growth-oriented and satisfying. Without leadership, the best facility will lie idle while program offerings fail to meet their potential.

Areas and facilities. The next important element, perhaps, is the provision of properly developed recreation areas to meet the leisure needs of citizens. "Areas" refer to park and recreation play spaces of varying types, while "facilities" refer to buildings, fields, pools, special structures, and equipment that are a part of these areas.

Knowledge of the facility and equipment requirements of activities is required in effective program planning. The environment can contribute to the mood for having fun. Quite often, the failure of program activity can be attributed to the space problem. Many types of programs demand a special or unique area, specialized equipment and tools; without them success of the activity will be diminished.

Finance. Sufficient funds are needed to provide adequate recreation opportunities for all the people. Many activities cannot be conducted successfully unless money is available to pay for the cost of leadership, equipment, supplies, and other items of expense. How much money is available to support a balanced program? The cost of providing an activity must be carefully considered before it is implemented.

Activities. The component parts of any program are the activities or events which provide the appeal and interest of the program. Only through activity can people satisfy their leisure-time interests and desires. In planning programs, the leader must consider the suitability of various activities for people of different age, sex, and skill, as well as groups of different sizes.

APPROACHES TO PROGRAM PLANNING

Through the years, there have been numerous approaches and practices used in planning and organizing recreation programs. While most of them have proven to be of significant value, indi-

vidually, each approach is considered vulnerable to weaknesses and ineffectiveness. Recreation leaders who have organized successful programs have employed a combination of approaches and theories in planning their activities. They have not limited their planning to a single approach.

1. *Current practice.* Find out what other recreators and program directors are doing and take advantage of their successful methods and ideas.

2. *Expressed desire.* Determine what the people are interested in and give them what they want.

3. *Traditional practice.* Learn what programs have proven successful in the past and present the same activities.

4. *Authoritarian approach.* Refuse to allow participants to share in planning the program because the administrative staff already have made the decisions.

Used individually, these four approaches could result in unsound planning, but combined with good judgment, they are highly effective.

Nothing can spark a program more than a varied, rich, creative, and challenging approach to planning and leadership. Conversely, programs that show lack of imagination and initiative, and offer a narrow range of recreation interests, will attract few participants.

DEPARTMENTAL PLANNING

The general planning of the recreation program is a major responsibility of the recreation administration, but planning is also a cooperative effort in which the entire professional staff should contribute.

Workers at the individual playgrounds and centers contribute valuable suggestions, because they are close to the people and therefore are familiar with the desires and needs of the neighborhoods they serve. Supervisors will submit for approval a tentative program for their respective divisions. Giving the people of a community or neighborhood a share in planning programs intended for their benefit is a desirable democratic procedure; it is also a

Activities should not be initiated and groups organized unless sufficient leadership, time, interest, and necessary financial support are available. Occasionally, a department will "spread itself too thin." Staff members will schedule or start more events than they can effectively conduct. For a new program, in particular, it is very important to be successful in a few activities rather than have a program with far too many activities and have it ineffectively conducted.

BASIC PRINCIPLES IN PROGRAM PLANNING

The following are just a few of the principles which can serve as a guide to program planning. Chapters 13 and 14 will present some of the ways in which these planning principles can be used.

1. The program should consist of many and varied activities related to the needs, interests, and abilities of people of both sexes and of all ages.
2. The worth of an activity should be assessed in terms of its effects upon people. *The program should be people centered.*
3. The program should consist of activities that develop values sought by leadership.
4. Programs should be developed that are acceptable to the culture, customs, and tradition of the community.
5. An effective program must provide activities in which people are interested and strive for more satisfying and rewarding experiences.
6. The program should provide life-time activities in which interest will continue over many years.
7. Equal opportunities should be extended to everyone, regardless of race, creed, social or economic status.
8. The program should emphasize activities that relate to one another.
9. Effective leadership is the backbone of any successful recreation program.
10. Leaders should invite participants to share responsibility for program planning. *Involve the participants.*

Fig. 12-4 SHARING IN THE PLANNING. Leaders at the playgrounds and centers who are close to the people and are aware of their desires and needs can contribute valuable planning suggestions. By allowing the children to share in the planning, the playground staff can achieve strong participation from them.

means of assuring their participation in the activities.[4]

The scheduling of major city-wide events requires special procedures. The agency as a whole participates in these events, and normally, schedules them on a monthly basis. The planning of events by various major divisions, must be coordinated by department heads. Daily, weekly, and seasonal schedules must be drawn up so that conflicts and unnecessary problems are kept to a minimum.

---

[4] Butler, op. cit., p. 274.

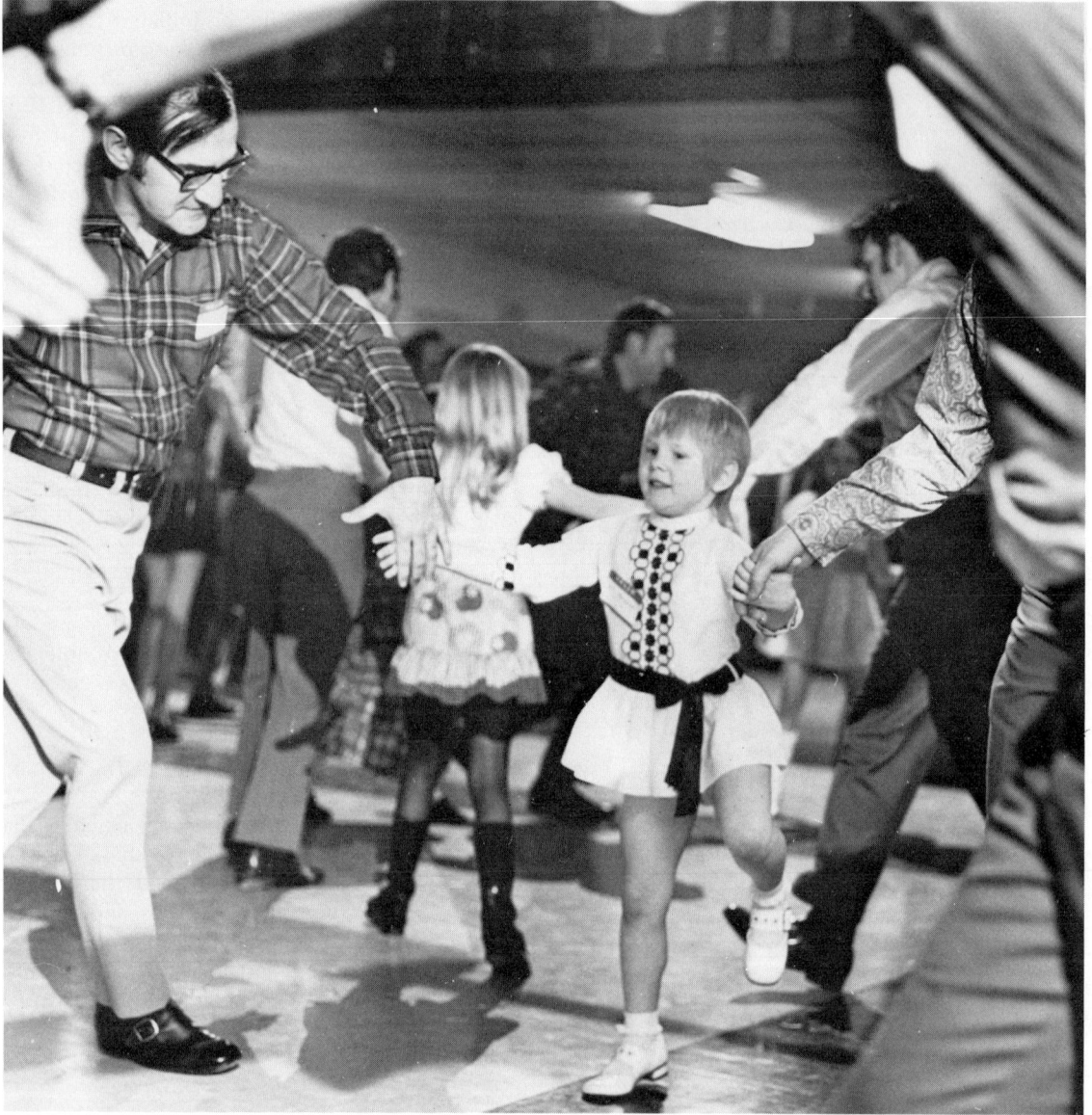

Fig. 12-5 FAMILY FUN. Opportunities should be provided in the recreation program for the family to play together. The Daddy–Daughter Date Nite is an annual special event sponsored by the Naperville Park District, Illinois.

11. The program should be sufficiently flexible to permit adaptation to varying situations.

12. Grouping is a significant factor in programming.

13. Program development should be positive in direction but gradual in pace.

14. Adequate financial support is necessary for the success of any activity or program.

15. Safe and healthful conditions should be provided all recreational activities.

16. Continuous evaluation is a major factor in program improvement.

17. Opportunities should be provided for a family to play together.
18. Programs should offer relaxing activities as well as active forms of recreation.
19. The needs of the ill and handicapped should be served with a well-rounded program of activities.
20. Overplan rather than underplan.
21. Have a keen eye for details. Use a check list in most areas of planning and organization.
22. All recreators shoud have a sound knowledge and understanding of the policies, rules and regulations stated in the department's policy manual.

SPECIAL FACTORS IN PROGRAM SUCCESS

In addition to the correct execution of guidelines and principles such as those just listed, there are a number of special factors or ingredients that are essential to a dynamic program.

Creativity

Creative thinking can be a great asset to any recreation staff. William Penn Mott, Jr. believes that the best recreation program is one that fosters ". . . the type of climate that encourages imaginative, positive thinking, new ideas and a desire to excel." According to Mott, "We must dare to try new ideas to meet the great social changes of our time. If he is timid and afraid to accept and try new ideas, even the most imaginative person soon becomes frustrated and discouraged."[5]

Although some educators believe "you are either born with it or you are not," Charles L. Nunnelly firmly believes that "Everybody is creative. The problem is how to get it out, but you are not going to get creativity from me. You are not going to get the tingle from me—neither can you search for creativity. You just have to live your life, openly and freely, with interest and vigor

and excitement, and you will be creative. The whole concept of creativity is bringing things together that never existed before."[6]

The following are some of Mott's guidelines that can start any department along the path of creative programming:

- Permit free and open discussion of all problems.
- Give department heads equal opportunity to review all plans.
- Encourage the flow of magazines, periodicals, and books through all departments. Read!
- Encourage employees and provide incentives and opportunities for them to receive continuing education. Think!
- Hold regular staff meetings and general meetings of all employees. Communicate!
- Encourage ideas and act upon them giving due credit; or, if rejected, give reason.
- Encourage inquisitiveness.
- Create an atmosphere of urgency and action. Make things happen!
- Allow employees the freedom of judgment and permit "calculated risk" decisions.
- Review your operations. Are they up-to-date? Or are you just satisfied?[7]

There is just one ingredient for a successful program that no formula can provide—imagination. The creative leader has the imagination, vision, and ingenuity to think or dream up all types of imaginative happenings and fun situations. The leader sees things through the eyes of his followers. He puts himself in their shoes and helps them make their dreams come through. Keeping in mind what the needs and desires of the participants are, he strives to inject into his program spontaneous, fresh activities and even an occasional crazy stunt.

The imaginative and creative leader is particularly popular on the playground where a child's ability to dream and imagine knows no bounds. The leader simply has to draw it out. Bringing to the playground "Captain Bloodybones" or some

---

[5] William Penn Mott, Jr., "The Creative Approach to Parks and Recreation," *Recreation Magazine,* September 1965, p. 340.

[6] Charles L. Nunnelly, "The Creativity of Creative Thinking," taken from his keynote speech of the 1972 Fall Conference of CAL-SPRE, November 10, 1972, Santa Barbara, Calif.

[7] Mott, op. cit., p. 340.

Fig. 12-6 EXCITING FUN-FILLED ACTIVITIES like the wet sponge throw can provide considerable appeal to the playground program, particularly if one of the leaders has to be one of the targets.

Fig. 12-7 GOOD COMMUNICATION. The use of a public address system is highly effective when large numbers of participants are involved in a recreation event. This portable P.A. unit is ideal for those activities in which the leader has to be mobile.

fictitious character will excite every child's interest and fancy.

Communication

Success or failure in leadership is often determined by how well leaders communicate with their followers. Basically, communication is the process by which one person influences another.

The following are some important steps to better communication:

1. Think clearly before you speak.
2. Listen intently to your group.
3. Make sure your group can see and hear you.
4. Speak persuasively, with feeling and assurance.
5. Know your subject, what you are talking about.
6. Be brief, concise, and to the point.
7. Choose your words wisely.
8. Use your voice to the best advantage, loud and clear when necessary.
9. Have good diction, enunciate, and emphasize key words.
10. Use a proper pace, rather than rapid chatter.
11. Speak with confidence and a positive frame of mind.
12. Have an idea what you want to say, then go ahead and say it.

Flexibility

Program plans should be flexible enough so they may be revised to cope with changing conditions and unexpected needs. The alert leader anticipates difficulties and prepares for them.

Flexibility calls for some important foresight and anticipation on the part of both the planning staff and the leaders. The necessary alternatives and resources for flexibility must be available. For example, a picnic group, in the event of rain or inclement weather, should have adequate indoor facilities with which to change from an outdoor setting to an indoor one. The leader who has a wide assortment of games, program materials, and

Fig. 12-8 ENCOURAGEMENT AND PRAISE. A child's self-confidence can be greatly bolstered by the encouragement and praise of leaders. This ring throwing activity took place at a Halloween costume party.

> SOME MEN SEE THINGS AS THEY ARE AND SAY, WHY? I DREAM THINGS THAT NEVER WERE AND SAY, WHY NOT?
> *Robert F. Kennedy*

> A CHILD'S SELF-CONFIDENCE, THE FEELING HE CAN DO WHATEVER HE SETS OUT TO DO, IS BUILT ON PRAISE AND ENCOURAGEMENT.
> *Elizabeth Post*

offerings will have the flexibility to make appropriate changes and adjustments when necessary.

Praise and Encouragement

No other tactic can achieve the result that praise and pleasure in an individual's accomplishment can provide. Desire can be greatly diminished or destroyed completely by lack of response or by discouragement by the leader.

Leaders should give praise when their participants do something good. People respond quickly and affirmatively to praise. The leader must never let the learner get frustrated and give up. "Keep working, Jimmy!" "You can do it!" should be steadily repeated by the leader.

Learning from mistakes should take place in a friendly and relaxed atmosphere. Participants should not be unduly embarrassed, ridiculed, or humiliated because of errors they make while learning. Therefore, by praising what they do correctly, the leader can encourage his pupils to keep trying until they master the skill.

Motivation

The ability to persuade people to participate is one of the most important qualities of leadership.

Leadership involves the ability to motivate and persuade people to take some kind of action. The leader's ability to motivate his group is often determined by his skills of communication.

Dedication and Courage

The dedicated leader has great pride in himself, his organization, and profession. He is never satisfied with "an adequate performance," merely getting the job done. He is continuously striving for excellence, giving 100 per cent. He is ready to give extra effort at all times.

Courageous and devoted to a high level of service, he will never give up, but always strive for progress and a better program. The leader who will "hang in there" even under difficult circumstances can set a great example for both his followers and fellow staff members.

THE ART OF LEADERSHIP

A leader is one who has the ability to guide and direct others in activities that are desirable and wanted by his group. He has the ability to initiate, "to make things happen." A dependable and responsible individual, he has a strong determination to carry the activity through to completion.

A leader is a person who can influence other people to want to follow him or his advice. A good leader steers his followers towards the right goals and helps them arrive there. A self-starter, he can create plans and set them in motion. Punctual and responsible, he knows how to make things happen!

Recreation leaders are involved in the conduct of activities with outcomes that go far beyond fun, enjoyment, and relaxation. They must be concerned with total outcomes—with human relationships; social, moral, and ethical impacts; emotional responses; intellectual outcomes; and physiological values. Howard G. Danford wrote:

A boy playing softball on a playground team is having fun, but since the "whole person" is involved, many other things are also happen-

ing to him. He is active, therefore physiological outcomes, either good or bad, are certain to result, and skills, either properly or improperly executed, are engaged in. His intellectual operations may involve the learning of rules and the making of intelligent decisions during play. These intellectual operations interlock with the development of social behavior as he responds to his teammates, his opponents, the officials, spectators, and to his coach, or leader. The emotions may be aroused in many of these responses. Moral and ethical choices may have to be made.[8]

Thus, the true worth of recreation can best be judged in terms of its total effect upon the whole individual, not merely upon a few parts of him.

In teaching children to play a game of tag, the accomplished leader will strive for more values and goals than just the fun of it. He realizes that good physical fitness can be promoted through vigorous running, but he also realizes that by teaching them to tell the truth when they are tagged, he can strengthen the moral fiber of the children. Thus, activities should be selected and conducted by leaders for the specific purpose of achieving certain values. As a result, the leaders should be careful in their selection of activities through which these goals are to be achieved.

The goals of the participant sometimes differ with those of the leader. As Danford explained, "A boy may enter a track meet solely to win a ribbon and status, but the leader may seek fitness and fair play as well. Probably no volleyball player ever entered a game to strengthen his moral fiber, but the good leader teaches him to call the foul if he touches the net."[9]

Types of Leadership

Four major types of leadership exist in American recreation:

---

[8] Howard G. Danford and Max Shirley, *Creative Leadership in Recreation*, 2nd Ed. (Boston: Allyn and Bacon, Inc., 1970), pp. 31–32.

[9] Ibid., p. 61.

Fig. 12-9 TAG GAMES can involve more values than just fun. In addition to the promotion of better physical fitness, teaching the children to tell the truth when tagged can strengthen their moral fiber.

1. *Activity and group leadership.* This type of leader works directly with people as they participate in recreation activities.

2. *Administrative leadership.* This leader's role is primarily an executive one involving organizing and administering.

3. *Civic or community leadership.* These are lay leaders who may serve as members of boards, commissions, councils, committees, or other citizen groups that can provide effective support to the local recreation department.

4. *Educational leadership.* Typically, this is the recreation educator in the colleges and universities among whose chief responsibilities is the professional education of recreation personnel.

Qualifications of Successful Leadership

A good, qualified leader is essential to a successful community recreation program. The following are qualities expected of all professional recreation leaders:

1. An understanding of the interests and needs of people.
2. A pleasing, friendly person who is liked by his followers.
3. Belief in the worth and dignity of every human being.
4. A good sense of humor.
5. Organizing and planning ability.

6. Ability to understand, communicate, and get along with people.
7. Good character and personal and professional integrity.
8. An abundance of energy and contagious enthusiasm.
9. Dependability, capable of assuming responsibility.
10. The desire and determination to give 100 per cent on the job. An employer can ask for no more.
11. Demonstrate the game briefly if necessary.
12. Always patient, has strong concern for the growth of the individual.
13. A capacity for patience, imagination, flexibility, creativity, and ingenuity.
14. The ability to be flexible, to adapt and adjust activities when needed.
15. The ability to delegate responsibility and authority to make decisions.
16. To provide an environment for character growth and development.
17. To lead democratically by accepting the opinions and personalities of others, by being open-minded.
18. The ability to remain calm and cool during moments of excitement and occasional difficulty.
19. Having a wide range of skills and interests.
20. Ability to conduct oneself in an ethically consistent and prudent manner.

Fig. 12-10 WHEN LEADING GAMES that involve parallel lines, the leader (Ronald Degler) stands between the lines at the end. This exciting water balloon tossing game is highly popular with both participants and spectators.

21. The talent to be productive, make things happen, to get things done.
22. The talent for teaching the basic skills of activity, in addition to social and moral behavior.
23. Possesses a broad repertoire of activity ideas and continually adds to it.
24. Knows his own leadership objectives and continuously evaluates their attainment.
25. Takes pride in his program and the organization he represents.

Effective Game Leadership

Successful leadership of a low organized game does not occur just by chance. A well-conducted game is the result of the correct execution of a list of leadership guidelines and principles. Used by outstanding recreation leaders, the process of successful game leadership is comprised of the following helpful hints:

1. Pick the activity that is appropriate for the occasion.
2. Understand the rules and procedures of the game.
3. Get the players into the basic formation or group needed to start the game.
4. Use some signal to secure the players' attention and to start activities.
5. Make sure you have the "complete attention" of the group.
6. Introduce yourself and tell the group the name of the game.
7. Have them take the appropriate formation or divide into teams, lines, or other arrangements.
8. Explain the game in as lively and enthusiastic a manner as possible.
9. State simply and clearly the directions for playing the game.
10. Make sure *everyone* in the group can hear you. *Sound off!*
11. Demonstrate the game briefly if necessary.
12. Give a brief explanation of the game.
13. Ask the group if they have any questions.
14. Have a good starting cue to begin the game, such as "Get ready, set, go!"

15. Cut the game off while interest in it is still fairly high.

Group Formations

Formations of groups have important psychological effects on the players and should be employed to the best advantage. The following diagrams are group formations used often by recreation leaders:

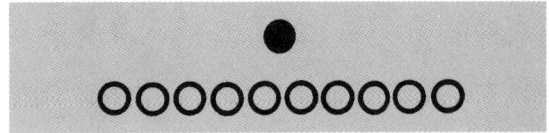

EVALUATION OF A PROGRAM

The aim of evaluation is to determine the extent of progress toward specific goals. It is used to measure objectively what a program is trying to accomplish. Each recreation leader should periodically take a look at the job he or she is doing in planning, programming, and operating the program. While the results need not be announced to the public, the leader should form an opinion for his own use, as well as future action.

In conducting the program, the recreation leader might ask himself these questions. Does the program:

- afford opportunities for all children to engage in play?
- allow boys and girls to let off steam, and play without repressions?
- give every age a fair chance, girls equal with boys?
- develop a variety of skills, give all levels of ability a chance?
- consider varied interests—music, arts, nature?
- always offer something interesting to do?
- make fair play the rule—do all have an equal opportunity?
- hold safety and health paramount?
- include passive as well as active forms of recreation?
- provide activities for different periods of free time?

A. One line—the leader stands in front of the group.

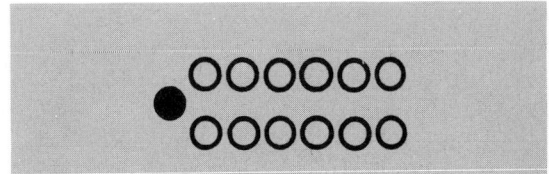

B. Parallel lines—the leader stands between the lines at the end.

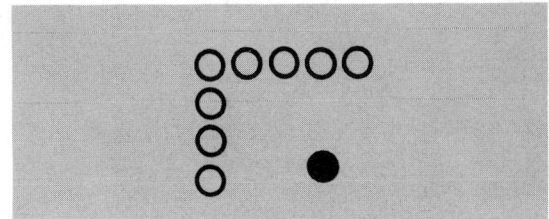

C. The corner—the leader stands in front of the corner.

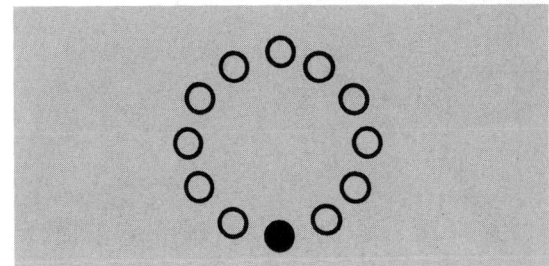

D. The circle—the leader is part of the circle.

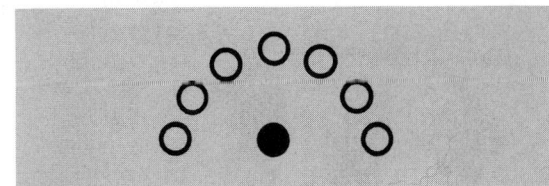

E. Semi-circle—the leader stands before the group in center.

13

Program Areas and Activities

The great variety of activities and events that occupy the leisure time of people is called recreation. Indeed, the evergrowing field of recreation and leisure services is limitless, ranging from the low organized type to those requiring highly organized planning, from individual to group enjoyments. Some activities can be physical; others are characterized by mental or social skills and interests.

Recreation activities can be grouped in a number of ways. The traditional approach, however, is to classify activities according to several broad areas or types of recreation interests. In an attempt to provide a satisfactory coverage of the vast number of recreation activities and programs, they have been classified into the following "Big Ten in Program Areas":

1. Arts and crafts
2. Dancing
3. Dramatics
4. Music
5. Hobbies
6. Sports and games
7. Outdoor recreation
8. Social recreation
9. Clubs
10. Special events

All types of recreation have one characteristic in common: they provide an important outlet for some basic urge or need. There are additional characteristics that allow grouping into the various types.

Recreation activities can be classified by the age or sex of the participants, level of skill, season of the year, or organizational structure. Activities are often classified between indoor and outdoor conditions, while participation can be formal or informal. Some activities are highly competitive, others are more passive.

Recreation programs cover a wide range of opportunities. Because of the varied backgrounds of people, the differences in education and skill levels, agencies and organizations responsible for providing recreation and leisure services have had to develop programs as broad as human interest. Likewise, satisfying recreation interests in the home setting are countless and unending.

ARTS AND CRAFTS

With the exception of games and sports, arts and crafts are one of the oldest forms of recreation

Fig. 13-1 WINTER SPORTS FOR THE ENTIRE FAMILY. Oglebay Park in Wheeling, West Virginia, has been "a winter wonderland" for millions of outdoor recreation enthusiasts. Following a day of ice skating, sleigh riding, and skiing, participants are eager to warm up in the comfortable ski lodge. (Courtesy of the Wheeling Park Commission.)

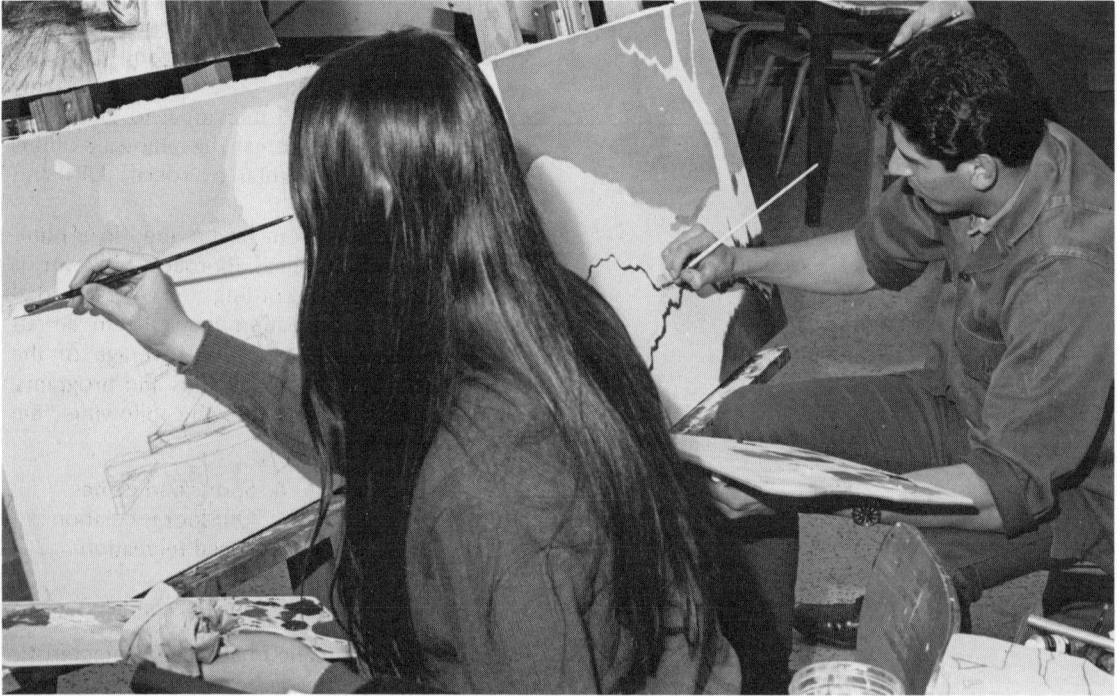

Fig. 13-2 THE JOY OF CREATION. Experiences in arts and crafts should be of a progressive nature. As skills increase, participants may seek specialized training and experiences requiring more advanced methods.

activities provided by public recreation and park agencies. The sand gardens of Boston, established in 1885, included simple arts and crafts such as woodworking, sewing, and weaving for children.

Arts and crafts are almost unlimited in scope, and may range from painting a paper bag mask for a holiday affair to the intricate three-dimensional design of stage sets; from sand modeling to wood and soap carving; from jewelry to ceramics; from random finger painting to the painting of landscapes; or from simple whittling to building boats.

Many people do not realize their latent creativity, nor are they aware of opportunities offered by recreation agencies to work in the arts, not as professionals but as amateurs. Arts and crafts experiences have contributed to the development and enrichment of personality, and in doing so, to the cultural attributes of community life. Therefore, leisure agencies must explore ways and means through which people may understand their own capabilities, and discover that they can paint

pictures or design jewelry. Children, teen-agers, adults, and senior citizens should all be included in community-wide art programs which offer drawing, painting, ceramics, sculpture, stitchery, spinning and weaving, jewelry, print making, and photography.

An individual's experiences in arts and crafts should be of a progressive nature. Beginning with projects involving elementary skills, he should be provided with opportunities that demand more advanced instruction and skills.

Although activities in arts and crafts can involve expensive projects, some of the most satisfying are the most inexpensive ones. Scrap or discarded materials such as old tires, bottles, tin cans, and box crates can be obtained for nothing and used to create interesting works of art.

Values

People have always had the need to express their creativity and communicate it to one another. In

> TO HAVE REACHED THE AGE OF 40 WITHOUT EVER HANDLING A BRUSH, TO HAVE REGARDED THE PAINTING OF PICTURES AS A MYSTERY, AND THEN SUDDENLY FIND ONESELF PLUNGED IN THE MIDDLE OF A NEW INTEREST WITH PAINTS AND PALETTES AND CANVASES, AND NOT TO BE DISCOURAGED BY RESULTS, IS AN ASTONISHING AND ENRICHING EXPERIENCE. I HOPE IT MAY BE SHARED BY OTHERS.
>
> *Winston Churchill*

no other area of the recreation program does an individual come as close to the job of creation as in arts and crafts activities. From primitive etchings to contemporary art, various media have been used to express the artist's feelings. By utilizing their abilities and expressing themselves through art, people can reduce some of the tensions of modern living, and as a result, develop a sense of fulfillment.

Some of the more positive values that often result from involvement in arts and crafts activities include:

> Appreciation and recognition
> Personal satisfaction
> Pride and accomplishment
> Creative expression
> Working with the hands
> Hobbies

Role of the Leader

A successful leader need not be a highly skilled artist or craftsman. He should, however, know how to do many of the crafts himself. More important than being a skilled performer is his ability to teach. The key to good leadership is effective communication—the ability to transmit ideas both directly and indirectly.

The arts and crafts leader must understand that the values received by the participant through the activity itself are more important than the

> MORE ARTS FOR A BETTER COMMUNITY

object being made. The spirit of adventure is a great attitude for leaders of arts and crafts to have, and they must encourage their participants to acquire this same exploratory frame of mind.

The quality of the experience is most essential to the success of the program. This, of course, rests to a great extent upon the type of leadership. Once started under good leadership, a simple program will expand through its own enthusiasm.

The leader is an initiator, provider, encourager, and motivator. He emphasizes creativity, the personal satisfaction and joy of doing, rather than perfection of the product. He helps everyone to realize success as early and as frequently as possible. He praises children for work well done, but withholds praise unless it is merited. He motivates primarily through praise and the display of finished products. The display or exhibit is very important as it gives recognition to every child and contributes to his developing sense of personal adequacy.[1]

Creativity and Art

In working with children, the leader should not demand, "Do it this way." In drawing, coloring, or painting, it is best to leave the child to his own devices as much as possible. When the child has finished his work, the leader should not confuse the issue with exaggerated praise.

The creative potentialities of children can best be achieved when the leader emphasizes original thinking, planning, and doing. "A young child's drawing is not art but reality," said Virginia Clark. "He is portraying the world as he sees it."[2]

Activities in Arts and Crafts

A good leader will provide a variety of activities and allow participants freedom of choice. Each

---

[1] Howard G. Danford and Max Shirley, *Creative Leadership in Recreation,* 2nd Ed. (Boston: Allyn and Bacon, Inc., 1970), p. 298.

[2] Virginia Clark, "Keep Creativity Alive," *Recreation Magazine,* April 1964, p. 199.

Fig. 13-3 ENTHUSIASM AND APPROACH to activities by the leader are very important. If he is enthusiastic about creating beautiful things, the group in all likelihood will be, too.

individual should be permitted to engage in activities that are most meaningful to him.

The most commonly offered arts and crafts activities for children in order of frequency are papercraft, clay modeling, leathercraft, weaving, drawing, painting, woodwork, metalcraft, ceramics, needlecraft, and plastics.[3] The five most popular activities among adults are ceramics, painting, leathercraft, drawing, and needlecraft.[4]

A complete list of arts and crafts activities is as follows:

Aluminum foil
Basket-making
Beadwork
Block printing
Braiding
Candlemaking
Carving
Cards and Christmas decorations
Ceramics
Chair caning

China painting
Clay modeling
Collage
Découpage
Drawing and sketching
Etching
Feltwork
Fiberglass
Finger painting
Flower arrangements
Furniture refinishing
Graphics
Hat-making
Jewelry making
Knitting
Lapidary
Leatherwork
Macramé
Metalwork
Model-making (wood, clay, sand)
Mosaics
Needlework
Origami (paper-folding and cutting)
Painting (oil and watercolor)
Papercraft
Papier-mâché
Photography
Picture framing and matting
Plastic craft
Pottery
Printing and bookmaking
Puppets
Rugs
Sewing
Scrap crafts
Sculpture
Silk-screen fabrics
Sketching
Stenciling
Stitchery
Tincraft
Upholstery
Weaving

[3] Donald E. Hawkins, *Recreation and Park Yearbook, 1966* (Washington, D.C.: National Recreation and Park Association, 1966), p. 55.

[4] Ibid.

Playground Activities

Arts and crafts have played a key role in the success of summer and after-school playground programs. Today, the playground leader has at his disposal an almost unlimited array of activities and projects from which to choose. As with other recreation activities, the leader must offer children a steady diet of satisfying, imaginative projects and activities which will enable the individual to express himself creatively and artistically. Indeed, recreational activities can take on new dimensions when joined with the arts.

Craftmobiles have been used effectively by recreation departments to increase participation and to reach areas more distant and remote from a park or playground. Following a regular schedule, the craft specialist might visit as many as six playgrounds in one day. Using a bus or house trailer, the craftmobile contains various machines and electrical devices along with an assortment of craft materials and tools.

On the playground, the typical arts and crafts program usually serves the needs of two groups:

1. *General activities.* Designed for the majority of playground participants, a varied program of arts and crafts activities is scheduled through the summer season. Some type of activity is offered almost daily, as the arts and crafts area makes a major contribution to the entire playground program. Many craft projects are designed to support or contribute to other phases of the program or special events such as a puppet show, carnival, or circus.

2. *Special activities.* Children who desire experiences of a more specialized and advanced level are given an opportunity to participate in special classes, usually conducted by an arts and crafts specialist or coordinator. Crafts are often organized in special-interest classes and workshops under the direction of specialists.

Indoor Center Activities

Since indoor centers are open throughout the year, they can offer a more diversified and specialized program in arts and crafts than can playgrounds. Children have the opportunity to sign up for classes to develop their skills in painting, drawing, woodworking, clay modeling, and soap sculpture. Some of the most popular activities for teenagers and adults involve ceramics, sculpture, pottery, macramé, silk screen, and stitchery.

Special Arts and Crafts Centers

In response to the tremendous popularity of arts and crafts, many cities have constructed elaborate buildings and facilities in which to conduct their steadily growing programs. Many of these buildings feature well-equipped craft rooms where activities in ceramics, weaving, and other craft projects take place. Normally, a room is set aside for art instruction.

Workshop classes have proven very popular among the young and old alike. One example is the increasing number of junior workshops for boys and girls eight to sixteen. Courses are offered on Saturday mornings throughout the year and include such areas as puppetry, jewelry making, metal crafts, and other activities.

Arts and Crafts Exhibits

The highlight or climax of an arts and crafts program is often the exhibit held annually or at the end of each season. On occasion, articles made at the playgrounds or centers can be shown in the neighborhood stores, but recreation agencies have found it more fitting to make the exhibition city-wide and hold it at one central location. Quite often, the displays are accompanied by interesting demonstrations of various activities by groups from the playground or centers. Many agencies, near the close of the summer playground program, combine an art exhibit with an aquacade or talent show in the pool nearby.

Community Art Show

A community art show or festival can be a showcase for the park and recreation agency. For both the amateur and the professional artist, as well as the viewing public, it can provide a stimulating educational and aesthetic experience.

The community art show is usually distinguished from the more formal museum exhibits because it is open to the general public for both viewing and participating.

An art show has the following specific purposes:

- Stimulate interest in the arts
- Provide a showcase for the work of the agency in the fine and performing arts
- Encourage participation in agency programs
- Provide greater recognition and encouragement to local artists
- Provide an outlet for artists, such as the purchase of art for use in home, office, industry, etc.[5]

DANCING

During the last two decades, there has been a spectacular increase in the number of persons and groups participating in various kinds of dancing. Increased leisure has been a contributing factor to the growth of dancing, but perhaps more significant has been the establishment of public recreation and school programs employing leadership skilled in the dance arts.

In many communities, there has been a close relationship established among schools, recreation agencies, commercial dance studios, private associations and clubs, and nationality and ethnic groups. This cooperation has led not only to an interchange of leadership, program ideas, and dance patterns, but has promoted a higher level of appreciation and participation in community-wide events or performances.

Throughout the nation, large numbers of children, teenagers, and adults have enrolled in classes in ballroom, folk and square dancing, tap, ballet, and acrobatics. Some groups even arrange their own dances.

Social dances, pageants and festivals, barn dances, and old-fashioned square dances are highly popular events which are playing a major role in America's recreation movement.

While hard rock is still with us, many teenagers have turned back the clock with increasing interest and proficiency in ballroom dancing. In many communities, youngsters are dancing the foxtrot, waltz, cha-cha, swing, and the samba, to name just a few.

Ballroom dancing waned as the anti-establishment movement began rocking the nation in the early 1960s. "Dancing, like all art forms, is an expression of the times," according to Mary Molaghan, board chairman of the American Ballroom Company, "and the times were mean. The music therefore got mean and the dancers danced apart, doing their own thing."[6]

But now the revolution is over and the foxtrot, waltz, and other steps are re-emerging, as the nation's young people are seeking out the big-band music. Record-breaking crowds are turning out across the nation to listen and dance to the bands of Tex Beneke, Harry James, Les Brown, Dick Jurgens, and Freddie Martin—and Lawrence Welk is threatening to become the latest teenage hero.[7]

The big, thirty-three-year-old Hollywood Palladium has increased the number of its dances by about twenty per cent a year as a response to the rising popularity of touch dancing among the young.

A Community Program of Dance

Dance activities should begin at an early age. From kindergarten through the sixth grade, rhythmical skills should be taught to all children. In the pre-school and kindergarten, the child should have an opportunity to listen to rhythms and to practice the fundamental rhythm skills. These basic rhythms include running, jumping, walking, marching, hopping, and skipping. The primary grades are a good time for children to create simple dance patterns to music.

Beginning with the intermediate grades, boys and girls should be given an opportunity to express fundamental rhythms in folk and square dances. These two forms of dance are particularly popular with fourth- and fifth-grade children.

Social or ballroom dancing is generally taught in the sixth and seventh grades. There has been some criticism in the past of offering social dance

[5] "Community Art Shows," *Parks and Recreation*, April 1966, p. 336.

[6] Al Martinez, "Dancing Together," *Sacramento Bee*, September 9, 1973.

[7] Ibid.

at this age level; however, it should be pointed out that much of the difficulty in teaching the social dance in later grades can be attributed to its late introduction. By not giving them social dance experiences at an early age, children can acquire such learning problems as shyness and self-consciousness.

Recreation agencies and the schools have a responsibility of coordinating their programs to provide outlets for junior high school boys and girls to use their skills in social dance. Co-recreational activities should be offered in physical education classes, school recreation programs, parties and socials.

In the city of Fresno, California, there was not a place in the city where black or Mexican young people could enjoy social dancing on a regular basis. As a result, officials of the Park and Recreation Department developed such dances, working with committees of young people from the various neighborhoods.

Values of Dance

The many types of dance offer numerous values and rewards to those who participate regularly. Many people like to dance simply for fun and enjoyment; others feel dancing provides a release of tensions. Certainly, the values in dancing involve a significant contribution to both mental and physical well-being. The development of poise, self-confidence, and personal adequacy are additional values to be gained through social dancing. For many, it offers an opportunity for dating and getting to know members of the opposite sex.

Through folk dancing, people can develop an understanding and appreciation of various cultures. As part of their cultural heritage, dancing can be a source of great pride and interest to those with minority and ethnic backgrounds, such as black Americans and Mexican Americans.

Leadership in Dance

For instructional classes in dance, the trained leader or instructor is most desirable. He or she must have the ability and background to plan and conduct a well-rounded program of activities. Generally, the dance teacher has the responsibility to teach effectively the basic skills and to provide wholesome social experiences.

Hiring a regular recreation leader to serve as a dance instructor rather than a dance specialist can be a serious mistake. A more sensible solution would be to increase fees and use the additional funds to employ a more qualified person. However, playground leaders should be qualified to provide limited instruction in rhythms and folk dances for children, or the more simple square and social dances which are a regular part of the playground or center program. Still, when the public is charged a fee, they deserve a qualified leader who can meet a near professional level of proficiency.

Qualified dance instructors are often obtained through the schools or commercial or private dance studios in the community. Colleges and universities that prepare professional recreation leaders usually place considerable emphasis on teaching of dance skills.

In the ideal dance class, the teaching climate and such factors as time and space available are such that the teacher can maintain a continual awareness of the individual's rate of progress. The alert teacher can then encourage natural creativity which is so often lost before the age of twelve.

Classification

A recreation dance program should be developed to meet the needs and interests of the community and should offer a wide range of dance activities.

The following is a list of dance activities offered by many recreation agencies:

Ballet
Creative rhythms for children
Dance mixers
Ethnic dance
Folk dance
Hawaiian dances
Tap and clog dance
Jazz dance
Latin American dance
Modern dance
Rock dance

Fig. 13-4 SOCIAL DANCING provides an opportunity for both sexes to meet and to develop acceptable social manners. This instructional class of sixth and seventh graders was taught by professional dance teachers.

Social or ballroom dance
Square dance

Social Dancing.   Social or ballroom dancing is offered in the program of more recreation agencies than any other type of dance. As a co-recreational activity, it has had tremendous appeal with people of all age groups. Classes for instruction cover such popular dance movements as the foxtrot, waltz, polka, jitterbug, and the Latin steps in the rhumba, mambo, samba, and tango.

Social dancing varies in form and movement according to the age group. Teenagers have demonstrated a preference for rock and novelty dances. During the 1960s, a new form of social dance emerged among teenage groups. Partners were separated and dancing became a physically energetic activity involving new freedom of expression and total body movement. Today, however, touch dancing appears to be re-emerging among the nation's young people.

Generally, adults participate in less vigorous and more conservative dance steps, while senior citizens prefer foxtrots and waltzes to familiar old-time tunes.

Square Dancing.   A form of folk dance, square dancing has become extremely popular with young and old alike. With two couples facing one another in a square, various figures are performed alternately, until the dance is completed. A caller directs the group by calling out each figure in

characteristic language. Square dancing is not difficult to learn once the fundamental figures are mastered and the terminology understood.

The number of square dance groups and associations in the United States is growing rapidly. Many cities regularly schedule square dance nights. Square dances appeal strongly to older adults, and handicapped groups have effectively modified the activity to fit their needs.

Every Saturday afternoon at the Western Dance Center in Spokane, Washington, a group of 150 to 200 youngsters from the fifth grade through high school participate in square dance lessons by age groups. Sponsored by the Spokane County Department of Parks and Recreation and the Western Square Dance Association, the well-disciplined classes are held in a spacious building erected for the exclusive use of square dancers. The adults take over in the evenings.

Folk Dancing.   Essentially, the varied and colorful folk dances are to dancing what folk music is to music. Many of the folk dances in America came from countries in Europe, originating out of everyday life. Through folk dancing, a person ". . . can express his convictions about religion, work, war, and the various customs and rituals of the people."[8]

Folk dancing has enjoyed much popularity and significance in playground and center programs, particularly in pageants or festivals. Folk dance festivals are especially suited to preschool children, playground activities, and even to groups for the aging. In addition to those sponsored by recreation agencies, typical folk dance groups represent schools, 4-H clubs, dance clubs, and studies.

Typically, folk dance participants attend their activities and festivals dressed in gay and colorful national costumes. The traditional songs are furnished either by a "live" group of musicians or by recorded music.

Modern Dance.   Especially popular with girls and women, modern dance deals with the art of creative expression. Communicating ideas through movement, the individual expresses himself creatively and esthetically through free exercise

---

[8] Danford, op. cit., p. 255.

movement, creative dance, and choreography. A typical approach to modern dance is the creation of a story, telling of the story, and then communicating it through movement with musical accompaniment.

An effective leader or instructor is essential to the success of modern dance programs. In order for the participant to gain a satisfactory creative experience, the instructor must be able to assist her in understanding the use of movement for expression.

Rhythms for Children.   Creative rhythms for children provide satisfying and wholesome opportunities for many experiences in expression through movement. In expressing himself creatively to music, the child engages in such basic natural movements as running, walking, skipping, hopping, sliding, and galloping.

In general, creative rhythms are limited primarily to younger children, ages six to eight years. Fundamental rhythms involving basic dance movements have been successfully offered to all elementary age levels.

Children are delighted by opportunities to interpret their impressions of animals or highly imaginative characters to music. Portraying an elephant or a rabbit, a fairy or a dwarf, the child can be introduced to a new world of exploration and imagination.

Ballet.   Ballet can be a popular and important phase of a community dance program. Ballet has been very beneficial in developing poise, self-assurance, and pleasure on the part of girls and increasing numbers of boys.

Ballet in a recreation activity should involve only the most simple ballet skills, and they should be done with a freer, more creative approach than in formal ballet. The younger child is given experience in simple body movements and adaptations of these movements to tell a story.

DRAMA

Drama is a form of recreative expression as old as man himself. Contributing to the release of tensions, drama gives temporary escape from reality and is a powerful source for development of creative interests not always found in other forms of human activity. The tools necessary for its expression are for the most part, voice and body.

The strong relationship between recreation and drama is not coincidental. Both spontaneous and planned programs of drama may be seen in almost all community recreation programs. Drama activities may be the simple and unpretentious children's story hours, the unsophisticated development of dramatic play of the young child, the organizing of play reading clubs, the construction of puppets or marionettes, the elaborate presentation of an annual pageant or festival involving all of the performing arts and hundreds of skilled players, or bringing into the community professional dramatic or musical comedy productions of national reputation.

In meeting the growing demands of the public for "the performing arts," many public recreation and park agencies have improved existing drama and theatre activities, and have initiated new programs under various auspices. There has been closer cooperation among public recreation agencies and various community groups and people concerned with the drama field.

Attendance studies have indicated that more and more people are practicing the dramatic arts which were once conceded to be the prerogative of the professional few. As communities initiate and encourage people to take the opportunities afforded by leisure, people are finding greater satisfactions, not only as participants, but deeper understanding and appreciation for the dramatic performances of others.

In recent years, added emphasis is being placed on theatre arts in colleges and universities, as well as increased support of drama in elementary and high school curricula. Adult education has taken an active role in the improvement of skills and appreciation by offering instruction in speech, play reading and production, acting, and techniques of radio and television.

Values of Drama

Drama in the recreation program offers participants opportunities to express themselves through imaginative and dramatic play.

Children can develop poise and self-control from training and experience on a stage. Qualities such as tolerance and empathy can also be stimulated and enriched through participation in a drama activity. A new sympathy and respect for one another is developed. Being a part of a group where everyone is working together toward a common goal can give a child a feeling of belonging he may never have had before.

Pre-school children are surprisingly creative when they are given a familiar story to act out in their own words. Every exercise in creative thought and self-expression is an excellent opportunity to release the pent-up feelings children often have no way to express.

Drama activities can provide a framework for channeling the creative drives of young people. Experience and participation in drama can stimulate, inspire, and direct the talents of young people so they may achieve the realization of their own abilities.

Drama also provides entertainment for the passive participant. Through the various drama presentations, the viewer often finds escape and leisure entertainment in the unfolding drama or lively, musical comedy productions.

Drama also has an important place in numerous social recreation activities. The element of drama can make a game highly enjoyable to all ages. Dramatic games include guessing games, charades, and singing games. The action and dialogue of skits can be very exciting.

Organizing a Drama Program

The development of a diverse program in the dramatic arts cannot be accomplished in a few years; it requires a base of progression in program approach which might take longer.

Generally, the drama programs conducted by recreation agencies are primarily for children of elementary school age. The objectives of most playground programs are based on the assumption that drama activities should not be limited to talented children but should be for all children. Many drama programs begin at the pre-school age level and are integrated with music, rhythms, and puppetry. Through these early ex-

periences under qualified leadership, interests and appreciations can be developed and maintained throughout life.

Simple creative elements of play acting, storytelling, rhythms, music, and pantomime serve as introductory activities, while story acting and elementary performances based on familiar situations and associations prepare the children for more highly developed and formal productions. The total program is planned to give progression from informal to more formal activities.

The recreation department's approach to drama should not be based solely on the development of play production and performance. Instead, the program should be broad and varied and built on a progressive development of skills from pre-school age children through elementary, junior high and high school youth to adults. Activities may include informal story acting, rhythmics, creative drama and dramatics, as well as stage crafts and stage arts, talent shows, skit nights, storytelling and puppetry.

Teen Troupe

An increasing number of recreation departments have sponsored Teen Troupe programs, consisting of approximately 100 youth who participate in summer stock and workshop experience during the summer vacation. The Troupe is a training program as well as a recreation activity for teenage youth. In turn, certain children's plays are developed by these young people and trouped to various playgrounds and centers in the city. In preparation, the Teen Troupers attend classes in producing and directing plays, acting and stagecraft, playwriting and selection, as well as costume design and makeup. The program is open to any teenager in junior or senior high school. Scheduled for ten weeks, classes are held daily both morning and afternoon. At least one new play is produced each week for theatre production and two or three trouping plays are developed each season.

At the close of the summer, a three-act musical production is staged, which is the highlight and triumph of the season. A social affair for the troupe members is held after the closing performance, at which time special recognition is given and diplomas are awarded to all who have successfully completed the summer program.

Drama on the Playground

As an integrated playground activity, drama can include informal group singing, pantomime, singing games, rhythmic play with music, play acting with storytelling, creative development of stories told by the children, and dramatizations using paper bag puppets.

Although in some instances plays with scripts can be produced, for the most part drama should maintain a spontaneity which comes from imaginative play acting. Verse choirs, folk plays, and dramatization of ballads and folk stories can all be included.

Most community drama programs take place the year round, with the majority of the activities occurring during the summer months. Although drama should be scheduled at all community playgrounds during the summer, major productions, such as children's dramas, can be held at community centers or outdoor theatres.

Facilities

Although many drama activities occur at city playgrounds during the summer, the major productions are held at recreation or community centers, or outdoor theatres. Outdoor settings can be quite adaptable to children's dramatic activities.

Recreation and parks have a long record of activity in outdoor, children's theatre, and mobile theatre units. However, few new outdoor theatres have been constructed in recent years, and it is becoming apparent that there is a significant need for communities to modernize outdoor theatre facilities.

Mobile units serve a number of purposes in the recreation drama program. Facilities for puppet shows, children's theatre performance, talent and variety shows, and other types of performances are transported on these vehicles to various sections of the community.

Leadership

The leader of a children's drama program should have a working knowledge of creative dramatics and of children's literature and plays. Equally important, they should know children and understand the viewpoints of parents and teachers.

A specialist trained in the drama area is, of course, ideal; however, the well-rounded and experienced recreation leader can become a good drama leader, provided he has in-service or supplementary training, with emphasis on the philosophy and techniques of creative dramatics, the technique of acting, and of play production. The leader must keep an open mind and learn from the children as the program progresses.

For the community theatre, though, trained professional leadership is absolutely essential. Drama specialists are recruited from several sources, but the main source is from local colleges. Students majoring in drama find this type of work an excellent opportunity to gain experience in an atmosphere where creativeness is given freedom for expression.

The successful drama leader should have genuine enthusiasm for working with children and the ability to improvise and create much out of little.

In-service training in drama should be provided for all recreation leaders, under the guidance of the drama specialist. On the playground, the recreation leader is usually the director of the play, although occasionally, someone trained in drama may volunteer for the role.

List of Drama Activities

Since drama has acquired such a universal interest and such a variety of forms, the following activities are only a partial list:

Adult repertory theatre
Ceremonials
Charades and dramatics games
Children's theatre
Choral speaking
Community theatre
Creative dramatics

Demonstrations
Dramatic games
Dramatizations
Experimental theatre
Festivals
Formal dramas
Grand operas
Impersonations
Light operas
Mask-making and marionettes
Monodramas
Monologues
Musical comedies
One-act plays
Operettas
Pageants
Pantomimes
Plays
Play readings
Puppetry
Scenery-making and stagecraft
Shows
Shadow plays
Skits
Story reading
Storytelling
Stunts
Theatre parties
Theatre-in-the-round
Variety shows
Water pageants

Drama for Children

The following drama activities are for children between the ages of five and twelve and are ideal for playgrounds and recreation centers:

Creative Drama. In creative drama, the players improvise their own lines and movement. The players' enjoyment is the prime purpose, not the entertainment of an audience. Much of the drama activity of children should be made up of creative drama. The leader can stimulate creative thinking by asking questions which the children respond to.

Formal Drama. Formal drama for children involves set plays, with lines to be memorized and

rehearsals. The play is usually prepared for an audience.

The Play. The play is a story acted before an audience by players on a stage, and it is usually the final goal of any drama program. Plays given for recreational purposes should be short and simple. A play may consist of one act or may be divided into several acts.

Monologues and Monodramas. Popular in the theatre and on television, these drama activities provide unique opportunities for the individual. In the monologue, one speaker usually maintains a simple characterization; in a monodrama, one person, through a series of dramatic monologues, impersonates several characters who tell the story.

Puppetry. A puppetry program involves all types of puppets, including marionettes, hand puppets, and stick puppets. Children can create their own plays and carry out the activity from the initial construction of the puppets to the actual staging.

The best hand puppets for playground activities are those that can be made quickly. Heads are usually molded or stuffed. Each child constructs the type he or she feels is best suited to the character to be portrayed.

A puppet specialist usually spends one week at each center, demonstrating puppeteering, assisting the children with the construction of the heads, sewing and fashioning the costumes, planning the puppet show, and staging it.

Shows can be given before civic groups, social clubs, audiences of children and adults for a variety of occasions.

Storytelling. Everyone likes to hear and tell stories. The setting in which the story will be told is an important factor. In selecting a story to tell, the leader should consider the age, sex, and background of the group with whom it will be shared.

Pantomime. Pantomime is the expression of an idea or emotion without use of the voice.

Shadow Play. Similar to puppetry, figures can be cut out of cardboard, mounted on sticks, and held so that their shadows are reproduced on a screen.

Fig. 13-5 DRAMA FUN WITH PUPPETS. Creative drama for children should be allowed to evolve easily into harmonious expression through puppetry, music, and rhythm. This puppet show climaxed a two-week workshop conducted by the Sacramento Parks and Recreation Department.

MUSIC

In every culture and nation of the world, music has been an integral part of life. Indeed, music is universal in its appeal, providing emotional responses which have given people great pleasure and rewards.

Music in recreation occurs in a wide assortment of settings and activities. It can satisfy any age, sex, taste, mood, or level of ability. On the playground, music may consist of informal sings in

the late summer morning or afternoon. The construction of instruments and the creation of a playground orchestra can be challenging and satisfying to children. Teenage choral and orchestral groups can be organized in community centers. Music is often used with other activities, accompanying civic celebrations, pageants, sports events, and ceremonials.

According to Richard Kraus, "Participation in musical activities in American schools and colleges has grown to an all-time high. By the early 1960s,

> PEOPLE SINGING AND PLAYING INSTRU-
> MENTS AND MAKING MUSIC FOR THEIR
> OWN ENJOYMENT IS A GREAT AMERICAN
> TRADITION.
>
> *Richard Kraus*

it was estimated that there were 35,000 orchestras, 50,000 bands, and 100,000 choruses in public secondary schools in the United States."[9]

The number of amateur musicians in the United States is overwhelming. There are an estimated 46,000,000 active amateur musicians in America "doing their thing." According to Thomas Yukic, "Over 20 million pianos, 4 million guitars, 3 million violins and strings, and over 2 million brass and woodwind instruments are in use."[10]

Indeed, unlimited opportunities for listening to good music are available to the American people. In addition to radio and television, the majority of American citizens have stereo record players, band concerts, and various other musical presentations at their disposal.

Scope of Music

Many types of music programs and activities have been made available through public recreation and park agencies. They include informal group singing, community choruses, and other vocal ensembles, children's rhythm bands with simple percussion and melody instruments, games with music, concert and marching bands, symphony orchestras and ensembles of many kinds, instrumental and vocal soloists, and development of musical arrangements and compositions.

Combinations of these are found in community musical productions such as festivals and pageants, operettas and oratorios, musical plays and holiday celebrations, and outdoor and indoor theatre performances. In many communities throughout America, musical productions have become a part of the cultural tradition and are anticipated annual events.

The growing trend toward the construction and establishment of community art or music centers is indicative of the significance and priority public recreation agencies have placed on music and the performing arts. In these art centers, facilities and leadership are brought together in one building or group of buildings where music, drama, dance, and dimensional arts are merged. An excellent example of such a facility is "The Great Hall" of the new Krannert Center for the Performing Arts on the University of Illinois' Urbana-Champaign campus. Built in 1969 as an acoustical environment for music, it is recognized as one of the world's great concert halls.

In the schools, music instruction makes a vital contribution to music by ". . . arousing children's interest in music and by developing skills which enrich the child's life outside the school and in later life."[11]

Oak Park, Illinois, with a population of over 70,000, offers its residents a wide range of musical activities, including the Civic Symphony, summer band concerts, a musical theatre, a sing-out group, a recorder society, and an aeolian choral association.

For 22 years, Westchester County in New York has sponsored a six-week Summer Music and Dance Center. The program is designed to give students an awareness of music as a living art. Class training in 17 instruments, under the instruction of 30 paid teachers, is offered 500 young people, ranging in age from 7 to 16.

In the adult black community of Fresno, California, there was a genuine interest in hearing "adult music." When officials of the Fresno Recreation and Park Department investigated, they learned that the demand was for jazz, not rock. As a result, a series of jazz concerts have been introduced, not only in the summer but throughout the year. These concerts have attracted a wide

[9] Richard Kraus, *Recreation Today, Program Planning and Leadership* (New York: Appleton-Century-Crofts, 1966), p. 164.

[10] Thomas Yukic, *Fundamentals of Recreation* (New York: Harper & Row, 1970), p. 119.

[11] From *Introduction to Community Recreation* by George D. Butler. Copyright © 1967 by the National Recreation Association, Inc. Used with permission of McGraw-Hill Book Company. P. 396.

> MUSIC IS THE UNIVERSAL
> LANGUAGE OF MANKIND.

variety of ages from the black community, as well as from the Mexican-American community and the white community.

Values

The unique appeal and interest of music has provided mankind with many values. "No other activity in the recreation program can weld a group together as does music in a community sing," said John H. Jenny. "The mood of music is able to change the mood of man. Tone, melody, rhythm, harmony, mood, meter, all have an especial appeal to man. Music helps to supply man's need and desire for self-expression." [12]

The pleasure of hearing or participating in music provides considerable enjoyment. Even more appealing is the on-going, pulsating rhythm of music, which invariably causes a humming, singing, or whistling response on the part of the listener.

The effects of music can instill a sense of personal well-being, which ". . . can release tensions, bringing a freer flow of energy and a lift of spirit. The individual is more thoroughly alive and inwardly at ease." [13]

The Role of Leadership

Effective use of music by the entire recreation staff can offer a recreation program much needed spirit and enthusiasm. Through group singing, rhythmic movement, and the playing of many types of musical instruments, leadership can create the type of atmosphere that no other area of recreation can match. Easy-to-remember songs can be highly pleasing for both children and adults to sing. Playing one's own musical instrument can be a challenging and exhilarating experience.

[12] John H. Jenny, *Recreation Education* (Philadelphia: W. B. Saunders Company, 1955), p. 76.

[13] Ibid., p.198.

On the playground, the use of rhythm instruments can be one of the most delightful and pleasing experiences children can have. The typical playground orchestra includes drums, tom-toms, and shaking instruments such as tambourines, clappers, and rattles.

Especially popular is informal group singing before special events during the summer recreation program, particularly when large numbers of children and adults are in attendance.

Classification of Music Activities

The variety of the kinds of music activities is almost unlimited. Recreation agencies have categorized music activities into several general groups. [14]

Singing. Informal singing, community sings, choruses, quartets and other ensembles, glee clubs, a cappella choir, Madrigal groups, solos, singing games.
Playing. Rhythm instruments, simple melody instruments, simple harmony instruments, fretted instruments, bands, orchestras, ensembles, and chamber music groups, solos.
Listening. Incidental, hearing, home music, records, tape recorder, cassettes, radio and television, live concerts.
Rhythmic movement. Purely rhythmic, simple interpretive singing games, play and party games, folk dances.
Creating. Song making, other music making.
Combined activities. Folk dancing, musical charades, shadow plays, festivals, seasonal and holiday programs, pageants, caroling, community programs, variety shows, talent shows, sports events, swimming and skating, park concerts, operettas, opera, workshops.

Singing

Almost everyone likes to sing—in the shower room, at work, at play, at school, at church, or just

[14] Second National Workshop, op. cit., pp. 200–201.

Fig. 13-6 THE USE OF RHYTHM INSTRUMENTS can be an enjoyable experience for children. The instruments shown are often used to accompany recorded music or group singing.

when good friends get together. Since almost everyone likes to sing, the task of organizing a singing group is relatively easy.

The leader's first concern is to provide the conditions that make people feel like singing. In order to accomplish this goal, he should be "genuinely cordial, warmly moved himself to sing, have full, vivid sense of the melody mood and rhythmic life of the song, know it by heart if he can, and be confident and at ease."[15]

Community Singing. Community singing is informal singing brought to community dimensions. All it needs is a good leader and an able accom-

panist who can play a given song in any key with or without the printed music.

Danford listed the types of songs which have proven especially popular for community singing:[16]

Popular songs
Action songs
Folk songs
Rounds
Hymns and carols
Spirituals
Patriotic songs
Songs of sentiment

Quartets. Involving musical harmonization, a quartet requires four voices of some individual

[15] Ibid., p. 202.

[16] Danford and Shirley, op. cit., pp. 245–48.

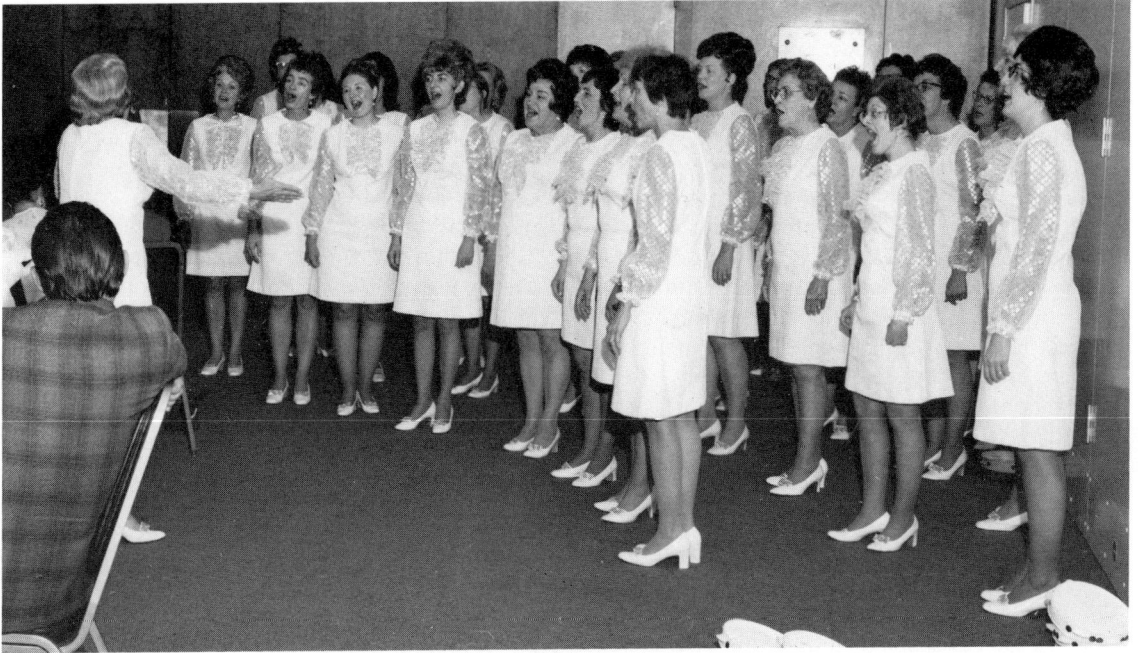

Fig. 13-7 SWEET ADELINES HAVING FUN! This Sweet Adeline group, the Sacramento chapter, comprised of mothers and housewives, receives particular delight from its barbershop harmony and singing engagements.

ability singing four-part harmony. The Barber Shop Quartet, characterizing the "gay nineties," is perhaps the most famous of musical groupings with thousands of quartets in existence in America.

Glee Clubs. Glee clubs are mostly associated with college and high school groups, involving both male and female singers. In groups of twelve or more voices, their repertoire consists of a varied assortment of choral material. An effective leader or coach is most essential to the success of a glee club.

Choruses. Representing probably the widest field for choral opportunities, a chorus involves a formal type of musical expression. Through concert programs and special functions, choruses of outstanding talent have contributed noteworthy services to the local community. A cappella choral groups, which function without instrumental accompaniment in the style of church or chapel music, have proven particularly popular.

Madrigal Singers. Originating in Elizabethan England, madrigal singing groups are again popular. Madrigals are sung in two or three parts and are usually unaccompanied.

Playing. To play music, is ". . . to produce musical sound with an instrument by pounding it, blowing into or across it, or by scraping strings stretched over it. Instrumental activity of all kinds enables the player to enjoy, understand and re-create music of all types."[17]

SPORTS AND ACTIVE GAMES

The growth of sports has been one of the most remarkable trends in the recreation and leisure field during the past two decades. In participation, the sharpest increases have been in swimming, bowling, tennis, baseball, and softball. Track and

---

[17] *The Recreation Program*, op. cit., p. 207.

field, volleyball, golf, horseback riding, skiing, and ice skating have also shown considerable growth. Hunting and fishing continue to be popular among outdoor sports enthusiasts.

Although millions of people enjoy spectator sports, participant sports have an even greater appeal. The sharp growth in sports participation can be attributed to such significant factors as increased leisure time, growing affluence, emphasis on the importance of physical fitness, and television coverage of sports events. Jogging has increased considerably among both men and women.

Millions of Americans enjoy spectator sports. According to attendance statistics, football is currently America's top spectator sport, from the professional level down to the Pop Warner caliber of play. Baseball and basketball follow football in the latest polls.

The range of sports programs, for all age groups, has greatly expanded. New and exciting activities such as scuba diving, surfing, and recreational motor vehicles have attracted great numbers of participants.

Many traditional sports have had significant adaptations which have made them suitable for those previously considered too young, too old, or handicapped. Slow-pitch softball, for example, has been a tremendously popular activity among men too old to play fast pitch softball or baseball. Even though teens, collegians, and women are playing ball more than ever before, it is the middle-aged businessman out for a quick workout and the fading hardball star who seem the most eager to belt some long flies.

The physically handicapped have found wheelchair bowling and basketball very much to their liking, while the mentally retarded enjoy swimming, softball, and roller skating.

Recreation agencies are being confronted with greatly increased demands for ball fields, tennis courts, golf courses, marinas, swimming pools, skating rinks, and other sports facilities.

Commercial recreation continues to soar. Bowling has moved from the smoke-filled establishments of the 1930s to ultramodern, multi-lane centers, with its popularity rising accordingly. In addition to bowling, a great number of Americans are participating in roller skating, miniature golf,

or golf practice at driving ranges. Artificial ice skating rinks are being built in growing numbers throughout America.

Handball is in the midst of a renaissance similar to bowling, moving from the confines adjacent to the locker room to handsome athletic centers built by universities and community organizations.

Tennis and golf have literally exploded in regard to greatly widened participation in the United States. Their rapid growth in recent years can be attributed to age group clubs and leagues and the competition such clubs provide. The spectacular increase in young tennis players and the resulting high caliber of play can be credited in part to the Youth Tennis League, the National Junior Tennis League, and the President's Council on Physical Fitness and Sports.

The Youth Tennis League and National Junior Tennis League were initially patterned after Little League baseball. In baseball, competition has proven to be the lifeblood of the sport. If a player can compete on a team at any age level, his interest in the sport is nurtured from year to year.

The same type of growth and development with a similar youth age group structure has taken place in golf. Many recreation agencies, in conjunction with private and public country clubs, have been conducting clinics for junior players.

Water sports continue to grow rapidly, accompanied by new demands for increased facilities. The great numbers of water skiers, skin divers, sailing, and speed boat enthusiasts have enabled many commercial enterprises to reap huge profits.

Similarly, winter sports programs have attained tremendous popularity in both cold and warm climates. The popularity of professional ice hockey has resulted in a "hockey boom on the local level." Northern regions of the country have natural settings of snow and ice, but cities and areas in warmer climates have developed outdoor and indoor facilities that employ artificial ice and snow. The popularity of snowmobiles has resulted in many enjoyable activities for the family, group, or individual.

Sports for girls and women have grown tremendously during the past decade, and indications are that the sharp rise will continue in the future. The number of sports programs for girls is not only increasing among recreation agencies, but schools are accelerating their programs. Consequently, those in charge of sports for girls and women are demanding fairer share of the program necessities.

Organization of Sports and Games

Typically, the sports program of public recreation agencies is comprised of two sections: (1) activities organized and conducted on the playground or neighborhood level, and (2) city-wide events.

Playground Activities. In addition to team games such as flag football and basketball, children participate in a variety of low organized games and relays which call for considerable running and throwing. Tetherball, table tennis, and horseshoes are typical games which involve elimination tournaments which in turn often lead to district and city-wide championships. League competition is offered in the various team sports.

League competition involving the various team sports is held among area playgrounds. Children participate according to age, or grade, with the largest participation between nine and fourteen years of age.

Some of the highlights of the year-round sports program on the playground are such special attractions as league play-offs, Junior Olympics, play days, and various skill contests.

City-wide Programs. For those interested in a higher level of competition, many leagues in numerous sports are formed among local clubs, churches, industries, and other groups representing the entire community. In cities and towns across America, diversified programs of team, individual, and dual competition are keeping sports facilities busy and often filled with both participants and spectators. As a result, the assignment of ball fields, courts, and indoor facilities often requires the undivided attention of a sports supervisor and staff.

The common approach to the organization of a city-wide sports program is through an association that represents the leagues, teams, and players. In cooperation with the recreation agency, the association will group the teams for league play, develop rules and policies, and conduct the post-season tournaments. Although officials of the recreation department provide overall administrative control of these associations, considerable assistance is rendered by the officers and committees of the sports associations.

Values

People participate in sports and games primarily for fun; they also participate for the enjoyment that comes from participation and athletic achievement. Indeed, the urge to play for enjoyment, satisfaction, accomplishment, and fellowship accounts for the majority of participants. Sports participation provides much needed physical exercise to keep our bodies strong and healthy. Muscles strengthen, reactions quicken, and breathing eases, as exercise and sports develop and improve the human body. As a person's physical being improves, so does his mental state and general well-being.

For many people, taking part in a sport as a member of a team contributes significantly to the development of wholesome attitudes toward those they play with. Sport becomes a challenge as one competes against himself and against others.

On the playground level, boys and girls have the opportunity to experience competitive sports activity and to develop beneficial behavior skills such as sportsmanship, fair play, and team play. The chance to be a member of a team can be a most rewarding social experience particularly when one considers the lack of belonging and commitment on the part of so many of our youth today.

Psychologically, sports provide participants an opportunity to "let off steam." By entering into vigorous, competitive play, individuals are able to express their aggressive or combative instincts. More than any other area, it is in athletics that people's competitive instincts come into play.

While "playing to win" is normal, competition and the winning element must not dominate a sports program. In too many sports programs, the goal is to win at all costs, resulting in an overemphasis on winning. As a result, the more important goals and ideals of sports are almost com-

Fig. 13-8 THE POPULARITY OF BASEBALL. This multiple-use ball field in Alameda, California, is used around the clock by baseball leagues for all age groups. After the boys leave the field, the popular men's slow-pitch league of fifty teams plays its games under the lights.

pletely ignored. The novice or player lacking in skills must be given the opportunity to compete on his own level.

Competitive athletics contribute to qualities of leadership. Through sports activity, opportunities are provided for accepting responsibility and making decisions.

Types of Sports Activities

Sports activities are classified under the following major groups:

Team Sports.   Team activities provide participants with the opportunity to "play on a team."

Baseball
Basketball
Field hockey
Football (tackle,
    flag, touch)
Hockey (ice, floor)
Lacrosse
Polo (field, water)
Rugby
Soccer
Softball
Swimming

Track and field
Volleyball
Wrestling

Individual Sports.   Activities that can be played on an individual basis include the following:

Archery
Auto racing
Bicycling
Bowling
Canoeing
Casting
Curling
Fishing
Golf
Gymnastics
Handball
Hiking
Horseback riding
Roller skating
Skating (ice)
Skiing
Shooting (rifle, pistol)
Squash
Swimming
Track and field
Weight lifting

Fig. 13-9 FOOTBALL IS AMERICA'S TOP SPECTATOR SPORT. From the National Football League down to the Pop Warner variety, football is enjoyed by millions of spectators and participants each year. Here, a ball carrier on the Washington Redskins team finds running room through the defense of the San Francisco '49ers.

Dual Sports. Sports that involve two or more participants include:

Badminton
Bowling
Boxing
Fencing
Golf
Handball
Horseshoes
Judo
Racquet ball
Table tennis
Tennis (racquet, paddle)
Wrestling

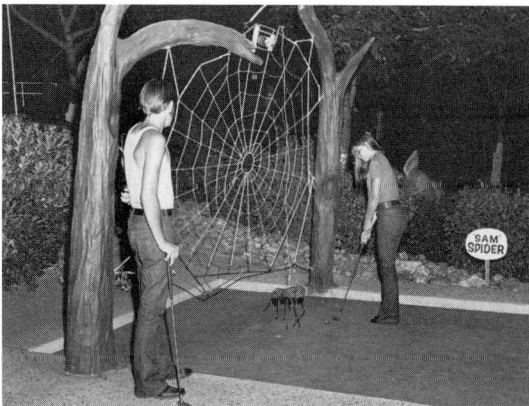

Fig. 13-10 GREAT NUMBERS OF AMERICANS are participating in golf at public and commercial courses and driving ranges. Miniature courses like this one have proven highly popular throughout the nation.

Low Organized Games and Contests. This type of game activity has proven very popular on playgrounds and at recreation centers. They require few rules and little organization. For children, they serve as a fine lead-up experience for the highly organized sports and games.

Bat ball
Croquet
Deck tennis
Dodge ball
Drop the Handkerchief
Follow the Leader
Four Squares
Hide and Seek
Hopscotch
Kick ball
Jumping
Lead-up
Line ball
Long ball

Fig. 13-11 INTEREST IN ICE HOCKEY SOARS. The great popularity of professional hockey has resulted in the sport's rapid growth on the local level. The exciting action shown here took place in the Naperville Ice Hockey League for boys conducted by the Naperville Park District. (Courtesy Naperville, Illinois, Park District.)

Maze
Midnight
Pinball
Red Rover
Relays
Roofball
Rope jumping
Running
Skittles
Speedball
Strike-out
Table golf
Tag games
Tetherball
Twenty-one
Work-up

Equipment Games

Baton twirling
Billiards
Bocci
Broom hockey
Caroms
Checkers
Chess

Croquet
Darts
Horseshoes
Ice hockey
Jacks
Marbles
Mok hockey
Paddle tennis
Shuffleboard
Squash
Table games
Tetherball

Aquatics. During the past several decades, aquatic or water-related sports have enjoyed a sharp growth. This significant increase in programs and participants can be attributed to more elaborate facilities and, unquestionably, the far-reaching exposure of swimming and other aquatic sports over network television.

Bathing (sun)
Boating
Diving
Fishing
Lifesaving

Fig. 13-12 PARTICIPATION IN SPORTS BY GIRLS AND WOMEN has risen sharply in the schools and throughout the community. Track and field clubs, such as Will's Spikettes of Sacramento, have developed many outstanding female athletes for international competition.

Rowing regattas
Skin and scuba diving
   (exploration)
Surfing
Swimming (recreational,
   competitive)
Synchronized swimming
Water ballet
Water polo
Water safety
Water skiing
Yachting (sailing)

Physical Conditioning Activities.   Regular physical conditioning activities are being done by an increasing number of Americans. However, too many of those who need exercise remain passive. The biggest roadblock to adult participation is excuses, usually lack of time or rationalization. Daily exercise is now being accepted as not only beneficial but also as necessary.

Exercise classes
   (slimnastics)
Gymnastics
Jogging
Stunts and tumbling
Trampoline

Combative Sports.   This group of activities basically involves direct combat—one person against another. During the past decade, wrestling, judo, and karate have grown significantly in interest in America, while it appears that boxing, as a recreational sport, has steadily diminished in popularity, particularly in the schools.

Boxing
Fencing
Judo
Karate
Wrestling

Co-recreational Sports. A sports program would not be complete without opportunities for co-recreation sports at the various age levels. Having boys and girls or men and women play together on the same team offers important social rewards, such as mutual understanding. Co-recreational sports that provide the greatest benefits include:

Archery
Badminton
Bicycling
Boating
Diving
Ice skating
Riding (horse)
Shuffleboard
Skiing
Sledding
Swimming
Table tennis
Tennis
Volleyball

Types of Sports Tournaments

In organizing competition, one of the first steps is selecting the tournament best suited to the sport. Several different types of tournaments exist, and they require a close examination before making a selection.

Among the factors that will determine the type of tournament to be used are the number of entries, the time allotted for playing the tourney, the available facilities, and the advantages and disadvantages of each tournament structure.

Seeding. The method of seeding can play an important role in elimination tournaments. A "seeded" team or player is considered to be highly rated in skill. The purpose of seeding is to prevent the highly skilled entries from eliminating each other in the early rounds. This is accomplished by placing the seeded teams, or players, in separate brackets. Generally, two out of every four entries are seeded.

Byes. A bye is a dummy team, or player, that is placed in the tournament and matched against an opponent, but does not compete. If the original number of contestants is an exact power of two (2, 4, 8, 16, 32, etc.), the use of a bye or byes is not required. But, when the total number of contestants does not balance out to an even power of two, the system of byes is used to make up the difference. If there were only 13 teams, which is not a perfect power of two, the number of byes to be used would be 16 minus 13, or 3. Seeded teams are usually awarded the byes. A team that is awarded a bye automatically advances to the second round.

Preliminary Qualifying Rounds. Where there are a great number of contestants, it may be necessary to conduct preliminary qualifying rounds to cut down the field. The teams that play in this "pre-tournament" are drawn by lot or chosen because of poor or unknown ability. After the necessary number of rounds are completed to reduce the field to the desired number, the regular elimination tournament can be charted and scheduled.

Single Elimination Tournament. This is a quick and simple method of determining a champion. Because losers are eliminated, half of the contestants in each round are immediately removed from further play. The single elimination tourney is valuable when the number of entries is large, the tourney period is short, and the facilities are limited.

Consolation Tournament. The consolation tournament is set up to give the losers of first matches in the single elimination tournament an opportunity for further competition by placing them in consolation rounds. Weaker teams who may have drawn (and been defeated by) a seeded team in the first round and teams who have traveled long distances are given a second chance to compete.

Double Elimination Tournament. This tournament requires a much longer period of play than the single elimination. Each team must be defeated twice before being eliminated from further competition. As shown in Diagram 13-3, the championship bracket is carried on in the usual manner,

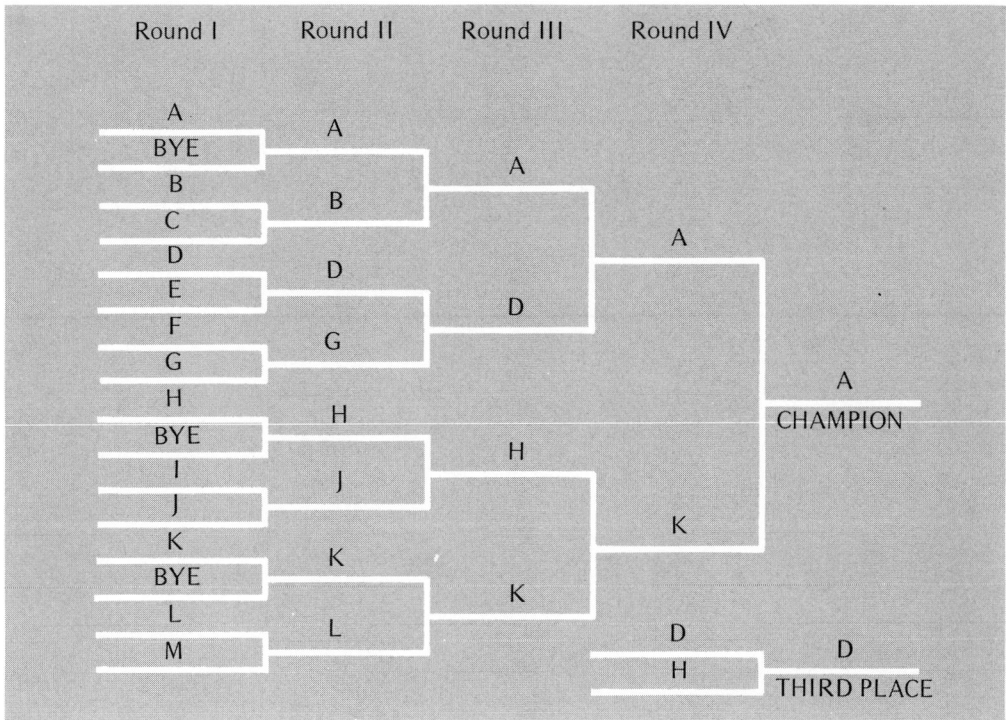

Diagram 13-1. Single elimination tournament.

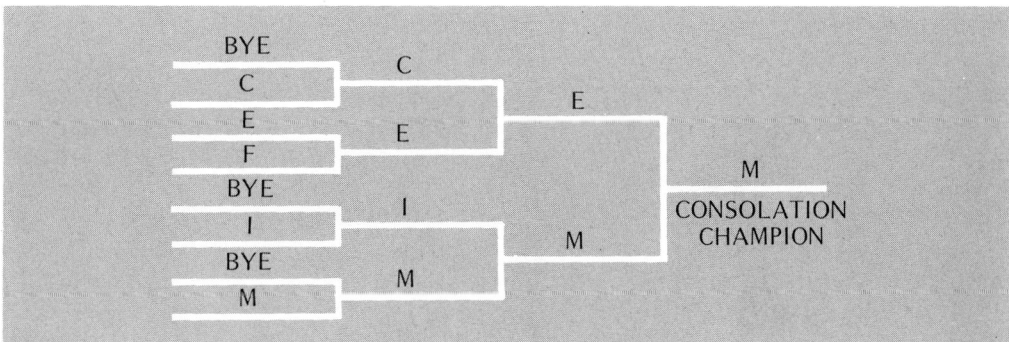

Diagram 13-2. Consolation tournament.

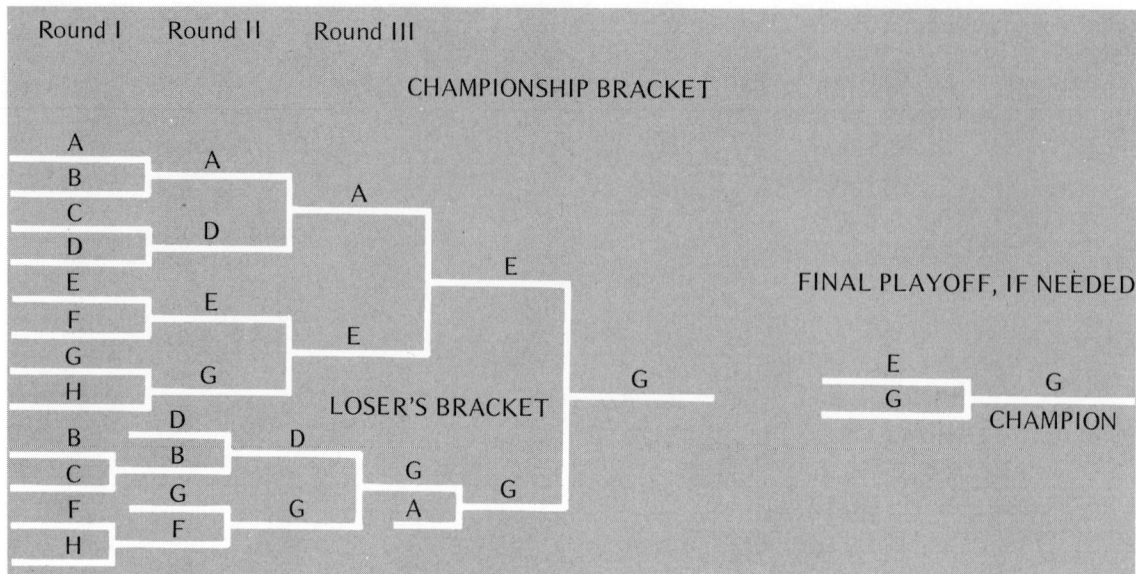

Diagram 13-3.   Double elimination tournament.

with the defeated teams dropping into the losers' bracket. The teams that win out in both brackets are matched for the championship.

Considering all types of tournaments, double elimination is probably the best to use in determining a regional, area, or national championship. Since it guarantees each entry two matches before being eliminated, this tournament is readily accepted.

Round Robin Tournaments.   Requiring a longer period of time for completion, the Round Robin tournament provides more participation for every contestant than any other type of tourney. Every player, or team, competes against every other player, or team, which stimulates interest throughout the playing season. The Round Robin tournament is best suited to league play, since it is important for each team participating to play every other team at least once.

Perhaps the easiest method for arranging a Round Robin is the rotation method. In arranging a draw for an even number of teams—six as an example—number one remains stationary and the others rotate around it counterclockwise until the original combination is reached.

Eight-Team Schedule							
A	5-6	3-4	7-8	7-5	1-3	3-6	8-2
B	3-8	1-7	6-2	6-1	4-2	4-5	7-3
C	4-7	8-6	4-1	2-3	5-8	2-7	1-5
D	2-1	2-5	5-3	8-4	6-7	8-1	6-4

(Field or Court)

Diagram 13-4.   Round robin tournament.

When teams do not have "home" fields or courts, a Round Robin schedule should be adjusted so that each team plays approximately the same number of games on each field or court. The schedule in Diagram 13-4 has been so balanced.

The final outcome of such a tournament is decided on a percentage basis. The winner is determined according to the percentage of victories, which is obtained by dividing the number of victories by the number of games played.

Ladder Tournament.   One of the best known of the extended type of tournaments, the ladder tournament can be used very effectively at playgrounds, camps, or clubs to develop and sustain interest in tennis, handball, table tennis, horseshoes, and similar activities. Usually this type of tournament continues for several months, since the object is for each entry to reach his highest level on the ladder. Contestants are permitted to challenge one and two positions above their own.

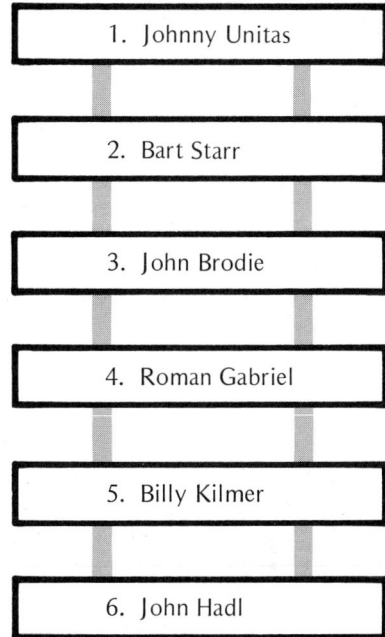

1. Johnny Unitas

2. Bart Starr

3. John Brodie

4. Roman Gabriel

5. Billy Kilmer

6. John Hadl

Diagram 13-5.   Ladder tournament.

OUTDOOR RECREATION

The urge to enjoy outdoor living has been an important concern of the American people for years, but it has been only recently that outdoor recreation resources have been made available to the great majority of the people. More leisure time, increased mobility and affluency of a greater majority of the people have caused a much greater demand for outdoor recreation opportunities. There are strong indications that this escalation will continue in the future.

Indeed, outdoor recreation has become a vital part of American life. In fact, this area of organized recreation service has expanded dramatically during the past decade. On all levels and in every outdoor recreation setting, new areas, facilities, and programs have been developed.

According to estimates reported by the Bureau of Outdoor Recreation, the American people participated in the major forms of summertime outdoor recreation activities in 1960 on 4.28 billion occasions. In 1965, five years later, the total had increased 51 per cent to 6.48 billion. Officials

of the bureau have predicted that by 1980, the number of participants in summertime activities will have soared to over 10 billion occasions, an increase of 137 per cent over the 1960 figure.

Although many outdoor recreation activities are expensive and complex, it appears that Americans enjoy the simple pleasures of leisure time most. According to the U.S. Department of the Interior, pleasure driving and walking account for about 40 per cent of the total outdoor participation annually. Other activities that require little preparation or specialized equipment are playing games, swimming, sightseeing, fishing, bicycling, viewing sports events, and picnicking. Ranking low in participation frequency are sports that require specialized equipment or skills such as skin diving, sailing, skiing, and mountain climbing.[18]

---

[18] U.S. Department of the Interior, *Outdoor Recreation Trends* (Washington, D.C.: U.S. Government Printing Office, 1967).

What Is Outdoor Recreation?

Basically, outdoor recreation can be defined as "the leisure-time interaction between people and the resources of nature." According to Richard Kraus, outdoor recreation consists of ". . . those recreational activities that can best be carried on out of doors, and which have in some way a direct relationship or dependence on nature, or that place the participant in direct contact with the elements."[19]

Values

Outdoor recreation activities offer participants numerous experiences that are both satisfying and rewarding. Participation in outdoor recreation also contributes to the enjoyment, appreciation, and use of the natural environment.

Among the many values outdoor recreation activity will develop in the individual, are these:

1. A sense of responsibility for the preservation, care, and wise use of the natural environment.
2. An awareness and understanding of nature.
3. An understanding and appreciation of man's heritage of outdoor living, skills, and pursuits.
4. Good outdoor citizenship.
5. A contribution to physical and mental health.
6. Resourcefulness, self-reliance, and adaptability.[20]

Classification of Outdoor Recreation Activities

As mentioned earlier, outdoor recreation experiences are extremely varied. Therefore, the list of activities and program services is equally numerous and diversified.

Astronomy
Backpacking
Bird walks
Boating
Camping

Caring for pets
Cave exploration
Coasting
Conservation sessions
Cycling
Day camp
Dog obedience
Driving for pleasure
Family camping
Fishing
Flower shows
Gardening
Glider soaring
Hiking
Horseback riding
Hunting
Ice boating
Ice skating
Indian lore
Kite flying
Mountaineering
Nature clubs
Nature trails
Nature museum
Nature study
Nature walks
Outdoor cooking
Outdoor games
Oyster roasts
Pet shows
Picnicking
Recreation vehicles
Resident camp
Sailing
Skiing (snow, water)
Skin and scuba diving
Snowshoeing
Snowmobiling
Snowtracking
Surfing
Swimming
Target shooting
Terrariums
Travel
Trap shooting
Tree identification
   trips
Underwater
   exploration

[19] Kraus, op. cit., p. 130.

[20] *The Recreation Program*, op. cit., p. 240.

Fig. 13-13 THE ENJOYMENT OF OUTDOOR ACTIVITY. Walking for pleasure is not only America's favorite pastime, but the desire for fitness, adventure, and exploration has contributed to a big increase in hiking and backpacking. This beautiful scene shows Glacier Lake in Montana's Flathead National Forest. (Courtesy of the U.S. Forest Service.)

Walking for
  pleasure
Watching outdoor
  sports events

Nature Activities. There is a wide range of nature activities that provide leisure-time enjoyment. Activities in natural science include the following:

Care of animals
Clubs and classes
Collections
Discovery and exploration
Experimentation
Exploration
Gardening
Nature arts and crafts
Nature games
Nature literature
Observation

Sightseeing
Special events
Talks and demonstrations

Trips and Outings. Many forms of trips and outings are part of the outdoor recreation program. Some trips are taken simply for the enjoyment of scenic beauty; others are made in order to reach a suitable location for a specific activity.

Bird walks
Group camping
Hiking
Historical sites
Informal outings
  free play
  informal games
  picnics
  visits to zoos, gardens
  walks
Nature observation

Parks
Pleasure driving
Snowshoeing
Tours and travel
Travel camping
Tree identification

Camping or Outdoor Living. Camps vary with the purposes of their establishment and organization. Perhaps the most prominent category are publicly owned campgrounds such as those found in national, state parks and forests, or locally operated areas. Resident camps for children are another well known area of camping. Day camps are designed to provide children with outdoor recreation experiences similar to those found in resident camps. In privately owned camp grounds families can pitch tents or park trailers or campers for a fee.

Plant Culture and Husbandry. A major outdoor activity among Americans, plant culture and husbandry involves such satisfying activities as growing plants, caring for animals, lawn care, gardening, and the development of land.

Animal care
Club activities
Experimentation
Forestry projects
Gardening
Land care
Landscaping
Special events
Trips and excursions

Outdoor Sports

Outdoor-related sports apply to those outdoor activities that involve the use of natural resources. The demand for outdoor recreation sports has increased at a spectacular rate in recent years.

Snow and Water Skiing. Once considered for only the young and the most daring, skiing is now enjoying growing popularity on land and water for members of the entire family. For those fortunate to get to the ocean fronts, surfing has provided many thrills and excitement.

Sailing and Boating. The increasing interest in boating and the ability of many people to own their own boat have been responsible for the increasing number of yacht and boating clubs of all kinds. Outboard motor boats of various types and sizes are found in boat clubs; sailboats and inboard motor cruisers can be found at yacht clubs.

Hunting and Fishing. These are two of the oldest forms of outdoor recreation activity, and they are still highly popular. In meeting the tremendous interest generated by these two outdoor pursuits, recreation agencies regularly schedule instruction in the use of guns, in bait fly casting, and in the use of other fishing equipment.

Hiking, Climbing, and Cycling. The urge for outdoor activity, adventure, and exploration can be attributed to the great increase in these outdoor pursuits. Interest in walking, jogging, and hiking has risen sharply, motivated, no doubt, by a desire for health and physical fitness. There has been a big increase in hiking and cycling trails in urban areas. Bicycling is one of the fastest growing outdoor recreation activities in America.

Underwater Exploration. Interest in skin and scuba diving has resulted in a booming business for industrial firms that manufacture the wide range of recreational equipment for exploring the natural environment under water.

Horseback Riding and Backpacking. The keen interest in horseback riding has resulted in the growth of riding clubs and the desire of people for their own horse. Although backpacking on horses or burros is highly popular, the number of hikers who enjoy "roughing it" have made backpacking by foot even more widespread.

Recreational Vehicles. Motorized vehicles of all kinds have contributed greatly to the growth of outdoor recreation. Providing increased mobility to outdoorsmen are motorcycles, travel trailers, campers, motor boats, snowmobiles, four-wheel drive cars or jeeps, mini-bikes, sail boats with auxiliaries, and others.

Despite the considerable fun and enjoyment they can provide, some of the recreation vehicles, such as snowmobiles and motorcycles, have created problems. Damage of wild lands, conservation neglect of our natural resources, and disruption of the quiet and peacefulness of the outdoor environment are some of the problems that call for appropriate regulatory measures.

Cross country skiers are increasingly critical of noisy snowmobilers who buzz by and zip over the next hill. The buzz-saw noise made by snowmobiles seems to be the main complaint voiced by skiers. Skiers and conservationists have also complained that snowmobiles are chasing off wildlife and in many instances have harmed plants and burrowing animals.

Apparently, the time is fast drawing to a close when owners of motorcycles, dune buggies and four-wheel-drive rigs can enjoy the freedom and exhilaration of tearing off indiscriminately across public land. State and federal agencies, along with conservation groups, are looking hard for ways to curb damage being caused by the swelling numbers of off-road vehicles in the back country.

The U.S. Forest Service and Bureau of Land Management have set up off-road vehicle recreation management plans for their lands. The bureau has set aside a million acres where the machines can be used without restriction, but bars them completely from another 825,000 acres, and limits travel to existing roads on the balance of the land.

Although he agrees that some controls are needed, Jack Edwards, administrator for the California Association of 4-Wheel Drive Clubs, is fearful that the estimated 10,000 four-wheel drive club members in California will be left out in the cold if "some common sense" is not used in drawing up the rules. Meanwhile, federal and state agencies are striving to work out regulatory provisions that will allow all outdoor recreation groups and clubs to "do their own thing."

Outdoor Recreation Enterprises

In 1962, the Outdoor Recreation Resources Review Commission (ORRRC) made an extensive study of private outdoor recreation facilities in the United States. The study revealed much useful information on the role and significance of privately sponsored outdoor recreation.

Among the findings of the study were that the majority of guest ranches, campgrounds, hunting and fishing camps, and shooting preserves are owned by private individuals or families. Most of the resorts and resort hotels, beaches, ski areas, and industrial employee recreation areas are owned by companies or corporations.

Swimming is the most frequently offered activity and the most popular at outdoor recreation enterprises. Camping, fishing, hiking, picnicking, boating, and golf are other highly popular activities.

The study indicated that a growing number of private land owners are increasing their income by developing the recreational potential of their property and resources.

Recreation Resorts. Perhaps the most widespread and lucrative privately owned enterprises are recreation resorts ranging from motels, cottages, and waterfront hotels, to huge harbor-bay or oceanside resort complexes. While the resort industry has been hurt by the fuel shortage, an easing of the energy crisis will make this area one of the most promising in the leisure industry.

Guest Ranches. A large number of ranches in the United States still provide recreation and vacation facilities for their guests. Many of these are working ranches that also offer entertainment and leisure services.

Shooting Preserves. To meet the continued growth and interest in hunting, there has been a steady increase in the number of privately owned shooting preserves where game is raised and later released for hunting purposes.

Vacation Farms. Vacation farms have provided city residents with a view of a different way of life. Increasingly, farm families are making their homes and nearby meadows, streams, and woods available to paying guests.

Shoreline Homes and Developments. In many areas of the country, the shorelines of lakes and rivers have been developed with private homes, many of them for vacation purposes. Hotels, motels, and private clubs, particularly, have developed large areas of private waterfront.

Company-Resort Areas. Industrial firms and union organizations are providing outdoor recreational areas at lakes and oceanside sites for their employees. Many of these vacation resorts provide comprehensive recreation programs for the company employees or union members and their families. Elaborate recreation facilities and services are offered year-round, for vacation and weekend use.

SOCIAL RECREATION

The wide range of opportunities for social life among people of all ages indicates the importance of social recreation experience in daily living. Essentially, the primary value of social recreation in a recreation program is its contribution to the social life of the participant.

Social recreation includes activities that help create a spirit of fun, fellowship, and sociability. A child's birthday party; teen centers and dances; trips by the family to the lake; watching sports, music, and drama events; adult square dances; and Golden Age Club activities are prime examples of the tremendous interest in social recreation opportunities.

Some of the most popular social recreation experiences take place at the following:

Coffee-tea hours
Co-recreation sports nights
Dances
Dinners and banquets
Drop-in centers
Family recreation
Game room activities
Outings and trips
Parties
Picnics
Social conversation
Special events

People of all ages have a need for social recreation. Children and adolescents find social activities exciting and satisfying. Young men and women need opportunities to meet and become acquainted with persons of the opposite sex.

Social recreation is practiced through an informal approach, which is adapted to the interest and ability of the participants. The imagination and ingenuity of the leader are important elements, but the needs and interest of the group should dictate the type of activities offered.

No one needs advance preparation to participate in social recreation activity. They should be able to use whatever skills they have. Emphasis on skill and winning should be minimized. Group fun and enjoyment are far more important than who wins or who loses.

Values in Game Play

Many important personal and social values and outcomes can be achieved from participation in games. The outstanding leader has definite goals in mind in organizing and conducting games for every occasion. Players can learn to:

Play according to the rules
Accept boundaries
Develop new skills and interests
Take turns
Accept defeats as well as victories
   in good spirit
Develop good sportsmanship
Cooperate with others
Be decisive

Objectives

The personal objectives of social recreation are to provide opportunities for the development of:

Worthy use of leisure time
Emotional releases and relaxation
A sense of personal worth
New friendships
Identification with others
A sense of belonging
Experiences in democratic living
Self-expression
Creative experiences
Leadership qualities

Classification

Social recreation consists of many different activities and events. Space will not permit separate descriptions of them individually; rather, they will be covered from a general approach.

Social Game Categories. The following are the major categories of low organized social games:

Active games
Ball games
Brain teasers
Card games
Circle games
Creative fun makers
Dance games
Defrosters
Dramatic games
Drawing games
Family games
Floor games
Ice breakers
Indoor naturettes
Magic tricks
Marble game
Memory games
Mental games
Musical quizzes
Mystifiers
Novelty contests
Party type games
Pencil and paper games
Picnic games
Puzzles
Quiet games
Quizzes
Sense alerters
Singing games
Skits
Socializers
Social mixers
Stunts
Relays
Table games
Tag games
Water games
Word games

Social Events

Amateur nights
Banquets
Barbecues

Basket suppers
Birthday parties
Card parties
Carnivals
Clambakes
Family nights
Father-son (or
   daughter) parties
Fun nights
Hayrides
Ice cream social
Marshmallow roasts
Masquerades
Mother-daughter
   (or son) parties
Picnics
Pot-luck suppers
Progressive parties
Scavenger hunts
Social dancing
Social games
Table games
Talent shows
Treasure hunts
Visiting
Wiener roasts

Planning the Program

Careful planning is the key to a successful program of social recreation. In planning activities and events, the social recreation leader should know:

Age and sex of participants
Number in group
Skill, education, social levels
Interests and needs
Facilities available
Equipment and supplies
Type of program, length, time
Funds available for program
Program assistance available
Financial status of participants

Planning Parties

Successful party leadership depends upon careful planning. Activities, wisely selected, must be bal-

Fig. 13-14 THE FUN AND EXCITEMENT OF PIÑATA have made this traditional Mexican game highly popular in America, too. After a close miss by this young lady, the next participant brought the candy down to the floor where anxious children scrambled after the goodies.

anced with both active and passive games, and with good continuity and progression effectively presented to reach a fitting climax.

Committees can be appointed to plan the program, refreshments, and decorations. Under the direction and guidance of the party chairman, the group should determine the theme and object of the party, setting the tune and place of the event. Invitations, decorations, and refreshments can be built around a theme.

Game Leadership

To be effective, the social recreation leader must master the art of game leadership. The following are eight of the most important points in successful game leadership:

1. Select the right activity.
2. Get the complete attention of the group.
3. Move the players into a formation in which you can best communicate to them.
4. Introduce yourself and the name of the game.
5. Explain the game clearly and enthusiastically.
6. Have the players take the appropriate formation, that is, teams, lines, circles, etc.
7. Before beginning, ask for questions to clear up any uncertainty.
8. Stop the game before it starts to drag.

Psychological Effects of Game Formations

Game formations have definite psychological effects on the players. In their book *Social Games for Recreation*, Evelyne Borst and Elmer Mitchell listed some of these effects:

Standing or sitting in a circle has a unifying effect on the players by giving them a feeling of belonging and being a part of the group.
The action of assembling, scattering, and reassembling has a defrosting effect, minimizing self-consciousness by keeping everyone busy.
Standing in a line creates in individuals a feeling of "action," for the line frequently is the springboard for activity.
Standing in files, one player behind the other, symbolizes relays-group competition.[21]

---

[21] Evelyne Borst and Elmer Mitchell, *Social Games for Recreation* (New York: The Ronald Press, 1959), pp. 5–6.

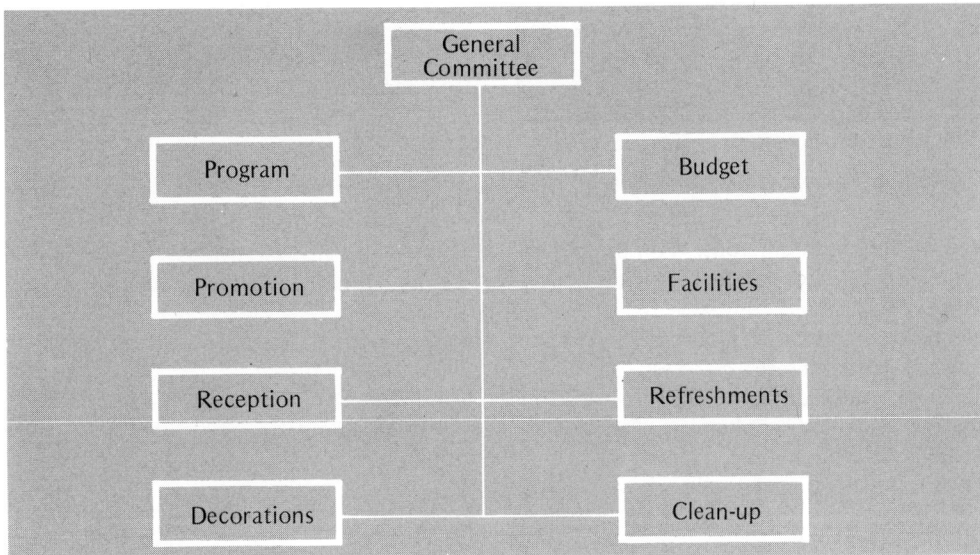

Diagram 13-6.   Organization chart for conducting a party or social event.

Starting, guiding, and stopping are three important techniques of game leadership in capturing the interest of the participant and keeping the tempo moving. The leader must be able to start and accelerate the opening activity and maintain a spirit of fun and cooperation. Then, with good continuity, the leader can guide the players from one activity to the next.

- Were the leaders friendly and enthusiastic?
- Did they have good rapport with participants?
- Were they aware of group reactions?
- Were they flexible and tactful in handling mistakes or emergencies?
- Did everyone have a good time?
- Did the event finish with a climax or a pleasing ending?

Evaluation

In evaluating a social event, the following questions should be used to determine its success, with emphasis on suggestions and recommendations for future planning.

- Was there evidence of careful planning?
- Was the event organized?
- Was there variety and continuity?
- Did the event show unity and interest?
- Was it started on time?
- Were the activities suited to the group?
- Did the leaders share responsibilities?
- Did the activities follow the central theme?
- Did the activities move smoothly from one to another?

CLUBS

Club activities have an important place in a well-rounded recreational program. They differ from other recreation activities in that they usually have a slate of officers and a constitution, charge dues, keep attendance records, and have membership qualifications.

Normally, the purpose of a club involves a particular interest around which the organization is developed. Quite often, a club is created from a special interest or several people have expressed a desire for organized activity. The extent of organization varies with the size of the group, its major purpose, and the interests and needs of the members.

> TO BELONG TO, FEEL SECURE IN, AND WANTED BY A GROUP IS ESSENTIAL TO HUMAN JOY AND WELL-BEING.

> LIFE'S HAPPINESS IS LARGELY FOUND AND SHARED WITH OTHER PEOPLE.

Values

The values of clubs are numerous. With prime emphasis on pleasurable activity, they provide opportunities to:
Have fun and enjoyment.
Learn new skills and interests.
Perfect previously learned skills.
Gain new knowledge of people, places, and ideas.
Provide service to other people.
Develop friendly relations with others.

Types

There is no limit to the number and nature of clubs. A common interest is all that is necessary to group people into a club. The following is a partial list of clubs that have operated successfully:

Airplane
Archery
Art
Athletic
Bicycling
Bird watching
Boating
Book review
Bowling
Camera
Card
Chess
Chorus
Church
Debate
Dramatics
Fitness
Fly and bait casting
Folk dancing
Garden
Golf
Glee
Golden Age
Health

Hiking
Hobby
Homemakers
Model railroad
Music
Opera
Orchestra
Painting
Photography
Riding
Rifle
Rock
Scuba diving
Service
Sewing
Social
Skating
Skeet shooting
Skiing
Square dancing
Stamp collecting
Teen
Tennis
Woodwork
Women's
Yacht
Youth

Organizing a Club

Interest in starting a club can come from a group of five or more people. With this nucleus of interest, an informal meeting can be scheduled. The initial group should determine the tentative name, purpose, time, and meeting place, and the feasibility of a sponsor for the activity. A time and place should be set for a gathering of all other individuals who might be interested in joining.

Attendance at the organizational meeting can be publicized by telephone, letter, posters, flyers, news media, or word of mouth. Normally, one of the initial organizers presides at this opening meeting.

The Officers. Club officers should be selected and elected because of their qualifications and willingness to serve the group. Much too often, the most popular individuals rather than the most capable become the elected officers. The sponsor or one of the organizing leaders can help to correct this situation by serving on the nominating committee and encouraging the best slate of officers possible.

The list of officers includes the president, vice president, secretary, and treasurer. It is important that their duties and responsibilities be spelled out in the governing rules or constitution. The usual procedure is for a small committee to be appointed to draft up a simple constitution.

The Constitution. The constitution should consist of the following articles:

Article I.   Name
Article II.   Purpose
Article III.   Membership
Article IV.   Officers
Article V.   Meetings
Article VI.   Amendments

Parliamentary Procedures. All meetings should be conducted according to proper parliamentary procedures, such as the *Roberts' Rules of Order*. A meeting should follow an agenda which includes:

The call to order
Reading of the minutes of
   the last meeting
Committee reports
Old business
New business
Announcements
Adjournment

Committees. Effective committee organization is most essential to the success of any club operation. Committee members can be appointed either by the president, committee chairman, or by accepting volunteers.

The Program. Club programs should be determined by the needs and interests of the group. The program committee has the prime responsibility of choosing program speakers and topics, but they should also listen to the suggestions of the group. Interesting programs, refreshments, and enjoyable activities can do much to keep attendance high.

Fund-Raising Activities. Most clubs are confronted with the problem of raising money to help support their activities and projects. Some projects or activities that have proven successful in making money are:

Art shows
Benefit sports contests
Candy sales
Car wash and wax
Carnivals
Cake sales
Christmas candy or
   card sales
Magazine subscriptions
Rummage sales
Selling scrap paper
Sports tournaments

Evaluation. The programs and activities of the club should be evaluated regularly by the officers and members. A simple check list questionnaire can be used to obtain information as to how the club can be improved.

HOBBIES

A hobby is a leisure-time activity in which interest is enjoyed over a length of time. "Basically, a hobby is an individual recreation pursuit which permits the hobbyist to start and stop when he chooses. It can and often does lead the hobbyist into group participation."[22]

No hobby should be forced on an individual; however, it is desirable for recreators and their agencies to offer both motivation and leadership to those with hobbies. Much of the leadership is applied indirectly, although hobby clubs and shows can be sponsored by an agency.

Recreation agencies have encouraged more adults to develop a hobby by sponsoring clubs or group activities with a common hobby interest. In

---

[22] *The Recreation Program*, op. cit., p. 179.

doing so, they provide the leadership and furnish a place where such groups can hold meetings.

Gardening, for example, is one of America's most expensive hobbies. Millions of amateur gardeners spend billions of dollars each year on this hobby. In meeting the needs and interests of those who enjoy this leisure-time activity, recreation departments have sponsored "green thumb" clubs and activities.

Hobby shows are an excellent means of arousing interest in various hobby activities and the recruitment of prospective hobby club members. Demonstrations of hobbies such as art, photography, and underwater exploration skills can arouse keen interest in the activities of the club. The shows can exhibit the various articles hobbyists have made or collected.

Values

A hobby provides ways in which an individual's social and psychological needs are met. The real value of a hobby depends to a large extent on how well these needs are met and how much satisfaction is gained through participation. Hobbies are a means of relaxation, but they also help alleviate boredom. They can provide opportunity for creative expression as well as knowledge and learning skills. Above all, hobbies can lead to social acceptance and recognition and can enhance the joy of living.

Classification of Hobbies

The range and variety of hobbies are as broad as human interest. Fundamentally, hobbies have been classified into four major categories.

Collecting. Collecting is a natural habit for many people. The two most popular collection hobbies are stamps and antiques. Collection hobbies are almost unlimited in scope and include coins, books, clocks, china, dolls, paintings, matchbooks, autographs, stamps, sea shells, Indian relics, and weapons. Historic relics are a favorite among collectors.

Creating. People have a great urge to create, construct, or make. People's desire to create has been largely met by painting, writing, composing, inventing, designing, and making objects of various types. Hobbies constitute one of the most effective ways to satisfy the creative urge. A list of creative hobbies includes:

Ceramics
Cooking
Crafts
Gardening
Home arts (knitting,
    sewing, stitching)
Home mechanics
Leatherwork
Metal work
Model making (airplanes,
    railroads, boats, cars)
Music
Painting
Photography
Puppetry
Textiles
Woodworking
Writing

Educational. This large variety of activities involves the acquisition of knowledge and the learning of skills. Two of the most sought-after rewards of educational hobbies are adventure and exploring. Quite often, an educational hobby will also involve collecting. Educational hobbies include the following:

Reading for pleasure
Study of plant life
Study of stars, planets, etc.
Study of animal life
Study of trees
Learning craft skills
Learning to dance
Learning sports skills
Learning to play instruments, sing,
    and dance

Performing. Performing hobbies are based on the use of skills and have enjoyed spectacular popularity since the "cultural arts explosion" began in the 1950s. Many people receive satisfaction from performing for others. Some examples of performing hobbies include:

Acrobatics
Backpacking
Baseball
Basketball
Boating
Bowling
Camping
Canoeing
Checkers
Chess
Choral singing
Dancing
Fencing
Fishing
Football
Golf
Hiking
Horseback riding
Hunting
Magic tricks
Orchestras
Roller skating
Sailing
Swimming
Tennis

Factors in Selecting a Hobby

The selection and enjoyment of a hobby is often determined by a number of factors. These factors include the following:[23]

Space needed
Time available
Available money
Suitable temperament
Interest of hobby
Enjoyment gained
Cooperation of other people needed
Acceptability of hobby
Skills required
Materials needed

---

[23] Ibid., p. 189.

SPECIAL EVENTS

Special events are often referred to by recreation professionals as "frosting on the cake." Special events are perhaps the most enjoyable and appealing phase of the entire recreation program. They are considered "the spice" and the highlight of the year's program.

A special event is one that departs from the normal routine and requires special planning and assistance. It should be related to the program being conducted; however, it should not dominate or interfere with the other important phases of the program. Ideally, an event should be built around a special occasion, celebration, or holiday, thus giving it added meaning.

The variety of special events is almost unlimited. The only limiting factor is the imagination and creativity of the leaders. The cost of the event and the interests of the public, though, are factors to be considered in the choice of special events.

Values

Special events can generate a unique interest and enjoyment among both participants and the leaders. Playground-sponsored events have proven highly effective in promoting the overall program, encouraging greater numbers of participants and spectators. In many instances, a special event is the culmination of a much larger program. As a result, the public spotlight is focused on events that can capture the interest and imagination of the public. Quite often, the major objective of the event is to raise funds for some specific purpose, such as support of the handicapped or underprivileged.

An event planned around a special occasion or holiday can provide considerable interest and excitement to the day's festivities. Often, an event is designed to provide a demonstration and appropriate display of what the program has accomplished.

Special events can provide a strong incentive for those on the playground or organization to become more involved in the program, in addition to motivating others who have been unaware of the activities. As a note of caution, however,

> ANY GOOD EVENT IS THE DIRECT RESULT OF GOOD PLANNING.

too much emphasis, in the way of money and staff, can prove detrimental to a department or overall program. While they should be presented with verve and distinction, a zealous, all-out approach can often cause an imbalance and neglect in other program areas.

America's Top Special Events

1. The Christmas (or New Year) party
2. Easter egg hunt
3. Fourth of July picnic
4. Halloween party
5. Labor Day weekend trip
6. World Series (baseball)
7. The street parade
8. The social dance
9. The arts and crafts show
10. The bazaar (rummage sale, flea market)

Other Special Events

The following events have proven popular with people of all age groups.

Anniversaries
Antique shows
Arbor Day
Art shows
Auctions
Award nights
Baking contests
Balls
Band concerts
Banquets
Barbershop quartet songfests
Basketball free throw contests
Bazaars
Birthday parties
Box socials
Carnivals
Catch, throw, run
Christmas parties
Community sings
Coronations

County fairs
Craft shows
Dinner parties
Dog obedience shows
Doll shows
Dress-up days
Duck calling contests
Easter egg hunts
Exhibition games
Family nights
Fashion shows
Film festivals
Flea markets
Flower shows
Fourth of July picnics
Halloween festivals
Hayrides
Hikes
Hobo days
Hootenannies
Horse shows
Ice cream socials
Las Vegas nights (casino)
Mardi Gras Festivals
May Day Festivals
Model boat regattas
Movie nights
Olympics
Open house
Parades
Pass, punt, kick contests
Penny hunts
Pet shows
Picnics
Play days
Puppet shows
Recitals
Reunions
Rock concerts
Rodeos
Rummage sales
Sandcastle sculpturing contests
Scavenger hunts
Science fairs
Social dances
Soap box derbies
Sports days
Sports tournaments
Square dances

Fig. 13-15 THE BICYCLE RODEO, an annual event in most communities, is a challenging test of riding skills and safety practices that has been solidly supported by law enforcement agencies and service clubs. School assemblies and classroom study should precede the rodeo event.

Star gazing nights
Swap meets
Talent shows
Theatre productions
Tours
Trade shows
Treasure hunts
Trips
Variety shows
White elephant sales
Winter carnivals

Favorite Playground Events

Penny Carnival. A popular playground event is a home-made carnival with booths manned by the children. Everything costs a penny (or a nickel?). A series of easily constructed booths can be erected for contests, demonstrations, acts and skits, including side shows such as fortune teller, hula dancers, fish pond, beauty chorus, snake charmer, target throw, food booth, and the ticket booth.

Frog Jumping Contest. Children can enter frogs in jumping competition, similar to the big event in California's Amador County. The frog is placed at the center of a circle, and the farthest point is measured after the frog makes three jumps. Or, the kids can make believe they are frogs.

Big Toe Contest. The "big toes" of the participants are painted and dolled up. Each youngster decorates his "big toe" in the most impressive fashion, competing in a variety of appealing categories. Ribbons or awards are given to the winners.

Sculpturing Contests. Although some beach cities get thousands of people participating, a sandcastle sculpture contest can be run on a small scale in sand boxes at local playgrounds.

This is a favorite with little children. Have them build their favorite castles, pyramids, mountains, houses, and so forth. Be sure to moisten the sand well just before using. Ice sculpturing is another event which has proven very popular with children.

Space Circus. An outer-space circus is an excellent event to take advantage of the strong interest in space travel, planets, and the astronauts. Making space costumes and preparing acts can arouse considerable spirit and help the children get acquainted with each other. Crafts can include finger painting "space pictures," space peepshows, and large paper-sack masks. Ball throws, animal acts, best costume contests, penny tosses, and refreshments from other planets can get the summer program off to a great start.

Balloon Space Contests. Participants send up helium or hot-air balloons with self-addressed postcards to be mailed back by the finder. Awards are given to the first one back, the one from the farthest place, and other achievements. The launching is, of course, most of the event, with the returned postcards coming in days later.

Pirate Day. To participate in a treasure hunt, every youngster should dress up as a pirate—eye patch, pirate hat, bandannas, flag, along with cardboard swords. "Captain Bloodybones" can be an exciting character to visit the playground. He can leave a "treasure clue" that will lead to many other clues on the playground. Or, each child can receive a map which will assist them along the way. The theme can be carried out by a huge "treasure chest of goodies," and "Pirates Rum" (Kool Aid) for refreshments.

Hobo Cookout. All the children come in hobo costumes. Tasty treats include hot dogs and roasted marshmallows. The "hobos" climb trees, roll down the grassy hills, and sing enjoyable songs. Getting dirty and not being scolded for it is an experience too good to pass up.

Fish Derby. The children can enjoy splashing after cork fish in the wading pool. Two or three foot long poles, paperclip hooks, and three feet of string can serve as the fisherman's gear. Each child can "angle" after three sizes of cork fish floating in the pool. Points are totaled with the winners receiving ribbons.

Scavenger Hunt. Each youngster on the playground should be given a list of goodies to bring back to their leader. The list can include: 20 blades of grass, 15 finger-size rocks, 1 living ant, 1 fly (dead or alive), 2 white rocks, 1 stick, and 1 wild flower.

Star Gazing Evening. With so much interest today in the moon, stars, planets, and even our satellites, an enjoyable evening in the park can make a big hit with the young and old alike. Make sure, however, that powerful telescopes are available. An astronomical society or club or a professor from a nearby college may be a good source for loaning telescopes. Since darkness does not arrive until 8:30 or 9:00 during summer evenings, the event can be combined with an all-family barbecue with picnic or playground contests, and group singing to lead up to the "star gazing" time.

First Ice Cream Cone Day. Commemorating the "first ice cream cone ever" can be a real social treat in July at the playground. Have the children bring a dime or quarter to pay for the ice cream. "The first cone ever made" took place on July 23, 1904, at the St. Louis World's Fair. A three-act play and group singing from the early 1900s can be tied into the afternoon or evening program.

Junior Olympics. This very colorful event has been one of the highlights of summer playground programs, featuring track and field competition for boys and girls six to fifteen years of age. The colorful Olympic Parade and torch lighting ceremony provide the pageantry so important for well-attended sports events. Competition is held in three divisions of events: field events, dashes, and relays. Medals and ribbons are awarded to the top contestants.

Aquacade-Art Exhibit. An evening synchronized swimming show in water ballet can be combined with a few comedy or talent acts. This popular event for the entire family can be held near the end of the summer program so that an exhibit of arts and crafts projects completed on the playground can be combined with the aquacade.

Pet Show.   Have the children enter their favorite pets in a show, with categories for dogs, cats, birds, rodents, and miscellaneous (fish, turtles, snakes, etc.). Awards can be given for the largest, smallest, oldest, fattest, most unusual, and prettiest.

Trips and Excursions.   Experiences of this type can provide considerable appeal and interest to any playground program. Most recreation agencies confine their trips off the playground to places requiring little, if any, expense, such as trips to the zoo, fire station, the TV studio, art gallery, or to some historical site. Major league baseball clubs, for years, have invited groups of children to watch their games free of charge or at a reduced price.

In many Los Angeles communities, a different excursion is scheduled once each week on a fee basis. These include such entertainment attractions as Disneyland, Magic Mountain, a Princess Paddle-Wheel cruise in Long Beach Harbor, tour of Universal Studios, visit to Sea World in San Diego, visit to Lion Country Safari, a wiener roast at Newport Dunes, visit to Knotts Berry Farm, and possibly a performance of the touring Ringling Brothers Circus.

14

Organizing and Conducting Activities and Events

Since recreation activities are so diverse in nature, their organization and conduct require the use of many different methods and procedures of implementing and conducting the various activities. In addition to a general knowledge of the major activities and areas in recreation, the leader should possess a thorough understanding of principles in program planning. The leader must then apply these principles of organizational planning and conduct the program accordingly.

The art of staging a successful event is similar to that of successful party-giving: whatever is planned moves so smoothly that the guests remark how effortlessly the leader or host entertains. One key to the impression of effortlessness is the amount of constructive, effective effort put into the event. Any good event is the direct result of good planning, regardless of the effort. All the hard work in the world cannot offset poor or incomplete planning.

Staging a successful event involves three levels of activity. Level one is *decision-making*, without which no further steps can be taken. Level two is *coordination*, which provides central triggering of activities and maintains the overall order of events. Level three is *clerical support*, without which various activities cannot be implemented.

SEASONAL SCHEDULING

Through the year, most recreation and park departments plan their total programs into either two, three, or four major periods. A winter program will involve chiefly indoor activities and programs, and the summer season will offer primarily outdoor activities. Generally, the program is broken down into the four seasons: winter, spring, summer, and fall.

Summer Programs

Many cities, large and small, offer extensive activity schedules during the summer season. Summer programs place strong emphasis on playground aquatic activities, in addition to day camping,

Fig. 14-1 PROGRAM PROMOTION AND MOTIVATION. Records and accomplishments of individuals and the team can be posted on attractive training aids such as this "swim ladder." The times and records should be kept up-to-date (Ron Degler).

Fig. 14-2 FUN CAPITAL OF THE NEIGHBORHOOD. Summer recreation programs place strong emphasis on playground activities. This tot lot at Westmoor Park in Daly City, California, offers an assortment of playground equipment, located next to a much-used multipurpose recreation building.

outdoor sports, and special events. Since many families go away for vacations during the summer season, attendance is irregular and unstable. As a result, the attendance often varies from one week to the next and makes program planning difficult.

Special summer program features include teenage dances, instructional dance classes, drawing and painting classes, tennis and golf instruction, jogging and fitness activities, preschool classes, and softball and baseball leagues on various age levels.

During the summer months, aquatic programs of all types are featured at various times during the week. They include recreational swimming, learn-to-swim classes, lifesaving and diving classes, and swimming and diving league competition. In recent years, water polo, sailing classes, fishing derbies, and surfboard competition have been highly popular in communities throughout America.

Fall and Winter Programs

During the fall and winter months, greater stress is placed on instructional classes and special group activities in community centers or on playgrounds. Social clubs and cultural activities such as arts and crafts or the performing arts, are very popular during the fall and winter season.

Flag football, basketball, and volleyball leagues for boys and men are typical offerings in most communities. Competition is often available in open and recreation league classifications. City-wide tournament action follows league play.

A well-rounded array of gymnasium activities are carried on at various schools or recreation centers throughout the city. These activities include gym and volleyball, handball, table tennis, women's volleyball and slim 'n' trim, girls' gymnastics, weight training and conditioning, judo, wrestling, and basketball.

Music, dance, and other performing arts require special instruction and supervision. Many class and club activities are carried on through clubs and organizational groups. Instrumental or choral music, dramatics, and arts and crafts are often conducted as group projects with regularly scheduled classes and special instruction. Most social clubs, such as photography, bridge, and square dancing, are self-operated membership groups which meet regularly.

During the winter season, many dinners, dances, parties, and fine arts concerts are sponsored by the recreation department, either directly or by merely providing the facilities and equipment.

PLANNING A PLAYGROUND PROGRAM

Imagination, planning, and organizational ingenuity combined with enthusiastic leadership can produce an exciting and stimulating program that will keep children returning to the program day after day. Children go where they have the most fun, and if the leaders can develop the playground into the "fun capital of the neighborhood," that is where children will be found. However, should the playground bring the same routine activities day after day, the leaders will find themselves in "quiet village." Dull, routine, unimaginative, and uninspiring activities will drive attendance down more than anything else. The program should produce something new and different every day, along with lots of surprises.

Generally, the unsuccessful, poorly attended playground program is one that lacks variety and diversity. Instead, a well-balanced program of activities should be sprinkled with special features that will capture the interest and imagination of the children and keep them coming back.

Of major importance to any successful playground operation is what happens to each and every boy and girl who is involved with the program. A leader should always remember that his playground activities are not an end in themselves. They are merely the tools with which many wholesome aims and objectives can be reached.

Supervised playground programs are offered on weekdays from mid-June to the end of August. Hours of play vary from 9 A.M. to 4 P.M. or 11 A.M. to 5 P.M. A typical weekly playground schedule is given on page 278. A summer playground program is usually planned on a weekly basis with the following factors in mind:

1. *Selecting activities for schedule.* Playground activities are selected on the basis of type, age level, and group size. They are then fitted into the weekly schedule in appropriate time blocks. Activities such as softball or track and field, which require at least an hour to play, should be placed into a major time block; story telling might require a shorter time period.

The standard pattern of developing a playground program includes:

Fig. 14-3 DEPARTMENT-WIDE PROGRAMS such as this Halloween Costume Contest draw participants from areas throughout the city. These special events require more extensive preparation and promotion.

1. The departmental-wide program which covers city district activities and special events.
2. The seasonal-neighborhood program which is based upon the interest and enthusiasm of the children for particular low organized games and activities such as hopscotch, tetherball, and checkers.

2. *Use of areas.* In scheduling activities, the leader must plan effectively in setting aside appropriate areas for participation. A typical playground scene might include the following: tables for arts and crafts; playfield and blacktop areas for group games, softball, volleyball, or tetherball; a wading pool; an area for game equipment; and a shady tree area for story telling and quiet games. In assigning areas, a noisy volleyball game should not be scheduled next to a story telling or singing activity.

3. *Dividing day into major time periods.* The daily playground program is scheduled according to specific major time blocks. Typically, the schedule should include at least one time block of an hour during the morning and possibly two during the afternoon. Shorter time periods should be worked in to allow for activities that require less time, for setting up and collecting equipment, for free play, and for various other responsibilities.

4. *Scheduling simultaneous activities.* Generally, most playground programs involve more than one group scheduled at the same time. This is particularly true when there are enough children on the playground to justify dividing them into groups.

Some activities require direct supervision; others can be carried on under general supervision. Having learned the activity, a group involved in a quiet game need not be given close leadership, but an activity such as folk dancing would require direct supervision.

5. *Younger children must not be overlooked.* Playground leaders will often give much of their attention to the older boys and girls because they are easier to organize and stronger in expressing their desires. It should be remembered, however, that the younger children need leadership as much as the older boys and girls.

Activities of an informal nature appeal to children in the younger age group. However, it is still necessary for the leaders to organize and plan activities for this group. Low organization games and activities that allow for imagination lend themselves well to young children.

6. *Time for routine responsibilities.* Playground leaders must set aside time to handle staff responsibilities and routine functions. These include the inspection of equipment and facilities before opening the playground, clean-up, staff meetings, filling out forms, and similar details.

7. *Assigning activities to appropriate time periods.* The weekly playground schedule should be based on intelligent planning. The leader must also keep in mind a number of important factors. Active games and strenuous activities should be scheduled during morning hours; quiet activities are usually offered in the afternoon periods. Generally, two physical activities should not be held one after another. Instead, a less strenuous activity could separate the two. For example, an arts and crafts period could be fitted in between a gymnastics activity and a softball team practice.

Activities that have proved more popular could be offered daily, whereas some programs could be presented just once or twice a week. Special events and trips are usually scheduled during afternoon hours, but there are some exceptions in which an event is held in the morning.

8. *Special weekly themes.* Designating a special theme each week to the summer playground program has been a popular practice of recreation departments. The theme system has been effective in giving a purpose to activities and events.

Not only is the special event or trip based upon this theme but other activities such as arts and crafts, music, and dancing may carry out the theme. Quite often, a special event on Thursday or Friday will culminate the special weekly program schedule.

Weekly theme titles should be geared to the overall theme for the entire summer season. Some examples of overall theme titles are "Fun in '74," "Blast off to Summer Fun," and "A TV Guide to Summer Recreation."

SUMMER PLAYGROUND PROGRAM
Overall Theme — "Blast Off to Summer Fun"

Week	Theme	Special Event
1	Hawaiian Aloha	Hawaiian Night Luau
2	Pirate Week	Treasure Hunt
3	Hobo Week	Hobo Cookout
4	Safari Week	Pet Show
5	Sportsman Week	Fishing Derby, Trip to Big League Game
6	Camp Week	Overnight Camp-out
7	Western Week	Frontier Day
8	Astronaut Week	Outer Space Circus
9	Olympic Week	Junior Olympics Meet
10	Cultural Arts Week	Art Exhibit, Aquacade, Dance and Drama Festival

LEADERSHIP

Only with competent leadership can the playground contribute to the development of socially acceptable conduct, democratic ideals, and happiness for the children who attend it. The leader is in charge of the playground and is responsible for making sure that maximum recreational service is rendered to those who use the playground.

Are leaders ready for the children when they arrive? Or, are they sitting back and looking at their empty bulletin board? If the latter is true, the leaders also will very likely be looking at an empty playground.

To a large extent, the successful operation of a playground depends on how much the leaders and their program satisfy the recreation needs and desires of participants. Careful planning and preparation is one of the secrets of success in playground leadership. The playground should be alive with the drama of creativity and imagination, featuring exciting and fun-filled activities.

Appearance

The leader's personal appearance can make a major impression upon those who come to the playground. Therefore, leaders should be neat and well groomed. Emblemed shirts or blouses that indicate department identification may be worn. Shoes should be appropriate, such as tennis shoes for sports.

Guidelines for Leaders

The following are some of the most important guidelines or responsibilities playground leaders should keep in mind while performing their job:

1. Leaders should make a strong effort to win the friendship and respect of all who use the playground.
2. Leaders should encourage all persons attending the playground to enter into various activities.
3. Be a leader, not merely a custodian. The leader should teach the children how and what to play and occasionally play with them.
4. Register each child on a registration card on opening day and continue to do so throughout the summer.
5. Make everybody feel at home. Teach the children your name and try to learn their names.
6. Encourage children to tell others about the playground.

> **WHEN YOU'RE FIRST AND OTHERS FOLLOW, THAT'S CALLED *LEADERSHIP*.**

7. Watch for new children and give them a word of welcome.
8. Get acquainted with your neighborhood and the parents of children who attend the playground.
9. Check supplies each day and see that everything is put away properly. *Check inventory daily.*
10. Provide for neat and orderly storage.
11. Report immediately any serious damage to playground equipment or apparatus.
12. Be aware of any problems or misconduct in the restrooms.
13. Cooperation with maintenance men is highly necessary for smooth-functioning activities programs.
14. All supplies should be carefully collected at the close of each session and locked up.
15. All leaders are expected to attend regularly scheduled staff meetings and other special meetings.
16. In the event of illness or an emergency, a leader should call the district office or immediate supervisor so that a substitute leader can be arranged.
17. The leader should be thoroughly professional in relations with coworkers. Playground service is basically a cooperative project.
18. The leader should always recognize the dignity and integrity of each individual. The leader should never ridicule or disparage any participant under any circumstances.
19. Smoking is not permitted while leaders are on duty.
20. The first aid kit should be kept adequately stocked at all times.
21. Leaders should stop and discourage all undesirable activities, such as gambling, profane language, vandalism, rowdyism, and destruction.
22. The grounds must be kept clean and sanitary. Have periodic cleanup days with a spirit of fun.

23. The leader should involve as many people as possible in planning and in the program.
24. Any activity that is scheduled should be carried out.
25. The rules and regulations of the playground should be posted.
26. The leader should be a good example—mature attitude, sense of humor, patience, and enthusiasm. A smile can be an important asset for any leader.
27. Using a check list should be a regular practice, particularly for higher organized events and activities.
28. Generally, visits by friends of leaders should be discouraged unless their appearance serves a useful function.
29. When children are taken off the playground for excursions, permission releases must be signed by their parents.
30. Be firm, fair, and decisive. Develop the ability to make quick and accurate decisions.
31. Are the leaders sensitive to the interests and needs of the patrons?
32. Keep your program interesting and flexible by introducing "new activities."
33. Do leaders offer patrons sufficient opportunities for instruction and practice?
34. Leaders should inject new games and ideas frequently, in addition to different variations into old activities.
35. The interests of the weak, timid, and small should be adequately protected from aggressive and domineering children.
36. All employees should have a copy of the Department Leader's Manual and know what is in it.

Building Good Rapport with Children

The following are ways to build a positive playground atmosphere:

• Learn names
• Be a good listener
• Use a non-challenging way to correct children
• Talk at their level
• Show a genuine interest in each child and their projects

• Make the child feel important
• Be firm, fair, impartial, and consistent

Volunteers

Volunteers can make the difference between a good program and an outstanding one. Volunteers can be found everywhere; the task is to recruit and train them. Volunteers can be responsible for such duties as the following:

• Checking out equipment
• Poster making and other publicity chores
• Counting attendance
• Furnishing transportation
• Providing leadership at special events
• Forming a telephone committee, addressing flyers, etc.

Volunteers should be recognized for their valuable service, and they must be made to feel their services are important. On a day to day basis, the regular leaders should thank them personally. Later, a thank you note, certificate of service or recognition should be extended them.

Evaluation

An effective personnel evaluation program is essential to the success of the department and its employees. Leaders should continually evaluate their own progress. They must recognize their strengths and weaknesses. Normally, the supervisor or leader in charge is responsible for filling out a rating scale at the close of the peak summer season. Questions such as the following might appear on such a rating scale:

• Did you schedule activities for children of all ages?
• Were you cheerful and friendly to everyone?
• Did you arouse and maintain interest?
• Did you listen to people and hear what they had to say?
• Did you use people with special abilities?
• Were you flexible enough to make the necessary adjustments when emergency situations arose?
• Were you creative in introducing new program features?

- Did the activities contribute to the best interests of the children?
- Was the program well-balanced and varied?
- Did you cooperate effectively with other employees on the staff?
- Did participants develop wholesome skills and attitudes?
- Did you publicize your programs sufficiently and keep everyone informed?
- Were you prompt in submitting reports, requisitions, weekly schedules, etc. to the district office?
- Did you consider the needs and interests of your children?
- Were you flexible and open minded to suggestions and ideas to improve the program?
- Did you involve the children in planning and the organization of the program?
- Did you use all the available community resources, such as places to visit, voluntary help, and available supplies, equipment, and facilities?

Fig. 14-4 LOW ORGANIZED GAMES AND ACTIVITIES such as this Chinese Checkers game should be a major part of every neighborhood playground program. In addition to the traditional favorites, leaders should inject new games and ideas frequently.

OPENING THE PLAYGROUND

Leaders should report for duty fifteen minutes before the scheduled opening time. Necessary gates and doors should be unlocked. The grounds should be inspected for any dangerous hazards such as broken glass or holes. Notices should be posted on bulletin boards, equipment and facilities checked, and game materials inspected and arranged for scheduled activities. Registration records should be filled out on all children.

CONDUCTING THE PROGRAM

Since morning hours are comparatively cooler, the more active games and sports should be offered during this session. The morning is also a good time for leaders to devote more time to the very young children. Singing games, simple crafts, storytelling, and play activities such as playing house and store are good activities for this age group.

Generally, older children who come to the playground during the morning session can be given equipment for softball and other self-organizing activities, unless there are enough leaders to actually work with this age group. With two or three leaders, activities involving different age groups can be offered simultaneously. Ideally, two vigorous activities should not be scheduled back to back.

Noon time should consist of free play, usually a quiet hour. Individual or quiet table games, such as chess and checkers, can be taught. Posters can be made at this time or some other necessary chore.

Afternoons are the best time for dancing, dramatics, handicrafts, club activities, and other similar activities. A quiet games hour is also good during this hot period.

Typical sports activities on the playground include four squares, softball, kickball, tetherball, basketball, flag and touch football, gymnastics, volleyball, table tennis, and junior track and field.

Low organized games include circle games, tag games, guessing games, "magic" games, relays and stunts, ball games, music and drama games. Table and board games, horseshoes, jump rope, hopscotch, jacks, croquet, shuffleboard, and the

Time	Sun.	Mon.	Tues.	Wed.	Thur.	Fri.	Sat.
9–10 A.M.		Low organized games (Practice) Team games	Gymnastics–Tumbling Broom hockey	Low organized contests (Tournament action) Team games	Gymnastics–Tumbling Broom hockey	Low organized contests (Tournament action) Preparation for next week event	
10–11 A.M.		Arts and crafts Sport clinic (featuring guest coaches and athletes)	Puppetry Musical games	Arts and crafts Surprise feature (activity or visitor)	Puppetry Musical games	Softball game	
11–12 A.M.		Softball practice Storytelling	Track & field practice Nature hike	Softball practice Play activities	Track & field practice Group games	Singing games	
12–1 P.M.		Free play Quiet hour	Free play	Free play Preparation for pet show	Free play	Free play	
1–2 P.M.		Folk dancing Rhythm band practice	Swimming Visit to the local pool	Rhythm band practice	Pet show	Folk dancing Club meetings	
2–3 P.M.		Drama activity (skits)		Drama activity (one-act play rehearsal)		Dept. staff meeting	

Chart 14-1. Typical weekly schedule of a summer playground program.

Fig. 14-5 FRONTIER DAY has been a popular attraction for boys and girls at the playground. The special event is ideal to culminate Western Week, the weekly theme title.

beanbag throw are additional games which can be available on a daily basis.

Crafts can feature painting, block printing, mural painting, finger painting, papier mâché, and various "scrap crafts" if supplies run short. Puppet shows and storytelling are very popular with younger children. The drama program can offer pantomimes, skits, charades, and one-act play competitions. Musical activities can include singing, marching, and rhythm bands. A varied repertoire of action songs, folk songs, rounds, and ballads can be enjoyed. Dance activities involving activity and instruction can include folk and square dances, reels, jigs, and modern dancing.

The highlight of the outdoor-nature program can be an overnight campout, in which the girls go one night and the boys the next. Camp activities offered can include campfire skits, singing, swimming, hiking, and outdoor cooking.

City-wide tournaments provide the challenge and incentive for intense competition. City cham-pions can be recognized in low organized games such as tetherball, four squares, chess, checkers, hopscotch, jacks, and table tennis.

A colorful dance festival can feature exhibitions dances, dancing for all children, junior leader certificates presentation, and refreshments. Children from each playground can make its own mural depicting its playground.

Playground Surprises

Surprise and suspense are two elements that can captivate the interest and imagination of children and should be exploited to the fullest on the playground. A special feature every other day should be a "surprise activity or visitor." A water-melon eating contest, bubble-blowing, ice sculpturing, making snow cones, apple bobbing, or some other imaginative activity can keep children in a state of anticipation and suspense.

Fig. 14-6 NEW GAMES AND IDEAS can stimulate any playground with interest and excitement. The great popularity of professional hockey has resulted in the formation of many local hockey leagues. This broom hockey league, conducted by Lou Quint of the Daly City Recreation and Park Department, plays its games indoors with broomsticks and plastic balls.

Adventure Play

Since children have the urge to build and create their own play environment, the adventure playground can meet this important need. The finished product is of little interest on an adventure playground; it is the period of creation that is most important. Any type of building materials can be used, including empty wooden boxes, old furniture, rolls of wallpaper, bits of rope, and paint. A regular supply of waste material can be collected from factories, shops, and stores; a sufficient number of hammers, saws, and pliers should be available.

The key factor in the success of an adventure playground is leadership. An effective leader can use a wide assortment of building materials to encourage children's creative urges.

According to Drummond Abernethy, one of the originators of the adventure playgrounds in England, "There are lots of injuries at adventure playgrounds, such as nails in feet and an occasional broken arm, but the creative, adventuresome learning experiences the children receive far outweigh the negative aspects of these exciting

and rewarding play areas. Yet, the number of serious injuries at adventure playgrounds are significantly less than the injuries suffered at school football and rugby contests. Effective supervision is the key, and we lock up these facilities when leadership is not available."[1]

Among the many popular features of adventure playgrounds are:

* Constructing and building
* Swinging from tree to tree on a pulley-cable
* Riding on a small box car
* Climbing up sloped structures and buildings
* Sliding down a hill in open plastic boxes
* Walking on elevated rope lines, hung from tree to tree
* Cooking food on a fire
* Enjoying water fights with buckets and wet sponges

---

[1] Drummond Abernethy, "*Adventure Playgrounds in England*," taken from his lecture sponsored by California State University (Sacramento), November 10, 1973.

CLOSING THE PLAYGROUND

All equipment and supplies should be checked in fifteen minutes before closing time. All gates, windows, and doors should be properly locked. Reports, including time sheets and attendance reports, should be filled out, and all damages, defective equipment and needed repairs should be reported. Normally, the leaders should see that all participants have left the grounds.

PUBLICITY AND PROMOTION

The best playground program in the world can be wasted unless the children and their parents know about it. The following are some methods and materials for promoting activities and events:

1. *Bulletin boards.* Announcements of activities and coming events should be attractively displayed. Material should be kept up-to-date with fresh features added regularly. Daily and weekly schedules should be posted along with colorful illustrations which will attract the attention. Records and accomplishments of individuals and teams can be posted.

2. *Monthly bulletin.* A monthly bulletin with a name such as the "Recreation Reporter" can prove a highly popular publication for any recreation department. Many agencies distribute as many as several thousand copies monthly.

3. *Flyers.* The flyer can help sell the playground program. It is a handbill and can be given directly to participants. It can also be sent home with the children as a program of coming events that may be of interest to others in the neighborhood.

4. *Posters.* Posters can be placed in buildings, on fences, or outside of buildings. They can be made of tagboard, butcher paper, or construction paper. Make them big (3' by 6') and use a letterspray kit. The children can help paint posters the leader sketches out.

Fig. 14-7 SPECIAL FEATURES can do much to keep children at the playground in a state of anticipation and suspense. This Ice Sculpturing Contest proved a big hit for children at playgrounds in Ottawa, Ontario. (Courtesy Ottawa Recreation Department.)

5. *Photos of playground.* Photographs of activities and the children can be valuable to the interest and morale on the playground. Pictures can be placed in a scrapbook or displayed on the bulletin board. Later, pictures can appear in reports to the administrator. Colored slides can be very effective for group talks and at board meetings.

6. *Playground newspaper.* This newsy little publication can provide considerable interest and appeal to children and their parents. In addition to publicizing playground activities, the newspaper can develop much needed morale and spirit.

7. *News media.* Newspaper, radio and television releases, featuring articles and pictures, will help build sound public attitudes and inform the public. All news releases and pictures must be sent through the supervisor, never directly to the newspaper.

8. *Announcements.* Posters or flyers publicizing a particular activity or event should be placed in prime locations such as recreation centers, schools, and store windows. Verbal and

285

Fig. 14-8 DISCIPLINE AND CONTROL. Rules must be followed and obeyed. With children who attend the playground regularly, however, it is seldom necessary to do more than call attention to their misconduct or disregard for rules.

written announcements, direct mail, the telephone, bulletin boards, and banners are other methods.

9. *Personal contacts.* Contact with the public should be made by talks before community groups and organizations and through informal chats with people who visit the recreation agency.

10. *Exhibitions, demonstrations and clinics.* These are ways to acquaint the public with the various program offerings and instill an interest to participate. Motion pictures and filmstrips can create interest in the program.

DISCIPLINE

The most desirable relationship between a leader and playground patrons is one of mutual respect and cooperation. A deep understanding and appreciation of the facilities and purpose of the program should reduce disciplinary action to a minimum. The word "discipline" is *not* synonymous with punishment. Good discipline is control and direction of behavior—listening, informing, structuring, and responding. The goal of discipline is self-control. A good leader is firm but friendly, not harsh or punishing, not lax or hesitant. Repeated warning without action weakens the leader's position in the eyes of the children.

The need for enforcing discipline is least evident when there is a great amount of interesting activity. The best way to secure good discipline on the playground is to start the first day in a businesslike manner. Everyone should be kept busy. Rules must be followed and obeyed, though, and the leader must insist that they be obeyed. They must be clear, concise, and practical. The wise leader will first try every means of correction before resorting to suspension—a warning on the first offense, a penalty on the second. He is aware that when the child leaves the playground, he can no longer try to help the youngster, and the child may get into more serious difficulty.

To be of value, discipline must be positive and constructive and in direct relation to the offense committed. First, the leader must be certain that he or she has the facts of the case and be sure who committed the offense. Second, the offender must understand why he or she is being punished and that it is done as a means of correction, not revenge. Punishment should be used as little as possible, and the objective should be educational.

The following methods of disciplining can be employed:

- Talk to the child and explain "rule" infringement.
- Keep the child out of the activity for 15–30 minutes.
- Exclude the child from the playground for one or two days.
- Exclusion for a longer period of time must first be discussed with the district supervisor.
- If possible, anticipate serious problems and discuss them with your supervisor.

In building a positive playground atmosphere for more effective control, leaders should:

- Learn the names of participants.
- Encourage children to talk with leaders.
- Make the child feel important.
- Be a good listener.
- Use a nonchallenging way of correcting the children.
- Be firm as well as fair and impartial.
- Be consistent in your application of rules and regulations.
- Identify and work with "natural leaders."
- Show a genuine interest in individuals.

SAFETY

Safety on the playground is essential. At no time should the program be initiated without observing essential rules to ensure the safety of all participants and spectators. Instruction should be given by leaders in the correct methods of play. Enforcement of simple rules will eliminate many potential hazards. "Safety First" should be the deciding factor in the selection of all activities.

ACCIDENTS

One of the best ways to prevent accidents is for the leader to be on the job and alert at all times. In situations involving injury, a judgment must be made by the leader as to the seriousness of the overall situation. First aid assistance should be given immediately. If it appears the accident is serious, the patient should not be moved and should be made as comfortable as possible.

In case of serious accidents, the police department, sheriff's department, or fire department should be called for ambulance service. The family should be notified of the circumstances surrounding the accident and what has been done. An accurate accident report should then be made out by the leaders, including testimony by witnesses, and delivered to the district office within twenty-four hours.

Generally, playground staff are directed never to call for or send an injured person to a local doctor or a private hospital, unless directed to do so by the parents. Since regulation cards are available on every child, including their parents' telephone numbers, the leader can contact the parents soon after first aid and a careful diagnosis has been rendered.

NEGLIGENCE

A leader must exercise *reasonable* prudence in the performance of his duties, since an injury of a patron on the playground could possibly result in a law suit because of negligence. Situations of this type are not common; however, a leader could be held liable if negligence can be proven. Therefore, he must protect himself with prudent actions at all times. Reasonable prudence is practical wisdom or plain common sense.

AWARDS

The granting of trophies or other awards tends to emphasize winning rather than participation. Therefore, there are many professionals who feel trophies should be kept to a minimum. In no case should awards or prizes be offered as the main inducement to participate in playground activities. Group awards of plaques or cups are recommended since they emphasize group cooperation. The general feeling among professional recreators is that inexpensive awards are justified because they serve as an incentive to participation and improvement. In fact, in city sports leagues income from fees paid by participants is used to purchase trophies and other awards. Most recreation departments have a variety of playground award certificates, ribbons, and participation cards that can be given to winners in contests, tournaments, and so forth.

RAINY DAYS

In the event of rain, playground areas without buildings should be closed. The decision to remain open is up to the area supervisor or leader.

1. Employees are required to report to their respective playground regardless of weather conditions.
2. Leaders and assistants are to remain on the job until notified by their immediate supervisor.
3. Rainy-day hours should be used for storytelling, quiet games, and for special rainy day programs that should be "canned up" and ready to use.
4. These hours can also be well spent in repairing equipment, checking records, registrations, etc.

FORMS

The object of a form is to provide information. If it is incorrect, it is of no value. Only a well-developed form will be of value to the department. Accurate playground attendance must be taken daily at the peak of attendance during both the morning and afternoon sessions.

The following forms should be used by the leader in conducting a playground program:

- Registration card (for each child)
- Attendance report
- Accident report
- Employee time sheet
- Requisition order
- Property damage
- Parent's permission release

FINANCING RECREATION

Finance and budget are essentially the responsibilities of the administrative staff; however, all department personnel should have an understanding of budget procedures, policies of finance, and the control of expenditures and incoming revenue. Since many agencies follow a program budgeting approach, all staff members should be prepared to carry out the procedures of accounting and control as directed by the administrator.

Some of the financial areas of concern that supervisory and face-to-face leaders are involved with are:

- Keeping accurate financial records in the collection of fees and charges.
- Following department policies in requesting the purchase of supplies and equipment; using authorized requisition or purchase order forms.
- Channeling all financial matters through the business office.
- Assisting the administrator in making financial and budgetary estimates for the fiscal year ahead.

SPECIAL EVENTS

This exciting phase of recreation can add zest to the activity program, giving participants something to look forward to and plan for. Special events also provide the opportunity for parents and friends to visit the grounds and see their children taking part.

Enough special events should be offered to challenge the interest and cooperation of those on the playground. Usually one special event a week is sufficient, and it should be scheduled at the times most convenient for the group to be served.

```
+-----------------------------------------------------------+
|                                                           |
|        City of Torrance Recreation Department             |
|                                                           |
|           R E G I S T R A T I O N   C A R D               |
|                                                           |
|   Name _____          |
|                                                           |
|   Address_____         |
|                                                           |
|   Phone_____ Age_____Grade_____         |
|                                                           |
|   Parent's Business Phone _____          |
|                                                           |
|   Neighbor's or Relative's Phone in case of emergency     |
|                                                           |
|                                                           |
|            _____             |
|                                                           |
|   Comments: _____         |
|                                                           |
|            _____         |
|                                                           |
+-----------------------------------------------------------+
```

Form 14-1. A registration card should be filled out by *all* the children who use the playground. This is a *must*, in case emergencies arise.

The following factors should be considered in planning and conducting a special event:

Program Schedule. The program should be varied and well balanced. Start it on time and keep the momentum moving, employing smooth transitions from one activity to the next.

Publicity and Promotion. To attract people to an event, an effective publicity campaign should be organized and conducted. Starting two or three weeks before the event, the campaign should include flyers, posters, news releases to the news media, banners, a telephone committee, and group visitations "to get the word out and beat the drums."

Musical Accompaniment. A must for any special event, background music will provide the atmosphere so necessary in developing the proper spirit and tempo. Music, appropriately selected (like a spirited Sousa march at a pet show or "Around the World in 80 Days" at a fashion show), will spark up any event.

Safety. A careful check for potential dangers or hazards should be conducted prior to the event. The condition of chairs and bleachers, the play areas, and equipment and apparatus should be closely inspected.

Leadership Needed. Leaders for special activities should be dependable, friendly, and like to work with people. Important responsibilities should be delegated to selected leaders by the chairman. However, the overall individual in charge, such as the chairman, must "call the shots" and be responsible for keeping the momentum going, for "trouble shooting," and for coping with possible "emergency situations."

Objectives and Aims.   A special event should strive to achieve designated objectives. Most special events are planned or developed around a central theme; program activities should be related to this theme, as well as meet the needs and interests of the age and sex of the participants.

Finances.   A budget of anticipated income and expenditures should be prepared, item by item. Essentially, the resources that can be utilized must be in relationship to the finances available. Of course, a low budget often motivates recreators to get out and get some donations and contributions. A low budget can also spur a leader to do some creative "mooching" and to make things that cost nothing.

The supervisor or leader in charge of a program should take into consideration the following expenditures: leadership needs, maintenance of facilities, purchase of supplies and equipment, and transportation. Should a fee be charged? If so, how much?

Equipment and Supplies.   Detailed checklists should be prepared for both equipment and supplies needed for the event. Never forget that "little things mean a lot." Items should be boxed up and ready for use the day before the event so that the chairman may check them off.

Reception.   This is an often neglected responsibility, and its practice is very effective in providing the friendly and warm greetings so essential for those who attend the event. Ideal for this important chore are a couple of personable, friendly young women or men who can make everyone relax and feel at home.

Facilities Needed.   Facilities for the event should be reserved well in advance, and reservation papers should be filled out. To provide flexibility in the event of adverse weather, indoor accommodations should also be available if outdoor activity is impossible. Is the facility large enough for the anticipated number of participants? Electrical outlets should be carefully checked. Lighting and P.A. systems may require extension cords.

Evaluation.   In addition to continual evaluation throughout the event, the chairman, assisted by his committee chairmen, should prepare an evaluation report. The final typed report, including a summary of highlights, strong points, weak points, and recommendations, should follow the evaluation meeting, which should be held immediately after the event. This report can then be filed until the following year when it can be carefully studied.

CONDUCTING INDOOR ACTIVITIES

Indoor facilities for recreational use are of major importance in any year-round community recreation program. Such facilities as community centers and neighborhood recreation buildings provide for a variety of physical, social, and cultural activities that necessitate an indoor setting.

Generally, indoor-center activities are more specialized and diverse than those engaged in on a playground. This is partly because a recreation center is designed to meet the needs of the entire neighborhood. People of all age groups visit the center throughout the year.

Rooms are provided for low organized games, reading, television viewing, and club activities. Most recreation centers feature a large game room in which table tennis, billiards, shuffleboard, and a variety of table games are enjoyed. A lobby and lounge are additional areas found in most centers. An important asset to any community center is a large activity area for dancing and active games. A portable stage that can be removed when necessary provides much needed flexibility to the large multi-purpose room. A juke box can provide the necessary musical atmosphere.

In addition to multiple-use facilities, many buildings designed for a single purpose are located throughout the community. These can include facilities for swimming, target shooting, crafts, bowling, and for an aquarium.

There are numerous other buildings not used solely for recreation purposes, many of which the recreation department operates jointly with other agencies or organizations. Organized recreation activities are carried on in schools, churches, libraries, industrial buildings, and other public buildings. The schools, through park-school joint-use agreements, provide a great many indoor rec-

Fig. 14-9 INDOOR CENTER ACTIVITIES are typically informal and self-directing in nature and offer a wide range of activities. This teen center features such recreational activities as pocket pool, pinball machines, a juke box, and table tennis.

Fig. 14-10 INSPIRED LEADERSHIP. Successful sports programs such as the Alameda Baseball League demand cooperation of the supervisor (Sam Spear) and staff. They teach skills and wholesome attitudes, supervise areas and facilities, and conduct the games.

reation facilities such as gymnasiums, swimming pools, classrooms, and industrial arts shops.

Many recreation departments, in fact, are dependent upon schools for many of their indoor areas and facilities. The physical plants of elementary and secondary schools have the resources to make a major contribution to a well-rounded community recreation program.

Increasingly, schools are serving as recreation centers during non-school hours—evenings, weekends, and particularly during the summer months. The "community school concept" has been highly effective in serving the needs of all the people. The park-school concept has enabled communities to provide both recreation and educational programs more effectively because of the availability of a more adequate system of facilities and space.

ORGANIZING A COMMUNITY SPORTS PROGRAM

A community-wide sports program should provide for players of all age groups and skills. Opportunities in a broad range of sports activities should be made available for those who want to participate informally and those who are interested in the highly organized type of competition.

Fig. 14-11 UNSUPERVISED FACILITIES. Many sports facilities are available to the public without supervision. These college students take time out from their studies to enjoy a game of basketball at a local park.

Generally, in most large cities, the area of sports and athletics is under the direction of a recreation supervisor, who in turn is responsible to the superintendent of recreation. The primary duties of the supervisor are to direct and organize a year-round program of leagues in many sports and be responsible for the supervision of staff, facilities, and equipment.

Department Role in Sports

A recreation department has many functions in administering a varied sports program in the community.

Unsupervised Sports Facilities. A recreation department has a responsibility to provide facilities for public use on an unsupervised basis. Softball fields, tracks, golf course, tennis courts, basketball courts, and similar areas are available to the public without supervision. There are a number of instances when use of a facility is granted on a permit basis, which may require a fee.

Competitive Leagues. League competition is offered in many sports throughout the year, either sponsored by the department or in cooperation with various organizations in the community. Examples of youth leagues include Little League baseball and Pop Warner football; City League basketball and volleyball serve adult men.

In cooperating with an organization, the recreation agency provides such administrative assistance as scheduling facilities, officials, and publicity; the organization is responsible for coaching assignments, player recruitment, and financial support.

Instructional Classes and Clinics. Instructional training classes and clinics for youth and adults are sponsored during the year in sports activities. Classes in golf, tennis, and bowling are typical offerings taught by department instructors, while the major team sport programs place considerable emphasis on basic instruction and training.

Special Events. Recreation departments sponsor a variety of sports tournaments and events that meet promotional and competitive needs. Sports tournaments often require considerable organizational skill and leadership staff, which recreation departments have the resources to provide. Sports workshops and demonstrations can significantly improve the caliber of play.

Training Programs. Successful programs in sports demand trained coaches and officials to direct and supervise the various activities. As a result, many departments offer a series of workshops and classes for sports officials, coaches, life guards, instructors and other necessary personnel. In swimming, the Red Cross and the YMCA have sponsored many training and leadership programs that have contributed much to swimming proficiency and water safety.

INITIATING A COMMUNITY RECREATION PROGRAM

In starting a community recreation program, a meeting should be called which representatives of all local organizations and interested citizens are asked to attend. The following organizational steps were suggested by George Butler in implementing a new program:

1. Survey the needs and interests.
2. Communicate the importance of recreation and the need for community action.
3. Point out the success of recreation programs in other communities.
4. Appoint a committee to make a study of local recreation resources and needs and give recommendations.
5. Determine the type of managing authority under which a program can best be administered.
6. Provide financial estimates and the local community's ability to provide the necessary funds.
7. Discuss the recommendations and findings of the study at a public meeting.
8. If given general approval, submit and publicize recommendations to the appropriate local authorities.
9. Pass a resolution or local ordinance creating a recreation department or bureau, thereby implementing the following action:
   a. Appoint a recreation board or commission.
   b. Appropriate necessary funds.
   c. Assign recreation areas and facilities.
   d. Employ a recreation administrator and staff personnel.
10. Initiate a community recreation program.[2]

[2] From *Introduction to Community Recreation* by George D. Butler. Copyright © 1967 by the National Recreation Association, Inc. Used with permission of McGraw-Hill Book Company. Pp. 278–79.

V

The Recreation Profession

15

The
Professional

One of the newest and most rapidly growing vocational fields in America is the recreation and parks profession. As the recreation industry prepares for a "leisure"-oriented society, the recreation field is steadily moving toward the full status of an established profession.

Serving an industry which annually exceeds $140 billion in expenditures, professionally trained workers in over sixty different occupations are involved in the provision of leisure services. However, not everyone engaged in recreation and leisure services is considered a recreation professional. Indeed, leisure services involve a multitude of businesses and professional activities that employ millions of personnel. Travel, nightclubs, restaurants, professional sports, and many other services are very much a part of the exploding leisure market; their staff and leaders, however, are not regarded as recreation professionals.

Recreation professionals are people in leadership, supervisory, and administrative capacities who are employed primarily with public and voluntary agencies that provide nonprofit recreational services and opportunities. Such professionals have college degrees in recreation or related fields and are employed as administrators or supervisors. "These are the people who are generally regarded as recreation professionals," wrote Richard Kraus, "assuming that they have appropriate educational qualifications and are employed at a professional level of service."[1]

The successful recreation professional is versatile, enterprising, and flexible. This is because he often works with people of all ages, the able-bodied as well as the handicapped. Depending on the situation, the professional recreator is a promoter, a planner, an organizer, a teacher, and a motivator. No wonder, those who work in the field find the profession challenging, exciting, and rewarding.

A PROFESSION

A profession is regarded as a rather broad field, within which there are areas of specialization.

Fig. 15-1 A FAVORABLE PUBLIC IMAGE. The public is becoming more aware of recreation as a profession—an image of effective leadership, professional competency, community responsibility, and service.

[1] Richard Kraus, *Recreation and Leisure in Modern Society,* © 1971 by Meredith Corporation. Reprinted by permission of Prentice-Hall, Inc., Englewood Cliffs, N.J. P. 104.

According to Morris L. Cogan, "A profession is a vocation whose practice is founded upon an understanding of the theoretical structure of some department of learning or science, and upon the abilities accompanying such understanding."[2]

Each profession must have a body of common knowledge, a core content, to which is added material pertaining to the specialized branches. Medicine, for example, includes surgery, neurology, pediatrics, and other branches. Similarly, recreation has numerous branches, such as municipal, industrial, therapeutic, and correctional recreation.

There are several ingredients that are basic to the development of a profession:

- Specific body of knowledge
- General acceptance of the field
- Professional preparation
- Research

- Certification
- Personnel standards
- Recruitment
- Professional organizations

A PROFESSIONAL IMAGE

A major goal among those in the parks and recreation field is the development of a favorable public image—an image of leadership, professional competency and responsibility. Indeed, a powerful force in any democracy is public awareness and favorable opinion.

Actually, there is a definite lack of public understanding of the field of recreation, and the problem is primarily one of image. Most Americans are not yet fully aware that recreation is a distinct area of professional service. "Ask any high school senior to locate and identify a doctor," wrote Thomas L. Goodale. "He might reply: 'You'll find him in his office or hospital, probably wearing a white jacket and carrying a black bag.' An architect? 'At his office drawing plans or at the site inspecting and supervising construction.' A recreator? 'A *what?*' Most young people, by the time they start sorting through career possibilities, have met and been in contact with many recreation professionals, with perhaps one of two results—they don't identify those they have met as recreation professionals, or they do not project or envision the profession beyond the camp, pool, or playground with which they are familiar."[3]

Several factors, however, indicate that recreation is attaining professional status. There has been a general acceptance on the part of the public of recreation as a community responsibility and service. In addition, there is increased awareness in the community for the need for competent leadership with special preparation and training.

Indeed, the public is becoming more fully aware of recreation as a profession. This awareness, no doubt, can be attributed to the great increase in the number of recreation and park agencies and with the growth of college and university curricula. Kraus suggested that "what remains is for the field itself to clarify its role, so that a single clear image emerges."[4]

THE PROFESSIONAL RECREATOR

There are a number of competencies that a professional recreator should have. Among the most important are the abilities to speak and write effectively. In addition to having a wide range of skills, the professional should possess a sound knowledge of principles, policies, and procedures that can be used in planning and conducting recreation activities and events.

In dealing with the public, the professional should use good judgment, tact, even restraint when encountering difficult situations, complaints, or criticism. Always conscious of the value of good public relations, he or she should be an able interpreter in describing department programs and activities to the public.

---

[2] Edward H. Storey, "Education for Leisure," Position Statement of the Society of Park and Recreation Educators, September 1972, p. 4.

[3] Thomas L. Goodale, "The Manpower Muddle," *Parks and Recreation,* February 1969, p. 29.

[4] Kraus, op. cit., p. 108.

Fig. 15-2 RECREATIONAL PROFESSIONALS AT WORK. This scene of an instructional swimming program in Alameda, California, effectively illustrates all levels of recreational leadership. As the instructional staff carry out their responsibilities, the administrator confers briefly with the pool supervisor and head instructor.

✳ Additional competencies of the "Professional Person":

- Reads constantly.
- Joins professional associations, pays dues and attends meetings.
- Seeks new ideas and trends in the field.
- Accepts membership on professional committees and is an active participant.
- Conducts himself or herself with dignity and in a way that commands respect.
- Bases his or her behavior on high moral and ethical principles.
- Works effectively with all organizations and individuals in the community.
- Demands high standards of excellence.
- Is receptive to suggestions and ideas from others.
- Enjoys life!

Personal Characteristics

Successful recreation leaders have many personal characteristics in common. Thomas Yukic listed the following traits as most important:[5]

[5] Thomas S. Yukic, *Fundamentals of Recreation* (New York: Harper & Row, Publishers, 1970), pp. 156–57.

- Common sense
- Pleasing personality
- A sense of humor
- A sense of human worth
- Productive energy
- A desire to serve people
- Ability to get along with others
- Good physical and mental health

TYPES OF PROFESSIONAL RECREATION LEADERS

Generally, recreation leaders may be divided into three categories: administrator or executive, supervisor, and leader.

Administrative Positions

This position involves major responsibility for planning and administering a recreation and park program to meet the needs and interests of the area served. The title may be administrator, general manager, director, or superintendent of parks

Fig. 15-3 THE RECREATION ADMINISTRATOR directs the total operation of the department, usually administering both the park and the recreation program operations. Paul Hagan, administrator of the Cordova Recreation and Park District, stands proudly in front of one of his newest parks in Rancho Cordova, California.

and recreation. Most administrators today are responsible for both the program and the park operations.

In addition to the administrator, there are also superintendents or directors of separate divisions, such as the superintendent of recreation or the director of park maintenance. These positions involve a high level of responsibility and are considered administrative.

Specific responsibilities of the administrator include:

1. Administering the work of the department in accordance with governing policies.
2. Recruiting, selecting, training, assigning, supervising, and evaluating the department staff.
3. Acquisition, planning, construction, improvement, and maintenance of areas and facilities.
4. Preparing budget, directing, controlling, and accounting for all expenditures, revenues, and fiscal operations.
5. Effective public relations.
6. Organizing, directing, and controlling all program activities.

7. Maintaining and preparing records, and reports.
8. Evaluating, performing research studies.
9. Motivating and inspiring personnel.

Comparable positions in park maintenance and facilities construction call for administrative and supervisory responsibilities. The person responsible for the operation and maintenance of physical facilities is often given the title of park superintendent or park foreman. While in the past, individuals have been assigned to either recreation or park responsibilities, today, an increasing number of cities are assigning recreation and park supervisors the responsibility for both areas..

Qualifications. The qualifications of an administrator usually include graduation from a recognized college or university with a bachelor's degree in recreation administration, park management, or a closely related field, plus successful experience over a period of years in recreation supervision and/or administration.

300

Fig. 15-4 OVERSEEING THE USE OF FACILITIES AND AREAS is among the many responsibilities of recreation supervisors. Chorley Park in Sacramento has been recognized nationally for its outstanding "adventure playground" design and operations.

Supervisory Positions

Representing a secondary level of administration, supervisors are responsible for the overall recreation or park operations, usually within a major category of program service.

Recreation Supervisor (general).   A general recreation supervisor is responsible for all phases of the recreation program within an area and for the supervision of all personnel in the area. His primary function is coordinating and directing the work of others, scheduling activities, and serving as liaison between the administrator and leaders in the field.

Specific responsibilities include:

1. Assisting the administrator and superintendent of recreation in administering programs.
2. Planning programs to meet the needs of the district.
3. Supervising, training, and evaluating personnel assigned to him.
4. Overseeing maintenance and use of facilities and areas.
5. Maintaining good public relations, publicity, and promotion.
6. Planning, research, and evaluation.
7. Assisting in budget preparation.
8. Maintaining records and preparing reports.

Special Supervisor.   A recreation supervisor who has more specialized responsibilities would be involved with a specific area of activity. A special supervisor's main functions might include being in charge of a large community center or other recreation complex or overseeing a major area of activity, such as athletics, aquatics, performing arts, or outdoor programs. He might also be responsible for programs involving special groups such as the handicapped, the aging, or youth.

Qualifications. Normally, the qualifications for supervisors include graduation from a recognized college or university with a degree in recreation, or recreation and parks, or a closely related field, along with a specified period of professional experience in recreation.

Leadership Positions

Some departments have several grades of recreation leaders, such as Leader I, II, and III. Many employ a senior leader in addition to the regular leaders. A senior leader often is required to supervise part-time personnel. Leadership jobs call for generalists as well as specialists.

Recreation Leader. A full-time, professional position, the recreation leader is responsible for planning, organizing, and supervising recreation programs. He or she may work in one or more facilities as a general leader, or in a particular area of activity, or may function as a specialist in a leader or teaching capacity.

Working directly with groups, the leader is responsible for the organization, direction, and supervision of recreational activities. In some situations, the leader is in full charge of the program, having been delegated various responsibilities by the supervisor. As a rule, however, the leader is responsible to the supervisor, who should always be kept informed. The duties of the recreation leader are listed on pages 00–00 in Chapter 14.

As a specialist, the recreation leader is responsible for a given area of activity and will promote the activity throughout the district. He may be responsible for a special tournament, show, or event.

Qualifications. For full-time positions, civil service qualifications for recreation leader have specified a college degree in recreation or a related field or a minimum of two years of college study. Part-time or summer leadership positions are being filled by upper and lower division students, particularly those majoring in recreation. Increasingly, community colleges are providing personnel on this level of service through leader or technician training programs.

CAREERS IN RECREATION AND PARKS

Rapid growth in the recreation and park profession is creating many career opportunities for men and women graduates of college and university training programs. The need for professionally trained and educated personnel has grown proportionately with the increase in the number of organizations and agencies involved with recreation and leisure services.

The local government level, including city, county, and district recreation agencies, constitutes a major source of employment, from administrative positions down to specialist and leadership roles. State government positions are not as numerous as local positions, but they have increased significantly in relation to the growth and development of a broader range of recreation services. Similarly, the federal government offers a diversified scope of job positions that appeal to young men and women graduating from colleges and universities.

Increasingly, professional recreators are assuming attractive job positions with commercial recreation agencies. Their training and background have made them ideal candidates for management and supervisory roles at golf and country clubs, bowling alleys, ski resorts, camps, beach resorts, housing development recreation areas, sports organizations, and the many recreation communities currently being developed.

Through classification and standardization of job titles, public agencies have been able to establish a career ladder which provides opportunities for promotion. The top administrative staff is usually directly appointed and not a part of the Civil Service system.

Fig. 15-5 THE PARK MAINTENANCE MAN is responsible for the maintenance of park areas and facilities. While there has been a trend toward developing mobile maintenance teams, many departments still employ the traditional procedure of having maintenance personnel assigned to specific parks.

FIELDS INVOLVING RECREATION AND LEISURE SERVICES

Public Recreation (Municipal)
School Recreation (Camp–School)
Group Work Recreation (Serving Youth)
Commercial Recreation (Amusements)
Therapeutic Recreation (Medical)
Resort Recreation (Travel)
Company Recreation (Industrial Employee)
Institutional Recreation (Correctional–Prison)
Private Recreation
Armed Forces (Military)

Career Options

Within the college or university curriculum are numerous options available to students in the recreation and parks field.

General Option. Sufficient diversification is provided to enable a student to enter any of several professional fields in recreation.

Recreation–Park Administration. This option places an emphasis on public administration, business, planning, and the natural sciences. Students are prepared for employment in recreation and park agencies at the various levels of government.

Therapeutic Recreation. The student is prepared for recreation employment in hospitals, convalescent homes, centers for the physically and mentally handicapped, or in specialized programs offered by local recreation and park departments.

Corrections. Emphasizing the fields of sociology, psychology, and law enforcement, this option meets the general requirements for employment in correctional institutions at the local, state, and federal levels.

Outdoor Recreation. Emphasis is on management, conservation, interpretation, and utilization of forest, wilderness areas, waterways, fish and wildlife.

Private Recreation. Professional recreators are needed to manage and supervise employee recreation programs, athletic clubs, golf courses, gun clubs, marinas, and other recreational facilities.

Armed Forces. Civilian and military employment opportunities are available for the direction and supervision of service clubs, libraries, sports, hobby shops, bowling alleys, and music for military personnel and their dependents.

Voluntary Service Agencies. Recreation leadership is the backbone of most youth-oriented groups such as the YMCA, Boy Scouts of America, Girl Scouts of America, Campfire Girls, and other activity-minded organizations. Group work agencies need professionally trained personnel for positions as executive directors, workers and leaders, specialists, field and regional secretaries, and research specialists.

Fig. 15-6 WORKING DIRECTLY WITH GROUPS, the recreation leader organizes, directs, and supervises activities on the playground. This scene shows several children enjoying free play during supervised playground hours.

Careers in the National Park Service

Headquartered in Washington, D.C., the National Park Service has a permanent staff of approximately 6,000 year-round employees. Employment opportunities are available in the following professional positions: park ranger, park naturalist, historian, archeologist. Design profession positions are available as an architect, landscape architect, and engineer.

Selections are made usually during the months of January through June, and those selected for uniformed positions normally enter the service in groups of forty-five at a time at the Horace M. Albright Training Center at Grand Canyon National Park, Arizona.

After successfully completing training, these uniformed employees are assigned to appropriate park locations for further training and development during their first year with the service.

A person in a career in the park service may wish to gain at least one summer season of actual work experience in a park or office of the National Park Service while still pursuing his or her education.

Interested applicants can obtain a copy of the examination announcement covering the position for which they wish to apply at their local post office or an office of the Civil Service Commission.

Opportunities in Other Federal Agencies

In addition to the National Park Service, there are numerous forest ranger and federal game management agent positions. Applicants interested in these positions should contact the Forest Service, U.S. Department of Agriculture, Washington, D.C. 20250 (for forest ranger); and the Bureau of Sport Fisheries and Wildlife, U.S. Department of the Interior, Washington, D.C. 20240 (for game management agent).

Summer Jobs in Federal Agencies

Each summer there are a limited number of opportunities for summer jobs with the federal government. These positions vary from office jobs to park rangers and are located throughout the United States.

Most appointments available in the Forest Service are limited to students majoring in the fields of forestry or related sciences. Each National Forest does its own selecting and hiring.

The National Park Service has a limited number of park ranger, park technician, and park aid positions available for applicants eighteen years of age or older. Applications should be sent to the superintendent of the park where the individual desires employment.

Various federal agencies have special work-study programs. Applicants who are appointed participate in specific training programs during vacations and attend college full-time during the academic periods.

Each year the federal government participates with private industry in providing summer jobs for educationally and economically disadvantaged youths aged sixteen through twenty-one. This program is specifically designed to provide jobs for young people from low income families and for youths who need incomes from summer jobs in order to return to school in the fall. Young people who are interested in these summer jobs should register with the local office of their state employment service.

Federal Jobs Overseas

Employment opportunities in recreational work are available overseas with such employers as the United States Army, Air Force, and Navy. Overseas positions are normally filled through the reassignment of Army career employees from the United States.

Most vacancies are filled by the appointment of local eligibles who qualify in competitive civil-service examinations which are announced and held in the local area.

Copies of the examination announcements, containing full information on how and where to apply, and application forms, can be obtained from the U.S. Civil Service Commission, Washington, D.C. 20415, and from its regional offices.

The Peace Corps

The Peace Corps provides opportunities for skilled Americans to serve in developing nations overseas. More than 13,000 people have served or are serving as Peace Corps Volunteers in 46 nations overseas. While most of the volunteers work in educational and community development programs, there are positions available in more than 300 separate skill areas. Recreation leaders are needed to organize scouting and youth activities programs, begin boys' clubs, build recreation facilities, and develop programs in camping, crafts, and water safety. A college degree is not required.

Applicants must be at least eighteen years of age and American citizens. Married couples are eligible if they have no dependents under eighteen. For further information on opportunities for service, and instructions for application, write the Office of Public Affairs, Peace Corps, Washington, D.C. 20525.

RECRUITMENT

The success of any profession depends on the quality of the individuals who are attracted to the field. With the intense competition of other more established professions, it is extremely important that recruitment for recreation leadership begin early so as to enable the field to recruit youth who have the strongest leadership abilities.

The advantages and rewards of recreation as a career should be effectively interpreted by the counseling services of secondary schools. Ideally, those who enroll as a recreation major at a college or university have had some prior leadership experience as a leader or aide on a playground or a drop-in center. Young people who enjoy working in aquatics, playgrounds, camps, Little Leagues, and in other recreation activities are excellent prospects for the professional recreation field. Whether the on-the-job training experience is part-time, on a paid or volunteer basis, the importance of such experience will prove most beneficial later on. With such a background, the student is much better oriented and ready to engage in a career of job preparation. Leadership experience in scouting, 4-H club activities, and sports is also highly beneficial to a prospective professional recreator.

There have also been substantial increases in the salaries of people in the recreation and parks field. Entry level pay for the holder of a bachelor's degree in recreation is generally over $8,500. Administrators are earning from $12,000 to $38,000 annually.

PROFESSIONAL ASSOCIATIONS

There are a large number of national and state-wide organizations that are contributing to the recreation movement. While space will not permit a description of all, there are a number of professional organizations that have promoted significantly the development of parks and recreation.

Fig. 15-7 MORE CAREER OPPORTUNITIES for young men and women are becoming available each year as the number of agencies and organizations involved with recreation and park services increases. Here, park rangers and maintenance staff discuss their day's work at Folsom Lake State Park in California.

National Recreation and Park Association

A nonprofit service, research, and education organization, the NRPA offers services to develop and support the administrative and technical abilities of professional members. Keeping all members informed of events that affect the quality of park and recreation services, the association provides services through publications, institutes, and workshops, and direct consultation and technical assistance.

"The NRPA is dedicated to the improvement of park and recreation leadership, programs and facilities everywhere," said Dwight F. Rettie, the organization's executive director. "The Association seeks to build public understanding of this important human mission."[6]

More than sixty state and regional organizations are affiliated with NRPA and provide members the opportunity to be active at the local,

state, and regional level. NRPA encourages joint membership in both the national and state affiliate.

The Association's membership of over 16,000 belong to the following seven branches: American Park and Recreation Society, Armed Forces Recreation Society, Commissioners-Board Members, National Conference on State Parks, National Student Recreation and Park Society, National Therapeutic Recreation Society, and Society of Park and Recreation Educators.

Regional staff help develop local and state programs and services through consultation and technical assistance to individual members, affiliate organizations, municipalities, counties, and states.

For further information, write: National Recreation and Park Association, 1601 North Kent Street, Arlington, Virginia 22209.

American Camping Association

The ACA is a nationwide, nonprofit organization of persons interested in the values and importance

---

[6] Taken from presentation of Dwight F. Rettie, tape recorded at 1973 Congress for Recreation and Parks, Washington, D.C., October 1, 1973.

of organized camping. Members include camp directors and owners, camp staff, educators, clergy, and others interested in camping and outdoor education programs.

The ACA is organized into sections to insure personal participation and close contact with its members. A section usually includes one or two states. These sections are grouped into seven regions

Accredited ACA camp members include resident camps, day camps, travel camps, and other special purpose camps. These camps are operated under the auspices of private ownership, organizations, churches, and special groups.

The association can be contacted by writing: American Camping Association, Bradford Woods, Martinsville, Indiana 46151.

American Association for Health, Physical Education and Recreation

The AAHPER is a professional organization involved with four major areas of interest: health, safety, physical education, and recreation. AAHPER's membership of over 50,000 is made up largely of physical education teachers, as well as an increasing number of recreation teachers and supervisors from secondary schools, colleges, and universities.

With headquarters in Washington, D.C., the full-time staff is headed by an executive secretary and assisted by several professional associates. Among the programs and projects sponsored by the association are workshops and institutes held in various regions in the country.

Further information can be obtained by writing: American Association for Health, Physical Education and Recreation, 1201 16th Street, N.W., Washington, D.C. 20036.

Athletic Institute

One of the principal service organizations in the field of recreation is the Athletic Institute. Founded in 1934, the institute's primary objective through the years has been to stimulate participation in sport activities in America; however, the functions of the institute have since been broadened considerably to include recreation and physical education.

Supported financially by the manufacturers of athletic, sports, and recreation equipment, the operations of the institute are under the direction of a board of directors and an advisory committee.

The institute has been involved with three major fields of service: visual aids, financial support of sports programs, workshops, and projects, and publication of numerous publications and texts.

This service organization can be contacted by writing: Athletic Institute, Room 805, Merchandise Mart, Chicago, Illinois 60600.

National Industrial Recreation Association

The NIRA is the leading organization in the field of industrial-employee recreation. The association serves over 800 major companies that provide recreation programs for their employees. According to estimates compiled by the association in 1967, "There were 1,000 full-time industrial recreation directors and 500 park and recreation center managers employed by industries throughout the United States."[6]

The Association's mailing address is: National Industrial Recreation Association, 20 North Wacker Drive, Chicago, Illinois 60600.

---

[6] Kraus, op. cit., p. 97.

Public.
City
County
State
National

PARK#REC.
CPRS
ACA
NRPA
NIRA
AAHPER

CREATIVITY
MR. CHARLES NUNNELLY
McDONALD-DOUGLAS CORP.

WEL
RECREATIO
OF CAL

16

Professional Preparation

A dramatic and sharp growth in professional preparation in recreation and parks has occurred during the past decade. Today, over 300 colleges and universities provide curricula in the park and recreation field. Since the field is comprised of numerous subject areas and interests, college curricula offer many specialties of training and education.

The first specialized training in recreation and park administration took place during the 1920s, when the National Recreation Association sponsored a one-year graduate training institute. However, it was not until a decade later that colleges and universities entered this field of professional service.

Soon after World War II, a number of institutions initiated curricula for undergraduate and graduate recreation majors, usually as a part of the health and physical education department. In 1950, approximately fifty colleges were offering programs for recreation majors. Following a period of relative stability, recreation and park enrollments began to rise sharply in the 1960s.

The expansion of professional preparation was the result of the steady expansion of municipal recreation and park programs throughout America and the growing demand for more and better personnel. According to a survey conducted by the National Recreation and Park Association in 1967, 183 institutions reported park and recreation curricula—a huge increase over the 46 institutions reported in 1960.[1] Of this number, 45 two-year colleges were offering programs. Since the survey was made, over 100 other institutions have initiated recreation curricula.

NEW STANDARDS

Professional leaders and supervisors today must meet new and stronger standards than those of their predecessors. In large measure, the upgrading of leadership and management can be attributed to the efforts of professional organizations and their committees and to those institutions

Fig. 16-1 PROFESSIONAL GROWTH is the underlying theme of the annual fall conference of the California Society of Park and Recreation Educators. Here, Charles Nunnelly speaks on "Creativity" to educators from both the four-year and two-year colleges and universities.

---

[1] Educational survey conducted by the National Recreation and Park Association, 1967.

Fig. 16-2 STRONGER STANDARDS OF PROFESSIONAL PREPARATION. Dr. Allen Sapora, head of the Department of Recreation and Park Administration at the University of Illinois, is one of many outstanding recreation educators in America.

that have provided recreation curricula. Additional training in the form of workshops, institutes, courses, and in-service training have been responsible for raising the standards of the recreation field significantly.

There is a greater awareness on the part of the general public as to what constitutes effective leadership and program services. As a result, they have come to expect a higher caliber of recreation leadership and organization.

Professional curricula in colleges and universities are superior to those offered a decade or two ago, and there are those who believe that present training programs in such a young field as recreation and leisure services have yet to reach their potential.

The establishment of a code of ethics has contributed to the development of status and integrity for the recreation profession. Many of the professional organizations have adopted codes, which in addition to providing more effective services to the people, should prove instrumental in gaining professional recognition for the field. Two major problems still exist, however. First, the standards are not being accepted by all professionals, and second, the present means of enforcing adherence to the codes are not adequate to achieve their specific purpose.

There is an urgent need to improve the quality of preparation of recreation majors so as to better understand and serve disadvantaged groups as well as to recruit and prepare minority and low income students for recreation careers.

PROFESSIONAL EDUCATION

The professional recreation curricula offered by two-year and four-year colleges and universities have assumed the major responsibility for preparing personnel for the growing number of job positions that demand recreation skills and background. Opportunities at all levels of service are available depending on the type and extent of educational preparation.

The three programs offering professional recreation education are as follows:

1. *Two years in a community or junior college* will prepare an individual for a position as a leader, technician, or specialist with career ladder opportunities to climb upward. Graduates can begin as recreation leaders, recreation center supervisors, and special facility technicians.

2. *Four years in a college or university* will provide preparatory training for a professional career as an administrator or supervisor, or numerous other jobs based on the type of curriculum. With experience, students completing a bachelor's program can qualify as program specialists, assistants to directors in park and recreation departments, or directors in smaller communities.

3. *Postgraduate courses and degrees* will qualify the individual for higher levels of responsibility in top positions in one of the professional fields of specialization. Top administrative, educational, and research positions require advanced degrees on the master and doctoral level. Increasingly, many professional recreators are returning to the campus for advanced education and more specialized training.

UNDERGRADUATE PROFESSIONAL CURRICULUM

Undergraduate preparation should contribute a solid background for future growth and the mini-

Fig. 16-3 REGIONAL CONFERENCES ON LEADERSHIP held in 1969 were instrumental in upgrading and implementing community college training programs. Featured panelists at the four conferences, including this meeting at American River College, were two outstanding recreation educators, Dr. Douglas Sessoms and Dr. Peter Verhoven, far left.

mum competencies for beginning professional service.

In training majors in recreation, the trend is toward a greater emphasis on general education. Fifty per cent of the course work is devoted to general education, the humanities, language arts, physical and social sciences; the remaining one-half is allocated to professional recreation education and its related areas.[2]

The undergraduate student should receive numerous laboratory and work experiences which will result in the learning of greater skills and a close familiarity with the professional field of recreation. In order to gain some specialization, he should take a sufficient number of elective hours.[3]

After conferences with his advisor, the student should be able to choose an effective integration of courses in allied disciplines, as well as in laboratory and in theoretical experiences.

Field work offers the student-leader laboratory situations in which he is confronted with practical situations. Field work should be a cooperative effort between the student, the institu-

tion, and the agency or department he is working for. Directed field experience is divided into two types: (1) observation and participation, (2) internship.

PROFESSIONAL COMPETENCIES

A Professional Preparation Conference, which met in Washington, D.C., early in 1962, enumerated competencies essential to the recreation profession.

1. Understanding the concepts of leisure, the philosophies of recreation, and the development of a personal and professional philosophy of recreation.
2. Knowledge of the nature, history, and development of the recreation movement.
3. Knowledge of the place, scope, and importance of recreation in the community setting.
4. Knowledge and understanding of the interrelationships and relationships to the recreation profession of social institutions.
5. Appreciation of the roles of the leader and the leader's function in the guidance and counseling of the individual in social, personal, and leisure concerns.
6. Personal experiences, practical application, and skills in various program areas.
7. Knowledge of the planning and operation of park and recreation facilities.

---

[2] Report of a national conference, "Professional Preparation in Health Education, Physical Education, and Recreation Education" (Washington, D.C.: American Association for Health, Physical Education and Recreation, 1962), pp. 89, 90.

[3] Ibid.

8. Ability to train, supervise, and utilize both volunteers and professionals.
9. Ability to interpret the role of the recreation profession to colleagues, community groups, and participants in recreation programs.
10. Knowledge of professional, service, and related recreation organizations.[4]

Specialization

Indeed, the recreation and parks field has become quite extensive in scope. The field is so broad that it has become an impossibility to prepare students for all specialties. For years, it was felt that anyone possessing talent in recreational activities would be capable of setting up a program. Professionals in the field, of course, know this is ridiculous; still, it has taken decades for this erroneous thinking to be replaced with an image of an established profession. As a result, the specialized training of recreation leaders has been recognized only recently.

Internships

Professional internships or trainee programs involve a special program of on-the-job supervision and training. Normally, internship at a four-year college or university is not less than nine months, nor more than twelve months' duration. Supervision is provided by college and agency supervisors.

Salaries

Starting salaries are determined by job responsibility, size of the department, and the individual's education and experience. The geographic location is a factor since salary scales vary to a degree according to region and state.

Generally, an individual with a bachelor's degree starts between $8,000 and $9,000. Administrative positions in small communities, requiring a year or two of experience, can pay from $10,000

to $12,000. Middle- to upper-level positions range from $12,000 to $22,000. Top salaries start at $22,000 and may go as high as $40,000. Starting salaries and the range of salaries are continually being upgraded.

GRADUATE PROFESSIONAL PROGRAM

With the new demands for stronger standards for recreation personnel, graduate study has become essential. The larger agencies in many communities now require a master's degree for their top administrator. Generally, teachers, research specialists, and program planners are now required to have graduate degrees.

The objectives of a graduate program include the following:

Administrative techniques
Research and investigation
Specialization in an area
Observation and survey
Problem solving
Professional growth

Graduate preparation should capitalize on the previous experiences of the candidate. Students should be given opportunities to plan, organize, and supervise programs. They need to become more familiar with basic evaluative and research techniques, as well as the ability to make oral and written presentations. They must gain an understanding in the following areas:

• Philosophy and principles of recreation
• Administration of recreation
• Research and evaluation
• Personnel management
• Public relations

GROWTH OF COMMUNITY COLLEGE PROGRAMS

Professional preparation in recreation and parks has experienced a sharp growth during the past decade. In 1968, a manpower study conducted by the National Recreation and Park Association re-

---

[4] Ibid., pp. 88–89.

Figs. 16-4 and 16-5 PREPARING PERSONNEL for jobs in the recreation and parks field has been assumed largely by four-year and two-year colleges and universities. While community colleges train young men and women for jobs at the program leader level, the four-year schools are providing the field with personnel to fill administrative and high-level supervisory positions.

vealed that forty-five two-year community colleges were offering degree programs in recreation and parks. Many more institutions indicated that they were planning to initiate such programs in the near future.

Indeed, the community college movement offering associate degrees in recreation leadership has been a most significant trend. This development can be attributed to two major factors: (a) the rapid expansion of two-year colleges, and (b) the need for direct leaders and program technicians.

Offering an associate of arts degree, the role of the two-year program is to prepare students for direct face-to-face leadership or technical jobs in the field of recreation and parks. This role involves the preparation of the student for both early entry into the field and/or transfer to a four-year program to continue his education toward a bachelor's or master's degree.

Early Entry Program

Graduates of the two-year curriculum can find employment in leadership roles where they can move into positions of more responsibility through experience and additional education.

Increasingly, community colleges are training people for para-professional entry-level jobs with leisure service agencies. With a growing number of career opportunities available to qualified associate professionals, the community college has responded to the need by providing vocational or career-oriented curricula. In achieving this end, the two-year curriculum contains the basic knowledge and training skills to prepare the student to function effectively in a face-to-face leadership capacity in a variety of recreational settings.

Transfer Program

Two-year college graduates can continue their education at four-year schools for a bachelor's degree. The four-year institution offers full-fledged professional competencies, with extensive training provided to prepare students for the higher salaried supervisory and administrative positions.

While the major objective of the curriculum is to produce recreation leaders, the two-year program offers the basic professional courses in rec-

313

reation which will be acceptable and transferable to four-year schools.

Community college students are prepared sufficiently in the area of recreation skills. In addition to the core courses in recreation, they have many general education requirements to meet, such as social and natural sciences, psychology, art, music, and language arts. Recreation centers, playgrounds, schools, and parks are a few of the places where the student may work in directed work experience on the leadership level.

While it is difficult to provide students with broad professional training, community college programs in recreation leadership have been able to impart the basic skills and knowledge needed for many specialized jobs.

Storey noted that "the national trend in universities toward a division of the four-year program into general education (the first two years) and professional studies (the third and fourth years) seems to present difficulties for the Associate Degree recipient who will want to pursue the Baccalaureate. The Associate Degree programs appear to be developing in dissimilar directions to the first two years of the Baccalaureate program." ... "Increased articulation between associate degree and baccalaureate programs is essential if these conflicts are to be minimized," concluded Storey.[5]

INCREASED ARTICULATION

The California Society of Park and Recreation Educators took a major step toward improved articulation on March 4, 1972, by "agreeing to accept, with intent to support, the report from the Articulation Committee." The member colleges and universities, from both two-year and four-year institutions, further pledged to implement the provisions of the report at their respective schools.

Acceptance of the report by the recreation educators of the community colleges and four-year institutions of California has provided a new

dimension in the professional preparation in recreation and parks.

The Articulation Committee recognized a need to clarify the objectives of professional preparation in recreation and leisure services, and to improve curricular content, organization, and staffing. In addition, the report stated that "it should be the aim of the committee to assist community college students in making a smoother transfer to the four-year school."

ACCREDITATION

With the rapid growth of recreation curricula, there is an apparent need to determine their degree of effectiveness and to strengthen them. If they are to be improved, the accreditation of college and university programs is essential.

Accreditation is a process established by a professional organization to enable a college or university to be recognized as having met certain predetermined standards. For example, the California Council of Park and Recreation Accreditation was established by the California Park and Recreation Society, Inc., following an eight-year study. The council administers a plan for volunteer accreditation of colleges and universities in the state of California that have established recreation curricula.

In most professions, the process of accreditation indicates that the institution is meeting existing standards of training. The process entails the following criteria:

- Establishment of standards
- Development of evaluative criteria or schedules
- Inspection by accrediting agency
- Enforcement of standards

The development of an accreditation program, similar to that of the National Council on Accreditation of Teacher Education, has been proposed.

Proponents of accreditation claim that it sets a minimum standard of educational quality and relevance in relation to broad educational goals excluding professional preparation. Critics of

---

[5] Edward H. Storey, "Education for Leisure," Position Statement of the Society of Park and Recreation Educators, September 1972, p. 5.

the accreditation process are concerned that it may lead to an early establishment of a status quo in professional development that does not permit flexibility they feel is essential to development of a professional program for a profession that is itself inadequately defined, growing in scope and stature, and facing challenges that demand experimentation, creativity, and new techniques in its practice.[6]

Despite reluctance in some quarters to accept accreditation, strong efforts to establish it are receiving increasing approval of educators and professional practitioners alike. The critical issue in accreditation is for the professional and for educational programs alike, the determination of relevant and practical criteria as a basis for determining the accredibility of curricula in this field.[7]

Accreditation criteria must be kept broad and sufficiently general to permit continued experimentation in curriculum development.

STUDENT INVOLVEMENT

Faculty at both undergraduate and graduate levels are encouraged to seek student involvement in departmental affairs and curriculum planning. Student evaluation during and at the end of each course can be most helpful.

Students should be assisted by members of the faculty in establishing and maintaining a student club and developing its programs. However, students should be responsible for the affairs of the club.

CERTIFICATION AND REGISTRATION

Certification is another effort to upgrade the standards of the recreation profession. Some states, such as California and Michigan, have successfully

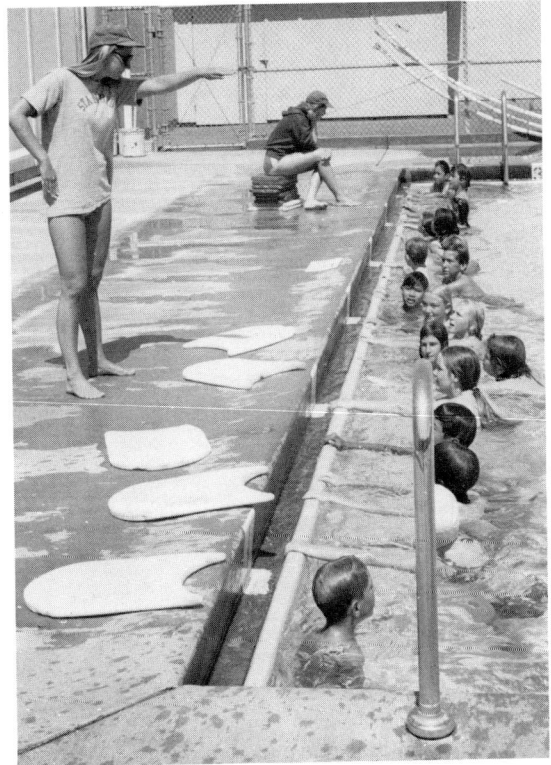

Fig. 16-6 FIELD WORK offers the student valuable laboratory situations, like this summer season of instructional swimming.

implemented voluntary registration programs. New York state has a plan with standards established by the New York State Recreation and Park Society, on nine levels of responsibility. Yet, the problem with such plans is that they are more voluntary than compulsory.

However, legislation expected to be enacted by the state of California will go far beyond voluntary registration and certification. If pending legislation passes, all park and recreation professionals in the state will be required to be licensed. Those who pass the examination will be issued specialty certificates by the State Park and Recreation Commission. According to the Public Resources Code, the commission would require an applicant to demonstrate such degree of experience and general knowledge of the park and recreation profession.

Private agencies have developed standards

[6] Storey, op. cit., p. 5.

[7] Ibid., p. 6.

Fig. 16-7 MORE LABORATORY RESEARCH. Institutions of higher learning are devoting increasing emphasis on research projects and studies, such as the above "creative teaching" presentation by Dr. William Niepoth, to recreation educators in California. Using a response panel, the group responded to thirteen quotations that involved creative teaching.

that involve certification of their personnel. Civil Service commissions, for years, have required comprehensive examinations for those applicants seeking positions in governmental agencies. However, there is a need to improve Civil Service hiring.

The dilemma of certification and registration can be attributed in part to the fact that opportunities in recreation are so vast and job positions vary so widely in type and content. Those who support such legislation maintain that these measures will hasten the day when the recreation profession is accepted universally as one with priorities on the level of education and law.

IN-SERVICE TRAINING

The professional advancement of the practitioner and educator should never end. Experience on the job should be combined with a well-organized in-service education program. In-service programs can be conducted independently or jointly with other agencies. Increasingly, colleges and universities have been cooperating with agencies in providing opportunities for in-service training.

Techniques that are often used include: conferences, staff meetings, seminars, institutes, workshops, symposia, individual or committee projects, and home study or correspondence courses. Professional periodicals and bulletins, textbooks, films and slides, radio, and television are other sources of learning and training.

RESEARCH

Recreation as a field has been rather weak in conducting research and study. As a young profession, it has had to rely too long on various other disciplines for information and answers to its problems. Most responsible for creating more emphasis on research has been the establishment of graduate programs in recreation and leisure studies in our colleges and universities. "A graduate program of study has little meaning if it is not supported by qualified research faculty," said Storey. "When possible, undergraduate students should be given the opportunity to participate in research projects."[8]

[8] Ibid., p. 7.

In addition to institutions of higher learning, many governmental agencies on the local, state, and federal levels have conducted recreation research, including industry, foundations, and various service organizations. Public recreation departments, on occasion, conduct studies in an attempt to secure information and data, and to solve some of their problems.

In the judgment of Carlson, Deppe, and MacLean, ". . . colleges offering graduate degrees in parks and recreation are best equipped with skilled technicians, laboratories, and qualified faculty to take the lead in recreation research. The results to date, . . . have been far from what is needed if recreation is to maintain status as a profession. The gap between researcher and practitioner must be narrowed if studies are to become a meaningful adjunct to the profession."[9]

[9] Reynold Carlson, Theodore Deppe, and Janet MacLean, *Recreation in American Life* (Belmont, California: Wadsworth Publishing Company, 1972), pp. 370–71.

WE MUST LEARN TO HONOR EXCELLENCE, INDEED DEMAND IT, IN EVERY SOCIALLY ACCEPTED HUMAN ACTIVITY, HOWEVER HUMBLE THE ACTIVITY, AND TO SCORN SHODDINESS HOWEVER EXALTED THE ACTIVITY. AN EXCELLENT PLUMBER IS INFINITELY MORE ADMIRABLE THAN AN INCOMPETENT PHILOSOPHER, AND THE SOCIETY WHICH SCORNS EXCELLENCE IN PLUMBING BECAUSE PLUMBING IS A HUMBLE ACTIVITY AND TOLERATES SHODDINESS IN PHILOSOPHY BECAUSE PHILOSOPHY IS AN EXALTED ACTIVITY WILL HAVE NEITHER GOOD PLUMBERS NOR GOOD PHILOSOPHERS, AND NEITHER ITS PIPES NOR ITS THEORIES WILL HOLD WATER.

John Gardner

VI

Challenges of the Recreation Movement

17

Issues and Problems Facing Recreation

The rapid development of the recreation and leisure movement, in progressing toward professional status, has not been without numerous problems and major issues. However, when one realizes the infancy of the field, the phenomenal speed of its development, combined with the growing complexities of modern life, the problems and seemingly difficult issues become challenges.

Despite inflation, the high cost of living, the energy crisis, taxes, Watergate, and numerous ecological problems, Americans have not lost their enthusiasm for a good time. Today, the nation is riding the crest of a "leisure boom."

The park and recreation movement has faced and will continue to face a crisis, but it is not alone in the struggle for local, state, and national priorities. Business, industry, agriculture, and education have also been affected.

If it faces up to the many challenges and problem areas, the recreation and leisure movement has great promise as an emerging profession. Students who have chosen recreation and leisure services as a career can either accept these challenges with a firm commitment to meet them, or they can sit on the sidelines and allow their chosen field to fail to live up to its tremendous potential.

THE USE OF LEISURE

The majority of the American people are experiencing greater amounts of leisure time. Many of these people actually do not know what to do with their increased leisure. They need guidance in determining how to make their lives more enjoyable and rewarding, to learn how to relax.

Whether leisure will be a blessing or a curse will in all likelihood be determined by man's knowledge and ability to use leisure constructively and creatively. Much will depend on our educational system, which has always been geared to preparing our young people to "make a living." In a leisure-oriented society, education's job will be to prepare people for meaningful leisure, in addition to a career job.

Fig. 17 1 NEW FORMS OF ETHNICALLY ORIENTED ACTIVITIES are reflecting racial demands, such as Afro-American arts and Chicano cultural programs. This scene took place at a conference of the California Recreation Educators, in which black students had earlier demonstrated some of their traditional culture and leisure activities.

Fig. 17-2 EDUCATING PEOPLE to use leisure wisely and constructively will continue to be recreation's No. 1 challenge. Here, a young couple enjoys a relaxing ride through a park.

Educating people to accept and use leisure will continue to be recreation's major challenge. The goal of every recreator should be to change people's attitudes toward a higher value for leisure. The use of leisure should be made an important part of an individual's daily living and throughout one's lifetime.

Solutions

Education for leisure should be part of every curriculum—elementary, junior and senior high, community college, and college–university.

The park and recreation profession, in a community-wide effort with all levels of education, must provide leisure skills, knowledge, and opportunities for all people.

There is a need to find ways of interpreting to the public a more accurate and complete understanding of what professional recreators are trying to do.

The mass news media should be used to spread "the good word," to create a greater public awareness for the need for constructive, enjoyable leisure time activity and experience.

Guidelines for Each Individual to Know

- His or her basic needs.
- The importance of leisure in daily living pattern.
- Factors that motivate choice of activities.
- An inventory of present leisure skills and activities.
- Available outlets for leisure in the community.
- Changes to make in his or her living pattern.
- Developing a more enjoyable leisure living plan.

INCREASED LEISURE

Leisure in America continues to grow at a more rapid rate than the people's capacity to use it intelligently. For many labor workers, the forty-hour work week is expected to drop to thirty-five or even thirty-two hours per week. Management and professional occupations, though, will not experi-

> THE MOST DANGEROUS THREAT TO AMER-
> ICAN SOCIETY IS THE RISE OF LEISURE
> AND THE FACT THAT THOSE WHO HAVE
> THE MOST LEISURE ARE THE LEAST
> EQUIPPED TO USE IT.
>
> *Eric Sevareid*

ence such a decrease in their working time. How-ever, even they can expect more holidays, vaca-tion time, and other benefits that result in more free time.

As for a shorter work week, a recent survey indicated that 45 per cent of men of all ages would like to make the switch to a four-day/forty-hour work week. This, of course, involves a three-day weekend every week of the year. While the majority of working women are opposed to the plan, the new schedule appears to be catching on in some areas.[1]

Those who favor a four-day work week claim that: (a) a shorter work week would provide a longer weekend; (b) families would have more time together; (c) there would be more oppor-tunities for leisure projects; and (d) increased job efficiency and morale would result.

Those opposed to the change feel that ten hours a day is too grueling a pace, and people have too much leisure time now.

Labor union leaders are seeking a shorter work week one way or another. Actually, author-ities believe the 35-hour work week will be prev-alent in the not too distant future. Many workers are already on this kind of schedule.

The vacation of the average American has increased from 1.8 weeks to 2.2 weeks per year.

EFFECTS OF AUTOMATION

Mass production of goods and services has had a major effect on the American economy, making life easier and providing increased leisure time. Due to technological and automation advances, however, there has been a great reduction in the number of hours of work. Less work has meant

[1] J. D. Hodgson, "Leisure and the American Worker," *Leisure Today*, 1972, pp. 5–6.

Fig. 17-3 TEACHING WHOLESOME LEISURE SKILLS AND ATTITUDES must be a responsibility that both schools and park and recreation agencies share. Lifetime, carry-over sports, like tennis, golf, and bowling, should receive major emphasis.

more free time. The boredom and monotony of automated work has caused much dissatisfaction with large numbers of workers; for others, auto-mation has caused unemployment.

Solutions

Use the increased leisure time wisely and con-structively.

Create new jobs for those unemployed because of automation.

Provide some means of achievement and satis-faction in boring and monotonous work.

Provide a more comprehensive recreation pro-gram for industrial workers, such as enjoyable activities during breaks and lunch hour, and challenging and creative leisure experiences during weekends, off-hours, and vacation time.

INCREASED INCOME

While the cost of living continues to rise, personal income also continues to increase at a rapid rate.

This has had a tremendous effect on the recreation and leisure services market. Leisure expenditures, recently estimated at over $140 billion, are expected to go beyond the $200 billion figure by 1980.

With more leisure time and more income, commercial businesses, industries, and recreation services will continue to have ever increasing profits and achievements.

As income rises, the standard of living, likewise, will improve in many ways. However, as far as the great majority of Americans are concerned, it is discouraging, indeed, to know that an elite few—only 4.4 per cent of the population—own most of America's wealth. They have a third of the nation's personal cash, a fourth of the real estate, and 40 per cent of non-corporate business assets.[2] "I'm not saying there should be a perfectly equal distribution," says Professor James D. Smith, Pennsylvania State University economist. "But there should be more evenness in the distribution."[3]

POPULATION GROWTH

The rising population in America will continue to have a major effect on the recreation and leisure market. Now well over 200 million, the population is expected to reach 300 million by the year 2000.

Along with this has been a large increase in the number of people over 65 years of age. The average life expectancy continues to rise, providing the challenge for society to make the "Golden Years" more meaningful and satisfying.

POPULATION CHANGES

There has been a major transformation in America from a rural to a predominately urban population. Urban sprawl and a mass exodus of middle-class citizens to the suburbs have been additional

---

[2] William Chapman, "Elite Few Own Most of Wealth," *Sacramento Bee*, September 24, 1973.

[3] Ibid.

Fig. 17-4 OUR DESIRE FOR MOBILITY AND TRAVEL. While the automobile will still be the chief means of travel, restrictions will increase in many state and national parks. Alternate transportation will be provided in many instances.

changes in the population. There has been a strong influx of racial minorities to central city ghettos. Within the next decade, it is expected that at least 85 per cent of the population in the United States will live in metropolitan areas.

Solutions

A sense of community spirit must be developed.
A feeling of acceptance and belonging must be cultivated among the newcomers.
New leaders must be developed to replace those who move away.

GREATER MOBILITY

With increased transportation services, people can now travel quickly to a variety of recreation sites. New super highways and freeway systems have contributed to a transportation network which has given man great mobility. The automobile will still be the chief means of travel for the individual and family, but air travel is expected to increase greatly by the end of the century. More than 8 million Americans traveled abroad in 1973, compared to 7.4 million in 1972.

Bike rides, horseback trips, picnicking, backpacking, and hosteling will become common leisure activities, and will contribute still further to our desire for mobility and travel.

On the playground level, mobile units are being used increasingly to serve the needs of congested or remote areas.

ENVIRONMENTAL CRISIS

The quality of the environment will be one of the major issues of the next decade. People must be made to realize the need to protect their environment. The cause of land, air, water, and noise pollution and the ugliness of our cities is people. Today, pollution experts call the once magnificent Mississippi River the garbage dump of mid-America. Hundreds of towns and cities use it as a sewer. Within many of our cities are unkept vacant lots, poorly maintained residential areas, unclean streets, and cluttered public areas. Therefore, to improve the environment, people must change their behavior. Just as they have polluted their environment, they can also de-pollute it.

Experiencing the sight of natural beauty, breathing deeply of clean, fresh air, can be cherished leisure experiences. Yet, these experiences are becoming rare for many Americans because the environment in many cities and areas of the country has become ugly and polluted.

The establishment of policies and controls at the local level are needed to clean our cities, towns, and natural environment. Their acceptance and enforcement will require the cooperation and efforts of each and every responsible citizen and agency. The issue is simply: Do enough citizens want to clean up their environment?

Solutions

Develop individual concepts of the importance of beauty and an attractive environment.

Protect our precious resources of air, water, and land against pollution.

Preserve for future generations the wildlife and scenic beauty.

Fig. 17-5 THE KEY TO ENVIRONMENTAL QUALITY is people rather than nature. While the pollution problem at Lake Tahoe is not as serious as in eastern lakes and rivers, unified action is needed to protect this magnificent resource of nature.

> IT IS THE RESPONSIBILITY OF EVERY CITIZEN TO PROTECT THE BEAUTY AND PURITY OF THE LAND, THE WATER, AND THE AIR.
>
> *Clayne R. Jensen*

Encourage unified action by community groups and organizations in controlling pollution and the ugliness of our environment.

Develop political awareness and support that involve the passage and enforcement of laws at various levels. Without political action, little can be accomplished.

Discover what federal grants-in-aid and technical assistance from state agencies are available to help local governments.

A responsible citizen can do his job by taking the following action:

> IT IS A DISMAL FACT THAT WE NOW HAVE POLLUTED ALMOST EVERY LARGE RIVER, LAKE, AND BAY IN THE ENTIRE UNITED STATES.
>
> *Clayne R. Jensen*

Write to congressional leaders informing them of the dangers of pollution and environmental destruction.

When questionable actions by agencies occur, write to the department head.

Organize citizen protest meetings.

Join local conservation organizations and citizen advisory planning committees.

Seek injunctions against agencies which attempt to use park areas for non-recreational purposes.

DETERIORATION OF OUR CITIES

Our great urban centers are in social turmoil, suffering from marked physical deterioration. Many American cities are physically obsolete, crime ridden, dirty, polluted, torn by racial conflicts, suffering from unemployment and corruption. Their deterioration has been a major cause in the mass population shifts the nation has experienced since the 1950s.

Recreation and park agencies can play a major role in making cities livable again, particularly if middle-class whites continue to move back to the city.

A bigger portion of the budget should be spent in low-income areas, providing new programs for areas and facilities in low-income neighborhoods. More facilities and programs must be made available "closer to people's homes."

The following "Master Plan" might be used by the nation's cities:

New and beautiful waterfront areas for residential development, sightseeing, and many other leisure uses.

New parks, playgrounds, and plazas to provide much needed appeal.

Exciting and attractive shopping malls, vistas, and park boulevards.

Bicycle paths built through scenic city routes.

Attractive, imaginative forms of urban design.

> THE FIGHT TO SAVE "OPEN SPACE" SHOULD BE A RESPONSIBILITY SHARED BY ALL CITIZENS.

OPEN SPACE

The overcrowding and congestion experienced by the cities must be prevented in the suburban areas, where there is an urgent need to preserve open space and create parks.

Land use legislation is vitally needed to meet the increasing pressure of industrialization, technological advances, population growth, and rapid urbanization.

Meeting the recreational needs of an increasingly urbanized society will continue to receive major emphasis. Local, county, and state agencies should unify their efforts in a new "Parks to People" concept, providing new recreation areas near large cities.

Solutions

Reliable annual funding is vital to the development.

State legislation of an Open Space acquisition fund, based on a 1 per cent real estate transfer tax, would provide regular monies to cities and counties for parks and open space purchase.

Another bill would authorize cities and counties to condemn land for open space uses.

Planning operations should be coordinated jointly among the various governmental units, particularly those that overlap and conflict with each other.

OVERCROWDED PARKS

In recent years, there has been a phenomenal increase in national park visits. This heavy use has had a detrimental effect on the preservation and conservation of natural resources. By the year 2000, the census is expected to count 350 million Americans. At that time, based on recent rates of

Fig. 17-6 A DEPRESSING SIGHT is burning dumps, which have contributed in part to the deterioration of our cities. A massive effort is needed to renew the beauty and vitality of our urban centers.

increase, there would be more than one billion visits per year to the national park system.

Despite this increase, less than 10 per cent of the system's areas suffer from overcrowding at the present time, and most of this occurs during the peak summer months. Moreover, the parks are not so much overcrowded with people as they are with the cars, camper vehicles, trailers, and boats that people bring with them.

Solutions

While additional parks is one approach, park visitors could be encouraged to use some of the less crowded areas.

Many national and state parks already have maximum capacity levels which they rigidly enforce.

Reservations are made in advance and with the aid of computers, the number of park visitors is closely observed.

Separate visitors from their cars once they reach the parks.

Provide alternative transportation such as tramways, monorails, or railways.

FINANCIAL CRISIS

In a period of near recession and fiscal crisis, many recreation and park agencies today are faced with the problem of maintaining adequate financial

Fig. 17-7 NEW AND ATTRACTIVE SHOPPING MALLS and park boulevards are needed in many of our cities. Recreation and park agencies can make a major contribution.

support. Inflation has been the greatest cause of increased city expenditures. Along with job freezes and lay-offs, many budgets have been cut, and in many instances, capital development has been at a standstill.

Solutions

Get maximum productivity from the tax dollar.
Seek funding and assistance from federal or state governments.
Rely more on fees and charges.
Provide maximum service by securing joint planning and coordination among all agencies in the community.

POVERTY

While America is at its highest level of wealth, extensive poverty still exists. Consequently, those who lack equal opportunity to share in the nation's wealth are bitter and unhappy.

The nation's elderly, increasingly, have had to cope with poverty conditions. Even though Social Security payments have risen by 52 per cent since 1969, more than 3 million elderly Americans still live below the government-defined "poverty line."

There is no easy solution to the intolerable living conditions experienced by those in poverty; the following measures, however, would help alleviate their plight. As discussed previously, the problem has become even more difficult because of the financial crisis the nation is currently experiencing.

Solutions

Find meaningful employment for those who can work.
For the ill, disabled, and the elderly, provide the necessary financial assistance to allow them to live above the "poverty line."
A larger portion of the budget should be made available to areas in low-income neighborhoods.
Increased recreation and leisure services should be made available without fees and charges.
Provide equal opportunities for education and employment for those in need.

RACIAL MILITANCE

During the 1960s, racial militance and antagonism was a common occurrence in many large cities. Increased lawbreaking and vandalism in parks and recreation centers have resulted in the need to shift personnel from district to district, based on ethnic factors.

Solutions

New forms of programs and activities should reflect racial demands for ethnically oriented activities, such as Afro-American arts, black history, and Mexican-American cultural programs.
Special teams of older neighborhood youth should be hired to maintain control of youth gangs and problem youth.

328

Fig. 17-8 SHAMEFUL ACTS OF VANDALISM AND LITTERING have forced many agencies to take major corrective action.

New personnel adaptations and innovations should be used to cope with the problem.

VIOLENCE

Crime is at an all-time high in America. Flare-ups of violence are often the result of prevailing tension and antagonism among various groups in our society. Demonstrators for various causes or those involved in strikes and walkouts often resort to deliberate civil disobedience.

Solutions

Greater emphasis in schools on standards of good behavior, ethics, morals, and citizenship.

Citizens action programs involving meetings and activities.

Recreation programs should make a stronger contribution to the strengthening of citizenship and moral fiber.

A major effort should be made to build a wholesome climate in the community.

VANDALISM

Increasing at an alarming rate, vandalism has grown from a nuisance-level problem to a major-loss factor. Shameful acts of vandalism, deliberate arson, and littering are making it necessary to close or severely restrict the use of many parks. Most vandalism is caused by juveniles, particularly those between the ages of nine and fourteen. The problem has become so serious that agencies have been forced to take major corrective action.

Solutions

Security inspections of department facilities.
Tighter control on the issuance of keys to facilities.
Night lighting and intrusion alarm devices.
Park security officer approach.
Street counselor and special problems programs.
Making the community aware of the seriousness of the problem.

ALIENATION OF YOUTH

Youth rebellion, delinquency, school dropouts, and the widespread use of drugs and alcohol are the major forms of social upheaval among our youth today. There has also been a corresponding drop in respect for authority.

While there are other factors that can affect the behavior and attitudes of our young people, studies have indicated that active recreational participation can contribute significantly to maintaining emotional stability and well-being. In addition to offering pleasure and satisfaction, recreation can provide a sense of creative and personal accomplishment. Social and professional group experiences can give an individual a sense of belonging, so often lacking in today's society of broken homes or working parents too busy to properly take care of their children.

Solutions

Provide youth with more exciting and challenging recreation and leisure experiences.
Give them something constructive to do—get them interested in a job, a hobby, a leisure pastime.
Parents can help considerably by establishing a closer relationship with their children, by developing warmth, understanding, and mutual respect for each other.

Provide youth with the sense of belonging that results from friendship and sociability.
Membership in clubs and organizations is essential to the growth of young people, providing opportunities to learn to cooperate with others, accept group rules, and abide by the expressed desires of the group.

THE ENERGY CRISIS

Although the energy squeeze has had a profound effect on the entire leisure economy, the resort and tourist travel industries have experienced the most serious decrease in business.

Casualties of the world fuel shortage have been thousands of motels, restaurants, travel agencies, airlines, resorts, and ski areas. Due to the uncertainty over flight cancellations, filling-station closings, and gasoline-rationing schemes, the traveling public has been staying closer to home.

The energy squeeze has, therefore, had a definite effect on tourism. An estimated seventy per cent of all tourist travel is by automobile. Until the energy crisis is over, the tourism industry will operate at a significantly reduced schedule.

The gasoline shortage and tight money have put the brakes on the feverish development of campground facilities across the United States. In addition, campground operators have cut rates and have had to step up promotional efforts to offset the drop in business. The building of many resort and community development enterprises has been delayed or curtailed.

Due to the gasoline shortage, Americans have been taking shorter trips and are staying longer in the parks they visit. Park visits to areas close to urban centers have increased greatly. The general public will be relying more and more upon municipal recreation and park departments to meet their leisure-time needs.

The energy problem appears to be a long-term one. This means a continuation of the conservation attitudes and actions the nation adopted when the energy crisis broke wide open in the aftermath of the Arab oil embargo in 1973.

Solutions

More participation and emphasis in programs and activities by municipal recreation and park agencies.

Significant increase in the number of weekend programs at local parks and recreation areas.

More emphasis on day camps and campgrounds closer to urban centers.

Curtailment of night programs requiring electrical power.

Car pools to and from various classes and activities.

Less dependence on the automobile and greater emphasis on mass transportation.

Continued boom in bicycling which has prompted more bicycle programs, bike trails.

Reduction in travel abroad.

Conservation of power and natural resources by individuals and agencies, such as reduced driving speeds and greater use of the smaller, economy automobile.

Greater research, experimentation, and use of new sources of energy.

Containment of suburban sprawl, with a greater movement of middle-class whites back to the city.

Adaptation will be the theme for planning recreational resources and programs.

18

Trends in Leisure and Recreation

In the future, people will spend their free time in a more leisurely fashion and with less pressure than in the past. More people will be spending an increasing amount of time in the simple pleasures of life. More than ever before, leisure will be enjoyed by the masses, and not by only the few.

The public is becoming more aware of both the opportunities and the problems of increasing leisure time. This awareness appears to have contributed to the greater prominence of the recreation and leisure services.

People will continue to seek a more healthy and satisfying balance between work and recreation. They will also achieve a higher level of physical and mental health in which there will be a more wholesome balance between activity and passivity.

Increased emphasis will be given to the enjoyment of family recreation, with the hope that increased sharing of leisure experiences will result in a more harmonious and tighter-knit family. Family recreation activities appear to be on the upswing, a trend substantiated by the sharp rise in family rooms, recreation rooms, hobby equip-

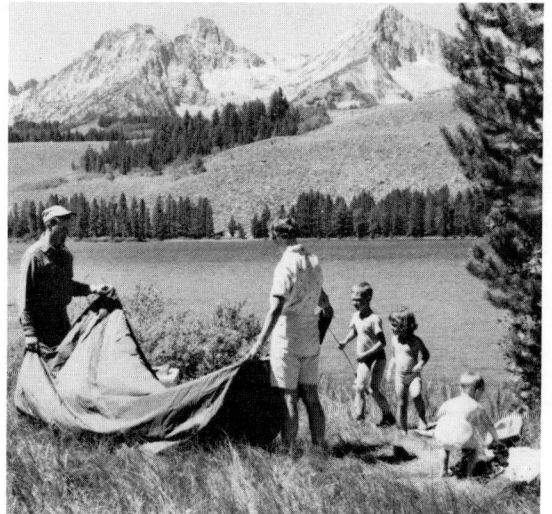

Fig. 18-2 THE DESIRE FOR FUN AND ADVENTURE will continue to grow. More families will be taking off on camping trips to outdoor areas such as Idaho's Sawtooth National Forest. (Courtesy of U.S. Forest Service.)

Fig. 18-1 OPEN SPACE AND PARK LANDS increasingly are receiving recognition as essential to the quality of life. Developing an environmental awareness and understanding should be a major objective of our schools and agencies involved with outdoor recreation.

ment, musical instruments, and backyard play equipment. With the three-day weekend closer to reality for many Americans, more families will be taking off on pleasure trips and making regular visits to outdoor recreation areas.

Water-related activities and experiences have been expanding at a sharp rate. Lakes, marinas, boating areas, and facilities for swimming, surfing, and skiing are being developed in great numbers.

While leisure will continue to increase dramatically, the distribution of this valuable gift will remain uneven among the people of the world for many years to come. Work will be more specialized and automated than in the past. Becoming increasingly intellectual in nature, work will require more education.

In time, the people of America will come to recognize leisure as a vital part of "the good life." In fact, for many, leisure will be more important than work in giving meaning to life.

MORE CREATIVE, CHALLENGING PROGRAMS

One of the biggest challenges of recreation professionals is to provide greater creativity and imagination in recreation programs. Rather than activities scheduled to fill idle hours, people's lives should be filled with exciting, creative activities that will challenge them to learn and develop.

Professional recreators should combine the traditionally successful programs with new ideas, greater variety, and popular changes that will provide much needed spark and appeal.

EXCITING, CHALLENGING PLAY EQUIPMENT

New kinds of play equipment are challenging the imagination and creativity of children and inspiring their interest and curiosity. Designers are developing innovations in play equipment that provide great appeal to children. There has been growing criticism of traditional play equipment

> CHARACTERISTICALLY, THE TYPICAL LARGE CITY PLAYGROUND IS AN UNBROKEN EXPANSE OF CONCRETE OR ASPHALT PAVEMENT, PUNCTUATED BY THE FORLORN PRESENCE OF METAL SWINGS, A SLIDE, AND SOME SEE-SAWS.
> *Richard Dattner*

and designs at many playgrounds. Critics have declared that most of the older playgrounds fail to appeal to children, contending that the equipment and designs are fixed, static, and provide little opportunity for creative and imaginative exploration.

SOME NEW TRENDS IN PLAYGROUND DESIGN

Theme Playgrounds. The entire playground is developed around a theme of interest to children. An example of such a facility includes a 65-foot-long Chinese junk, a Chinese wall maze, and play areas built to provide a stimulating environment reflecting Chinese culture. Other such facilities include a prehistoric park; a Mississippi River park complete with riverboat; a southwestern playground featuring a Spanish style fort; and a space age playground complete with space ships, rockets, and satellites.

Adventure Playgrounds. Adventure play areas provide creative play with a variety of challenges that require skill and agility from the children. Usually, adventure playgrounds involve little more than an empty lot, a pile of scrap lumber, waste materials, and some tools to work with. Children have the opportunity to build play environments that may change from day to day.

The so-called "junk playground" has been an exciting and controversial kind of adventure playground. Children play in rubble-filled lots with discarded equipment, lumber, ropes, and other scrap materials.

Steep Grades and Slopes. New approaches have been developed by designers in the use of levels in playgrounds. Increasing, play areas have

Fig. 18-3 IMAGINATIVE AND EXCITING PLAY EQUIPMENT. New approaches are being developed by playground designers, like this adventure play area involving rope swings or pulley rides.

steep grades and contrasts in levels, which provide opportunities for children to coast down the hill, hide, use rope swings or pulley rides, and climb along monkey bridges. Children can also pretend they are defending or attacking a fort.

Greater Use of Water. Increasingly, the key factor in outdoor recreation facilities and activities will be water. Participation in all kinds of activities involving water—boating, canoeing, sailing, surfing, swimming, water skiing, and under-

Fig. 18-4 AUTOMATED SURFING POOL. This remarkable wave pool facility built in Decatur, Alabama, involves the wave generation process similar to ocean surfing. The wave equipment can create three-foot-high waves and whitecaps. (Courtesy of the Charles M. Graves Organization.)

water exploration—will continue to soar. More parks and play areas will be featured by scenic water falls, jetting fountains, and reflecting pools and streams.

PROFESSIONAL DEVELOPMENT

If the goals of a new leisure are to be met, recreation professionals of the future must demonstrate a higher level of planning in developing exciting and imaginative programs and experiences. To accomplish this vital task, the professional must have a thorough understanding of the leisure phenomena in today's society and the sociological, economical, and psychological forces that affect it.

There are evidences of greater maturity on the part of recreation professionals. In solving the many problems and meeting the challenges of the future, those in the field will have to exem-

plify more maturity, creativity, and sophistication than ever before.

IMPROVING THE PROFESSIONAL IMAGE

The recreation and parks field is still not widely understood by the public as a specialized area of professional service. Not many people are aware of the importance and significance of professional recreation work. A more effective and revitalized National Recreation and Park Association, in cooperation and harmony with state societies and organizations, will hasten the professionalization of the field.

To improve the image of the recreation profession, progress must be made in the following areas:

- New and more creative uses of recreation and park personnel.

Fig. 18-5 STRONG DEDICATION TO CHILDREN on the part of America's recreation leaders can improve significantly the image of the recreation profession. This young leader received a farewell party and plaque of appreciation from the children.

- Greater professional recognition, public influences, and status.
- More competent program development, budget planning, and management.
- A new sense of dedication relative to the potential role of leisure programs.
- Certification and licensing of recreation and park personnel.
- More effective communication with people from the entire community.
- Getting the cooperation of newspaper editors, TV stations, service clubs, and the many agencies in the community.
- Challenging apathy with daring and imaginative program approaches.
- Moving more forcefully in solving the problems and ills of the community.
- Intelligent planning, hard work, teamwork, and cooperation.
- Constructive and creative leisure opportunities for people of all ages, races, and social backgrounds.

STRONGER CITIZEN INVOLVEMENT

One of the pressing needs of the parks and recreation field today is strong citizen involvement. Recreation needs the support of the people it serves more than ever before. Involvement will contribute to understanding, appreciation, and effective community leadership.

Broad community involvement and participation are needed in the planning of park and recreation programs. Without a coordinated effort, each segment of the community tries to do the job individually. What is needed is for the entire community to pull together in a unified effort.

Coordination councils serving in an advisory capacity have proven very useful in effectively involving citizens. To form such a council, each community organization should be requested to appoint a representative. The council should include representatives from service clubs, PTA groups, labor unions, businesses, church groups, and government organizations. All age groups should be represented, especially youth and the aging.

The primary function of such a council is to keep the recreation and park board and department aware of community needs and to help interpret the importance of recreation and park services. A council can be most useful in community projects and activities.

IMPROVEMENT IN QUALITY OF PREPARATION

A higher quality of course offerings and a greater depth of content should characterize the recreation courses offered by colleges and universities. Indeed, the lack of challenge has worked heavily against recruitment and retention of the more sophisticated and mature students in the recreation curriculum.

Curricula in recreation and parks are being challenged. The traditional approaches and methods are being questioned and examined and significant changes are occurring.

There is an increasing tendency for college recreation curricula to rely more heavily on courses in the behavioral sciences. Increased emphasis is also being given to the humanities, the social and natural sciences—areas that contribute to an understanding of people and of the relationship of people to their environment. As recreation personnel become more involved with the social behavior and welfare of people, professional preparation has a greater responsibility in teaching ethical behavior and morality.

One of the profession's greatest challenges should be training recreation personnel to meet the needs of special groups—the ill and handicapped, the elderly, the unemployed, and others.

LEISURE COUNSELING

Leisure counseling represents a relatively untapped area of recreation that can help assist people to use their leisure time wisely and constructively. The objective of leisure counseling is to help

people acquire not only skills and knowledge but the values and attitudes to enjoy a more meaningful and happy life. While counseling services have traditionally been the concern of those in therapeutic recreation, there is a growing feeling that others in the profession can also assume this role.

"The primary goal of leisure counseling is to establish a 'real' and an 'ideal' leisure profile," stated Gerald S. Fain, professor of therapeutic recreation at the University of Maryland. "The real is what a person actually does in his leisure; the ideal is what he would like to do. Bridging the gap between the real and the ideal is the counselor's role. In doing so, he should be concerned with the individual and his attitudes rather than with specific activities."[1]

According to Fain, "The need for leisure counseling is presently at a stage of development where if we in the recreation field do not become experts, others will. Guidance, rehabilitation, social work and other areas are broadening their scope to include leisure counseling in training and practice."[2]

In the years ahead, computers will be used extensively in determining the leisure needs of people. Background and aptitude data on an individual will be fed into a computer, and from it will come a program or schedule of suggested activities that will hopefully satisfy the leisure needs of the person.

Increasingly, computers are proving very useful to professional and industrial training programs in helping determine a student's proficiency and suitability for a particular career field of study.

Increased Interest in Research

Research, which has been one of the recreation field's weakest points, has recently shown an upsurge both in quality and quantity. Research can be a vital part of education for leisure, to help

[1] Gerald S. Fain, "Leisure Counseling: Translating Needs into Action," *Therapeutic Recreation Journal*, 7, no. 2, 1973, pp. 4–5.

[2] Ibid., p. 9.

determine how an individual can best use his leisure time. If recreators—practitioners as well as educators—are to operate effectively, much more needs to be done. Professional preparation, ideally, should depend heavily on the use of techniques and procedures validated through research efforts.

Professional recreators need to know how to measure and diagnose an individual's recreational needs and prepare an appropriate leisure-time program for him. For example, the characteristics of individuals could be fed into a computer to determine suitable activities for them.

A Higher Quality of Students

Sheer numbers are not the solution to the recruitment problems of the recreation profession. A higher quality of young recreators—more disciplined and intellectually mature—is needed. The recreation field must compete with the other more established professions for the limited number of bright young people seeking careers.

If recreation is to get its share of outstanding young people, the image of the field must be improved. In addition to a career ladder that will offer attractive opportunities for salary advancement, the nature and importance of one's work must command respect from the profession and the community.

The preparation of minority students for recreation service should be a challenge shared by all recreation educators. Colleges and universities are sadly lacking in the recruitment of capable minority students, particularly black students.

A MANPOWER CRISIS?

Perhaps the most nebulous aspect of the rapid growth of professional recreation has been the question of whether the field faces a manpower shortage. Many articles and publications during the past decade have declared that the field has faced and will continue to face a growing shortage of trained personnel. Recent studies have indicated, however, that this shortage is being drastically reduced through more extensive recruitment programs.

In some states and regions in the country, college graduates are experiencing problems in gaining employment in certain areas of the field, particularly jobs with municipal agencies. In recent years, for example, graduating seniors in California interested in employment in public recreation have had to cope with a tight job market. Yet, in many areas of the field, jobs are not only plentiful but are becoming increasingly attractive in salary, professional stature, and working conditions. Openings in significant numbers are available in such special areas as therapeutic, institutional, group work, and school recreation. Commercial and resort recreation enterprises have been attracting a growing number of professionals, and industrial and military recreation positions are more appealing today.

If the present trends and outlooks become a reality, the employment situation should become progressively more attractive and enticing to those seeking a career field. With the growing likelihood that recreation will attain full professional status and with the leisure market literally exploding, recreation authorities are predicting a vast number of employment possibilities for future graduates in a leisure-oriented society.

LIST OF TRENDS IN LEISURE AND RECREATION

The leisure and recreation movement has been characterized by a wide range of trends that have had a significant effect on its growth.

Leisure

- Leisure is expanding rapidly and occupying a greater portion of our lives.
- Continued technological and automated advancement is resulting in increased leisure time.
- More people are viewing leisure as an opportunity for a fuller life.
- There has been a spectacular rise in expenditures for commercial recreation.

- People of all ages are demonstrating a greater variety of interests.
- People are becoming more selective in their choice of leisure-time experiences.
- Participants are deriving greater significance from leisure-time activities.
- The energy squeeze is curtailing travel plans and causing more people to stay closer to home.
- Computers are programming the leisure needs of people.
- There is greater affluence, more discretionary income, and more available time among the American people.
- Off-the-job lives tend to be overscheduled.
- Changes in human behavior and personality are occurring.
- There are continuing changes in life styles and social values.
- There is an increasing number of private neighborhood recreation centers and clubs.
- New and exciting technological designs and innovations are being developed.
- Air travel is increasing greatly.

Education

- Schools are placing greater emphasis on education for leisure.
- There is growing use of school facilities for recreation purposes.
- The average educational level of the population has increased.
- The Community School concept is gaining wide acceptance.
- There is more emphasis on research needs in the park and recreation field.
- Computers are being used to help determine an individual's proficiency and suitability for a particular field of study.

Park and Recreation Departments

- There is a continuing trend in combining parks and recreation departments.
- There has been a steady increase in the number of new park and recreation systems.
- There is an increased level of priority in the allocation of the overall fiscal budget.

- Fiscal budgets have increased substantially.
- More recreation and park programs on a county or regional basis are needed.
- There is a need for more effective urban planning.
- The professional status of those in the field is gaining wider recognition.

Programs

- New and challenging leisure experiences are being provided people of all age groups.
- An increasing number of private firms are being hired by local and county governmental agencies, commercial, and resort companies to provide recreation services.
- There are greater opportunities for family recreation.
- Dynamic and creative ideas and programs are needed.
- There is greater demand for activities involving more intellectual content, such as art, opera, and drama.
- Making the arts available to more Americans will continue to be the goal of the recreation field.
- There has been a sharp increase in more expensive activities.
- Aquatic or water-related activities are expanding rapidly.
- The number of activities requiring a fee or charge is increasing.
- Stronger efforts should be made to provide recreation services for the aging.
- More activities with the elements of danger, daring, and adventure should be included.
- Greater participation by women and girls in sports is occurring.
- There is growing equality between the sexes.
- Special emphasis should be placed on the needs of minority and ethnic groups.
- Cultural attractions such as symphony orchestras, opera, and theatre are increasing.
- Due to the energy crisis, municipal departments are offering more comprehensive weekend programs and activities.
- More community-wide activities for the physically handicapped, mentally ill, the very young, the aged, and the poor should be undertaken.

What new trends

Fig. 18-6 RECREATION FOR THE AGING. During the decade ahead, an increasing number of programs and activities will be provided special populations, such as the elderly, the disabled, and the handicapped. These student volunteers conducted a birthday party at a convalescent home for the aging.

- Activities of a community service nature are increasing.
- Agencies at all levels of government are increasing recreation planning and services.
- Popularity of lifetime sports such as tennis, golf, and bowling is growing.
- Increased planning efforts on an international scope are being made.
- More effective recreation activities are gradually being established in many of our nation's jails and prisons.

Work

- The four-day work week is spreading.
- There is a trend toward the shortened workday and work week, with longer vacations and sabbaticals.
- There are increases in fringe benefits such as improved working conditions, pensions, and longer vacations.

- Retirement at the age of 38 may be commonplace by the year 2000.
- Sabbaticals, year-long leaves, may become an industry practice, similar to practices in the education field.
- Work is becoming less and less the central goal in life.
- Large numbers of bored young people are becoming dissatisfied with work, play, and family life.

Parks

- There will be new, more innovative designs in parks and playground facilities and equipment, such as:

  A floating marina, providing a safe harbor in the face of extreme weather.

  Air support structures, used to enclose tennis courts, swimming pools, and ice skating rinks.

  New, exciting amusement rides, such as the flume log ride which uses a constantly recirculating water system to carry riders down a sensational 2,100-foot waterway flume in a hollowed-out log.

  Cloverleaf baseball complexes, four diamonds in a cloverleaf shape with a huge ultra-modern clubhouse in the center.

  Inland surfing facilities, the new inventions that involve the wave generation process similar to ocean surfing.

- More parks and play areas will be made available closer to people's homes.
- There will be an increasing use of water in parks and play areas.
- Space will be used to a better advantage, transforming roof tops and parking lots into neighborhood playgrounds.
- There will be a big increase in facilities for walking and bicycling.
- Integration of park and recreation facilities has become the rule.
- There will be a greater number of multi-use facilities that provide year-round use, such as the new outdoor swim-skate facility in New York's Central Park.

341

Fig. 18-7 PRESERVATION AND USE OF OUR NATIONAL PARKS. While most Americans favor both use and preservation concepts, the use must be controlled in such a manner that areas such as Yosemite Park are preserved in their natural condition for future use. The awesome granite cliffs of El Capitan contribute to the beauty of Yosemite Park, one of the world's scenic wonders.

- More effective safety and design standards are being established for playground equipment.

National and State Parks

- Increased use of state and national forests and parks will occur as mobility increases—particularly if and when the energy squeeze eases.
- There will be greater emphasis on ways to separate visitors from their cars once they reach parks.
- Alternative transportation will include tramways, monorails, and railways.
- Expanded recreation services on public lands will be made through efforts of federal and state governments.

- Wiser use of flood plains has contributed to the decrease of environmental disasters.

Environment

- There will be increased emphasis on "saving our environment," restoring and preventing further destruction.
- Man will make gradual progress in restoring and maintaining a wholesome environment on earth.
- There is a trend toward urban blight and sprawl —cities are disintegrating rather than growing.
- An environmental awareness and understanding among people is developing.
- The energy problem is a long-term one that

will mean a continuation of conservation attitudes and actions.

Outdoor Recreation

- There is a growing emphasis on more active forms of leisure activities, such as hiking, bicycling, and jogging.
- Increased mobility of our population has resulted in extensive travel and participation in outdoor recreation activities.
- Organized camping, particularly day camping, has expanded.
- Use of recreation vehicles is booming, with a wide range of vehicles. Off-road vehicles, though, will face tighter restrictions by state and federal agencies.
- A great surge of popularity is occurring in camping, backpacking, hiking, and mountain climbing.
- The energy shortage is forcing more people to have their outdoor recreation experiences closer to home.

Professional Preparation

- Recreation as a field and as an area of study is moving toward professional status on a level with medicine, law, and education.
- Standards of the recreation profession will rise substantially, and services will be vastly improved.
- A general upgrading in the effectiveness of leadership will occur.
- New occupations will evolve in the field of leisure services.
- Recreation majors will be prepared to better understand and serve disadvantaged groups.
- Instilling in students an awareness, sensitivity, and a commitment to social issues will be a major aim of recreation education.
- Minority and low income students in greater numbers will be recruited and prepared for recreation service.
- A greater number of career opportunities in parks and recreation are being promoted.

Fitness and Health

- There will be a greater concern for physical fitness and culture.
- Regular physical activity is contributing to longer life spans.
- Advanced medical and surgical care has contributed to a longer life.
- A normal and healthy life to the age of 90 or 95 is within the foreseeable future.

Textbooks on Recreation and Leisure

Allen, Catherine, *Fun for Parties and Programs.* Englewood Cliffs, N.J.: Prentice-Hall, 1956.

Anderson, Nels, *Work and Leisure.* New York: Free Press, 1961.

Arco Editorial Board, *Playground and Recreation Director's Handbook.* New York: Arco Publishers, 1964.

Bannon, Joseph J., *Problem Solving in Recreation and Parks.* Englewood Cliffs, N.J.: Prentice-Hall, 1972.

Beal, George M.; Bohlen, Joe M.; and Raudabaugh, J. Neil, *Leadership and Dynamic Group Action.* Ames: Iowa State University Press, 1967.

Borst, Evelyne, and Mitchell, Elmer D., *Social Games for Recreation.* New York: Ronald Press, 1959.

Brightbill, Charles K., *Man and Leisure: A Philosophy of Recreation.* Englewood Cliffs, N.J.: Prentice-Hall, 1961.

Brockman, C. Frank, *Recreational Use of Wild Lands.* New York: McGraw-Hill, 1973.

Butler, George D., *Introduction to Community Recreation.* New York: McGraw-Hill, 1967.

————, *Pioneers in Public Recreation.* Minneapolis: Burgess, 1965.

Caillois, Roger, *Man, Play and Games.* London: Thames and Hudson, 1961.

Carlson, Reynold E.; Deppe, Theodore R.; and MacLean, Janet R., *Recreation in American Life.* Belmont, Calif.: Wadsworth, 1972.

Case, Maurice, *Recreation for Blind Adults.* Springfield, Ill.: Charles C. Thomas, 1966.

Chapman, Frederick M., *Recreation Activities for the Handicapped.* New York: Ronald Press, 1960.

Clawson, Marion, *The Bureau of Land Management.* New York: Praeger, 1971.

Clawson, Marion, and Knetsch, Jack, *Economics of Outdoor Recreation.* Baltimore: Johns Hopkins Press, 1966.

Corbin, H. Dan, *Recreation Leadership.* Englewood Cliffs, N.J.: Prentice-Hall, 1970.

Corbin, H. Dan, and Tait, William J., *Education for Leisure.* Englewood Cliffs, N.J.: Prentice-Hall, 1973.

Danford, Howard G., revised by Max Shirley, *Creative Leadership in Recreation,* 2nd Ed. Boston: Allyn and Bacon, Inc., 1970.

Danford, Howard G., *Recreation in the American Community.* New York: Harper, 1953.

Dattner, Richard, *Design for Play.* New York: Van Nostrand Reinhold, 1969.

deGrazia, Sebastian, *Of Time, Work and Leisure.* New York: Twentieth-Century Fund, 1962.

Depew, Arthur M., *The Cokesbury Game Book*. New York: Abingdon Press, 1960.

Doell, Charles E., and Fitzgerald, Charles B., *A Brief History of Parks and Recreation in the United States*. Chicago: The Athletic Institute, 1954.

Doell, Charles E., and Twandzik, Louis F., *Elements of Park and Recreation Administration*. Minneapolis: Burgess, 1968.

Donnally, Richard J.; Helms, William G.; and Mitchell, E. D., *Active Games and Contests*. New York: Ronald Press, 1958.

Douglas, Robert W., *Forest Recreation*. New York: Pergamon Press, 1969.

Dulles, Foster R., *A History of Recreation: America Learns to Play*. New York: Appleton-Century-Crofts, 1965.

Dumazedier, Joffre, *Toward a Society of Leisure*. New York: Free Press, Collier-Macmillan, 1967

Duran, Dorothy B. and Clement A., *The New Encyclopedia of Successful Program Ideas*. New York: Association Press, 1967.

Edwards, Myrtle, *Recreation Leader's Guide*. Palo Alto: National Press, 1967.

Eisenberg, Helen and Larry, *Omnibus of Fun*. New York: Association Press, 1969.

Everhart, William C., *The National Park Service*. New York: Praeger, 1972.

Fischer, David W.; Lewis, John E.; and Priddle, George B., *Land and Leisure*. Chicago: Maaroufa, 1974.

Fish, Harriet V., *Activities Program for Senior Citizens*. West Nyack, N.Y.: Parker Publishing, 1971.

Fitzgerald, Gerald B., *Community Organization for Recreation*. New York: A. S. Barnes, 1948.

———, *Leadership in Recreation*. New York: A. S. Barnes, 1951.

Frye, Mary V., and Peters, Martha, *Therapeutic Recreation: Its Theory, Philosophy, and Practice*. Harrisburg: Stackpole Books, 1972.

Gabrielsen, M. A., *Sports and Recreation Facilities for School and Community*. Englewood Cliffs, N.J.: Prentice-Hall, 1958.

Green, Arnold W., *Recreation, Leisure, and Politics*. New York: McGraw-Hill, 1964.

Guggenheimer, Elinor C., *Planning for Parks and Recreation Needs in Urban Areas*. New York: Twayne Publishers, 1969.

Hanson, Robert F., and Carlson, Reynold E., *Organizations for Children and Youth*. Englewood Cliffs, N.J.: Prentice-Hall, 1972.

Harris, Jane A., *File O'Fun* (Card File for Social Recreation). Minneapolis: Burgess, 1970.

Hawkins, Donald E., and Vinton, Dennis A., *The Environmental Classroom*. Englewood Cliffs, N.J.: Prentice-Hall, 1973.

Hindman, Darwin A., *The Complete Book of Games and Stunts*. Englewood Cliffs, N.J.: Prentice-Hall, 1956.

Hjelte, George, and Shivers, Jay S., *Public Administration of Recreational Services*. Philadelphia: Lea & Febiger, 1972.

Hormachea, Marion N. and Carroll R., *Recreation in Modern Society*. Boston: Holbrook Press, Inc., 1972.

Huizinga, Johan, *Homo Ludens: A Study of the Play Element in Culture*. Boston: Beacon Press, 1950.

Hunt, Valerie V., *Recreation for the Handicapped*. Englewood Cliffs, N.J.: Prentice-Hall, 1955.

Hutchinson, John L., *Principles of Recreation*. New York: Ronald Press, 1951.

Jacks, Lawrence P., *Education through Recreation*. Washington, D.C.: McGrath Publishing Company and the National Recreation and Park Association, 1972.

Jenny, John H., *Recreation Education*. Philadelphia: W. B. Saunders, 1956.

Jensen, Clayne R., *Issues in Outdoor Recreation*. Minneapolis: Burgess, 1972.

———, *Outdoor Recreation in America*. Minneapolis: Burgess, 1970.

Johnson, Elvin R., *Park Resources for Recreation*. Columbus: Charles E. Merrill, 1972.

Kaplan, Max, *Leisure in America—A Social Inquiry*. New York: John Wiley, 1960.

Kraus, Richard G., *Recreation Leader's Handbook*. New York: McGraw-Hill, 1955.

———, *Recreation and Leisure in Modern Society*. New York: Appleton-Century-Crofts, 1972.

———, *Recreation and the Schools*. New York: Macmillan, 1964.

———, *Recreation Today: Program Planning and Leadership*. New York: Appleton-Century-Crofts, 1966.

———, *Therapeutic Recreation Service*. Philadelphia: W. B. Saunders, 1973.

Kraus, Richard G., and Curtis, Joseph E., *Creative Administration in Recreation and Parks*. St. Louis: C. V. Mosby, 1973.

LaGasse, Alfred, and Cook, Walter, *History of Parks and Recreation*. Washington, D.C.: American Institute of Park Executives, 1965.

Larrabee, Eric, and Meyersohn, Rolf, *Mass Leisure*. Glencoe, Ill.: Free Press, 1958.

Lee, Joseph, *Play in Education*, 1905. Reprint.

Washington, D.C.: The National Recreation and Park Association, 1972.

Lee, Robert, *Religion and Leisure in the United States*. Nashville: Abingdon, 1964.

Lucas, Carol, *Recreational Activity Development for the Aging in Homes, Hospitals, and Nursing Homes*. Springfield, Ill.: Charles C. Thomas, 1962.

Machlis, Joseph, *The Enjoyment of Music*. New York: W. W. Norton, 1970.

Merrill, Toni, *Activities for the Aged and Infirm*. Springfield, Ill.: Charles C. Thomas, 1967.

Meyer, Harold D., and Brightbill, Charles K., *Recreation Administration, A Guide to Its Practices*. Englewood Cliffs, N.J.: Prentice-Hall, 1956.

Meyer, Harold D.; Brightbill, Charles K.; and Sessoms, H. Douglas, *Community Recreation, A Guide to Its Organization*, 4th Ed. Englewood Cliffs, N.J.: Prentice-Hall, 1969.

Millar, Susanna, *The Psychology of Play*. Baltimore: Penguin Books, 1968.

Miller, Norman P., and Robinson, Duane M., *The Leisure Age: Its Challenge to Recreation*. Belmont, Calif.: Wadsworth, 1963.

Miller, Peggy L., *Creative Outdoor Play Areas*. Englewood Cliffs, N.J.: Prentice-Hall, 1972.

Mitchell, Viola; Crawford, I. B.; and Robberson, J. D., *Camp Counselling*, 4th Ed. Philadelphia: W. B. Saunders, 1970.

Mulac, Margaret, *Games and Stunts for Schools, Camps, and Playgrounds*. New York: Harper & Row, 1964.

Murphy, James; Williams, John G.; Niepoth, E. W.; and Brown, Paul, *Leisure Service Delivery System*. Philadelphia: Lea & Febiger, 1973.

Musselman, Virginia, *Making Family Get-Togethers Click*. Harrisburg: Stackpole Books, 1968.

Nash, Jay Bryan, *Opportunities in Recreation and Outdoor Education*. New York: Vocational Guidance Manuals, 1963.

————, *Philosophy of Recreation and Leisure*. Dubuque: W. C. Brown, 1960.

————, *Recreation: Pertinent Readings, Guide Posts to the Future*. Dubuque: W. C. Brown, 1965.

Nathans, Alan A., *Maintenance for Camps, and Other Outdoor Recreation Facilities*. New York: Association Press, 1968.

National Conference on Areas and Facilities for Health, Physical Education, and Recreation, *Planning Areas and Facilities for Health, Physical Education, and Recreation*. Chicago: Athletic Institute, 1965.

National Recreation Association, prepared by George D. Butler, *Recreation Areas, Their Design and Equipment*. New York: A. S. Barnes, 1947.

National Workshop on Recreation, *The Recreation Program*. Chicago: Athletic Institute, 1963.

Nelms, Clarice, *Developing Leadership in Recreation*. Menlo Park, Calif.: Pacific Coast Publishers, 1968.

Nesbitt, John A.; Brown, Paul D.; and Murphy, James F., *Recreation and Leisure Service for the Disadvantaged*. Philadelphia: Lea & Febiger, 1970.

Neumeyer, Martin H. and Esther S., *Leisure and Recreation*. New York: Ronald Press, 1958.

Owen, Oliver S., *Natural Resource Conservation*. New York: Macmillan, 1971.

Parker, Stanley R., *The Future of Work and Leisure*. New York: Praeger, 1971.

Pomeroy, Janet, *Recreation for the Physically Handicapped*. New York: Macmillan, 1964.

Reader's Digest, *Book of 1,000 Family Games*. Pleasantville, N.Y.: The Reader's Digest Association, Inc., 1972.

Robbins, Florence G., *The Sociology of Play, Recreation, and Leisure Time*. Dubuque: W. C. Brown Co., 1955.

Rodney, Lynn S., *Administration of Public Recreation*. New York: Ronald Press, 1964.

Rosenberg, Bernard, and White, D. M., *Mass Culture*. Glencoe, Ill.: Free Press, 1957.

Sapora, Allen V., and Mitchell, Elmer, *The Theory of Play and Recreation*. New York: Ronald Press, 1961.

Schramm, Wilbur, *Classroom Out-of-Doors*. Kalamazoo: Sequoia Press, 1969.

Shivers, Jay S., *Principles and Practices of Recreational Service*. New York: Macmillan, 1967.

Slavson, Samuel, *Recreation and the Total Personality*. New York: Association Press, 1946.

Sloane, Eugene A., *The Complete Book of Bicycling*. New York: Trident Press, 1970.

Stein, Thomas A., and Sessoms, H. Douglas, *Recreation and Special Populations*. Boston: Holbrook Press, Inc., 1973.

Tilden, Freeman, *The State Parks, Their Meaning in American Life*. New York: Alfred A. Knopf, 1962.

Tillman, Albert, *The Program Book for Recreation Professionals*. Palo Alto: National Press Books, 1973.

Udall, Stewart L., *The Quiet Crisis*. New York: Holt, Rinehart and Winston, 1963.

U. S. Bureau of Outdoor Recreation, *Federal Outdoor Recreation Programs, the Nationwide Plan for Outdoor Recreation.* Washington, D.C.: U. S. Government Printing Office, 1968.

Van der Smissen, Margaret E., *Bibliography of Theses and Dissertations in Recreation, Parks, Camping and Outdoor Education.* Arlington, Va.: National Recreation and Park Association, 1970.

Van der Smissen, Margaret E., and Knierim, Helen, *Fitness and Fun through Recreational Sports and Games.* Minneapolis: Burgess, 1964.

Vannier, Maryhelen, *Methods and Materials in Recreation Leadership.* Philadelphia: W. B. Saunders, 1956.

Wackerbarth, Marjorie, and Graham, Lillian, *Successful Parties and How to Give Them.* Minneapolis: T. S. Denison, 1962.

Yukic, Thomas S., *Fundamentals of Recreation.* New York: Harper & Row, 1963.

Index

Anderson, Nels, 48
Anthony, Don, 160
Appalachian Mountain Club, 185
Aquatics, 252–253, 276, 299, 334, 336, 340, 341
Areas and facilities, 64–65, 87–88, 96–97, 155, 220, 290, 292, 303
Argentina, recreation in, 156
Arles, James, 63, 93, 97, 107
Armed forces, recreation in the, 63, 65–67, 135–138, 187
Army Overseas Recruitment Center, 137
Army Special Services, 136–137
Arnett, Ray, 116
Arousal-seeking theory, 14
Articulation Committee (SPRE), 314
Arts and crafts, 231–236
 activities, 233–235
 community show, 212, 235–236
 creativity, 233
 exhibits, 235, 272–273
 indoor center, 235
 handicrafts, 211
 leader, role of, 233
 playground, 234–235, 283
 special centers, 235
 values, 232–233
Assimilation, 20–21
Association, 249
Associations, professional, 305–307
 American Association for Health, Physical Education, and Recreation, 307
 American Camping Association, 306
 Athletic Institute, 307
 National Industrial Recreation Association, 307
 National Recreation and Park Association, 306
Astrodome, Houston, Texas, 37
Athletic Institute, 307
Attwell, Ernest T., 63
Auburn Dam, 133
Auckland Regional Authority, 160
Australia, recreation in, 159
Australian Parks Journal, 159
Automation, 48–49, 323
 effects of, 323
 solutions, 323
Automobile racing, 36
Awards, 287–288

B

Backpacking, 27, 259, 260, 343
Ball, Edith L., 190–191
Bankhead National Forest, Alabama, 45
Baseball, 35–37, 147, 153, 247, 250, 273
Baseball complex, cloverleaf, 341
Basketball, 195
Beckman, Norman, 95
Belgium, recreation in, 150
Bicycling, 10, 59, 142, 146, 158, 271, 331, 341, 343
Birthrate, 49–50
Bisham Abbey, 149
Black recreation movement, 50–52, 59, 61, 63, 65, 68, 70–72, 74, 105, 207, 237, 321, 328–329, 339–340, 342–343
Boards, 80–82, 91, 93, 96
Boating, 28–29, 31–32, 132, 260
Boating Industry Association, 37
Bolshoi Ballet, 152
Bond issues, 84, 105
Borst, Evelyne, 264
Boston Park and Recreation Department, 58–59, 208
Boston Sandgardens, 58, 232
Bowling, 35, 139, 155, 200, 247
Boy Scouts of America, 63, 181
Boys' Clubs of America, 182
Braucher, Howard, 61
Brazil, recreation in, 156
Brightbill, Charles K., 3, 8, 30, 59, 69, 117, 162, 178, 180–181
Brookline, Mass., 58, 147
Brown, Paul D., 59, 73
Bucher, Charles A., 16, 17
Budget, 39–41, 49, 65, 73, 82–83, 93, 97, 177, 289, 300, 326–328
Bulletin board, 285
Bullfighting, 159
Bureau of Indian Affairs, 125, 133
Bureau of Land Management, 125, 132, 261
Bureau of Outdoor Recreation, 37, 69, 134, 257
Bureau of Public Roads, 133
Bureau of Reclamation, 125, 130, 133
Bureau of Sports, Fisheries, and Wildlife, 132
Butler, George, 57, 64, 77, 78, 217, 221, 244, 293